IFS

An Annual Wealth Tax

C. T. SANDFORD
J. R. M. WILLIS
D. J. IRONSIDE

 Heinemann Educational Books · London

ISBN 0 435 84532 2

©1975   C. T. Sandford, J. R. M. Willis, D. J. Ironside

ISBN 0-435-84532-2

First published 1975

HJ
4113
.S3
1975

Published for the Institute for Fiscal Studies
by Heinemann Educational Books Ltd,
48 Charles Street, London W.1

Printed in Great Britain by George Berridge & Co. Ltd, London & Thetford

The Authors:

C. T. SANDFORD — Professor of Political Economy at the University of Bath. Author of various books on economics including: *Economics of Public Finance*, Pergamon, 1969, *Taxing Personal Wealth,* Allen and Unwin, 1971, and *Hidden Costs of Taxation*, IFS, 1973.

J. R. M. WILLIS — Professorial Research Fellow at the University of Bath and formerly a deputy chairman of the Board of Inland Revenue.

D. J. IRONSIDE — Visiting Fellow at the University of Bath. Chartered Accountant. Author of *Personal Taxation—the new unified system,* Institute of Chartered Accountants, 1972, and member of various national committees of the Institute of Chartered Accountants in England and Wales.

The three authors collaborated in a recent research study on *An Accessions Tax,* published by the Institute for Fiscal Studies in 1973.

Members of Advisory Committee:

A. B. ATKINSON — Professor of Economics, University of Essex.

J. F. AVERY JONES — Solicitor, Joint Editor, *British Tax Review.*

J. F. CHOWN — International Taxation Consultant.

J. P. LAWTON — Barrister, Joint Editor, *British Tax Review.*

G. McALLISTER — Chartered Accountant.

C. W. N. MILES — Professor of Land Management and Development, University of Reading.

A. ROWE — Chartered Accountant, Senior Lecturer in Accounting and Taxation, Oxford Polytechnic.

J. F. TURNER — Director, Estate Duties Investment Trust.

G. S. A. WHEATCROFT — Emeritus Professor of Law, University of London.

Acknowledgements

Our prime acknowledgement must be to the Leverhulme Trust and the Institute for Fiscal Studies which jointly financed the research study which the Institute sponsored. Our sincere thanks to both and to the University of Bath for assistance in kind.

Our main debt of a different kind is to members of the Advisory Committee whose names are listed below the authors on page iii. Each brought an expert knowledge to bear on some aspect of the study. The Committee met only once in full session, but its members individually made their advice available to the research team and commented (sometimes very fully and always very helpfully) on the draft report. The book would have been much poorer without their contributions. We must add, however, that the members of the Advisory Committee do not necessarily share the conclusions reached, which are the responsibility of the authors alone.

The dependence of this study on international comparisons is evident on almost every page and we can hardly over-state the assistance we have received from experts overseas. So many have helped that it is impossible to name them all; but we must thank the following officials and their colleagues: Dr. Bauer, Deputy Director of the Tax Department, Ministry of Finance, Federal German Republic; Mr. T. Dekker, Director General for Fiscal Affairs in the Netherlands; Mr. Gösta Ekman, Director General of the Swedish National Tax Board; Mr. E. Möller of the Danish Ministry of Finance; Mr. C. H. Murray, Secretary of the Department of Finance of the Republic of Ireland; and Mr. G. B. Skottun, Deputy Director of the Norwegian National Tax Board. No less helpful were the tax consultants abroad whom we approached, in particular the partners of McLintock Main Lafrentz & Co. in Amsterdam, Bremen, Copenhagen, Gothenburg and Oslo. Among our overseas helpers we must also mention Mr. J. van Hoorn and Dr. J. Booij of the International Bureau of Fiscal Documentation, Amsterdam; and Professor G. Rose and colleagues at the University of Cologne; last, but not least, Professor Göran Englund of the University of Lund; to Göran and Helga Englund we are indebted not only for intellectual fare but for a warm and generous hospitality that we shall long remember.

We are grateful to the Board of Inland Revenue and to the CBI for copies of material they had compiled on overseas tax systems; and grateful also to Sir Arthur Drew, and to Mr. F. Clive de Paula and Mr. A. E. Harman of the Agricultural Mortgage Corporation, for comments on parts of the draft report. We acknowledge with thanks the permission of the editor of *Accountancy* to reproduce as Appendix B material which, in substance, had first appeared in article form in that journal.

We acknowledge with gratitude the assistance of three present or former colleagues at Bath University—Peter Hardwick, Lecturer in Economics who helped particularly with the statistical work, and Dave Corney and Ken Buckingham, research assistants. Finally, no praise is too high for Sue Powell, Pauline Wright and Muriel King, who between them typed the many drafts of the report and whose goodwill and efficiency never failed despite the wholly unreasonable demands made upon them.

Cedric Sandford
Robert Willis
Donald Ironside

Contents

Introduction

Origin and Objectives

1. The study on which this book is based was commissioned by the Institute for Fiscal Studies following the announcement by the Chancellor of the Exchequer, Mr. Denis Healey, in March 1974 of his intention to introduce an annual net wealth tax. The prime object of the book is thus to offer an independent evaluation of the case for a wealth tax in the United Kingdom, examine the particular problems to which a wealth tax gives rise and suggest the directions along which solutions might be found. But, whilst the book attempts a thorough assessment of the Green Paper (Cmnd. 5704) presented by the Labour Government as a discussion document on the possible form of a wealth tax, it is intended to be more than that. The authors have sought to write a book of value for tax policy makers and students of taxation outside the United Kingdom as well as inside it, and not confined to the particular objectives or proposals set out in the Green Paper.

Structure

2. The book therefore has the following pattern. Part I aims to provide a theoretical perspective. Chapter 1 seeks to define and categorise; it reviews the arguments usually presented in favour of a wealth tax and the counter arguments, and indicates the relationship between objectives and form of tax. In the light of the distinctions set out in the first chapter, Chapter 2 assesses the possible macro-economic consequences of a wealth tax. The argument is conducted in general terms without reference to any particular wealth tax or set of proposals.

3. Part II reviews wealth taxes in practice, concentrating on Europe, and within Europe on the wealth taxes of Denmark, Norway, Sweden, Germany[1] and the Netherlands. The first chapter in this section compares the

---

[1] References to 'Germany' relate to the Federal German Republic throughout.

general characteristics of these wealth taxes with each other and with the proposals for the Republic of Ireland. As wealth taxes can only be adequately assessed in the context of other taxes on capital and investment income, these are brought into the picture and compared with taxation in the United Kingdom in 1974 (without a wealth tax). The next two chapters offer more detailed case studies of particular wealth taxes, those of Sweden and Germany. (Appendix C summarises the five Continental wealth taxes, the proposals for Ireland and the Green Paper proposals for a United Kingdom wealth tax, in tabular form, under a series of standardised headings).

4. The third part of the book consists of one chapter only which examines wealth tax proposals for the United Kingdom; it contains the background to the Green Paper, a summary of the proposals in it and an attempt to elucidate, in quantitative form, some of its macro implications. No attempt is made at this stage to reach any judgement on the Green Paper proposals; that comes only after Part IV.

5. Part IV, the largest section of the book, considers some of the main problems which a wealth tax generates: the scope of the charge; the appropriate threshold and exemptions; the issues raised by ceiling provisions; the crucial questions of valuation; the treatment of trusts; the special difficulties of private businesses and agriculture; the appropriate treatment for works of art and historic houses; administrative methods, operating costs and the dangers of evasion and avoidance. Whilst a formal pattern is not rigidly adhered to, each chapter seeks to consider the nature of the problem in general terms; to indicate how other countries with wealth taxes have tackled it; and to assess the nature of the problem in the United Kingdom, comment on the proposed solution in the Green Paper, and suggest, in the view of the authors, how best the problem might be met.

6. Finally, the one chapter in Part V concentrates on the United Kingdom. The conclusions on particular problems are summarised; the chapter considers what sort of wealth tax, if any, is appropriate for the United Kingdom; the Green Paper proposals are evaluated; and some alternative ways of achieving the same objectives are considered.

Methods and Constraints

7. If the book was to influence discussion on the Green Paper, and hence policy in the United Kingdom, it had to be available early; the research had therefore to be telescoped into a much shorter time than the authors or the sponsors would have wished. The timetable consequently allowed less than seven months from the start of work at the beginning of May to final typescript for the printers at mid-November; the time constraint was accentuated because the Green Paper was published later than expected. The tight schedule meant that some aspects of the research received less attention than

they warranted. The authors are particularly conscious of two deficiencies. They would have liked to undertake further statistical analyses in an attempt to measure more precisely some of the implications of the Green Paper proposals and of possible alternatives—though lack of data as well as lack of time limits what can be done. Secondly they would have wished to have studied more deeply the wealth taxes of the European countries in their individual social and economic settings. The authors are aware how easily misunderstandings arise because of lack of background knowledge; to mention just two instances of the importance of such factors: wealth taxes on the Continent have impinged less on agriculture than might be expected in the United Kingdom partly because farms are generally much smaller, and partly because the price of agricultural land has risen less, both because there has been less general inflation and because some European countries impose restrictions on the purchase of agricultural land. Again, in looking at a death duty (as a form of capital tax related to an annual wealth tax) the legal provisions about community of property bear crucially on effective tax rates on gifts or legacies between spouses and may have a determining influence on tax rates on bequests to children. The authors have the uneasy feeling that there may be factors of this kind which they have completely missed because of inadequate background knowledge.

8. For the reader's benefit the methods used in acquiring information on European wealth taxes should be stated. Besides consulting available published material, during the summer of 1974 at least two of the research team visited Denmark, Norway, Sweden, Germany and the Netherlands and in each country held discussions with leading tax officials and with a well-known firm of accountants; structured interview schedules were used, but the interviews were informal and the questions usually open-ended. By taking both an official and a taxpayer view it was hoped to obtain a fuller appreciation of the tax. In Sweden and Germany the wealth tax was also discussed with leading academics. In order to ensure, as far as may be, that no obvious factual errors had crept into the final report, at least one of our hosts in each country checked for accuracy the main references to the wealth tax in which he was a specialist.

9. It remains true, however, that the authors are alone responsible for any errors of fact as well as for expressions of opinion.

Part I
Economic and Social Perspectives

Chapter 1

The Case for an Annual Wealth Tax

What is a Wealth Tax?

1.1 It is a truism that 'a wealth tax' is a tax assessed on wealth. But this truism hides difficulties: we have to define wealth; we need to point out the various forms a wealth tax can take and specify more precisely which we are considering; and we need to dispel the confusion which leads to the assumption that a wealth tax is paid out of wealth.

1.2 By wealth we mean the total value of the net assets of an individual or a company or any other association or institution. Wealth can be taken as synonymous with capital or 'net worth'. It constitutes the value of the stock of all the assets, physical and financial, held at a particular point of time less liabilities. A wealth tax therefore relates to the generality of assets, not just particular kinds of property, and to their net and not their gross value. In this it contrasts with a 'property tax' (as in the USA) which is a tax on the gross value of one kind of asset only—real property. Of course, with any wealth tax there is likely to be a threshold level excluding from tax persons or institutions with net wealth less than a certain value; and most wealth taxes in practice exclude some kinds of assets. But in principle a wealth tax relates to the value of all assets and everything is treated as being included unless specifically exempted.

1.3 Wealth taxes can take various forms. A death duty is a wealth tax, based on the generality of net assets passing on the occasion of a death. Similarly a gift tax is a wealth tax. Both gift tax and death duty are forms of wealth transfer tax. More doubtfully a capital gains tax might be regarded as a wealth tax; but the tax base is not wealth as such but the appreciation in the value of wealth over a period of time, and such an appreciation may more properly be regarded as income.

1.4 However, the term 'wealth tax' in common parlance has come to be applied particularly to an annual tax on net wealth. Such a tax may apply to individuals or companies or both.

1.5 There are strong arguments against subjecting both individuals and companies to wealth tax, although some countries do so. To tax both means double taxation because the assets of the company are taxed both in the hands of the company and again in the hands of the shareholders through the value of their shares. To tax companies as well as individuals also means discriminating against the company form of business organisation. The Neumark Committee, whilst favouring a low annual wealth tax, considered that it should not be applied to legal entities[1]. To tax companies rather than shareholders has the disadvantage of leaving more scope for tax shifting onto the product; it puts companies at a disadvantage compared with other forms of business organisation; and it favours commercial firms as compared with manufacturing, which are likely to need both more fixed capital and larger stocks compared with turnover. Also it is difficult to make a wealth tax on companies progressive, in the sense of taxing richer persons more heavily. This can be done systematically with a wealth tax on individuals.

1.6 Apart from saying a little about a wealth tax on companies as well as individuals when (in Chapter 5) we examine the German wealth tax which applies to both, in this book we shall confine our consideration to personal wealth taxes.

1.7 There remains a source of possible confusion to be dispelled. It is some-times thought that a wealth tax has to be paid out of wealth. But it no more follows that a tax on wealth has to be paid from wealth than that a beer tax has to be paid from beer. 'Wealth' refers to the tax base, not the source of payment. A wealth tax may be met from income or it may be met from a disposal of assets, but there is nothing in the definition as such which pre-supposes either the one or the other.

1.8 Thus, this book is about an annual, personal, net wealth tax which, following common usage and as a convenient shorthand, we shall hence-forward refer to as a wealth tax. It is a tax on the total value of personal net assets, subject to any threshold and any specific exemptions. The tax base covers physical assets like a house, land, car and boat; it includes household possessions such as furniture, jewellery and paintings; it covers the business assets of a sole proprietor and of a partner; it includes financial claims like

---

[1] *The EEC Reports on Tax Harmonisation, Report of the Fiscal and Financial Committee,* trans by International Bureau of Fiscal Documentation, Amsterdam, 1963, pp. 127-8.

government bonds and national savings certificates and the value of shares in quoted and unquoted companies; it includes cash in the bank and cash in the house; and insurance policies and the accumulated value of pension rights if they are capable of being realised. In short the tax base, in principle, includes any assets able to be turned into cash[2], any potential control over economic resources, less liabilities, and it should apply to these assets (and liabilities) wherever they may be situated.

1.9 In concluding this section it will be convenient to sum up the characteristics of a wealth tax as compared with other taxes. Some of these distinguishing features we have already pointed out. A wealth tax is general, applying to all forms of wealth save those specifically exempted; it is imposed on net assets, i.e. the value of total assets minus liabilities; it is regular, imposed annually, as distinct from death and gift taxes which fall irregularly on property or property owners. In addition, unlike wealth transfer taxes which are concerned with gifts or legacies, it makes no distinction as to source of wealth; wealth derived from a combination of effort, enterprise and saving is treated on a par with wealth from legacies or capital gains. Finally, unlike wealth transfer taxes, or a capital gains tax levied on realisation, a wealth tax is levied at a point of time which is not associated with a transfer of ownership or an economic transaction or a flow of funds; it is from this feature that problems associated with valuation and lack of liquidity particularly spring.

Arguments for a Wealth Tax

1.10 Arguments advanced in favour of a wealth tax can be grouped under four main heads: horizontal equity, efficiency in resource use, reduction in inequality and administrative control.

Horizontal Equity

1.11 Horizontal equity is the principle that people of similar taxable capacity should be taxed the same. It would be widely agreed that income is the best single criterion of ability to pay taxation; but income, by itself, is an insufficient yardstick, for capital, or wealth, yields advantages to its possessor over and above the income derived from it—advantages of security, independence and opportunity.

1.12 Further, the additional taxable capacity of wealth cannot be adequately covered by levying income tax at a higher rate on income from property than on income from work. Certainly this distinction, long employed by some countries like the UK, originated in the recognition of the extra advantage that income from investment, tied neither to the health nor the working life

---

[2] Appendix A considers whether the capitalised value of future earnings ought to be included.

B

of its owner, had over earned income. But, whilst such differentiation may partly meet the additional taxable capacity of wealth, it falls short in two ways, one of which is really an extreme example of the other. An investment income surcharge does not touch wealth which yields no income, even though such wealth gives its owner potential control over economic resources; nor does it allow for different capital values which may yield the same income.

1.13 The equity case for taxing wealth which yields no income was vividly illustrated by Professor Lord Kaldor[3]. He compared the position of a beggar, who has neither income nor property, with that of a man (for convenience of reference let us call him a Maharajah) who keeps the whole of his wealth in the form of jewels and gold. Judging their taxable capacities by the test of income alone, the capacity of both is the same: nil. But the Maharajah, with his large potential control over resources, has a taxable capacity much higher than the beggar.

1.14 Another way of putting the argument for taxing wealth which, like jewellery or pictures, yields no money income, is to say that these assets yield a 'psychic' income to their possessor which gives him a satisfaction at least as large as that which he would have from the money income he could have obtained by putting his resources into an alternative investment. Or they are providing an equivalent investment for purposes of capital gain.

1.15 To illustrate the second point of differing yields on capital: two men, 'A' and 'B', may obtain the same investment income (say £1,000) from different amounts of wealth. Because they hold wealth in different forms 'A' may obtain the £1,000 income from an investment worth £10,000 whilst 'B', with a rate on return on his capital only half that of 'A', receives his £1,000 from an investment worth £20,000. It is clear than 'B' has a higher taxable capacity than 'A'; 'B' could sell his investment and replace it by the same kind of asset as 'A', retain the same income and be left with a 'surplus' £10,000 to dispose of how he wished, by consumption or by investing it to yield further income.

1.16 There are two further advantages claimed for a wealth tax under the heading of horizontal equity. First, taxing both wealth and income widens the tax base and reduces tax avoidance, in particular avoidance by means of a switch into assets yielding psychic income but not money income taxable to income tax.

1.17 Second, Professor Due has claimed that a wealth tax, 'while not taxing increases in capital values as such, does reach the higher values as they accrue.'[4] By contrast, a capital gains tax only reaches them when they are realised and thus creates an incentive to avoid realisation—the locked-in

---

[3] N. Kaldor *Indian Tax Reform*, Ministry of Finance, Government of India, New Delhi, 1956, p. 20.
[4] John F. Due 'Net Worth Taxation', *Public Finance*, Vol. XV, 1960, p. 316.

effect. Whilst true, this cannot be regarded as a very strong argument. A wealth tax is not an adequate replacement for a capital gains tax, of which the essence is the taxation of the gain as such, and the appropriate rates for capital gains tax approach more closely those of an income tax than the much lower rates of a wealth tax.

1.18 To sum up the argument: there is a strong case on grounds of horizontal equity[5] for supplementing an income tax with a wealth tax; and, if a country's income tax differentiates between earned and investment income by means of an investment income surcharge or an earned income relief, for replacing this differential element by a wealth tax. A wealth tax takes account of the additional taxable capacity which wealth confers over and above the income derived from it and is superior to an investment income surcharge because it not only taxes both capital which confers an income and that which does not; it takes account, too, of the different values of capital which may yield the same income; and by widening the tax base it checks or offsets avoidance of income tax by the purchase of non-income yielding assets.

1.19 The logic of the horizontal equity argument leads to a low wealth tax, essentially as a supplement to income tax, which might be proportional (like the 1973-4 15% investment income surcharge in the UK) or mildly progressive, and would have a low threshold.

Efficiency of Resource Use

1.20 The efficiency argument rests on a comparison of the effects of wealth tax and income tax; it considers a wealth tax as a substitute for income tax either in the sense that it partially replaces an existing income tax to maintain a given revenue, or that it is used as an alternative to increasing income tax to raise an equal additional revenue.

1.21 The main argument has both a negative and a positive aspect. Because the tax base, wealth, is related to past and not present effort, a wealth tax will restrict the supply of labour and enterprise less than an equivalent income tax. To put the point more simply, if a wealth tax were imposed as an alternative to higher income tax, people would not be deterred from working harder or from additional enterprise by the wealth tax as long as the object of their effort was extra consumption. (The question of saving we consider later).

---

[5] A refinement of the horizontal equity argument should be noted. There is a typical life-time pattern of wealth-holding by which people save during their working lives up to retirement and thereafter, when they no longer have any income from work, tend to draw upon their savings. Thus a 25-year-old with £100,000 wealth has a different taxable capacity from that of a 65-year-old with £100,000 wealth. This consideration is connected with the coverage of the wealth tax; if the wealth tax base includes the capitalised value of future earnings, then the difference in taxable capacity resulting from age is automatically taken care of. If not, there is a strong case for an age relief. (See Appendix A).

1.22 The positive argument advanced in favour of a wealth tax[6] is that, because it imposes a charge on wealth regardless of the income from it, and indeed whether it yields an income or not, a wealth tax encourages people to use wealth more productively. Owners of assets which were nil-yielding would find these assets adding to their wealth tax liability even though they generated no money income with which to pay the tax; hence owners would be encouraged to transfer into assets which yielded income; or, if they had assets which were low yielding, wealth tax might encourage them to move into high-yielding assets; the essential point being that the amount of wealth tax liability is the same for any asset of a certain value irrespective of its yield. The inducement to seek higher yielding assets would be the stronger if the wealth tax was a partial substitute for income tax, because then the income tax liability on higher yielding assets would be less.

1.23 Some examples may serve to demonstrate the point. A wealth tax may be expected to discourage the holding of idle money balances, which attract wealth tax and usually yield little or no income from which to pay it; thus the proprietor of an unincorporated business who is rather careless about the money balances he keeps on hand, is encouraged to assess more carefully his liquidity requirements. Similarly, a wealth tax is an inducement to the owner of a private business to adopt an efficient policy of stock control, to reduce the level of his stocks to the necessary minimum to free capital for more productive use. In these ways a wealth tax reinforces the profit motive to secure an efficient allocation of resources. A comprehensive wealth tax discourages 'investment' in jewellery, stamp collections, pictures and the like which yield no money income but carry liability to wealth tax. Again, a landowner pays no income tax on a piece of land which he leaves uncultivated and undeveloped; but he must pay wealth tax whether it yields an income or not. Hence he may be induced to cultivate it or develop it, or alternatively to sell it to someone who will cultivate or develop it. To take a final example: suppose a block of flats is owned by an individual and allowed to stand empty, in the hope of capital gain or higher rentals; if there is a wealth tax the owner will incur wealth tax liability on the net capital value of it and he may, therefore, be induced to sell or let it sooner than he otherwise would.

1.24 This characteristic of a wealth tax, that it imposes the same liability on a high-yielding as a low-yielding asset of the same capital value, has been generalised to the claim that a wealth tax would promote risk bearing more, or at least discourage it less, than an equivalent income tax. As Gulati puts it, 'a capital tax falls on investments with a severity which varies inversely with their riskiness'.[7] He argues (with figures reminiscent of past days) that if a 6% industrial equity and a 3% gilt-edged have the same capital value, then

---

[6] For some contrary arguments see paragraph 1.43.
[7] I. S. Gulati, *Capital Taxation*, Orient Longmans, 1957, p. 15.

a 1% wealth tax reduces the yield of the equity to 5% and the gilt-edged to 2%. The ratio of yields has changed from 6:3 to 5:2 or from twice to 2½ in favour of the equity; therefore wealth tax as compared with income tax is more favourable to risk investments. However, various economists have pointed out[8] the questionable nature of this conclusion. Under an income tax with loss offsets the Revenue is in fact sharing the risks, which it does not do with wealth tax; moreover the return to risk bearing often takes the form of capital gain, which annually enters into the wealth tax base but avoids income tax. The issue must therefore be regarded as open.

1.25 Professor Due[9] points out that a wealth tax has an advantage because it does not directly impinge on corporations, and is therefore less likely to influence business decision-making than a personal-corporate income tax system. Further, it is a virtue of a wealth tax that because it applies to the generality of assets it minimises distortion in investment decision-making save for its general encouragement to higher-yielding investments, already discussed.

1.26 As a final point in favour of a wealth tax as a partial alternative to income tax, Due[10] argues that it carries a psychological advantage; on assets yielding 5%, a one per cent wealth tax is equivalent to a 20% income tax, but wealth owners are more likely to be influenced to reduce their tax liability by the income tax than by a wealth tax which creates the same liability but sounds less oppressive.[11]

1.27 Like a wealth tax aimed at horizontal equity, one designed for efficiency in resource use might be expected to realise this objective most fully if the threshold were fairly low and the rates modest—either proportional or mildly progressive. High progressive rates might prove a deterrent to saving and investment.

Reduction of Inequality

1.28 A third main argument in favour of a wealth tax is that it can be used to reduce inequalities in the distribution of wealth. As a personal value judgement many people may consider the distribution of wealth in a country to be unacceptably unequal; a wealth tax may then be seen as an obvious way to reduce that inequality.

1.29 There are many problems of a conceptual and practical nature in measuring and assessing the distribution of personal wealth in a country, some of which are examined, in relation to the United Kingdom, in Appendix B. These apart, however, the use of a wealth tax for the purpose of reducing

---

[8] For example, J. F. Due, 'Net Wealth Taxation', *Public Finance* Vol. XV, 1960, p. 317 who also refers to Musgrave; and A. B. Atkinson *Unequal Shares*, Allen Lane, The Penguin Press, 1972, pp. 149-50.
[9] *Ibid* p. 317.
[10] *Ibid* p. 313.
[11] For a contrary view see paragraph 2.24.

inequalities of wealth needs further clarification; its advocates do not always specify their meaning exactly.

1.30 A wealth tax for the reduction of inequalities of wealth may have a limited and negative objective or an aim which is more radical and extensive.

1.31 In the limited sense a wealth tax may be regarded as reducing inequality of wealth in much the same way as a progressive income tax. Income and wealth are closely associated. Wealth usually generates income and the larger a person's income the more his scope for augmenting his wealth out of saving. A progressive income tax by itself, or a progressive income tax allied to a wealth tax, both met from income, mitigate inequality of wealth by reducing income inequalities and thus checking further accumulation by the wealthy. This limited interpretation particularly fits the views of many people who fail clearly to distinguish wealth from income and apply the term 'wealthy' to people with large incomes and little property as well as to those with net assets of high value.

1.32 The use of a wealth tax for reducing inequality in this limited sense could have a more specific meaning. An income tax, even with an investment income surcharge, may be less effective in restraining wealth inequalities than a combination of income tax and wealth tax, if many wealthy have been avoiding income tax by transferring into assets which yield no money income but carry the prospect of capital gain. A wealth tax in order to widen the tax base might then be a necessary component of a tax policy to mitigate inequalities. But there must be some doubt whether investment in pictures, collections, jewellery and the like would ever proceed on such a scale as to diminish seriously the redistributive effect of a progressive income tax. Moreover, if in these circumstances a wealth tax replaced an investment income surcharge, owners of high yielding assets would pay less total tax and would be in a better position to accumulate wealth. Whilst such a change might favour efficiency in resource use, it is doubtful if, overall, it would do more than the income tax to mitigate inequalities of income or wealth.

1.33 The other sense in which a wealth tax might be considered a method of reducing inequalities of wealth is the more obvious and direct: i.e. to impose a wealth tax at such a level that the wealthy can only meet it by parting with some of their wealth; they cannot meet their combined income tax and wealth tax liabilities out of income. Then inequalities of wealth are reduced because the wealthiest members of the community part with assets each year in order to pay wealth tax; every year their wealth is diminished.

1.34 A wealth tax, used in this way to bring about a direct and early reduction in wealth inequalities, differs in a fundamental way from the wealth taxes associated with the objectives of horizontal equity, of efficiency and of reduction in inequality in the more limited sense. These objectives all viewed a wealth tax as a supplement to income tax, an alternative to it and normally capable of being met from income even by the very wealthy; the use of a wealth tax directly to reduce wealth inequalities necessarily implies a combined income tax and wealth tax in excess of what the wealthy can meet from income.

1.35 There is a rider to the argument for the use of a wealth tax to reduce inequalities of wealth, which could relate to either the limited or the more radical objective, although it applies particularly to the latter. It can be argued that reducing inequalities is a necessary step in enabling certain policies to be effected in the community. Thus, unless some action is seen to be taken to reduce what are considered extreme and unjustifiable differences of wealth, wage earners will not accept limitations on wages necessary to check inflation. In other words the reduction of inequalities of wealth is a method of creating a more widespread sense of fairness in a society, so that the less well off are prepared to accept sacrifices for the common good; a wealth tax to reduce inequality is seen by some as a step towards this end.

1.36 Clearly a radical policy to reduce inequalities by means of a wealth tax points to a progressive tax and is compatible with a high threshold.

Administrative Control

1.37 A fiscal advantage of a wealth tax is that it generates data, which can be cross-checked with other information collected by the Revenue authorities, to tighten up tax administration as a whole and enable evasion to be more readily discovered and therefore reduced. Data on personal wealth can be checked for discrepancies against personal income; and wealth returns can further be cross-checked with returns of gift taxes and legacies. Not only ought wealth and investment income to match up, but if a person records an increase in wealth larger than is reasonable in relation to his total income, the tax authorities will be alerted to investigate its source and to see if it arose from a legacy or gift which has gone unrecorded. Similarly an acquisition shown by gift or death duty returns can be followed up by the Revenue authorities to see if it figures in the beneficiary's next wealth tax return.

1.38 As incidental merits, a country which wished to adopt a progressive expenditure tax or to tax accrued rather than realised capital gains would have the necessary information to hand in the wealth tax returns. At the same time, wealth tax data would have the further spillover benefit of providing a new source of information about the distribution of personal wealth in a country.

1.39 Anything like a comprehensive control system from wealth tax returns and the attainment of the incidental merits mentioned, however, would require returns on wealth to be collected from more or less the whole income tax paying population.

Arguments Against a Wealth Tax

1.40 The general arguments against a wealth tax can be grouped under two broad headings: practical difficulties and possible adverse economic consequences, particularly on saving.

Practical Difficulties

1.41 The critics of a wealth tax start from the basis that the advantages listed for it have been overstated because they are based on theoretical considerations and take insufficient account of the practical realities of administration and of the real world. In practice the advantages claimed are only very imperfectly realised.

1.42 The administrative difficulties of a wealth tax revolve mainly around problems of disclosure and valuation. Some assets, like valuable household possessions, jewellery, pictures, collections of stamps and books are difficult for the Revenue authorities to identify. In practice they are often omitted from the tax base or, if included, are grossly undervalued. Although the valuation of some assets, like quoted securities, present little difficulty, the valuation of others, like personal chattels, land and private businesses is very complex. In consequence the theoretical assumption that a wealth tax covers all assets at uniform valuations breaks down. But omissions from the tax base and discrepancies in valuation mean that the tax falls short in its attainment of horizontal equity and creates investment distortions detrimental to the efficiency objective.

1.43 The argument of efficiency in resource use implicitly assumes that efficiency is equatable with high yield and that resources are infinitely mobile. But this is not the real world. In practice, circumstances arise where a low yield is neither a sign of the inefficiency of the producer nor an indication that the national interest requires a transfer of resources. A new business with good prospects, but not yet profitable, an established business going through a bad patch because of the closure of an export market, a farm where the yield is low because of soaring land prices—in all these cases a wealth tax may be detrimental to efficiency and more harmful than an equivalent income tax. Even where there would be economic advantage in a transfer of investment, the specific nature of physical assets may make it impossible in the short run. Moreover, it is doubtful if a wealth tax will have much influence even on stock exchange investors. For one thing the very wealthiest contain a high proportion of older people who may be disinclined to change their investment habits. Further, although the wealthiest appear to hold a larger proportion of their assets in income-yielding form than the less wealthy,[12] where (as in the United Kingdom) there are high marginal rates of income tax and much lower rates of tax on realised gains, capital growth

---

[12] For statistics relating to the United Kingdom, see paragraphs 6.48-6.55.

rather than high yield will still remain attractive after the introduction of a wealth tax, unless there has been a big concurrent reduction in income tax.[13]
1.44 Similarly the argument of administrative control is less convincing in practice than in theory. Would-be evaders would surely avoid obvious inconsistencies between their investment income and their capital. The most likely area of evasion under a wealth tax is the under-reporting of assets, like jewellery, where no cross check is possible with income because they yield none. Again, the different branches of a revenue authority dealing with gift tax, death duties and a wealth tax, are likely to co-ordinate their activities very imperfectly; apart from other difficulties the officers lack the time for automatic and regular cross checks.

1.45 The practical problems of administration are such that the cost is likely to be high even though the results remain imperfect. Self assessment may reduce administrative costs to the Revenue, but only by raising compliance costs—the costs incurred by the taxpayer in meeting the requirements of the tax system—without necessarily saving any real resources.

1.46 Further, if some assets are difficult for the Revenue to identify, it follows that tax evasion by under-reporting is easy. If the taxpayer is required to submit his own valuations, he must be tempted to undervalue. On both counts a wealth tax threatens standards of tax morality.

1.47 Much of this book is concerned with the practical problems of a wealth tax so no more will be said at this point. Here we have sought simply to indicate something of the nature of the problems; an assessment of their significance must await their detailed consideration.

Possible Adverse Economic Consequences
1.48 The second general argument against a wealth tax is that it may have some adverse economic consequences, and in particular reduce the incentive to save. The tax base is accumulated saving. Therefore the tax may discourage saving and, insofar as effort or enterprise have accumulation as their objectives, it may discourage work and enterprise too. This is not a necessary result. Insofar as a wealth tax is substituted for income tax there is a countervailing influence: whilst saving adds to liability to wealth tax, the income from additional saving suffers less income tax. In such a situation the outcome is uncertain.

The Purpose and Structure of a Wealth Tax
1.49 We have sought in this chapter to present the general case for and against a wealth tax. But it is clear that both the merits and the disadvantages relate closely to the weight and structure of the tax. A tax radically to reduce inequality of wealth requires a structure different from that primarily

---

[13] For some examples, see paragraph 6.45 and tables 6.4(a), 6.4(b) and 6.4(c).

concerned with horizontal equity or efficiency in resource use. Similarly the administrative problems and cost will vary with the threshold and exemptions; the extent of evasion will relate to the structure of exemptions, the methods of administration and the height of the tax; and the effect on saving will depend not only on the height of the wealth tax but on any consequential reduction in income tax.

1.50 Whilst a number of the details of a wealth tax are clearly important in relation to its purpose and consequences, there is one distinction, already mentioned, which is crucial: whether or not the taxpayer is able to meet the tax from income.

1.51 As a matter of convenient shorthand we shall call the kind of wealth tax which can be met from income (after allowing for reasonable consumption requirements) as 'substitutive' and that which cannot as an 'additive' wealth tax. This corresponds to the reality that if a wealth tax were introduced into an advanced economy like that of the United Kingdom it is unlikely that the wealthy would be able to meet it from income unless there was some concurrent reduction in income tax. But the essential consideration is whether the wealthy can meet wealth tax and income tax from income or whether their payment requires a disposal of assets.

1.52 This distinction suffers from two defects. First it is imprecise for two reasons: it depends on the taxpayer's level of consumption and the disposition of his assets. A wealth tax becomes additive at a combined level of income tax and wealth tax less than 100% of income, for the taxpayer must live; but how much less is not clear-cut. Further, the distinction is imprecise because income, and therefore the tax on it, is not a fixed sum and the taxpayer could increase his disposable income by transferring to higher-yielding assets. Second, in relation to any particular tax, the distinction is a little artificial: it may be that most taxpayers can meet a wealth tax from income but the very wealthiest cannot; it may be that a wealth tax is partly substitutive and partly additive. Nonetheless the distinction is useful and is the core of our analysis of some economic consequences of a wealth tax in the next chapter.

Summary and Conclusions

1.53 'Wealth tax' is a shorthand for an annual personal net wealth tax. The arguments in favour of such a tax can be grouped under the headings of horizontal equity, efficiency in resource use, reduction in inequality of wealth and administrative control. Arguments against stress the practical problems which inhibit the full achievement of these objectives, the difficulties and cost of administration and the possible detrimental effects on saving. Apart from the aim of directly reducing inequality of wealth, the other objectives of a wealth tax can be realised by a tax with a low threshold and with rates such that income tax and wealth tax together can normally be met out of income even by the very wealthy. The wealth tax to reduce inequality is different; its logic leads to a progressive wealth tax which (taking into account income tax) cannot be met from income. The distinction between those wealth taxes which can and those which cannot be met from income is crucial to the attainment of the different objectives, the extent of the disadvantages and the economic consequences. For convenience the first kind will be referred to as a 'substitutive' and the second as an 'additive' wealth tax.

Chapter 2

Some General Economic Effects

Introduction

2.1 The previous chapter examining the main arguments for and against a wealth tax necessarily touched on some of its economic effects, especially on efficiency in resource use and on the incentive to save. In this chapter, in the light of the distinction between substitutive and additive wealth taxes, we pursue further some of the more general (or macro) economic consequences: we take up again the question of efficiency and incentives; we look at the demand effects of a wealth tax and at relative price effects. We also consider some of the economic implications of the circumstances of the introduction of a wealth tax, particularly under conditions of inflation. Some micro-economic consequences, such as the effects on agriculture and on the private business, we examine separately in Part IV.

Shifting a Wealth Tax

2.2 As a necessary prelude to our economic analysis we must seek to answer one question. How far can a wealth tax be shifted? If the incidence of the tax can easily be moved from the personal wealth owner elsewhere, then the analysis becomes more complicated, the effects of the tax less predictable and its use for a particular social or economic purpose more doubtful.

2.3 There is a considerable measure of agreement in the economic literature that, by and large, a personal wealth tax (as distinct from one on companies) is not readily shiftable, mainly because the tax is not levied in conjunction with an economic transaction such as the purchase or sale of a product or factor of production. If the wealth tax is part of a process of increasing total government revenue, then strictly we must examine the consequential actions of government, its expenditure, its changed borrowing requirements and so on before we can be sure. But at least the wealth tax does not carry the more immediate characteristics of shiftability, as a commodity tax does. However, economists have usually assumed a substitutive tax. The effects of an additive tax will be more pronounced and might lead to some shifting of the burden through falls in capital values which restored, or partially restored, the net of wealth tax yield on capital to its pre-wealth tax levels.[1]

Additive and Substitutive Wealth Taxes

2.4 As outlined in the previous chapter, the crucial economic distinction is between wealth taxes paid from income and wealth taxes which can only be met from sale of assets, which, for convenience, we designated substitutive and additive wealth taxes respectively. An additive tax is therefore one which, when taken in conjunction with income tax is in excess of 100% of income; or more accurately, where the disposable income net of tax is not enough to cover the taxpayer's reasonable consumption requirements.

Incentives to Save and Invest

2.5 The significance of this distinction for the incentive to seek high-yielding assets and the incentives to earn and save is shown by the following example of marginal rates (MR) of income tax (IT) and wealth tax (WT). It is marginal rates of tax (i.e. the tax on the additional earned income or investment income) which are particularly relevant to the incentive to earn more or save more.

2.6 Situation I
Consider an initial situation where the rate of tax on earned income and on investment income is the same and there is no wealth tax. A person 'A' has wealth of £200,000 and an income of £20,000 on which he pays the maximum marginal rate of income tax at 80%.

2.7 Situation II—An Additive Wealth Tax
Assume that a wealth tax is introduced at $2\frac{1}{2}\%$ (marginal rate) on £200,000 of wealth.
WT at $2\frac{1}{2}\%$ is equivalent to IT at 50% on an investment yielding 5% and to IT at 25% on an investment yielding 10%.
If 'A' earns additional income, MR of IT ... ...   = 80%
If 'A' adds to his saving out of income and invests it (or, perhaps more realistically, receives a gift which he does not consume) then, on the investment income,
at 5% yield MR of IT + WT ... ... =130%
at 10% yield MR of IT + WT ... ... =105%

---

[1] In this connexion see particularly the discussion of the crucial importance of changes in the price of agricultural land as a result of wealth tax, paragraphs 13.27-13.31.

In both cases his income has actually fallen because he has saved more.

2.8 Situation III—A Substitutive Wealth Tax
Suppose that, at the same time as WT is introduced, income tax is reduced, say to a maximum of 50%.
Then,
if 'A' earns additional income, MR of IT ... ... = 50%
If 'A' saves additional income and invests it, then on the investment income
at 5% yield MR of IT + WT ... ... = 100%
at 10% yield MR of IT + WT ... ... = 75%

2.9 Whilst the actual figures are hypothetical and not necessarily realistic, Situation III makes it clear that if a government sought to obtain the same total revenue from IT + WT as it had previously obtained from IT (Situation I), the effect would be to reduce marginal tax rates on earned income and on high yielding investments and to increase them on low or nil yielding investments.

2.10 Situation III is the kind of substitution which a government might undertake; a substantial reduction in income tax on earned income might well be considered politically feasible allied to a wealth tax to replace lost revenue. But in other respects the reference to changes in earned income makes the example a little unfair and is a red herring. Income tax on earned income could have been reduced without a wealth tax but with a compensating increase in income tax on investment income (say by an investment income surcharge). In assessing a wealth tax we should concentrate on the effect of investment income in the example and think in terms of a wealth tax either added to a given level of income tax on investment income, or replacing part of the income tax on investment income.

2.11 Theoretical analysis tells us that where a tax on income is increased there are two effects on the incentive to save, working in opposite directions: an income and a substitution effect. The income effect encourages saving where people are striving for a particular level of capital and disposable income in the future; to achieve their object they must save more. The substitution effect generates a response of reduced saving (and increased consumption or perhaps leisure) because saving at the margin is less rewarding. The example suggests an overwhelming presumption that an additive tax will be a powerful disincentive to save; for where the marginal rate of income tax and wealth tax combined exceed 100% of income (even at relatively high yields) the income effect is at best only partially applicable. Saving more will (temporarily) increase capital, but anyone who saves more becomes actually worse off in terms of income: both income and substitution effects work in the same direction—a reduced incentive to save. With the substitutive wealth tax the effect on the overall incentive to save is more open. One can certainly expect an incentive to seek higher-yielding assets with a substitutive wealth tax.

2.12 The example examines only marginal rates and our definition of an additive and a substitutive tax related aggregate tax to aggregate income. But on any tax scale likely to be envisaged, an additive tax, where payment of the combined income tax and wealth tax requires some disposal of assets, must imply marginal rates in excess of 100% of income even for high-yielding assets. Under a substitutive tax, depending on the rate structure, marginal rates might well be over 100% up to quite a high yield.[2]

Demand Effects

2.13 The distinction between an additive or substitutive wealth tax is perhaps of even more economic significance in its demand effects than in its effects on the incentive to save. Apart from the incentive to save, the question arises of the effects of a wealth tax on the capacity to save. In other words, how far will the payment of the tax be met from a reduction in consumption and how far from a reduction in saving?

2.14 If a wealth tax is substituted for the top rates of income tax to produce the same total revenue, one would expect the wealth tax to affect aggregate demand much as the income tax it replaced. If a wealth tax was introduced as an alternative to increasing the rates of income tax, one would expect that the taxpayer would meet either tax partly by reduced consumption and partly by reduced savings; either would reduce aggregate demand significantly, but by less than the full amount of the tax revenue.

2.15 An additive wealth tax would have very different effects. It could be met only to a very small extent by reduced consumption. To say that it would be largely met out of wealth or out of capital does not, of course, mean that any capital would be physically destroyed; it means that assets are transferred from the private to the public sector. The tax would reduce aggregate demand only by a very small proportion of the revenue raised. It would therefore do little to release resources from current output.

2.16 A tax may have two effects on aggregate demand; the most immediate and generally by far the more important is the 'income effect': the reduction in disposable income consequent upon the tax reduces the taxpayer's demand for current output to the extent that he reduces his consumption to meet the tax. The second or 'wealth effect' results from the taxpayer's reduction in saving, or his dissaving, to meet the tax; his wealth is less than if the tax had not been imposed and, in consequence, other things being equal, he may in

---

[2] Examples of the effect of different wealth and income taxes on aggregate income are given in Chapters 3 and 6 and Appendix D.

the future be inclined to consume a smaller proportion of his income. Further, insofar as the wealth holder has less wealth to pass on to heirs then, both because of reduced expectation and realisation, the heirs in turn may be inclined to save a larger proportion of their income.

2.17 The income effect of an additive wealth tax will be to reduce consumption very little. The wealth effect will be stronger than with most other taxes except gift tax and death duties; but the wealth effect in reducing consumption demand is diffused over time and is indeterminate. The main significance of this analysis is that, starting from an equilibrium situation, revenue from an additive wealth tax cannot be used on a pound for pound basis to reduce other taxes (except taxes, like death duties, paid from wealth); nor should it be used to finance government expenditure which makes calls on current resources, because the wealth tax does not appreciably reduce demand for current output. To use the revenue to increase family allowances or expenditure on the health services would be bound to be inflationary. The revenue from an additive wealth tax mainly adds to the government's capital account receipts and reduces its borrowing requirements.

2.18 As a demand stabiliser a substitutive wealth tax is probably more uncertain in its effects than income tax on investment income. A tax promotes fiscal stability if its revenue automatically rises more than proportionately when pressure of private demand is high and falls more than proportionately when demand is low. A progressive income tax can thus be expected to act as an automatic stabiliser. The reliability of a wealth tax for this purpose is likely to be less than income tax. Stock exchange prices often do tend to be high in periods of high demand and vice versa; but this is not invariably so (witness the 1974 Stock Exchange slump in the UK). Moreover, wealth taxes are often proportional or only mildly progressive with constant rates over wide bands; revenue will therefore tend to be proportional to fluctuations in asset values, though not entirely so because the fluctuations will bring some people into or remove them from the wealth tax net. Further, and possibly most important, a wealth tax payment normally relates to one specific valuation date each year. It will be based on asset prices which are out of date. At the bottom of a stock exchange slump, people will be paying wealth taxes on higher than current values. If the stock exchange slump coincides with a slump in the economy, wealth tax payments will be relatively high at a time when the need is to stimulate demand. However, it would be misleading to stress the possible de-stabilising effects of a wealth tax. Because the revenue from a wealth tax is so small (for example under 2% of total revenue from taxation in all the European countries which have wealth taxes) and, even with a substitutive tax, the demand effect is less than the revenue effect, any stabilising or de-stabilising influences are comparatively unimportant.

c

Relative Prices and Consumption Patterns

2.19 A wealth tax may be expected to have some effects on relative prices. Nil-yielding and low-yielding assets will be less attractive, high-yielding assets more attractive. We can expect a wealth tax to have an effect in reducing the prices of pictures, stamp collections and antique furniture; to raise the price of high-yielding securities and shares; and to increase the attractions of high yield as compared with capital growth. Also one may expect the holdings of cash balances to be less attractive, so that, on this score there may be a reduction in liquidity preference which, given no action by the monetary authorities, would raise the price of securities and thus lower interest rates.

2.20 These influences on relative prices would be felt both from a substitutive and an additive wealth tax, but with important differences. If a substitutive wealth tax was associated with a reduction in income tax, then the attraction of higher-yielding assets would be correspondingly increased. If an additive wealth tax had the effect of discouraging saving then there would be a counter movement to the effect on interest rates. Further, if many wealth holders were selling assets to meet wealth tax liabilities this might be expected to depress asset prices generally. However, this is not necessarily so, because the government's own borrowing requirements would be correspondingly reduced; the increased pressure to sell assets of wealth tax payers is matched by a reduction of government sales of new securities or even government purchase of debt. Thus the overall demand for assets might be expected to remain the same except to the extent of any reduction in the incentive to save; but the incentive to sell assets would not be evenly distributed across all assets; it would be concentrated most on the low- or nil-yielding assets which carried wealth tax liability with little or no income. Hence the effect on the relative prices of different assets, outlined above, might be accentuated.

2.21 In considering the effect of introducing a wealth tax in one country on the relative prices of different kinds of assets the extent of the market must be taken into account. Thus because the market in a nil-yielding asset such as 'old masters' is international rather than national, the relative price reduction would be less; whilst because the market in low-yielding agricultural land is mainly national, its relative price fall could be expected to be more pronounced.

2.22 Of course, any assets exempt from wealth tax, or relatively undervalued for wealth tax purposes, would tend to attract investment funds and their prices would tend to rise relatively to other assets.

2.23 If a wealth tax of either variety reduced the incentive to save, and even to some extent if it didn't, there would be a tendency to consume more single-use goods and services. If durable consumption goods (cars, washing-machines, furniture) entered into the wealth tax base, then expensive meals out and holidays abroad become relatively more attractive. If their supply was perfectly elastic in the long run, their price would not rise, but the pattern of consumption would change. Similarly if human capital is excluded from the tax base, then investment in education and training, yielding higher earned income, becomes relatively more attractive than investment in physical or financial assets, which are included in the tax base.

Circumstances of Introduction

Timing and Acceptability

2.24 'A wealth tax' has a pejorative sound about it. Whilst such a tax, presented as a substitute for top rates of income tax, is unlikely to cause much taxpayer resentment, an additive tax may well do so. An additive tax has the character of a minor capital levy except that it applies each year. Its acceptability to those who have to pay it will depend in part on whether they see a need for it. Just as it has always been held that a capital levy could only be used or justified in times of emergency (and most suggestions for or applications of levies have been in the immediate aftermath of major wars) so an additive tax has something of the same flavour about it.

2.25 If it fails to gain acceptability certain economic consequences may follow. Both its announcement and the attempt to apply it may have certain economic results. It could have a psychological effect detrimental to business confidence and to investment. Further it could lead to evasion and avoidance including the emigration of the rich and the transfer of their capital abroad. These are issues we explore further in Chapter 16.

A Wealth Tax and Inflation

2.26 Another circumstance relevant to the introduction and continuance of a wealth tax is the existence of inflation. It is sometimes argued that inflation makes a wealth tax more necessary, because inflation alters the relative prices of assets and generates huge gains for those holding wealth in particular forms, notably physical assets like land, buildings and precious metals. A wealth tax, it is said, is therefore necessary to tax the unmerited gains of those whom inflation has enriched. This is an unconvincing argument. The wealth tax base includes both assets which have risen more than average in price and those which have not risen at all, like cash and bank balances. It is adding to the discomfiture of the losers in the inflationary process to impose a tax on their depleted assets. If one seeks to tax the gains from inflation it would seem more sensible to strengthen and increase the rates of capital gains tax; at the same time it would be right to index it so that the acquisition value of assets was increased in proportion to the rise in the general price level and hence, on realisation, the tax was levied on the real, and not just the monetary gain.

2.27 In fact a high rate of inflation raises particular problems for the fair and efficient operation of a wealth tax. It accentuates valuation problems; with stable prices valuations would be easier and could be less frequent. Inflation generates problems where the productive capital of one man, such as the farmer, becomes the inflation hedge of another; the rise in price of assets used as a hedge against inflation and their correspondingly low yield, creates serious payment problems even with a substitutive wealth tax. Inflation at varying rates generates fluctuations in interest rates and much uncertainty about the level of future interest rates; yet some stability is required in interest rates if a sensible structure of rates is to be designed for a wealth tax; such a structure must be based on some appreciation of what is a reasonable rate of return to determine the combined burden of wealth tax and income tax. For example, with nil inflation a rate of interest on government irredeemable securities might be 3 or 4%; with inflation running at 5% per annum, 8% might be an expected yield; with inflation at 10% per annum, the same real yield would require interest rates of 13 or 14%. If inflation is running at 15 or 20% how does one design a wealth tax rate structure with a reasonable permanence? If wealth tax at top rate is intended to be the equivalent of a 50% income tax on the yield of a gilt-edged security, a rate that would meet that criterion at a time of high inflation would be enormously high if inflation were brought under control.

2.28 Whilst there is a strong case for indexing all taxes to ensure as far as possible that the real burden does not change simply as a result of a general change in the value of money, this need is greater for taxes like capital gains tax[3] (where a tax on a monetary gain may, as a result of inflation, be a tax on a real loss) and a wealth tax, especially of the additive kind. If no measures are taken to protect the taxpayer against inflation, the real burden of a capital gains tax or a wealth tax increases and the tax bites into, or more deeply into, the taxpayer's capital or wealth. This is more serious than the effect of inflation in raising the burden of income tax, because its effect is more permanent. If a wage or salary earner suffers an additional tax burden because income tax thresholds have not risen in line with prices, his loss consists of a part of the return to an asset, his earning capacity, but the earning capacity itself is unaffected. A subsequent raising of the threshold will restore his real income to its previous level and, if the threshold is raised sufficiently, he may even recover the lost income. But with a wealth tax or a capital gains tax the effect of inflation can be to deplete (or deplete more than was intended) the assets from which income is derived; a subsequent raising of the threshold cannot bring back the lost assets.

2.29 Inflation therefore causes particular problems with a wealth tax and inflation-proofing is particularly necessary if serious inequities are to be avoided. It is therefore highly desirable that each step of a wealth tax should

---

[3] A. J. Merrett, 'The Capital Gains Tax', *Lloyds Bank Review*, October 1965.

be related to an index of the general price level and automatically adjusted in line with changes in that index.

2.30 In what follows, for purposes of exposition, we shall assume a stable currency (or at any rate regard the general price rise as not more than 4%) save where inflation gives rise to some problem that needs special mention. The rates of return in our calculations should be interpreted in this light. As future rates of inflation are so very uncertain, any other solution for purposes of exposition seems hardly practical.

Summary and Conclusions

2.31 The distinction between a substitutive and an additive wealth tax (one where the taxpayer's disposable income net of income and wealth tax is not sufficient to cover reasonable consumption requirements) is crucial in the analysis of economic consequences. An additive tax, with marginal rates of combined income tax and wealth tax in excess of 100% even on high yielding assets, is very likely to act as a disincentive to saving; an additive tax will have little effect in reducing demand for current output so that revenue from it cannot be treated as freely available for current government expenditure; and both kinds of tax, but especially the additive, may be expected to effect changes in the relative prices of assets. The problems of introducing a wealth tax are accentuated by inflation and indexing the various steps in the tax is particularly necessary.

Part II
Wealth Taxes in Practice

Chapter 3

A Comparative Review of some European Wealth Taxes

An International Perspective

3.1 Wealth taxes are not a particularly recent fiscal innovation. Some twenty wealth taxes exist, many originating over half a century ago. About half the present wealth taxes are to be found in Europe; the remainder are all in developing countries, in the Indian sub-continent (India, Pakistan and Sri Lanka) and in a number of countries of Central and South America. No developed country outside Europe (e.g. USA, Canada, Australia) currently imposes a wealth tax, but under the influence of the Shoup Mission Japan introduced one in 1950, only to abolish it three years later.

3.2 In Europe, wealth taxes are to be found in all the Scandinavian countries: Sweden, Norway, Finland, Denmark and Iceland; in Germany, the Netherlands and Luxembourg of the original EEC countries; and also in Austria and the Swiss cantons. The Republic of Ireland is committed to a wealth tax planned to commence in 1975 and the main outlines of the proposed tax are available in the Irish White Paper on *Capital Taxation* as modified by ministerial statements.[1] The United Kingdom is the latest country to propose adoption of a wealth tax; the Labour Government hopes to legislate for it in 1976. Apart from a firm commitment to the principle of a wealth tax, however, the only other undertaking is that the threshold shall be £100,000 (Chapter 6).

3.3 Because of the very different social and economic circumstances of the countries outside Europe, this review will be restricted to European countries;

---

[1] White Paper on *Capital Taxation,* February 1974; modified by the Statement of Mr. Richie Ryan, Minister of Finance, on 15 May 1974.

within Europe it will concentrate on a group of five countries with wealth taxes: Norway, Sweden, Denmark, Germany and the Netherlands. The review thus includes three of the Scandinavian countries and all the EEC countries which have wealth taxes except Luxembourg. Additionally we shall include in the comparisons the two European countries committed to wealth taxes, the Republic of Ireland, using the fairly firm proposals now existing, and the United Kingdom with its 1974 tax system which does not include a wealth tax but does include an investment income surcharge.

3.4 The purpose of this chapter is to present an overall view of the main characteristics of the wealth taxes of the five countries and of the Irish proposals and then to compare the weight of taxation on capital and investment income of these countries with each other and with the 1974 (pre-wealth tax) situation in the United Kingdom. The wealth taxes of two of the countries, Sweden and Germany, will be presented in detail as case studies in the next two chapters. Also, more detailed accounts of particular aspects of the wealth taxes of these countries will be given in Part IV in considering particular problems. At this point in the book we seek to provide a meaningful perspective.

3.5 International comparisons are fraught with difficulty. Although all the European countries we are considering have advanced 'mixed' economies, they differ in history, social structure and economic organisation. Thus, for example, a wealth tax to reduce inequality may make sense in one country with large inequalities of wealth, whereas in another it would be otiose because wealth inequalities are much less pronounced. Likewise a wealth tax may raise serious problems for a particular form of economic activity (such as the owner-occupier in agriculture) in one country, whereas the same problem may not exist, or be much less important, in another, because of a different form of ownership or a smaller size of economic unit.

3.6 It therefore does not follow that if the purpose of a wealth tax, or the form of the tax, or the method of valuation, or the administrative arrangements, differ between one country and another, then one must be right and the other wrong. Each might be the most suitable for that country (or, of course, there might be a better way for both). Similarly, it may be that a method which works in one country cannot be successfully transplanted to another. Indeed, it does not even follow that, if one country has a wealth tax and another has not, one is right and the other wrong. Apart from different social and economic circumstances, the very fact that each country has a different established tax structure and administration may make it unwise for one to adopt the method of the other. Major changes in a tax system are expensive, not only in administrative costs to the Revenue, but also in the compliance costs to taxpayers and in rendering obsolescent the skills of tax advisers;[2] even if, say, a wealth tax is clearly preferable, in the abstract, to a surcharge on investment income, it does not follow it would be sound policy for a country to adopt the superior system. If the change is to be justified, the alternative must be better by a sufficient margin to outweigh the costs of change. There are some 'improvements' which are just not worth the bother. Considerations like this explain the adage that 'an old tax is a good tax'; though, in turn, they must not be used an an excuse for perpetuating serious inefficiency or inequity.

3.7 International comparisons of the weight of different kinds of taxes raise particular difficulties which we shall consider in some detail later in the chapter.

3.8 Nevertheless, one can expect international comparisons, treated with care, to be useful. At least they throw up questions about why one country differs in its practice from another and set us looking for satisfactory answers; they may reveal methods in one country that *can* with value be transplanted (possibly with some modification); they may offer examples to avoid as well as to follow; and they help to extend the vision of tax policy makers and commentators. They fulfil a further purpose; differences in the form of taxes and particularly big differences in the weight of taxation between countries influence the migration of labour and capital and may need to be taken into account by tax policy makers on that score.

3.9 It is, in particular, to be expected that a country embarking on a new tax will gain from examining the practices of those who have already trod that path. The inexperienced ought to be able to learn from the experienced. Thus, tax policy makers in both the Republic of Ireland and the United Kingdom can expect to benefit from a study of the wealth taxes of other European countries. There is an especial case for a close and careful study of European wealth taxes by the Irish and the British for, in both countries, the proposals for this fiscal innovation were accompanied, and partly justified, by frequent references to the existence of wealth taxes in other countries.[3] We must enquire how far the precedents are valid.

Characteristics of European Wealth Taxes

European Wealth Taxes as a whole

3.10 Several generalisations can be made about European wealth taxes as a whole. They are all substitutive in the sense of being supplements to income tax and alternatives to a higher rate of tax on investment income. The intention

---

[2] See C. T. Sandford, *Hidden Costs of Taxation*, I.F.S., July 1973, especially pp. 149-150.

[3] See, for example, the Irish Government's White Paper on *Capital Taxation*, p. 1 and p. 17; and the British Government's Green Paper on *Wealth Tax*, p. iii (The Chancellor's Foreword) and pp. 1 and 2; and the Labour Party advocacy of the tax, in pamphlets such as *Labour's Economic Strategy*, 1969, p. 48.

that payment should normally be met from the taxpayer's income is clear from the relatively low rates and the prevalence of ceiling provisions which limit the combined total of taxes on wealth and income to a percentage of taxable income; most notably, ceilings apply in the two countries, Sweden and Finland, with the highest rates.

3.11 Classified by reference to the rate structure of their wealth taxes, the European countries divide evenly into two, corresponding with geographical groupings. Half the European wealth taxes have maximum rates of over 1% and half of under 1%. The five Scandinavian countries (including Iceland) have rates rising above 1% and in all cases their wealth taxes are progressive (though Denmark only just qualifies on both counts, having recently changed from a 0.9% proportional rate to a two-band progression with a maximum rate of 1.1%). The remaining five European countries with wealth taxes all have rates which are proportional to taxable wealth except for Switzerland, where some of the cantons levy progressive wealth taxes at rates of a fraction of 1%.

3.12 Of the newcomers seeking to join the club, the Republic of Ireland has now settled for a proportional rate of 1%; the United Kingdom seems set on a progressive rate structure rising well above 1%.

Characteristics of Some European Wealth Taxes

3.13 Henceforward, our concentration will be on the five European countries of Denmark, Norway and Sweden, Germany and the Netherlands. A detailed comparison of the features of the wealth taxes of these five countries and the proposals for the Republic of Ireland and the United Kingdom is set out in Appendix C. Here we attempt to draw out some of the more important general characteristics.

3.14 A significant feature of this group of European wealth taxes is their age; all are over fifty years old. The youngest is the German wealth tax which first became law in 1922; but this tax can claim ancestry from the Prussian tax of 1893 on which it was modelled. If we take the earlier date for the German tax, then all the wealth taxes pre-date the first World War. Their age is an important clue to their purpose; it is no accident that these countries were introducing annual wealth taxes at about the same time that the United Kingdom was differentiating its income tax in order to tax income from property more heavily than income from work. Contemporary governments saw these measures very largely as alternative ways of promoting horizontal equity, recognising the greater permanence of income from property over income from work and the advantages of wealth itself in addition to the income it yielded. It follows that these countries with a wealth tax do not have an investment income surcharge.

3.15 The promotion of horizontal equity is still seen in all these countries as the prime purpose of the wealth tax. Considerations of administrative control are subsidiary and officials in the different countries vary in the importance they attach to it. Thus, in Denmark, its value is stressed and all income tax payers are required to return details of their wealth, even though they are below the threshold for wealth tax. On the other hand, in Germany (where wealth tax assessments are triennial and the returns, though they go to the same tax office, are separate from those for income tax) and the Netherlands (where only wealth tax payers complete a combined form for income tax and wealth tax) the advantage of a wealth tax for purposes of control, whilst acknowledged, was considered fairly minimal and supplementary to other methods.

3.16 In no case was it suggested to us that the Continental wealth taxes were valuable as a means of promoting efficiency in resource use; this may be partly because this function is to some extent negative, in the sense of being less detrimental to efficiency than an equivalent addition to income tax. We were given some indications that wealth taxes are beginning to be seen as instruments for reducing inequality of wealth, but only in the limited sense in which a progressive income tax can be said to do so (paragraph 1.31).

3.17 Broadly speaking, in all five countries, wealth taxes are levied on the world-wide assets of residents and apply to a more limited range of assets for non-residents. The main difference in the scope of the charge is that Germany and Norway also levy wealth tax on companies. The Norwegians also have a local as well as a national wealth tax.

3.18 All five countries aggregate the wealth of husband and wife (though they differ in whether the minor children are included within the tax unit). Despite this common feature of aggregation, the approach to the threshold of liability differs. Denmark and Sweden allow only the same basic tax free amount to a family as to a single person; Norway raises the tax free sum by one-third for a taxpayer with dependents; Germany and the Netherlands have more generous and elaborate provisions to give additional tax free amounts not only for a wife but also for dependent children and for the aged and invalid. These differences of treatment complicate a comparison of the thresholds, but if we take the simple case of single persons, in 1974 the tax free amount varied between a low of some £5,800[4] for Norway to a high of £31,500 for Denmark. Thus the highest threshold amongst these European taxes is less than one-third of that being proposed for the United Kingdom, and also not much more than one-third of the proposed Irish exemption limit (£70,000) if account is taken of the Irish proposal to exempt a principal private residence, which comes within the wealth tax base in all the other

---

[4] All sterling equivalents of foreign currencies are calculated at the exchange rates ruling on 1 July 1974 (See Appendix C).

countries. The threshold level in the five countries reflects the purpose of horizontal equity.

3.19 All five countries give exemptions for household chattels for personal use; but all, except Denmark, impose some limits on what may be included. Norway groups works of art, collections and jewellery together with other household goods and taxes them in excess of a certain aggregate value. Germany taxes those household goods deemed to be luxuries. The Dutch and Swedes exempt all household goods save for jewellery (in the Dutch case, grouped with precious metals), which is taxable above a specified sum. The Danes alone hold to the clear principle that 'the tax stops short at the doors'; thus in Denmark everything inside the house, be it work of art or jewellery of unlimited value, is outside the wealth tax base (unless used for business purposes).

3.20 As previously mentioned, the three Scandinavian countries have progressive rates rising above 1%, whilst those for Germany and the Netherlands are proportional at 0.7^5 and 0.8% respectively. All five countries except Germany have ceiling provisions. Norway abolished a ceiling provision in 1973 but the position remained under review and a provision was re-introduced in the Autumn of 1974 to apply to the income year 1974. Germany, with by far the lowest marginal rate of income tax, as well as the lowest rate of wealth tax, hardly needs one. Over recent years, the yield of wealth tax in all five countries has been under $1\frac{1}{2}$% of total taxes (including social security contributions). The 1971 figures range from 0.5% in Denmark to 1.3% in Germany (where companies are taxed as well as individuals).

3.21 In all five countries, the work of tax assessment and collection is decentralised; but a sharp distinction must be drawn between the Netherlands and the other four in administrative practice. In the Netherlands responsibility is placed on the taxpayer to value his assets; he is given no guide lines except that the values should be 'open market'. These values are then accepted or disputed by the local tax inspector, who has wide discretionary powers. The other four countries, whilst differing in detail from each other, all have in common the existence of specific rules and procedures for determining values. The taxpayer puts his own open market valuation on personal chattels, but the value of almost all other assets is determined in accordance with set rules. This feature is perhaps seen at its strongest in Germany, where a valuation law determines precise methods of valuation for a range of taxes. But in the Scandinavian countries also, whilst assessment and collection is local, guide lines are centrally laid down and uniformity of practice promoted by agencies like the Swedish National Tax Board. The valuation of shares in closely held companies and of unincorporated businesses generally follows procedures

---

[5] The rate of wealth tax on companies in Germany is to rise to 1% from 1 January 1974; but it is to remain at 0.7% for individuals.

based on income tax practice. Real property is valued by local assessment committees in the Scandinavian countries and by a specialist department (within the tax administration) of the Land governments in Germany, but in all cases in line with central directives. Save in Norway, a cadastral basis, which generally holds until the next valuation, is used for real property; and the value of a man's land or house for wealth tax purposes is determined for him by an assessment based on a detailed consideration of the characteristics of the house. In the Scandinavian countries each year specific wealth tax values are even put on farm livestock according to their kind.

3.22 The proposals for the Republic of Ireland and the United Kingdom approach much closer to the Dutch model, but with some important differences. The Irish or United Kingdom taxpayer is to be required to value his assets with few rules to guide him; but authority on the Revenue side is not to be de-centralised like the Dutch. The Republic of Ireland envisages a centralised system, the United Kingdom a regionalised system. In both cases, as the taxpayer's return may not be checked for some time after its submission, he may have to remain for long uncertain if his valuations have been accepted.

Comparison of the Weight of Taxation

3.23 A comparison of wealth taxes alone has only limited value for they need to be seen in the context of related taxes, especially if we seek to measure the weight of taxation on capital and on the return on capital.

Problems of International Tax Comparisons

3.24 The difficulties of such comparisons and their limitations must, however, be fully appreciated. The main problems can be grouped under five headings:

1. *The lack of a common currency.* To compare tax rates and thresholds, we convert them all into sterling at the exchange rates ruling at a specified date (1 July 1974). But a particular exchange rate is an imperfect measure of the relative values of goods and services which enter into international trade, let alone of the value of assets, many of which, like land and houses, normally do not. There is no simple way of correcting for this deficiency.

2. *What taxes to include.* We seek to compare the taxes on investment income and on capital. Clearly, this includes national income tax on investment income, national wealth taxes and death duties. But there are several marginal cases.

   In the three Scandinavian countries, local income tax is levied on taxable income at a proportional rate of 20% or more. In those countries, the local authorities undertake spending which elsewhere is financed from central government taxation. Moreover, local income tax is a major tax on investment income, which cannot be ignored. But if we include local income tax, why not local wealth tax (which is levied in Norway) and if local wealth tax, why not also local taxes on real property, which are levied on the capital value of real property in most of the countries, and on an assessed annual value in the Republic of Ireland and in the United Kingdom? In fact, we have decided to include the one local wealth tax (the Norwegian) but to exclude all forms of local realty tax. This can be justified on perhaps three grounds: the Norwegian local wealth tax is comprehensive, which realty taxes are not; the local wealth tax is taken into account in the determination of the Norwegian ceiling provisions, so that if we omit it we cannot calculate precisely when these provisions apply; and finally, though we cannot claim to have done an exhaustive analysis, our impression is that Norwegian local wealth tax is quantitatively more important than the local realty taxes. Some indication of the significance of the Norwegian local wealth tax and of the United Kingdom local rates is given in Appendix D.

Another problem is raised by gift tax, which is particularly irregular in its incidence—more so than death duties that apply once in a generation. In fact, all the countries now link gift taxes and death duties with some measure of cumulation, so without grossly over-simplifying we can regard gift taxes as being covered by death duties.

A further border-line case is capital gains tax. Of the seven countries with which we are concerned, five have capital gains taxes though not always named as such. The exceptions are Germany and the Netherlands, though even these countries tax some gains as income. The regulations on taxation of gains vary considerably between countries and are very complex.[6] Whilst the existence of capital gains taxes does increase the weight of taxation on wealth, there is no simple way to include them and they have been omitted from the attempt at quantitative assessment.

3. *Lack of a uniform tax base.* This difficulty applies to all the taxes included. Different tax systems generate different bases of taxation. To take some examples. All five European countries with wealth taxes impute an income to the owners of owner-occupied houses for income tax purposes, although the method of imputation varies. The United Kingdom, on the other hand, no longer imputes any such income. Again the tax base varies according to the number and size of allowances—thus there are different reliefs for income tax, wealth tax and death duties. For example, the United Kingdom has an income tax child relief, but Sweden does not, because there, child allowances are now wholly paid in cash. We have already mentioned the different practices on thresholds under wealth tax, varying in some countries, but not all, according to the number of persons in the tax unit. Exemption or otherwise of life insurance and of a private residence may significantly affect the weight of a wealth tax. Similarly there may be death duty concessions for particular kinds of property

---

[6] Some details are given in Appendix C.

(like woodlands or works of art) which lower the effective rate. Clearly too, differences in the amount of tax evasion and avoidance affect the effective rate of tax and distort international comparisons.

4. *Lack of uniform valuation.* More subtly, differences in valuation alter effective tax rates. For example, in every country with a wealth tax, it is recognised that owner-occupied houses are under-valued. In Germany, Denmark and Sweden with re-assessment at intervals, the initial assessments are cautious and between assessment dates the wealth tax value and market value have increasingly diverged. In Sweden, it is now provided by statute that real property is assessed for wealth tax at only 75% of the market value. In the Netherlands, houses are valued by the taxpayer himself. The basis is open market value, but where the house is let or occupied by the owner, the accepted value is about two-thirds of vacant possession value. Ireland is proposing to value the first £200,000 of a farm at only 50% of market value—and so on. If one country has relatively low valuations, this effectively raises its thresholds and reduces the burden of tax and so distorts any international comparison.

5. *Variant forms of tax.* The problems on this score are most obvious with death duties. All the countries except the United Kingdom tax the recipient of a gift or inheritance, not the donor or testator. Each inheritance tax contains several scales; so that the tax paid varies both according to the size of the shares into which an estate is divided and the relationship of the various beneficiaries to the deceased. Tax paid under the United Kingdom capital transfer tax[7] is the same, irrespective of the distribution of the estate or the size of the shares, except that gifts and legacies to a surviving spouse are duty free. Other less important differences of death tax form affecting the effective rates of tax are the nature and extent of cumulation of gifts with gifts and gifts with final legacy. The United Kingdom capital transfer tax cumulates all gifts and bequests from the same donor. The Irish capital acquisition tax proposes to cumulate all gifts and bequests from the same donor to the same donee, but to charge a 25% lower rate on gifts. The other countries all have some element of cumulation but of varying degrees. Another important difference is the treatment of a surviving spouse. Not only do taxing statutes differ, the position is affected by differing property laws. Thus, under Swedish laws on community of property, only half the joint property is assessed to death duty when a married person dies. In Norway, all joint property passes to the surviving widow without duty and when she dies

---

[7] At the time of writing, the United Kingdom death duties are in a transitional stage. The capital transfer tax came into effect for gifts from March 26 1974 and is to replace estate duty in the case of a death from the date at which the Autumn 1974 Finance Bill receives the Royal Assent. Our calculations are all based on the rates proposed for the new capital transfer tax.

her children are regarded as inheriting partly from her and partly from their father, so that the rate of duty is consequently less.

3.25 Table 3.1 offers a first approach to a perspective on the comparative weight of taxation on wealth and on investment income. The tax rates are the latest available, applying to the year 1974, 1974-5 or 1975 (where new rates have already been specifically approved at the time of our investigation, notably the German income tax). The minimum thresholds are the lowest tax free amounts that a single man[8] could obtain for wealth tax and death duty respectively. The 'minimax' is the minimum level at which the maximum tax rate (on income, wealth or inheritance) is applicable. To put the inheritance taxes and the capital transfer tax on a par, the death duty rates are those applicable when the whole of the estate passes from a parent to a child who has attained majority. In such a case an inheritance tax and a death duty levied on the total estate with the same rates generate the same tax liability.

3.26 To offer a general perspective on the overall weight of taxation for the countries considered, OECD figures are given of total taxes as a percentage of GNP at market prices. (A factor cost measure of GNP would have been preferable, but differing accounting methods complicate the factor cost comparison and for our broad purpose the market price measure is adequate.) The position of these countries in the OECD tax league (of 22 countries) is also included in the table.[9] It is clear that, with the exception of Ireland, we are dealing with countries around the top of the tax league.

3.27 The minimaxes in table 3.1 provides some corrective to misleading impressions derived from looking at maximum marginal tax rates on their own; to take the two extremes: the maximum rate of income tax in Denmark applies at a much lower income than in any other country and at a level less than one-third of the majority. At the other end of the scale the maximum rate of death duty in Germany only comes into effect (if it ever does) at the enormous inheritance of over £16m. The United Kingdom has the distinction of the highest marginal rate of income tax (which would be true even without the 15% investment income surcharge) and the highest marginal rate of death duty; but the other countries have wealth taxes in addition to income tax; and with the exception of Germany, the United Kingdom has the highest minimax for death duties.

3.28 Table 3.1, whilst helpful, conceals much that is important. It takes no account of the curve of progression of income tax (or death duty) which

---

[8] The comparison would be different if a family unit were taken, e.g. in the case of wealth tax, Germany and the Netherlands give additional tax free amounts for each member of a family, Sweden and Denmark do not (Appendix C).

[9] The make up of the OECD statistics can be found in *Revenue Statistics of OECD Member Countries 1965-71;* for commentary see *Economic Trends,* October 1973. Note that death duties are not included in the total of taxes expressed as a percentage of GNP.

Table 3.1 Comparison of Taxation on Wealth and Investment Income for various European Countries 1974/1974-5/1975

Country	Income tax on investment income		Wealth tax			Death duty (and gift tax)			All taxes (inc. social security contributions) % of GNP at market prices (average 1965-71)	Position from 22 countries
	Maximum marginal rate %	Minimax £	Minimum threshold £	Maximum marginal rate %	Minimax £	Minimum threshold £	Maximum marginal rate %	Minimax £		
Denmark	65	6,400	31,500	1.1	139,800	559	32	69,900	37	4
Germany	56	21,300	11,400	0.7	11,400	14,700	35	16,400,000	34	8
Netherlands	71	21,500	6,800	0.8	6,800	944	17	79,600	39	2
Norway	71	20,700	5,800	1.6+1*	44,200	769	35	30,700	38	3
Sweden	78	14,700	19,000	2.5	95,200	1,429	65	476,200	40	1
Ireland (proposals)	70	10,900	70,000	1.0	70,000	150,000	55	450,000	29	14
United Kingdom (pre-wealth tax)	98	20,600	—	—	—	15,000	75	2,000,000	35	7

NOTES:
* Local wealth tax.
Minimax: minimum level at which maximum rate becomes payable.
Income tax: rates for Denmark, Norway and Sweden include local income tax at average rates;
rate for Denmark also includes 4% for pension and social security contributions;
rate for United Kingdom includes 15% investment surcharge (on investment incomes over £2,000);
the allowances for the Netherlands are those applicable to the first half of 1974.
Death duty: rate for Germany is on a 'slab' basis (applicable to the total estate).
Rates of exchange: as at 1 July 1974.
Rounding: rates of income tax, death duty and total taxes as % of GNP are rounded to the nearest whole number; minimaxes are rounded to the nearest hundred.

affects the weight of tax at different levels of income (or estate); nor does it allow for the effect of ceiling provisions in reducing the combined burden of income tax and wealth tax. The following group of tables (3.2a, b and c) show income tax (IT) and annual wealth tax (WT) for each country at different rates of return and different levels of net wealth as a percentage of investment income, assuming, as with table 3.1, a single person with minimum allowances and investment income only. Table 3.2a compares tax on investment income and wealth for a net wealth of £100,000 for each country, assuming an average rate of return of 2% and of 5%. Table 3.2b shows wealth tax and investment income tax for a net capital of £1m assuming average rates of return of 5% and 10%. Assets yielding a nil monetary return (like household goods, houses, cars and boats) bring down the average rate of return and these nil-yielding assets will normally decline in proportion to total assets as the size of estate increases, hence the assumption of higher average rates of return for larger wealth holdings. Table 3.2c combines tax on wealth and investment income at various rates of return and different levels of net wealth. (The separate details of wealth tax and investment income tax are given in full in Appendix D).

3.29 Tables 3.2a and 3.2b show the heavy effect of wealth tax relatively to income tax when the rate of return is low, and its lighter effect at high rates of return. The lack of a wealth tax in the United Kingdom, and the limited progression in the income tax over the middle range of incomes, account for the low tax position of the United Kingdom compared with the other countries in table 3.2a; the introduction of a wealth tax in the United Kingdom at the proposed threshold of £100,000 would leave this situation unchanged. On the other hand, at net wealth of £1m (table 3.2b), at the 10% rate of return the United Kingdom emerges at the top of the league and at the 5% next to the top even without a wealth tax. The tables also show the significance of the ceiling provisions, applicable in Denmark, the Netherlands, Norway and Sweden, in reducing the combined tax burden. It should be recalled that the figures for Ireland assume no ceiling provisions, but the Irish Government has left open the possibility of introducing them.

3.30 These same points are reflected in the combined wealth tax and income tax figures in table 3.2c where, at each level of net wealth and rate of return, the lowest combined tax burden has been printed in bold, and the lowest in italic, type. The United Kingdom is at the bottom of the table on the lower amounts of net wealth where the return is lowest and at the top of the table for the largest amounts of net wealth, especially where the rate of return is highest.

Marginal Tax Rates

3.31 Economic behaviour on saving and investment is probably influenced

Tables 3.2 (a) and (b)

Comparison of Wealth Tax and Investment Income Tax as a Percentage of Investment Income at different rates of return (Single person with minimum allowances and no earned income)

percentages

(a) On Net Wealth of £100,000

Country	2% rate of return			5% rate of return		
	IT	WT*	IT & WT	IT	WT*	IT & WT
Denmark	33	31	48°	48	12	58°
Germany	17	31	48	27	12	39
Netherlands	17	37	54	29	15	44
Norway	19	111	28°	31	44	65°
Sweden	25	75	80°	43	30	73
Ireland—proposals	20	15	35	29	6	35
United Kingdom[1]	23	—	23	38	—	38

(b) On Net Wealth of £1,000,000

Country	5% rate of return			10% rate of return		
	IT	WT*	IT & WT	IT	WT*	IT & WT
Denmark	63	21	73°	64	10	73°
Germany	52	14	66	54	7	61
Netherlands	65	16	79°	68	8	76
Norway	64	51	88°	68	26	89°
Sweden	73	48	83°	76	24	84
Ireland—proposals	64	19	83	67	9	76
United Kingdom[1]	86	—	86	92	—	92

NOTES:
° After applying ceiling provisions.
* Includes local wealth tax for Norway.
1 Without wealth tax but including investment income surcharge at 15 per cent on investment income over £2,000.
Other assumptions for income tax as Table 3.1.

Table 3.2 (c)

Comparison of Combined Wealth Tax and Investment Income Tax as a Percentage of Investment Income at different rates of return on different amounts of net wealth

(Single person with minimum allowances and no earned income)

percentages

Wealth £'000	Denmark	Germany	Nether-lands	Norway[2]	Sweden	Ireland (proposals)	United Kingdom[1]
2% Rate of Return							
50	32c	38	44	0c	**46**	13	12
100	48c	48	54	28c	**80**c	35	23
200	65c	57	64	59c	**80**c	60	33
5% Rate of Return							
50	42c	28	33	40c	**45**	22	25
100	58	39	44	65c	**73**	35	36
200	70c	50	58	78c	**80**c	54	50
500	73c	61	74	85c	81c	76	73
1,000	73c	66	79c	**88**c	83c	83	86
5,000	73c	69	80c	90c	85c		**95**
10% Rate of Return							
500	73c	59	72	**88**c	83c	73	86
1,000	73c	61	76	89c	84c	74	**92**
5,000	73c	63	78	90c	85c	76	**97**

NOTES:

c After applying ceiling provisions.
The highest in bold type, the lowest italic type, in each row.
1 Without wealth tax but including investment income surcharge at 15 per cent on investment income over £2,000.
2 Including local wealth tax.
Other details as tables 3.2 (a) and (b).

less by average than by marginal rates of tax, i.e. the amount of tax payable on the incremental addition to savings or investment. Tables 3.3a, b and c are based on the same assumptions as 3.2a, b and c except in two respects. The tax rates are marginal, not average; the marginal rate of income tax is defined as the tax that would be paid on an additional £100 of investment income; the marginal rate of wealth tax is the tax that would be paid on that amount of additional wealth required to generate an additional £100 of income. Further, we include some examples of higher rates of return; the return on a marginal investment is not pulled down, like the average, by those nil-yielding assets necessarily included within a person's total wealth; and wealthier persons can afford to pay for the best investment advice and to take any risks associated with high yield.

3.32 The relationship between combined marginal income tax and marginal wealth tax rates needs to be clarified. The relevant ceiling provisions of Denmark, Sweden, the Netherlands and Norway are all based on 'average' criteria, though sometimes with special limiting provisions. Consequently, although before the ceiling provisions have come into force, the combined *marginal* rates of income tax and wealth tax can exceed the specified ceiling percentage (and, indeed, may exceed 100 per cent of income) once the ceiling provision applies, the combined marginal rate becomes synonymous with the ceiling percentage. To take the simplest example: in the Netherlands, combined income tax and wealth tax is restricted to a maximum of 80% of total income. The combined marginal rate of wealth tax and income tax on investment income may exceed 80%, as long as the combined tax is less than 80% of total income; indeed, for the ceiling to be reached at all, the combined marginal rates must exceed 80 per cent at certain levels of net wealth. But once the ceiling applies, the combined marginal tax rate is necessarily 80%. The use of marginal instead of average rates reduces the situations in which the United Kingdom emerges with rates amongst the lowest and increases the occasions in which the UK has the highest rates.

The Inclusion of Earned Income

3.33 Our examples comparing the weight of wealth tax and tax on investment income have so far assumed that the taxpayer's income was wholly from property. More typically the taxpayer will also have earned income, which may be large. As all the countries aggregate earned and investment income for income tax purposes, the effect of including earned income is to put the person with investment income into a higher tax bracket. In general, our assumption that the wealth owner has no earned income will have biased the comparisons towards under-stating the relative tax burden of countries with the highest marginal tax rates on high incomes. To give some idea of the extent of the bias, and to offer a corrective, the next two tables, 3.4a and b, assume a single person with minimum allowances, as before, but possessing £10,000 earned income; this might, perhaps, be regarded as a fairly typical executive or professional salary. To simplify the comparison we confine it to the United Kingdom and the two countries with wealth taxes which held the highest and the lowest positions in the OECD league (see table 3.1), i.e. Sweden and Germany (respectively). Table 3.4a expresses combined wealth tax and income tax as a percentage of total income. Table 3.4b expresses combined wealth tax and income tax on investment income as a percentage of investment income, taking investment income as the top slice of income.

3.34 The 'boxes' in the north-east and the south-west corners of the tables mark off calculations which are based on unrealistically high and low (respectively) rates of return for the size of net wealth. In table 3.4a, at the

Tables 3.3 (a) and (b)

Comparison of Marginal Rates of Combined Wealth Tax and Investment Income Tax as a percentage of Investment Income at different rates of return (Single person with minimum allowances and no earned income)

percentages

Country	(a) On Net Wealth of £100,000			(b) On Net Wealth of £1,000,000		
	IT	WT	IT & WT	IT	WT	IT & WT
	5% rate of return			5% rate of return		
Denmark	60	18	76°	65	22	73°
Germany	42	14	56	56	14	70
Netherlands	49	16	65	71	16	80°
Norway	46	52	90°	71	52	90°
Sweden	62	50	112	78	50	85°
Ireland—proposals	45	20	65	70	20	90
United Kingdom	48	—	48	98	—	98
	10% rate of return			10% rate of return		
Denmark	65	9	74	65	11	73°
Germany	50	7	57	56	7	63
Netherlands	63	8	71	71	8	79
Norway	61	26	87	71	26	90°
Sweden	73	25	98	78	25	85°
Ireland—proposals	65	10	75	70	10	80
United Kingdom	73	—	73	98	—	98

NOTES: as tables 3.2 (a) and (b).

Table 3.3(c)

Comparison of Marginal Rates of Combined Wealth Tax and Investment Income Tax as a percentage of Investment Income at different rates of return on different amounts of net wealth

(Single person with minimum allowances and no earned income)

percentages

Wealth £'000	Denmark	Germany	Netherlands	Norway[2]	Sweden	Ireland (proposals)	United Kingdom[1]
5% Rate of Return							
50	67	36	47	90c	83	35	33
100	76	56	65	90c	112	65	48
200	79	64	79	90c	80c	85	73
10% Rate of Return							
50	69	49	57	72	82	45	48
100	74	57	71	87	98	75	73
200	76	62	77	92	85c	80	88
500	76	63	79	90c	85c	80	98
1,000	73c	63	79	90c	85c	80	98
5,000	73c	63	79	90c	85c	80	98
15% Rate of Return							
500	72	61	76	88	85c	77	98
1,000	72	61	76	88	85c	77	98
5,000	72	61	76	88	85c	77	98

NOTES: as table 3.2c

lowest rate of return for the three smaller sizes of estate, there is little to choose between Germany and the United Kingdom with Sweden well ahead. At the 5% rate of return, Germany is lowest at all levels of net wealth, with the United Kingdom overtaking Sweden at net wealth levels of £1m and above. At the highest rate of return, the United Kingdom leads on estates of £500,000 and above. The main difference as compared with the situation with no earned income (table 3.2c) is to pull up the United Kingdom, both absolutely and relatively, in the proportion of income paid in tax at the lower levels of net wealth. In table 3.4b, where investment income is treated as the top slice of income, at 5% and 10% rates of return, the proportion of investment income taken in tax in the United Kingdom is higher than either Sweden or Germany at all levels of wealth holding; and it should be remembered that this is without including any allowance for a wealth tax in the United Kingdom.

Tables 3.4 (a) and (b)

(a) Comparison of Combined Wealth Tax and Income Tax as Percentage of Total Income at different rates of return and different levels of net wealth, for a single person with £10,000 earned income and minimum allowances

Wealth £'000	2% return			5% return			10% return		
	U.K.[1] %	Sweden %	Germany %	U.K.[1] %	Sweden %	Germany %	U.K.[1] %	Sweden %	Germany %
50	41	61	41	44	62	42	51	64	44
100	43	71	45	51	72	47	60	73	49
200	48	80	51	60	80	52	72	82	53
500	60	80	63	76	82	60	85	83	58
1,000	72	82	72	85	84	64	91	84	60
5,000	91	84	86	95	85	69	96	85	62

(b) Comparison of Combined Wealth Tax and Income Tax on Investment Income (assuming investment income to be the top slice of Income) as a percentage of Investment Income, for a single person with £10,000 earned income and minimum allowances

Wealth £'000	2% return			5% return			10% return		
	U.K.[1] %	Sweden %	Germany %	U.K.[1] %	Sweden %	Germany %	U.K.[1] %	Sweden %	Germany %
50	60	122	78	65	92	62	74	83	58
100	61	149	83	74	104	65	81	91	60
200	71	143	85	81	106	67	89	95	62
500	81	106	88	91	93	69	94	89	62
1,000	89	95	90	94	89	69	96	87	63
5,000	96	87ᶜ	91	97	86	70	98	85	63

NOTES:

1 Without wealth tax but including investment income surcharge at 15 per cent on incomes over £2,000. The bottom left hand box and the top right hand box represent very unrealistic situations.

ᶜAfter applying ceiling provisions.

Allowing for Death Duties

3.35 Apart from the references in table 3.1 to the maximum rates and thresholds of death duties, our comparisons of tax burdens have so far been confined to annual taxes on wealth and investment income; the difficulty of bringing death duties into calculations to compare the overall weight of tax on wealth and investment income is their irregularity; they apply to any particular property, on average, once in a generation. We now attempt to include death duties by converting them into an annual tax. This raises a number of difficulties: first, few taxpayers behave in relation to death duties as though they were an annual tax. Second, treating them as such creates unrealities in that the combined total of income tax on investment income, annual wealth tax and death duties (expressed as an annual tax) will often exceed 100% of the taxpayer's income; which means that, even if he wanted to, he could not make provision annually against death duties without reducing the capital on which they would be payable. Third, in converting death duties into an annual tax, various assumptions can be made of different degrees of sophistication.[10] We could, for example, calculate the amount, net of income tax, that the taxpayer would have to pay in annual premiums for an insurance policy equal to the tax on his estate at death (which estate would include the value of the insurance); or we could elaborate this calculation by reckoning that, because of people's time preference for the present over the future, from the taxpayer's point of view an annual tax equivalent to death duty ought to be taken as something less than the value of these insurance premiums.

3.36 In fact, we have adopted a simple solution. We wish to convert death duties into an annual wealth tax. In the Green Paper on the United Kingdom wealth tax (paragraph 6.17), the Government has suggested that in some cases the taxpayer might be permitted to defer wealth tax payment, plus interest, until death. This procedure changes an annual wealth tax into a death duty. To convert a death duty into an annual wealth tax, we adopt the same method in reverse: we need to see what annual sum, with interest, cumulated over a generation, would equal death duty liability. This still leaves some significant issues open, about the length of a generation and the appropriate rate of interest, on which some more or less arbitrary decisions have to be taken. We assume a generation of 25 years and have taken an interest rate of 3% (non-deductible from income for income tax purposes). Whilst in inflationary conditions 3% is well below a commercial rate, in such conditions the value of the property on which death duty would eventually be payable would also be likely to rise over the 25 years constituting a generation. We suspect that no income tax allowance against interest would be

---

[10] See, for example, N. Kaldor, 'The Income Burden of Capital Taxes', *Review of Economic Studies*, 1942.

Tables 3.5 (a) and (b)

Comparison of Wealth Tax, Investment Income Tax and Death Duties (as an annual equivalent tax) expressed as a percentage of Investment Income at different rates of return

percentages

Country	(a) on Net Wealth of £100,000 Death Duty: Assumption 1 (Estate left wholly to one child)			(b) on Net Wealth of £1,000,000		
	IT & WT	Death Duty	IT, WT & DD	IT & WT	Death Duty	IT, WT & DD
	2% rate of return			5% rate of return		
Denmark	48°	32	80	72°	17	89
Germany	48	9	57	66	8	73
Netherlands	54	19	74	79°	9	88
Norway	28°	43	70	88°	19	106
Sweden	63	56	119	83°	33	116
Ireland—proposals	35	—	35	83	23	106
United Kingdom	23	39	61	86	32	118
	5% rate of return			10% rate of return		
Denmark	60	13	73	73°	9	81
Germany	39	4	43	61	4	65
Netherlands	44	8	51	76	4	80
Norway	65°	17	82	89°	10	98
Sweden	72	22	95	84	16	100
Ireland—proposals	35	—	35	76	11	88
United Kingdom	38	15	53	92	16	108

Tables 3.5 (a) and (b) continued

percentages

(a) on Net Wealth of £100,000

Death Duty: Assumption 2 (Estate left equally to three children)

Country	IT & WT	Death Duty	IT, WT & DD
2% rate of return			
Denmark	48[c]	20	68
Germany	48	3	51
Netherlands	54	15	69
Norway	28[c]	32	60
Sweden	63	36	99
Ireland—proposals	35	—	35
United Kingdom	23	39	61
5% rate of return			
Denmark	60	8	68
Germany	39	2	41
Netherlands	44	6	50
Norway	65[c]	13	78
Sweden	73	14	87
Ireland—proposals	35	—	35
United Kingdom	38	15	53

(b) on Net Wealth of £1,000,000

Country	IT & WT	Death Duty	IT, WT & DD
5% rate of return			
Denmark	72[c]	16	88
Germany	66	6	71
Netherlands	79[c]	9	88
Norway	88[c]	19	106
Sweden	83[c]	28	111
Ireland—proposals	83	10	92
United Kingdom	86	32	118
10% rate of return			
Denmark	73[c]	8	81
Germany	61	3	64
Netherlands	76	5	80
Norway	89[c]	9	98
Sweden	84	14	98
Ireland—proposals	76	5	81
United Kingdom	92	16	108

Assumptions on Income Tax and Wealth Tax as in table 3.2 (a) and (b).

Table 3.5 (c) (i)

Comparison of Combined Wealth Tax, Investment Income Tax and Death Duties (as an annual equivalent tax) expressed as a percentage of investment income at different rates of return on different amounts of net wealth and assuming the estate is left to one child

percentages

Wealth £'000	Denmark	Germany	Nether-lands	Norway	Sweden	Ireland (proposals)	United Kingdom
2% rate of return							
50	59ᶜ	44	61	37	**105**	*13*	34
100	80ᶜ	57	74	70	**119ᶜ**	*35*	61
200	103ᶜ	71	85	104	**144ᶜ**	*68*	93
5% rate of return							
50	53	31	40	55	**65**	*22*	36
100	73	43	51	82	**95**	*35*	53
200	85ᶜ	56	67	96	**106ᶜ**	*47*	74
500	88ᶜ	68	83	104	**111ᶜ**	*91*	102
1,000	89ᶜ	73	88ᶜ	106	**116ᶜ**	*106*	**118**
5,000	90ᶜ	83	89ᶜ	109	**120ᶜ**	*117*	**134**
10% rate of return							
500	80ᶜ	62	77	97	**97ᶜ**	*80*	**100**
1,000	81ᶜ	65	80	98	**100ᶜ**	*88*	**108**
5,000	82ᶜ	69	83	99	**102ᶜ**	*94*	**116**

NOTE:
Assumptions as tables 3.5 (a) and (b).

permitted if the Green Paper proposals for deferment of wealth tax were introduced into the United Kingdom (for this is the procedure currently followed with the interest levied on death duty payments in the United Kingdom); but that the rate of interest fixed by the government would take this into account. Hence, 3%, non-deductible, does not seem unreasonable as a real rate of interest. Of course, if a higher rate of interest had been taken, the annual equivalent would be smaller.

3.37 With the warning of the element of artificiality and arbitrariness that they necessarily contain, tables 3.5a, b and c are presented. They match up with the data from 3.2a, b and c, with the addition of death duty, calculated as an equivalent annual tax on two different assumptions: (i) the whole estate left by a parent to one child; (ii) the estate divided equally amongst three children. Both seem reasonably typical situations. On assumption (i) the form of death duty, whether the estate duty type or inheritance tax, is immaterial—

Table 3.5 (c) (ii)

Comparison of Combined Wealth Tax, Investment Income Tax and Death Duties (as an annual equivalent tax) expressed as a percentage of investment income at different rates of return on different amounts of net wealth, and assuming the estate is divided equally amongst three children

percentages

Wealth £'000	Denmark	Germany	Nether-lands	Norway	Sweden	Ireland (proposals)	United Kingdom
2% rate of return							
50	50ᶜ	39	59	22	**69**	*13*	34
100	68ᶜ	51	69	60	**99ᶜ**	*35*	61
200	91ᶜ	64	81	99	**126ᶜ**	*60*	93
5% rate of return							
50	49	29	38	49	**51**	22	36
100	68	41	50	78	**87**	35	53
200	80ᶜ	53	65	94	**101**	54	74
500	86ᶜ	66	82	103	**106ᶜ**	77	102
1,000	88ᶜ	71	88ᶜ	106	111ᶜ	92	**118**
5,000	90ᶜ	79	89ᶜ	109	119ᶜ	114	**134**
10% rate of return							
500	80ᶜ	*61*	77	96	96ᶜ	73	**100**
1,000	81ᶜ	*64*	80	98	98ᶜ	81	**108**
5,000	82ᶜ	*79*	83	99	102ᶜ	92	**116**

NOTE:
Assumptions as tables 3.5 (a) and (b).

the tax burden is the same in either case. Assumption (ii) leaves estate duty unchanged, but reduces inheritance tax. The United Kingdom alone has a death duty on the estate (capital transfer tax); the other countries all have inheritance taxes, which offer scope for reduction of duty by dispersing estates more widely; indeed, under an inheritance tax, however large the estate, it is theoretically possible to reduce death duty to zero by spreading wealth at death sufficiently widely in sufficiently small parcels. On the other hand it must also be remembered that the inheritance taxes of all the countries we are considering provide for higher tax rates if property is left to distant relatives or strangers.

3.38 The pattern which emerges from tables 3.5c(i) and (ii) is clear-cut. At the 2% rate of return for all values shown, Sweden emerges as the heaviest taxed. At the 5% rate of return at all values of net wealth, up to, and including £500,000, Sweden has the heaviest tax burden on capital. At wealth levels over £500,000 at a 5% rate of return and at all levels shown for the 10% rate of return, the top place is taken by the United Kingdom with its investment income surcharge, but no wealth tax.

3.39 At the bottom end of the scale, the proposals of the Republic of Ireland offer the lowest burden on all wealth levels shown for the 2% rate of return and for the 5% rate of return up to and including £200,000 (table c(i)) or £100,000 (table c(ii)). In all other cases, Germany has pride of place for the lowest tax burden on capital. The relative positions are only marginally affected by the alternative assumptions about the disposition of the estate.

3.40 A comparison with table 3.2c shows the relative positions of the countries very little changed by the inclusion of death duties on the assumptions used.

Harmonisation of Wealth Taxes in the EEC

3.41 Any consideration of taxes in a European context can hardly proceed without some reference to the harmonisation policies of the European Community, even if that reference is entirely negative. To promote the EEC objective of economic growth by the free movement of goods and of factors of production within the Community, the Treaty of Rome makes explicit reference (Article 99) to the harmonisation of sales and excise duties. No other Articles specifically refer to taxation, but corporation tax and social security payments can be brought within the rubric of General Articles (such as 100 and 102) concerned with hindrances to competition and the free movement of workers and capital.

3.42 The Commission has had little to say about wealth taxes, either annual taxes or death duties. The Neumark Report[11] of 1963, a document not of the Commission but written for the Commission, contained some three paragraphs on an annual wealth tax. The Neumark Committee did not consider whether it was necessary for all tax systems of member countries to include a wealth tax. However, a majority of members of the Fiscal and Financial Committee expressed the view that it was expedient to have such a tax at low rates as a means of differentiating income according to source; they also mentioned the administrative advantage of being able to cross-check returns for income tax, wealth tax and inheritance tax. They further argued that to prevent a wealth tax bearing too heavily on small and medium-sized fortunes it should contain generous allowances determined by reference to the family circumstances and age of the taxpayers.

3.43 The Committee considered that if taxes were levied on wealth in the EEC they should be broadly aligned and that the relationship between income tax and wealth tax would need to be harmonised. Finally, they came

---

[11] *The EEC Report on Tax Harmonisation: Report of the Fiscal and Financial Committee* (The Neumark Report), Amsterdam, 1963, pp. 127-8.

down emphatically against applying a wealth tax to companies, both in order to avoid double taxation and to prevent distortion of competition because the tax would discriminate against businesses with high capital to labour ratios.

3.44 Clearly, the Committee saw a wealth tax very much as a supplement and partial alternative to income tax. The view currently held in the Commission appears to be that matters of personal taxation should generally remain within the discretion of Member Governments.

3.45 Of the original six EEC members, three (Germany, the Netherlands, and Luxembourg) have had wealth taxes for some considerable time. Of the three new members, Denmark has long had a wealth tax and now Ireland and the United Kingdom are proposing to have them; but there is no reason to believe that these decisions have any reference to their membership of the EEC.

3.46 In short, there is no EEC policy which need inhibit member states in their decisions on a wealth tax. Any prospect of harmonisation is, to put it at its highest, far distant. The Commission is at present making only slow progress with the harmonisation of those taxes where the economic case is strongest and the Treaty of Rome most explicit.

Summary and Conclusions

3.47 The European countries with wealth taxes all regard them as supplements to income tax, introduced primarily to promote horizontal equity; the relatively low thresholds, low rates and ceiling provisions support this interpretation. In assessing the burden of taxation on wealth and investment income, whether or not death duties are included, taxation in Norway and Sweden is the heaviest on small and medium wealth holdings with low and medium rates of return. The United Kingdom, even without a wealth tax, has the heaviest taxation for the largest wealth holdings at moderate and high rates of return. There is no likelihood of a harmonisation of wealth taxes within the European Community in the foreseeable future.

E

Chapter 4

A Case Study—The Swedish Wealth Tax

The Choice of Sweden

4.1 The Swedish wealth tax was a natural choice for a case study. First, wealth taxation has a long history in Sweden. Wealth first entered the base for annual taxation in 1910, when under 'the national income and wealth tax' one-sixtieth of the value of net wealth was treated as income for income tax purposes. In 1947 the tax acquired its present form, separate from income tax but accounted for in the same tax return. The Swedes thus have a lengthy experience on which to draw; and recently a capital tax committee has completed a review of the wealth tax along with other capital taxes.

4.2 Secondly the Swedish wealth tax is the highest on the Continent (at least nominally) with a top rate of $2\frac{1}{2}\%$. The next highest in Europe is Finland, with rates rising to 2%. Amongst the countries on which we are concentrating, the nearest rival is Norway at 1.6% (though Norway also has a local wealth tax of up to 1%). A tax with the highest rates might be expected to highlight any problems associated with a wealth tax. Further, the United Kingdom, if not any longer the Republic of Ireland,[1] seems disposed to go for maximum rates at or above the Swedish levels.

4.3 Thirdly, and perhaps most important, it is the Swedish tax that has been most frequently referred to as a possible model for the United Kingdom and

---

[1] The *Capital Taxation* White Paper of the Irish Government proposed rates of wealth tax up to $2\frac{1}{2}\%$; but since then the Minister of Finance has announced that the rate will be a flat 1%.

indeed for other countries.[2] It behoves us therefore to examine it with some care.

4.4 This chapter has two main purposes. First, to offer a detailed description and analysis of the Swedish tax. To help the reader through some fairly indigestible material and to enable him to concentrate on topics he finds of especial interest, we have plentifully endowed this section with headings and sub-headings and each main sub-section starts with a summary of its contents. Second, in the light of this detailed account, to attempt an assessment of the Swedish tax against the advantages and disadvantages of a wealth tax as set out in Chapter 1. We seek to answer the question 'how far does the Swedish tax achieve the advantages claimed for a wealth tax and with what disadvantages?'

Description and Analysis

Scope of the Charge

4.5 *Summary*. The Swedish wealth tax is essentially a tax on individuals, both resident and non-resident. Swedish companies are not liable to wealth tax, but the charge extends to Swedish family trusts and to estates of deceased persons in course of administration and also to certain non-family trusts ('foundations' and associations). Non-resident companies are also liable.

4.6 *A Swedish resident* is chargeable in respect of his total net wealth, subject to certain exemptions, wherever the assets are situated. A family trust is, in principle, taxable as an individual, but where, as is usual, the beneficiaries are entitled to specific shares of the trust income, the capital is attributed to the several beneficiaries in proportion to their respective shares of the income and taxed as if it belonged to them. It is possible to set up a trust for members of a family under which the trustees have discretion as to the distribution of the income, including power to accumulate; in such a case the trust is taxable as an individual on the part of the capital corresponding to the accumulated income. Such trusts, however, appear to be relatively uncommon, partly because gift tax or succession duty on the highest scale is attracted on their formation and partly because the wealth tax (on distributed income) falls on the beneficiaries, who have no access to the capital.

4.7 *An estate in course of administration* is similarly taxed as a single individual for the first four years. Thereafter, if the value of the estate exceeds Skr 100,000 (£9,523) or its income exceeds Skr 10,000 (£952) the capital is attributed to the various beneficiaries for wealth tax purposes.

---

[2] For example, M. Stewart, 'The Wealth Tax', *Bankers' Magazine* 1963 and NEDC *Conditions Favourable to Faster Growth*, HMSO, 1963, p. 42, both refer to the Swedish wealth tax as a possible model for the United Kingdom. N. Kaldor, *Indian Tax Reform*, 1956, drew on the Swedish tax quite heavily in proposing a wealth tax for India.

4.8 *The charge on non-family trusts and associations* is relatively unimportant. Foundations for charitable purposes and other purposes of public benefit are usually exempt from tax; other chargeable bodies, which do not qualify for exemption, are subject only to a very low rate of tax.

4.9 *The charge on a non-resident individual* is strictly limited. It extends only to real property (including long leaseholds) situated in Sweden and assets used in a business carried on in Sweden. Thus debts, for example, owed by a Swedish debtor, including mortgage debts on real property in Sweden, are not chargeable in the case of a non-resident, nor are shares in a Swedish company. The general intent of the charge on non-residents is to tax the possession of productive assets in Sweden; on this basis one might expect the charge to extend at least to Swedish shares. The committee which recently reviewed capital taxation in Sweden considered that there was a good case in principle for changing the rule and including shares within the charge on non-residents; but its conclusion was that in view of the practical difficulties of enforcing liability the existing position should be left undisturbed.

4.10 The charge on the non-resident is thus relatively narrow, and is further eased by the fact that, if he has chargeable property, he is taxed on the same scale as the resident and so does not attract liability at all unless the value of his chargeable assets exceeds Skr 200,000 (£19,048). The foreigner who comes to live in Sweden naturally becomes taxable as a resident on his total wealth, wherever situated; on the other hand, he would not, as he would in the UK, automatically become resident for a particular year merely by reason of spending six months in Sweden in that year. Broadly speaking, an individual is resident for tax purposes if he makes his home in Sweden; if his home was elsewhere he could, for example, own a holiday cottage in Sweden and spend his summer holidays there without being treated as resident. Up to three years after leaving Sweden, a resident is still seen as resident unless he can show that he has no 'essential connexion' with Sweden. After three years the onus is on the Swedish authorities to prove such connexion.

4.11 *A non-resident company*, unlike a Swedish company, is also liable to wealth tax, the scope of the charge being the same as in the case of a non-resident individual. In the case of a Swedish company the wealth tax is paid by the shareholders, all or the vast majority of whom will be Swedish residents; the charge on the foreign company with a permanent establishment in Sweden is in substitution for a charge on the shareholders, who being predominantly non-residents, cannot be reached. (A Swedish shareholder in a non-resident company operating in Sweden thus suffers, to some extent, a double charge of wealth tax, for which no relief is provided by Swedish law). If, however, the non-resident company forms a Swedish subsidiary to take over the business of its Swedish branch, the liability to wealth tax disappears, since Swedish companies are outside the charge. Some of Sweden's double taxation agreements with other countries, including the agreement with the United Kingdom, exempt companies of the other country with branches in Sweden so that, so far as wealth tax is concerned, it makes no difference whether the Swedish business is carried on through a branch or a subsidiary.

Rates of Tax, Threshold and Ceiling Provisions

4.12 *Summary.* Ignoring the specific exemptions, the wealth tax rises from a rate of 1% on wealth of Skr 200,000 (£19,048) to a rate of $2\frac{1}{2}$% on wealth of Skr 1,000,000 (£95,238). The wealth of husband, wife and minor children is aggregated for wealth tax purposes. A ceiling provision restricts the combined wealth tax, national income tax and local income tax to 80% of the first Skr 200,000 (£19,048) of income from all sources and 85% of the remainder, subject to a minimum charge.

4.13 *Rates.* The Swedish tax is graduated on the following scale:

Net Wealth			Rate (%)	Tax at top of range	
Skr		£		Skr	£
0 – 200,000		(19,048)	Nil	Nil	(Nil)
200,000 – 275,000		(26,190)	1	750	(71)
275,000 – 400,000		(38,095)	$1\frac{1}{2}$	2,625	(250)
400,000 – 1,000,000		(95,238)	2	14,625	(1,393)
Excess over 1,000,000			$2\frac{1}{2}$		

4.14 The above scale applies alike to individuals, whether resident or non-resident, to family trusts and undivided estates, and to non-resident companies.

4.15 Non-family trusts or other bodies liable to the tax are charged at a flat rate of 0.15% on the excess of their wealth over Skr 15,000 (£1,428).

4.16 *The wealth of husband and wife* is aggregated for wealth tax purposes; liability for the resulting tax is divided between them in proportion to their respective shares of the aggregate net wealth. *The wealth of children* under 18 living with their parents is also aggregated with the parental wealth. If the child's income exceeds the income tax exemption limit the proportionate share of the family's wealth tax liability is attributed to the child; otherwise the liability falls on the parent.

4.17 *The threshold of liability* for a married couple is the same as for a single person, Skr 200,000 (£19,048), notwithstanding that their respective assets are aggregated. By normal tests of taxable capacity one might expect the married couple to qualify for a higher threshold, and the capital tax committee in fact recommended that it should be 50% higher than the single person's. The Government, however, did not accept the proposal. (For income tax purposes a reduction of tax, running up to Skr 1,800 (£171) at the maximum, is given where one spouse's income is less than the amount of the basic personal allowance Skr 4,500 (£429).)

4.18 Relief is given where the aggregate amount of national and local income tax and wealth tax exceeds 80% of the first Skr 200,000 (£19,048) of taxable income and 85% of taxable income above that figure. The wealth tax and, if necessary, the national income tax are reduced by the amount of the excess, subject to the proviso that the remaining liability must not be less than the wealth tax which would be payable on taxable wealth equal to 50% of the taxpayer's actual wealth. There is no reduction of the local income tax. Before 1971 the 80% test applied to all ranges of income and there was a further ceiling limiting taxable wealth to thirty times income (subject to the same proviso).

4.19 Current rates of national income tax are set out below[3]; the local income tax, which is proportional, averaged 24% in the 1974 assessment year (1973 income year).

4.20 The operation of the ceiling provision can be seen from the following examples (all figures in Skr except where £ is indicated).

4.21 *Example I*

	Skr	£
Net wealth	2,000,000	190,476
Earned income	100,000	9,524
Investment income	122,000	11,619
Deductions	2,000	190
TAXABLE INCOME	220,000	20,953
National income tax (55,150 + 54% × 70,000) ... =	92,950	8,852
Local income tax (say 25% × 220,000) ... ... =	55,000	5,238
Net wealth tax (14,625 + 2.5% × 1,000,000) ... =	39,625	3,774
Combined tax if no ceiling provision	187,575	17,864

Application of ceiling provision:

80% × 200,000 + 85% of 20,000 ... ... =	177,000	16,857
187,575 − 177,000 ... ... =	10,575	1,007

Therefore wealth tax reduced by 10,575 (£1,007) from 39,625 (£3,774) to 29,050 (£2,767)

---

[3] Paragraph 4.75.

4.22 *Example II*

	Skr	£
Net wealth (mainly shares with very low dividends) ...	4,000,000	380,952
Earned income	Nil	Nil
Investment income	72,000	6,857
Deductions	2,000	190
TAXABLE INCOME	70,000	6,667
National income tax	16,550	1,576
Local income tax (25% × 70,000)	17,500	1,667
Net wealth tax	89,675	8,540
Combined tax if no ceiling provision	123,725	11,783

Application of ceiling provision:

	Skr	£
80% of 70,000	56,000	5,333

But combined income taxes and wealth tax must not be lower than local income tax (17,500) and net wealth tax on half net wealth (39,625) = 57,125 (£5,441). Therefore tax liability reduced to:

	Skr	£
National income tax	Nil	Nil
Local income tax	17,500	1,667
Wealth tax	39,625	3,774
	57,125	5,441

Exemptions

4.23 *Summary.* Exemptions cover life insurance policies, pensions and annuities, furniture and other household movables, works of art and collections if not for business use, jewellery and 'outdoor' chattels if less than Skr 1,000 (£95), housekeeping balances, trade names, goodwill, patents and copyrights not used in a business.

4.24 Certain classes of property are exempt from wealth tax. Of these, perhaps the most important is the *value of life insurance policies*. Such policies, whether payable only on death or payable at a given future date or on earlier death (endowment insurance), are exempt without limit of amount.

4.25 *The value of a pension or right to an annuity* provided by an employer in respect of past employment is also exempt, and the same applies to insurances taken out privately by an individual to secure a pension or annuity on his retirement. Again there is no limit on the amount of pension insurance which qualifies for exemption; further, the premiums are deductible for income tax purposes, even if paid out of capital.

4.26 *Furniture and other movables for use in the home* are exempt property, regardless of their value, as are works of art and collections (of books, paintings, stamps, etc.), provided they are not exploited commercially. The broad effect is that objects kept in the home are exempt whether they are of ordinary or exceptional quality, and there is, therefore, no need to decide whether a particular painting (for example) is an important work of art.

4.27 *Assets for outdoor as distinct from indoor use,* typically cars and boats, are chargeable; jewellery also is not exempt. There is, however, no charge if the aggregate value of these assets does not exceed Skr 1,000 (£95). Apparently a recent Court case has established that unmounted precious stones are exempt on the grounds that they do not come within the categories of taxable assets listed in the wealth tax return.

4.28 *Housekeeping balances,* in the form of cash in hand to meet the ordinary household expenses, are also exempt. There appear to be no set rules for determining at what point the balances should be regarded as more than is reasonably needed for housekeeping purposes. Correspondingly, no deduction is allowed for housekeeping debts.

4.29 *Goodwill and the value of analogous assets* such as trade names, trade marks and protected designs are not chargeable property.

4.30 *Patents and copyrights* not used in a business are also exempt, but the exemption only applies if the owner has not licensed the use of the patent or copyright by another person in return for royalties; where the patent or copyright has been licensed the capitalised value put on the property tends to be cautious, unless the duration and yearly amounts are reasonably certain, when a realistic valuation is possible.

Valuation

4.31 *Summary.* Except where provided otherwise, assets are intended to be valued at what they would fetch on an open market sale as at the last day of the year. Real property is valued every five years and the valuation for tax purposes is fixed at 75% of the open market valuation at that time. Unincorporated businesses and closely held companies are valued on a net assets basis with accelerated depreciation (in line with income tax procedures).

4.32 *Personal Chattels.* The valuation of the personal chattels included within the tax base (e.g. car, boat and jewellery) is left to the taxpayer and largely taken on trust.

4.33 *Real Property.* The valuation is on a capital value basis (not rental income) and is determined at regular quinquennial valuations. The last valuation came into force in 1970 for which the basis year was 1968 and the next will be in 1975 with 1973 as the basis year. In principle, the valuation for all real property is 75% of the open market value as between a willing buyer and seller; until recently, as a matter of administrative practice, houses and agricultural property were valued for tax purposes at 75% of open market value and apartment houses and business and industrial real estate at 80% of market value. As from 1975 the 75% will apply as a statutory provision to all real property. If there is no essential change in the property, the valuations remain unaltered for the five year period; the 75% rule is to guard against over-valuation and to provide a safety margin against falling values. Special provisions provide for new valuations where buildings are enlarged or new buildings constructed or where real property is destroyed by fire or other calamities. With newly erected houses the initial valuation is intended to equate with that which would have been made had the house been in existence in the basis year for the quinquennium during which it was built.

4.34 The valuation procedure for a dwelling house (what the Swedes classify as one-and-two-family houses) starts from a very detailed return by the taxpayer which gives information such as: total floor area; number of rooms of various types; various amenities, e.g. central heating; area of land associated with the house; age of the house; mode of construction; insurance value. A proportion of properties is also inspected.

4.35 All conveyancing of land has to be registered with the courts and full information on sales is made available to the tax authorities who produce detailed statistics of price variations between the basis years, classified by type of house, location, region, etc. These statistics (which categorise houses under certain standard headings, such as size, age, etc.) are used to assist the quinquennial revaluation process.

4.36 In principle, the same concepts are used for valuing agricultural land, but there is the added complication of varying fertility, which is taken into account in making the assessment. Such variation will also be reflected in sale prices.

4.37 Where there is standing timber, the value of the real estate includes the timber but, within the total, the land and trees are separately valued.

4.38 Assessments of real property distinguish between the value of the land and the value of the buildings. The owner-occupier of a house on a leasehold site is assessed to wealth tax only on the value of the building (but the value of the land plus building is used for the purpose of assessing imputed income for income tax purposes, the actual ground rent then being deducted).

4.39 The law provides for the possibility of taxing to wealth tax the owner of the unexpired portion of a leasehold interest in land or buildings, but in practice little attempt is made to do so.

4.40 The principles used to value domestic and agricultural property apply also to industrial real property. Industrial buildings may also be valued by reference to the cost of re-building, less an allowance for the age and condition of the building, including its suitability for the purpose for which it is used.

4.41 The valuations resulting from these procedures are used not only for wealth tax but also for succession duty and gift tax and as a basis for imputed rental income for national and local income tax. (For one-family and two-family houses the imputed rental is 2% up to Skr 150,000 (£14,286), 4% on the next Skr 75,000 (£7,143) and 8% on the excess.)

4.42 *Quoted companies.* The basis of valuation for wealth tax purposes of shares held by individuals is the quotation on 31 December each year (or the nearest date for which there are stock exchange quotations). The quotations are taken from a list drawn up by the association of Swedish stockbrokers.

4.43 *Unquoted Companies with actively traded shares.* The shares of a small number of companies, although not quoted, are sufficiently actively traded in arms length transactions to be valued on the evidence of the prices so obtained. The wealth tax valuation of these shares appears in a list drawn up by the association of Swedish stockbrokers. In other similar cases, price-earnings ratios are established which are related to those prevailing on comparable quoted shares. Statistics are published of the price-earnings ratios of quoted shares in various industrial classifications.

4.44 *Unquoted Companies with closely held shares.* No statutory border line is drawn between the unquoted companies valued on the basis of traded shares and the remainder which constitute the large majority of companies. These companies (mainly comprising family shareholdings) are valued on an assets basis, ignoring goodwill. The assets are not taken at open market value but, broadly speaking, at the values adopted for income tax purposes.

4.45 Land and buildings are included at their assessed value, but if physical conditions have changed the valuation is adjusted upwards or downwards, even though the new valuation has not yet been agreed with the taxing authorities.

4.46 Plant and machinery is brought in at the written down valuation for income tax purposes either on the 'book depreciation' or 'planned depreciation' methods. If obsolescence or other considerations have reduced the market value of the machinery below the written down value, the market value may be used.

4.47 With stock in trade, the starting point is actual or replacement cost, whichever is the lower. From this figure, a deduction is made to provide for obsolete or unsaleable items, or items where there is a risk of falling prices; this can be a percentage deduction (commonly 5%, but 10% where the risk is high) or a deduction on a line by line basis of the amount required to reduce cost to net realisable value. From cost, as thus reduced, a further deduction of 60% is made to arrive at the value for income tax and wealth tax purposes. There are two supplementary rules:

4.48 (a) If the net realisable value (reached in the way described) is less than the average of the corresponding value at the close of the two previous years (the 'comparable value'), the company may write its stock down by 60% of the comparable value rather than 60% of the value of the year in question.

4.49 (b) The company has the option to value raw materials or staple commodities at the lowest market price ruling during the income year or during any of the nine previous years and then to reduce that figure by 30% to give a stock valuation equal to 70% of the ten year low. Use of this rule prevents use of the comparable value rule.

4.50 Purchased goodwill and premiums paid on leasehold property were formerly included but are now disregarded completely. A deduction can be made for half of any unfunded pension liability.

4.51 Companies are valued at the balance sheet date. The returns are made in September and the value has to be settled by December and attributed to the shares. In December, the share value is notified to all tax offices (and presumably companies also notify their shareholders) so that any shareholder inquiring at a tax office may be told the value of his shares.

4.52 The primary responsibility for filing information about the company's value rests with the company and the company will normally conduct all negotiations with the tax office. However, a shareholder is free to dispute the value thus arrived at, but in practice is unlikely to succeed in displacing it.

4.53 Because the balance sheet date may not coincide with 31 December, there may have to be an adjustment to the value at the balance sheet date to take account of capital movements between a company and its shareholders between the balance sheet date and the 31 December at which the wealth tax return is being made (for example, if an additional call on shares was made by the company during that period).

4.54 *Unincorporated businesses.* The valuation of an unincorporated business, in its principal features, proceeds on the same basis as that of unquoted companies whose shares are closely held.

Administrative Procedures and Costs

4.55 *Summary.* Swedish tax administration is decentralised under the general supervisory authority of a National Tax Board for direct taxation. The administration of income tax and wealth tax is closely linked. For this reason and because of common valuation procedures for various taxes, it is not possible to calculate separate costs for the administration of wealth tax. The taxing authorities have wide powers to obtain information and a range of penalties for tax evaders. Compliance costs of wealth tax are generally small and non-deductible.

4.56 *The Tax Authorities.* The Swedish Ministry of Finance has practically no day to day function of tax administration. The executive work in the administration of the wealth and other direct taxes, lies with the National Tax Board and the Provincial Governors' Offices.

4.57 The National Tax Board is the supervisory authority for direct taxation. It has general powers to promote a uniform application of direct taxation throughout the country and to this end it issues advice and instructions.

4.58 Sweden is divided into Provinces, each with a Governor appointed by the national government. The assessment, auditing and collection of direct taxes in the Province is the responsibility of the fiscal department of the Provincial Governor's Office. The task of making assessments is delegated to Assessment Boards; the more complicated questions go to Special Assessment Boards, but the assessment of private persons is normally handled by Local Assessment Boards in local assessment districts, each Board normally handling between 1,500 and 3,000 taxpayers. The Chairman of each Board and one other member is appointed by the Provincial Governor; the remaining members, from three to 12 per Board, are elected by the municipal assemblies in the district concerned. None of the members is, as such, a salaried tax official. On the basis of the assessment made, the tax to be levied from each taxpayer is calculated by the tax offices, of which there are about 120 in the country.

4.59 The head of the fiscal department of the Province has the duty to satisfy himself that the assessments are correct and, if not satisfied, he can appeal to an independent tribunal, the Provincial Tax Court. The taxpayer may also appeal to that Court. Appeals from decisions of the Provincial Tax Court may go to one of the three Fiscal Courts of Appeal, and under certain conditions, there is a right of further appeal to the Supreme Administrative Court.

4.60 Besides the Local Assessment Boards, which are appointed annually and meet during the period from February/March to end June, there are Real-Estate Assessment Boards which have a similar composition but meet every five years to deal with the valuation of land and buildings.

4.61 *Administrative links.* Returns of income and wealth are made on the same forms annually, so there is an immediate cross-check of wealth, earned income and investment income. There is not as close a link between wealth tax and other capital taxes, i.e. gift tax and succession duty. As already indicated, there are important valuation links: assessed values for real property apply to wealth tax, succession duty and gift tax and are used in computing notional income for state and local income tax. The assets basis of valuation for unincorporated businesses and unquoted companies follows income tax methods. The valuation rules for unincorporated businesses apply for succession duty. Wealth tax valuations for unquoted shares are taken as a guide to valuation for gift tax and succession duty.

4.62 *Administrative costs.* Because of the link with income tax and the links with other capital taxes, no separate calculation of administrative costs for wealth tax is possible. The members of the Local Assessment Boards and the Real Estate Assessment Boards, all of whom are part time, are paid, but at relatively low rates.

4.63 There are currently some 280,000 – 290,000 wealth tax payers.

4.64 *Enforcement powers.* In enforcing tax regulations the Swedes have a number of powers:

4.65 (1) Banks paying dividends on bearer bonds and shares are required to give to the Revenue authorities details of the names and addresses of the persons entitled to the dividends. This information is actively used by the Revenue authorities.

4.66 (2) Banks can be required to reveal information on the balances of clients and this power is frequently utilised. The tax authorities write to the Head Office of the bank which then has to inquire from all branches about the affairs of any particular customer.

4.67 (3) Accountants likewise can be required to provide information on the finances of their clients.

4.68 *Penalties.* Rules regarding penalties for tax evasion have recently been revised and now fall into two categories.

4.69 (1) A special criminal law for tax matters where *intention* to evade must be proved to obtain a conviction. In addition to payment of tax due, penalties range from fines to up to six years' imprisonment for fraud.

4.70 (2) Powers possessed by the taxing authorities to recover the tax due plus a penalty charge equal to 50% of the unpaid tax. In 1972, the first year this provision applied, 43,000 taxpayers were subject to penalties and Skr 84 million (£8m) was collected in penalties. In 1973, the corresponding figures were 49,000 people and Skr 84 million (£8m). These figures related to all taxes. Information on the numbers penalised is given publicity to act as a deterrent to would-be evaders. Publishing information on tax payments is part of Swedish tradition; each year information is available from the tax offices of every person's income tax and wealth tax payments; and a commercial organisation, with information purchased from the revenue authorities, publishes in book form the names, addresses and wealth tax payments of the richer persons.

4.71 *Compliance Costs*. Businesses apart, professional valuers are little used by taxpayers in preparing their wealth tax return, but richer taxpayers will use accountants and may seek advice from barristers. Many Swedish taxpayers use 'tax preparers',[4] but it is probably the income tax part of the return rather than the wealth tax part which causes the most difficulty; in practice, the compliance costs of the wealth tax are so linked with those of income tax as to be hardly distinguishable.

4.72 Taxpayer compliance costs are not deductible from wealth tax (not even the costs of a successful court action) but they do, of course, reduce wealth. However, as in the United Kingdom, in practice compliance costs are often treated as deductible against income tax where taxpayers have business accounts prepared.

Yield

4.73 The wealth tax currently yields about 0.7% of total revenue from all taxes, local and national and including social security contributions.

Related Taxes

4.74 *Summary*. The most relevant related taxes are income tax on investment income, succession duty and gift tax, and capital gains tax. National income tax is a smoothly progressive tax, rising to 54% on a taxable income of Skr 150,000 (£14,286). Local income tax is a fixed proportion of taxable income, the rate varying with the locality; it averaged 24% in 1974. Succession duty and gift tax are charged on three different scales. The highest (marginal) rate for legacies to beneficiaries in the direct line is 65%, applicable on an inheritance (gift) of over Skr 5,000,000 (£476,190). There is no capital gains tax as such, but a proportion of certain gains is taxed as income.

4.75 *National Income Tax on Investment Income*. The rates of national income tax on taxable income, whether from work or investment, are as follows:

Taxable Income			Tax at top of Range	
Skr	£	Rate (%)	Skr	£
0 – 15,000	(1,429)	7	1,050	(100)
15,000 – 20,000	(1,905)	13	1,700	(162)
20,000 – 30,000	(2,857)	19	3,600	(343)
30,000 – 52,500	(5,000)	28	9,900	(943)
52,500 – 70,000	(6,667)	38	16,550	(1,576)
70,000 – 100,000	(9,524)	47	30,650	(2,919)
100,000 – 150,000	(14,286)	49	55,150	(5,252)
Excess over 150,000		54		

---

[4] 'Tax preparers' is the name used in the USA for the comparatively untrained persons who will help the taxpayer fill in his income tax return for a small fee.

4.76 Up to Skr 30,000 (£2,857) income there is a personal relief deduction of Skr 4,500 (£429). Above Skr 30,000 the relief is tapered down until it disappears at Skr 52,500 (£5,000).

4.77 There is a special fee for health insurance but it relates only to earned income.[5]

4.78 *Local Income Tax.* The local income tax is directly proportional to taxable income. It is fixed by the localities and in the 1974 assessment year (1973 income year) it varied between 19.90 and 27.80%; the average over all localities was 24.02% of taxable income.

4.79 *Succession Duty.* The succession duty is charged on the capital value of property which a person inherits. There are three different scales relating to three classes of inheritor:

4.80 *Class I.* Husband or wife, lineal descendants of the deceased, husband or wife of a child, surviving husband or wife of a deceased child, person who has lived together with the deceased if they have or have had a child together, step-child, adopted child, foster-child and their descendants.

4.81 *Class II.* Beneficiaries other than those assignable to Class I or Class III.

4.82 *Class III.* Charities, Swedish institutions for the public benefit, etc.

4.83 In Class I there is an exemption of the first Skr 30,000 (£2,857) for a surviving spouse or Skr 15,000 (£1,429) for others. If a lineal descendant is less than 18 years old, an extra amount of Skr 3,000 (£286) is free of duty for each year by which the child's age is under 18.

4.84 In Class II and Class III the duty free amount is Skr 3,000 (£286).

4.85 The rates are as follows:

Size of Inheritance Liable to Taxation				*Tax at Top of Range*	
Class I Skr		£	Rate (%)	Skr	£
0 –	25,000	(2,381)	5	1,250	(119)
25,000 –	50,000	(4,762)	10	3,750	(357)
50,000 –	75,000	(7,143)	15	7,500	(714)
75,000 –	100,000	(9,524)	22	13,000	(1,238)
100,000 –	150,000	(14,286)	28	27,000	(2,571)
150,000 –	250,000	(23,810)	33	60,000	(5,714)
250,000 –	350,000	(33,333)	38	98,000	(9,333)
350,000 –	500,000	(47,619)	44	164,000	(15,619)
500,000 –	1,000,000	(95,238)	49	409,000	(38,952)
1,000,000 –	2,000,000	(190,476)	53	939,000	(89,429)
2,000,000 –	5,000,000	(476,190)	58	2,679,000	(255,143)
Excess over 5,000,000			65		

---

[5] For 1975 the Finance Minister has proposed a new national income tax scale with a maximum rate of 56% at Skr 150,000 (£14,286). The personal deduction of Skr 4,500 (£429) is to apply at all levels of income and the special fee for health insurance is to disappear.

Class II

0	–	10,000	(952)	8	800	(76)
10,000	–	20,000	(1,905)	16	2,400	(228)
20,000	–	30,000	(2,857)	24	4,800	(457)
30,000	–	50,000	(4,762)	32	11,200	(1,067)
50,000	–	70,000	(6,667)	40	19,200	(1,829)
70,000	–	100,000	(9,524)	45	32,700	(3,114)
100,000	–	150,000	(14,286)	50	57,700	(5,495)
150,000	–	200,000	(19,048)	56	85,700	(8,162)
200,000	–	500,000	(47,619)	61	268,700	(25,590)
500,000	–	1,000,000	(95,238)	67	603,700	(57,495)
Excess over 1,000,000				72		

Class III

0	–	10,000	(952)	8	800	(76)
10,000	–	20,000	(1,905)	16	2,400	(229)
20,000	–	30,000	(2,857)	24	4,800	(457)
Excess over 30,000				30		

4.86 *Gift Tax.* In principle, this has the same rates and regulations as the succession duty. The first Skr 2,000 (£191) per year of gifts from each donor is duty free. Apart from this exemption, gifts and any legacy over a 10 year period from the same donor are cumulated to determine the rate of duty.

4.87 *Capital Gains Tax.* There is no capital gains tax as such in Sweden, but certain gains are included as income liable to the ordinary national and local income taxes.

4.88 Gains from shares and other movable property are subject to income tax if the property has been held for less than five years; if held for over two years only a proportion of the gain is chargeable (two to three years, 75%, three to four years, 50%, four to five years, 25%).

4.89 If shares and similar securities have been held for five years or more, 10% of the gross receipt is treated as taxable income unless it can be proved that the seller has made a loss or that the gain does not exceed 5% of the sales price. A sum of Skr 500 (£48) is deductible from that gain. If other movable property has been held for more than five years there is no tax liability.

4.90 Gains from real property are taxed as income, but if the property has been held for more than two years, only 75% of the gain is chargeable. In calculating the gain, the acquisition cost, together with the value of any improvements over Skr 3,000 (£286) per year, is increased in the same proportion as the rise in an index of consumer prices. Also Skr 3,000 (£286) per year can be added to the acquisition price.

F

Evaluation of Swedish Wealth Tax

Horizontal Equity

4.91 The Swedish wealth tax is seen by those who operate it as a tax on capital, designed to take into account the additional taxable capacity that capital bestows on its possessor, but to be paid from income. It is therefore primarily on grounds of horizontal equity that it should be judged.

4.92 The Swedish tax ensures that all those whose wealth brings them above a modest threshold pay more tax from their income-yielding capital than if the same income had been gained from work; it contributes to the objective that, where the same income is derived from two different capital sums, the higher taxable capacity of the larger sum is taken into account; also some nil-yielding assets are brought within the tax base, notably jewellery, boats and cars, above a small exemption limit.

4.93 It is in relation to assets which do not yield an income that the Swedish wealth tax most falls short of the theoretical ideal. Many such assets are wholly excluded from the tax base—works of art, collections of all kinds, furniture, regardless of its value. Moreover, where personal chattels are included, the valuation is left to the taxpayer and, because of the difficulties of checking, largely taken on trust. It is recognised that jewellery, which is included in the tax base, is widely under-reported; and where it is returned at all, under-valued. Indeed, had the maharajah, with his gold and jewels but no income, who vividly illustrated the theoretical case for a wealth tax to secure horizontal equity,[6] been a Swedish citizen, then he might not have reported his jewels; or if he had, they would have been returned at a nominal value; or he might even have secured their exemption as a collection.[7]

4.94 In other ways, too, the achievement of horizontal equity is less than perfect. Differences in valuation favour owners of some forms of wealth compared with others. Thus real property owners are favoured: at the time of the quinquennial assessments the value is set at 75% of an open market figure; before the next revaluation it may fall much below that percentage.[8] Again the assets valuation method for closely held and unincorporated business favours their owners as compared with shareholders in quoted companies, particularly by virtue of the very low values attributable to stock.

4.95 Further, the procedure by which wealth tax valuations are determined with respect to a single date in the calendar year may create inequities, e.g. the man whose whose shares happen to peak on that day will suffer; the

---

[6] See paragraph 1.13.

[7] Had the jewels been unmounted they would have been exempt; see paragraph 4.27.

[8] The position is not as bad as it might seem to UK readers. The Swedes have had less inflation in recent years than the United Kingdom; the purchase of agricultural land is severely restricted; and the Swedes probably have a surplus of housing. Consequently there has been nothing like the explosion in real property prices which occurred in the United Kingdom in the early seventies.

recipient of a legacy on 30 December is unfortunate compared with a legatee whose windfall arrives on 1 January, (and who can spend it before the next assessment date). Similarly, if a person takes up permanent residence in Sweden on 30 December, he is liable to wealth tax for the year because it is before 31 December; whereas by waiting until 1 January he would have been exempted from all liability until the following 31 December. It can be argued, however, that an average value for prices like stock exchange quotations would not necessarily be fairer. If valuation relates to liability day, at least the taxpayer had the means to pay on that day. If an average were used and the stock exchange fell, he might find himself facing a tax bill based on more wealth than he possessed. (For a discussion of this issue, see paragraph 10.62.)

Efficiency in Resource Use

4.96 The Swedes make no claim that efficiency in resource use is a particular purpose of their wealth tax; but it is important, nonetheless, to see what is achieved under this head, for the claim is made on behalf of a wealth tax that it avoids investment distortions, except the 'desirable distortion' of promoting investment in more productive assets.

4.97 Doubtless the Swedish tax may achieve something under this head, but it is easy to point out the limitations.

4.98 The advantage of no distortion rests on the assumption that a wealth tax is general and that valuation is uniform. In practice, this is far from true in the Swedish case. Consequently, investment is attracted to the exempt items (art objects, collections, insurance and possibly pension funds) and to the undervalued forms of capital.

4.99 Moreover, some of these are predominantly nil-yielding assets, so a stimulus is given to the very opposite forms of investment assumed by wealth tax theory. As it happens, in Sweden, even the purchase of insurance will do little to promote risk-taking and enterprise, for Swedish insurance companies are restricted by law in the range of their investments and required to keep 90% of their policy funds in investments of a gilt-edged nature; even the remaining 10% cannot be invested in ordinary shares, although surplus funds may be so invested subject to a maximum 5% holding in any one individual company.

4.100 The wealth tax, in practice, is also not neutral between different forms of business organisation. The net assets form of valuation, omitting goodwill, is, in normal circumstances, likely to be favourable for closely held companies and may be a discouragement to 'go public'.

4.101 The ceiling provisions also have an unexpected result which hardly makes for efficiency. The 80/85% rule relates to the proportion of income from all sources taken in national and local income tax and wealth tax combined. It therefore follows, that once the ceiling provisions have been brought into operation to give relief for a particular taxpayer, should he then earn an extra Skr 1,000 (£95) by additional effort or enterprise, his marginal tax rate is either 80 or 85%, (not the nominal 78% (assuming the average rate for local income tax)).

Reduction in Inequality

4.102 The Swedish wealth tax reduces inequality only in the limited sense discussed in Chapter 1 (paragraph 1.31) and is not intended to do more. The ceiling provisions mean that, in many cases, the very wealthy and the moderately wealthy pay much the same proportion of their income in income tax and wealth tax combined; and these provisions may also mean that, where two people have the same income from very different amounts of wealth, the wealthiest may pay no more in tax than the less wealthy (paragraph 9.12).

Administrative Control

4.103 Administrative control is regarded as a secondary objective. There is a direct cross-check of income and wealth, which are returned on the same form (but, of course, this is no help in checking evasion in respect of assets which are liable to wealth tax but yield no income). The relationship with other capital taxes is less close and the cross-checking more limited in practice. For example, if a person's wealth falls substantially between one return and the next, this suggests that he may have made gifts; the Local Assessment Board should inform the head of the Provincial Fiscal Department who forwards the information to the gift tax authorities; in practice this is probably often overlooked by busy Boards working to a tight timetable. Similarly, in theory, information on, say, a legacy of jewellery, could be passed from the succession duty authorities to the wealth tax authorities including a valuation (which for succession duty purposes has to be authenticated by a professional valuer's certificate) so that it could be checked in the beneficiary's subsequent wealth tax return. Since succession duty is administered by the courts, and not by the tax authorities, such information is rarely passed on. Thus the control advantages claimed for a wealth tax are imperfectly achieved.

Administrative Cost

4.104 If the protagonists of a wealth tax are less than fully vindicated by Swedish practice, the case of the antagonists is also less strong in practice than in theory. The Swedish tax is not considered expensive to administer. This is partly because some of the more difficult assets to value, like pictures, are left out of the tax base; and in other cases, like jewellery, valuations are largely taken on trust. But more, it results from the common bases of valuation used for a variety of taxes. Compliance costs of wealth tax appear to be generally low for very much the same reasons; also the formalised valuation methods used for many assets carry the advantage of certainty for the taxpayer.

Other Economic Consequences

4.105 It is impossible to assess whether the tax carries any serious economic disadvantages, but the authorities do not think so. The valuation methods and ceiling provisions prevent it hitting too hard at private businesses or at saving, although where the ceiling provision has not yet been brought into operation, a marginal rate of tax on the return on additional saving can easily top 100%.

4.106 There is no doubt that the tax is both evaded by under-reporting and under-valuation of personal chattels; and avoided by purchase of works of art and collections and by investment in insurance and in under-valued real estate. One form of avoidance has been to borrow money to make such purchases, the debts counting as a deduction in arriving at net wealth. For example, someone could borrow Skr 1,000,000 (£95,238) and use it to buy real estate which might have a wealth tax value of only Skr 500,000 (£47,619). As a result, the wealth of the purchaser is the same, but his taxable wealth has fallen by Skr 500,000 (£47,619). There is no provision that a loan has to be related to a particular asset with income or wealth tax liability, so that a man may borrow on an insurance policy which is exempt and still deduct the liability from his wealth tax base. Art objects have particular attractions because, not only are they exempt from wealth tax, but they are also exempt from tax on capital gains if held for more than five years.

4.107 The authorities are aware of these problems. The capital tax committee considered the inclusion of art objects within the wealth tax base but rejected it on the grounds of practical difficulty; it suggested an amendment of rules for capital gains, but no action has yet been taken. Another committee is currently considering the position on insurance. It is probable, however, that insurance is much less attractive as a loophole than in the United Kingdom, because the restrictions on the investments of insurance companies limit the chance of capital growth; also collective insurance is much more common in Sweden.

4.108 In general, the impression was gained that the Swedish tax authorities were concerned about evasion in general rather than specifically about evasion of wealth tax. This is suggested by recent special tax audits on doctors and architects which had revealed considerable evasion of income tax; and by the recent revision of penalties. The impression gained was that there was some avoidance and that evasion of a relatively minor character was fairly widespread, especially in relation to chattels.

Conclusions

4.109 In examining the merits of the Swedish wealth tax, we have compared it with the 'ideal' tax of the theorists; as such, it falls far short. On the other hand, the disadvantages are considerably less than the opponents of wealth taxes suggest. Assessed against a practical alternative, it is likely that the Swedish wealth tax is superior to a surcharge on investment income, especially in achieving horizontal equity.

Chapter 5

A Case Study—The German Wealth Tax

The Choice of Germany

5.1 The German wealth tax was a natural choice to complement our study of the Swedish tax. The German tax also has a long history, especially if its Prussian forebear is recognised and, like the Swedes, the Germans have recently undertaken a thorough review and re-assessment of their wealth tax[1].

5.2 Also Germany is the largest and economically and politically the most important of the EEC countries with a wealth tax.

5.3 Further, the German tax differs from the Swedish tax in some important ways. To mention only the immediately obvious, the Swedish tax in principle applies only to individuals; the German is levied also on companies. The Swedish tax has a progressive structure and includes the highest rate of any in Europe; the German tax is proportional, with the lowest rate of those wealth taxes we have been studying. Moreover the differences in rates of wealth tax reflect the differences in overall tax levels. As the OECD tax league table demonstrates, (paragraph 3.26, table 3.1) taking the average for the years 1965-71, Sweden emerged top of the league whilst Germany was eighth, the lowest position of those European countries with wealth taxes which we have been examining most closely.

5.4 This chapter has a similar purpose to that on the Swedish tax—to offer a description and analysis of the German wealth tax and then to attempt to evaluate it against the criteria outlined in our first chapter. However, we do not

---

[1] A detailed review of wealth tax proposals is included in the 1971 Report of the Tax Reform (Eberhard) Commission. Material examined by the Commission included a Report on the Reform of Direct Taxes, prepared in 1967, by the Technical Advisory Board to the Finance Ministry.

think it necessary to give as much detailed information about the German tax as about the Swedish, except for aspects of particular interest where there are notable differences between the two taxes.

Description and Analysis

The Scope of the Charge

5.5 The tax applies to individuals, companies and other bodies of persons and associations, both resident and non-resident. Exemption is however given to various public, social or religious bodies.

5.6 The German *resident* is taxable on all assets wherever situated, except assets situated in East Germany. An individual is resident if his 'domicile' (Wohnsitz) or customary place of abode is in the Federal Republic or West Berlin. Further, a stay of six months is sufficient to establish residence, but in exceptional cases the rule may be waived if the individual's 'domicile' is elsewhere and he is not working in Germany, provided his stay does not exceed a year.

5.7 The *non-resident* is generally taxable mainly on business assets and real property (including certain debts charged on real property) in Germany; also on German patents and similar rights and on interests in German partnerships. By a new rule, from 1 January 1974, the non-resident shareholder (individual or company) with a 25 per cent share-holding in a German company is liable to wealth tax.

5.8 The taxation both of companies and of their shares in the hands of the shareholders is widely regarded in Germany as double taxation. The Eberhard Commission (paragraph 5.1, footnote 1), reporting in 1971, did not go as far as to suggest the abolition of the charge on companies, but it proposed a reduction of the double tax burden by suggesting that shares in German companies should be assessed at half their value and that the exemption enjoyed by a company in respect of a substantial holding in another company should be extended so as to apply to shareholdings in excess of 10% instead of the current 25%. The committee did not advocate the complete exemption of the legal person, on the grounds that this would give an advantage to the corporate sector in terms of cash flow as compared with sole owners and partnerships; but their argument is somewhat unconvincing, for companies have the choice of modifying their dividend policies. The possibility of giving shareholders a credit, against their individual tax liability for wealth tax paid by the company, was rejected by the Committee on administrative grounds connected with the problem of non-resident shareholders and the need to pay some shareholders a cash refund.

Rate of Tax and Thresholds

5.9 Currently (1974) the wealth tax consists of a flat rate of 0.7% on both individuals and companies. On 1 January 1975 it is to be raised to 1% on companies but not individuals.

5.10 Before 1974 the charge had been 1% on individuals and on companies, but individuals had been able to deduct it from income for tax purposes. The tax had therefore been relatively heavier on those with low incomes because the deduction against income benefited the taxpayer according to the marginal rate at which he paid income tax. The reduction of the rate from 1% to 0.7%, together with the removal of deductibility, had the effect of increasing the charge on those with higher incomes and reducing it on those with lower.

5.11 *The wealth of husband and wife* and of minor children is aggregated for wealth tax purposes. Assets of children over 18 and up to age 27 are also aggregated with those of their parents (upon application of both parents and children) where the children have remained dependent, for example, where they are being educated or trained or are in voluntary social service or compulsory military service. Once a child ceases to be dependent, he is charged as a separate person. There is no age limit for children incapable of supporting themselves because of physical or mental incapacity.

Thresholds

5.12 For resident individuals, the threshold is DM 70,000 (£11,447) plus an additional DM 70,000 (£11,447) for wife and DM 70,000 (£11,447) for each dependent child as defined in paragraph 5.11. The threshold is increased by a further DM 10,000 (£1,635) allowance for an individual who is over 60 or incapacitated (unable to earn a living) for at least three years and whose wealth does not exceed DM 150,000 (£24,530). The allowance is increased to DM 50,000 (£8,177) for persons incapacitated or over their 65th birthday, if certain requirements on total means are fulfilled. These age concessions are, however, reduced mark for mark if the total taxable property exceeds DM 150,000 (£24,530). The limits are doubled in certain cases of married taxpayers.

5.13 No tax is levied on a resident company if its wealth is less than DM 10,000 (£1,635) but if it is in excess of that amount the whole of the value counts. For non-resident individuals or companies, the threshold is also DM 10,000 (£1,635).

5.14 For wealth tax purposes, valuations are always rounded down to the nearest DM 1,000 (£164).

5.15 There are no ceiling provisions.

Exemptions

5.16 Household furniture and other movable assets are exempt provided that they are not classified as taxable luxuries. For example, a mass-produced private car or yacht would not be regarded as a luxury, nor would furniture, however expensive, provided it was in private ownership for personal use. The taxpayer has a duty to list all articles over a certain value; the tax office then decides whether or not they should be regarded as for personal use.

5.17 There are a number of detailed provisions for exemptions and disregards: The first DM 10,000 (£1,635) of bank and savings accounts and shares is exempt, and there is an additional and separate exemption for the first DM 1,000 (£164) of bank and savings accounts. The first DM 10,000 (£1,635) of life insurance is also exempt. In addition assets of the following classes are disregarded if the aggregate value of the assets of the relevant class does not exceed the figure shown:

Jewellery and luxuries (DM 10,000 (£1,635))

Precious metals and stones (DM 1,000 (£164))

Art treasures and collections (DM 20,000 (£3,271))

Where the value exceeds the figure shown, tax is chargeable on the whole value. Art treasures and collections may also wholly or partly escape liability under provisions relating to items of artistic, historical or scientific importance.

5.18 The exemptions and disregards listed above are granted as many times as there are persons assessed jointly, e.g. a taxpayer with wife and two dependent children would be entitled to four times the figures given above.

5.19 *Pension Rights* provided by an employer are, in general, not liable to wealth tax either in the employer's or employee's hands whether during the period of employment or when the pension is being paid. Annuities of a similar type purchased by a taxpayer are also exempt provided that the annuity is not payable before age 60 except if the taxpayer is unable to earn his living for a period of not less than three years. Purchased annuities of other types are treated as insurance policies up to the date on which the annuity commences.

5.20 *Patents* owned by an inventor or his employer are not liable to wealth tax. If sold or licensed for a capital sum that capital sum is of course liable to wealth tax. If licensed in favour of third parties by the inventor or his employer in return for a royalty, the capitalised value of that royalty is not liable to wealth tax in the hands of the inventor or his employer. Persons who have purchased patent rights have to include the cost of those rights in their wealth tax base, less a writing down allowance. In exceptional cases licensees of patents should include the capitalised value of the obligation to pay royalties among their liabilities. Normally, however, these amounts cancel each other out. The position with regard to *copyright* is similar.

Valuation

5.21 The Germans lay down elaborate provisions for valuation in a specific Valuation Law which aims at securing uniformity of practice and at codifying substantive valuation rules for a variety of taxes on property. Thus the valuation rules for agricultural property, real property and business property apply to the wealth tax, the local realty tax, the real property transfer tax (in some instances), the inheritance tax and the trade tax on business capital.

5.22 *Personal Chattels,* if taxable (e.g. jewellery, luxuries) are some of the few assets that do not have an 'assessed value'; the valuation is supplied by the taxpayer and is intended to be the fair market value of the property.

5.23 *Real Property.* The present intention is that real property should be re-assessed every six years; but the current (1974) valuations are based on 1964 prices up-dated by 40% to allow for inflation since then, and before that valuations were based on 1935 prices. Valuations are carried out by specialist departments (within the tax administration) of the Land governments in accordance with detailed rules. The 1964 values were based on statistics of actual sales but using the lower end of the scale.

5.24 *Agricultural Property* has a separate basis of assessment from other real property. In principle, agricultural enterprises (apart from the residential properties thereon) are appraised on the basis of potential yield and the value of the enterprise is computed at 18 times the potential annual yield. However, individual appraisal of potential yield is rarely made; it is assessed by reference to a standard or model farm. A hypothetical agricultural enterprise with optimal yield is assigned an index figure of 100 and the potential yield of any individual enterprise is expressed as a percentage of the model after considering its nature (e.g. topography, soil quality, climatic conditions) and economic characteristics (e.g. size and organisation and the location of its component parts) and any special local factors affecting its profitability, such as local prices and wages. Representative farms are also selected in different localities with which the index can be compared. The value per hectare of land of the hypothetical model enterprise is then fixed by statute according to the type of product grown. The law allows for adjustments in the case of major discrepancies between the assumed conditions and those actually existing.

5.25 *Quoted Shares* are valued at the quoted price for 31 December.

5.26 *Unquoted Shares.* Shares of unquoted companies are valued by reference to transactions in those shares only if those transactions were very recent, at arms length and of a similar proportion of the company's share capital. In other circumstances the shares are valued by a formula ('the Stuttgart formula'), which uses the following expressions:

X   The value of the shares.

V   85% of the 'intrinsic' value of the assets of the company (i.e. net tangible assets) arrived at as described in paragraph 5.28, but including the value of any shareholdings exceeding 25% in other companies and deducting any liabilities relating to those shareholdings. V is expressed as a percentage of the share capital.

E   70% of the average earnings of the company after tax for the five most recent years expressed as a percentage of the share capital.

The formula is:

$$X = V + \frac{5(E - 10X)}{100}$$

that is to say 85% of net tangible assets plus five times the difference between 70% of average profit and 10% of the value of the shares.

In effect E represents estimated distributable profits so that the formula adds to 85% of net tangible assets five years purchase of the difference between distributable profits and 10% of the amount invested (the latter being regarded as the rate which could be earned in an alternative investment). The formula can be solved to become

$$X = \frac{66.67(V + 5E)}{100}$$

which is then simplified by rounding 66.67% to become 65%. If the five year average is a loss, that loss is substituted for 70% of average profit and becomes a negative figure.

Examples (in DM)

	1	2	3
Capital	90,000	90,000	30,000
Net tangible assets	120,000	120,000	100,000
85% thereof	102,000	102,000	85,000
As a % of capital (V)	113.33%	113.33%	283.33%
Average profit after tax (5 years)	9,000	(—2,700)	30,000
70% thereof	6,300	—	21,000
As a % of capital (E)	7%	(—3%)	70%
V + 5E	148.3%	98.3%	633.3%
65% thereof (% of capital) ...	96%	64%	412%
Total value	86,400	57,600	123,600
Price/earnings ratio	9.6	—	4.12
Price/assets ratio	0.72	0.48	1.24

The formula as shown above can be modified in some circumstances. It is intended for shareholdings which have an influence on the management of the company (holdings of spouses and infant children being aggregated for that purpose). For shares which do not have such an influence the deduction from net tangible assets to arrive at V is 20% instead of 15%, and average dividends replace 70% of average profit for E. Other special circumstances can be taken into account; e.g. a further deduction if profits are consistently low in relation to assets. But no deduction is allowed for the tax which would be payable if the shares were sold, nor are difficulties in selling shares or restrictions on transfer normally 'special circumstances' justifying a deduction. The Stuttgart formula is varied from time to time to take account of prevailing economic conditions. The most recent modifications (embodied in the above summary) were introduced in 1974 to apply to valuations at 31 December 1973.

5.27 The valuations are made at 31 December of each triennial period but with rights on both sides to reopen the valuations at the intermediate dates (paragraph 5.33). The return of net assets made by the company is that used as a basis for the wealth tax payable by the company itself (paragraph 5.28). The return incorporating the Stuttgart calculation is made by the company but individual shareholders can apply for different valuations based on special circumstances, as can the company itself if those circumstances are applicable to all shareholders.

5.28 All companies (as distinct from shareholders) pay wealth tax on their net tangible assets computed in the same way as for unincorporated businesses (paragraph 5.29). However in order to avoid treble taxation (since companies are already doubly taxed) holdings of over 25% owned by the taxpayer for at least 12 months in other German companies are not included and liabilities relating to those holdings are not deducted.

5.29 *Unincorporated businesses and partnerships* are valued by reference to net tangible assets. Land is taken at assessed value. In general plant and machinery is taken at the same value as used for income determination purposes although in theory a current going concern valuation could be substituted. No fixed asset still in use is to be valued at less than 30% of cost if acquired after 1959, even if it has been fully written off in the books or for tax purposes. Fixed assets bought before 1959 may be taken in at 15% of cost unless they have 'specially long lives'. There is no deduction for accelerated depreciation. Assets which cost less than DM 800 (£131) per item which are written off on acquisition are valued at 40% of the total of such acquisitions in the previous five years. Created goodwill is exempt; purchased goodwill is valued at cost unless it can be demonstrated that its value has fallen (this is said to be difficult). Patents and copyrights are dealt with as stated in paragraph 5.20. However, road transport licences have to be valued (corresponding to 'C' licences in the UK). Other assets and liabilities are mainly taken at the same values as used for income determination purposes (including stock and work in progress which is taken, broadly speaking, at cost including relevant overheads or net realisable value if lower). A deduction can be made for unfunded pension liabilities provided that it is also made in the books of the company. No deduction is allowed for the tax which would be payable if the business is liquidated. The valuations are made at 31 December of each triennial period but with rights on both sides to reopen the valuation at the intermediate dates (paragraph 5.33). The return of net business assets is made separately from the return of other personal assets.

5.30 *Life Insurance, endowment and annuity policies* are valued at the lower of two-thirds of total premiums paid since June 1948 or surrender value.

5.31 *Annuities,* other than those paid by insurance companies, are valued by prescribed methods based on a 5½ per annum compound yield. Thus a perpetual annuity is valued at 18 times the annual income. There are tables for fixed term annuities and very detailed rules for life annuities and life tenancies and other annuities of uncertain term.

Administration Procedures and Costs

5.32 *The Tax Authorities.* The wealth tax is administered locally but in accordance with the rules laid down in the wealth tax law and the Valuation Act. Taxpayers who feel they have been unfairly assessed have various rights of appeal; if a protest against the notice of assessment fails they can lodge an administrative appeal for a decision by the local fiscal office; against this decision an action can be taken to the Fiscal Court; failing satisfaction there, appeal can be made to the Federal Fiscal Court in Munich.

5.33 *Tax Assessments.* Wealth tax returns are separate from income tax returns and are normally only made every three years. No change in wealth tax is made in the intervening years unless the taxpayer's own wealth has changed by more than one-fifth or by more than DM 150,000 (£24,530) since the assessment date. If the value has risen, it must have changed by at least DM 50,000 (£8,177), and if fallen, by at least DM 10,000 (£1,635) to justify a new assessment. The taxpayer has no duty to make a return for a new assessment, though obviously it is in his interest to do so if his wealth has fallen. Local fiscal officers would require an additional return from a taxpayer if they thought that his wealth had risen sufficiently, and this possibility might be revealed by the income tax return (especially for businesses).

5.34 *Administrative Links.* Returns for income tax and wealth tax are on different forms but they go to the same office and are cross-checked; wealth tax information is also checked against gift tax and inheritance tax. As already indicated (paragraphs 5.21 and 5.26) there are important valuation links, partly through the common methods of assessment of businesses to income tax and wealth tax, but mainly through the common valuation methods for property taxes prescribed in the Valuation Act. The real property valuations on owner-occupied property are also used to calculate an imputed rent.

5.35 *Administration costs.* As with the Swedish wealth tax, because of the links with income tax and with other capital taxes no separate administrative costs are calculated for wealth tax. One of the biggest elements in the cost is valuation but the same procedures and values apply to all property taxes.

5.36 The number of wealth tax payers is currently approaching 500,000.

5.37 *Enforcement Powers.* The tax authorities have the power to visit people's homes to check on the accurate declaration of chattels, but very rarely exercise it. The authorities can also obtain information from banks about a client's accounts, but only if fraud is suspected.

5.38 *Penalties* for tax offences usually take the form of fines, only in rare cases imprisonment. Offenders may seek and be granted anonymity about their tax offences.

5.39 *Compliance costs.* In practice the large majority of wealth tax payers employ professional advice for both income tax and wealth tax—but it is the income tax which is by far the most important. Some compliance costs of wealth tax (as of other taxes) can be claimed as a deduction for income tax purposes. Where taxpayers employ professional advice for wealth tax, the consultants normally charge an overall sum for services in connection with both wealth tax and income tax. Personal wealth tax compliance costs are not heavy, but the calculations that businesses are required to make are more burdensome.

Yield

5.40 The wealth tax in 1971 yielded about 1.3% of revenue from all taxes including social security contributions.

Related Taxes

5.41 *Income Tax on Investment Income.* The same rates of tax are levied on income from work and income from property, although there are a number of small personal and income-related reliefs granted only against income from employment. A more liberal view than in the UK is taken in Germany on certain claims for expenses such as travelling to and from work. Overtime increments, within prescribed limits, are also exempted from income tax. The income tax liability is assessed using a number of equations. As from 1 January 1975 the position is as follows:

Range of Taxable Income	Tax Payable
(a) Up to DM 3,029. (£496)	Nil
(b) DM 3,030-16,019 (£2,622)	$0.22Y - 660$
(c) DM 16,020-47,999 (£7,856)	$[(-49.2X + 505.3)X + 3077]X + 2858$
(d) DM 48,000-130,019 (£21,280)	$\{[0.1Z - 6.07)Z + 109.95]Z + 4,800\}Z + 1626$
(e) Over DM 130,020 (£21,280)	$0.56Y - 12676$

where   Y=taxable income in DM

X=One-ten-thousandth of the excess of taxable income over DM 16,000 (£2,617)

Z=One-ten-thousandth of the excess of taxable income over DM 48,000 (£7,850)

Taxable income is first rounded down to the next lower figure divisible by 30 up to a taxable income of DM 48,000 (£7,856). For taxable income above DM 48,000 (£7,850) the steps are each DM 60 (£10).

German income tax thus consists of four basic zones:

Zone I (equation b) with a constant marginal rate of tax of 22%.

Zone II (equation c) is the lower progressive zone; the marginal rate of tax increases as the income increases.

Zone III (equation d) is the upper progressive zone; demonstrating similar patterns to Zone II.

Zone IV (equation e) has a consistent marginal rate of tax of 56%, the top rate of tax.

5.42 Administrators and taxpayers of course, have tables from which they read off the appropriate rate of tax.

5.43 The tax on married couples is calculated on the basis of twice the tax on half the combined income, e.g. if the combined income is DM 100,000 (£16,353) this is halved, to give DM 50,000 (£8,177). Tax on DM 50,000 (£8,177) is DM 17,220 (£2,816). Hence total tax due is DM 34,440 (£5,632).

5.44 *Inheritance and Gift Tax.* Tax rates are identical for gifts and legacies and are graduated both according to the size of accession and the kinship between the donor (testator) and donee (legatee). There are four classes as follows:

Class I — spouse, children and children of deceased children.

Class II — grandchildren and remoter issue (unless Class I).

Class III — parents, grandparents, parents-in-law, brother/sisters, sons/ daughters-in-law, divorced spouse and adopted parents.

Class IV — all others.

The tax is on a slab scale, by which the prescribed tax rate relates to the aggregate estate, and not just to the slice above the next lower rate band. A slab scale gives rise to the need for marginal relief to prevent a situation by which the heirs of an estate just above a point at which the rate changes receive less property after tax than if the estate had been smaller.

Inheritance and Gift Tax Rates (as from 1 January, 1974)

Slab Range
DM thousands (*after* reliefs)

Over	Not over		I	II	III	IV
0 —	50	(£8,183)	3	6	11	20
50 —	75		3.5	7	12.5	22
75 —	100		4	8	14	24
100 —	125		4.5	9	15.5	26
125 —	150		5	10	17	28
150 —	200		5.5	11	18.5	30

Class of legatee/donee
Rate %

200 — 250 (£40,917)	6	12	20	32
250 — 300	6.5	13	21.5	34
300 — 400	7	14	23	36
400 — 500 (£81,833)	7.5	15	24.5	38
500 — 600	8	16	26	40
600 — 700	8.5	17	27.5	42
700 — 800	9	18	29	44
800 — 900	9.5	19	30.5	46
900 — 1,000 (£163,666)	10	20	32	48

DM millions

1 — 2	11	22	34	50
2 — 3	12	24	36	52
3 — 4	13	26	38	54
4 — 6 (£982,000)	14	28	40	56
6 — 8	16	30	43	58
8 — 10	18	33	46	60
10 — 25	21	36	50	62
25 — 50	25	40	55	64
50 — 100	30	45	60	67
Over 100 (£16,366,612)	35	50	65	70

Marginal Relief. Tax payable is limited to that imposed at the top of the next band below plus a fraction of the excess of the actual taxable value over that limit. This fraction is one-half for accessions subject to a scale rate of up to 30%; three-quarters for scale rates 30%-50%; and nine-tenths for larger accessions.

5.45 Relief to child donees and legatees. As from 1 January 1974 a child receives a personal relief of DM 90,000 (£14,118) *plus* a 'maintenance' increment on the following scale:

Up to 5 years of age	DM 50,000 (£8,183)
From 5 years to 10 years of age	DM 40,000 (£6,547)
From 10 years to 15 years of age	DM 30,000 (£4,910)
From 15 years to 20 years of age	DM 20,000 (£3,273)
From 20 years to 27 years of age	DM 10,000 (£1,637)

This is, however, reduced, mark for mark, by the capital value of any tax-free statutory (social security) benefits and by any excess of the present and earlier aggregable accessions over DM 150,000 (£24,550).

5.46 Exemptions. Certain assets (e.g. works of art, collections, and household chattels) are either exempt or subject to a standard relief.

5.47 *Capital Gains Tax.* There is no capital gains tax as such, but certain gains attract liability to income tax, although in some cases at a reduced rate. For example, gains on the sale of a business are taxed to income tax at one-half of the taxpayer's average rate applicable to his total income including such

G

gains; (where the total gain is under DM 100,000 (£16,353) there is a reduction of DM 30,000 (£4,906) which is doubled for a taxpayer who is over 55 or retiring because of permanent incapacity). Short term ('speculative') gains, where the interval between acquisition and disposal is less than six months, or two years in the case of land, are treated as income and subject to the full rate of income tax.

5.48 *Local Taxes.* A real property tax and a trade tax are both regulated by federal law but collected by the municipalities which establish the effective rates. The trade tax has three bases: business profits, business capital and payrolls.

Evaluation of the German Wealth Tax
Similarity with the Swedish

5.49 The German wealth tax is seen as having the same primary purpose as the Swedish, to supplement income tax by taking account of the taxable capacity conferred by capital irrespective of any income derived from it. Administrative control is seen as a subsidiary advantage. The German tax, with its present (much increased) threshold—before 1974 it was only DM 10,000 (£1,637)—and by virtue of the exemptions for a wife and dependent children, will exclude from the tax many wealth holders who would be liable under Swedish provisions; and the low percentage rate also means that the tax is much lighter on persons than the Swedish. But, with a few exceptions, much the same points emerge in an evaluation of the two taxes.

5.50 The German tax contributes to the horizontal equity of the tax system, but falls short of the ideal, like the Swedish, especially in the taxation of nil-yielding assets. The Germans have in some ways made a more logical attempt to include nil-yielding assets within the tax base than have the Swedes, by seeking to tax 'luxury' goods and including, for example, works of art above a certain value. But, like the Swedish attempt to tax jewellery, it was accepted that in Germany there was much under-reporting of pictures, jewellery, gold coins etc.

5.51 Similarly, different bases for valuation create some inequities between taxpayers, favouring the owners of undervalued assets. In Germany, at any rate until very recently, this feature was more pronounced than in Sweden because of the completely out-of-date basis of German valuation of real property (paragraph 5.23). Another form of inequity applicable to Germany, but not to Sweden, is the double taxation effect of imposing the wealth tax both upon shareholdings and also upon the underlying corporate assets.

5.52 Clearly these differences also create some distortions. Undervalued assets attract investment funds, as do exempt assets or forms of wealth that can easily be hidden. The double taxation of company assets creates a bias in favour of the unincorporated business and as the Stuttgart formula is generally held to result in lower valuations than open market sales, there is some incentive for a firm not to 'go public'. Avoidance measures by firms may also take the form of an early dividend distribution (because, as a result of exemptions, the wealth tax liability of the shareholders as a body will be less than that of the company); and a company looking for shares in another company may seek a 'substantial' shareholding to gain the wealth tax (and corporation tax) benefit. But in general, probably because of its low rate and generally high yields, the German wealth tax is not considered to have much significance in affecting business or individual decision-making.

Evaluation of the Stuttgart Formula

5.53 One notable difference between the administration of the Swedish and German taxes is the formula the Germans have devised and applied over many years to obtain share values in unincorporated companies. It would seem worth while examining its effects more closely.

5.54 The Stuttgart formula includes an element of goodwill (as we have defined it in paragraph 10-33) but the valuation of unincorporated businesses and partnerships exempts created goodwill. This seems anomalous particularly as the net tangible assets of companies are doubly taxed and all the more so as in Germany there are many substantial businesses trading as limited partnerships[1] which in the United Kingdom would be companies. However, apart from the question of double taxation, we were interested to find that both taxpayers and revenue authorities appeared to be satisfied with the way in which the formula works. The price/earnings ratio shown in example 1 in paragraph 5.26 suggests that the formula can arrive at values (at least where the return on assets is comparatively low) which, even in relation to substantial but not controlling shareholdings, are high by United Kingdom standards. This leads us to wonder if the 'special circumstances' rule is applied fairly liberally. For companies with high earnings/assets ratios the rule appears to give a low price/earnings ratio (example 3). The current change from 1935 to updated 1964 valuations for real property (paragraph 5.23) may cause more dissatisfaction with the formula as net tangible assets are the dominant component in it. The valuations do not in general benefit from accelerated capital allowances as do the methods used in the three Scandinavian countries.

5.55 Although we believe that in Germany there are conventions with regard to management remuneration which are not applicable in the United Kingdom, it still seems to us that profit (and hence E in the formula) is liable to be influenced by remuneration paid to shareholders.

5.56 No doubt it can be argued that the Stuttgart formula is a crude method compared with the separate judgement of each case called for by present United Kingdom methods for estate duty and capital gains tax. But it rewards success

---

[1] Kommanditgesellschaft—abbreviated to KG.

and penalises failure and has the great merit of simplicity and certainty. Even if special circumstances are pleaded it seems to us that the basic concepts of the formula must serve as a reference point against which negotiations take place so that they are not as time consuming as in this country.

Administration

5.57 As with Sweden, the administrative procedures appear to work very smoothly (apart from the past failures to have regular re-valuations of real property) and the administrative cost to be contained mainly by the existence of a defined structure of procedures leading to common values for a range of taxes; and in part perhaps, by a measure of unconcern over the niceties of reporting and valuing personal chattels.

Conclusions

5.58 The German wealth tax, like the Swedish, fails to obtain the full advantages claimed by the theorist for an annual wealth tax; but nor do the administrative problems emerge as particularly burdensome.

Part III

Perspective on a Wealth Tax
for the United Kingdom

Chapter 6

Wealth Tax Possibilities in the United Kingdom

The Background to The Green Paper

6.1 A wealth tax can hardly be considered an innovation in Britain. J. A. Venn[1] records that, despite its name, the Land Tax of 1692 was at first a comprehensive property tax, covering, in the words of the original Act, 'Every person, body politic and corporate, having any estate in ready monies, or in any debts owing to them, or having any estate in goods, wares, merchandise or other chattel or personal estate whatever'. The Act was continued by aid of annual Bills for over 100 years, always covering the same forms of wealth, but the amount received under the headings of personal property steadily dwindled. The same story was true of the poor rate, the origin of the local rate; to quote Venn: 'As was the case with the Land Tax, all forms of property were covered at first and gradually all save land and buildings tacitly dropped out of assessment. Again, the explanation is the simple one that other forms of property were elusive, and also that the area of lands and the size of buildings formed an easier criterion by which to assess the wealth of individuals'.

6.2 More recently, in the twentieth century, especially after the First World War, there was a growth of interest in taxing wealth on a once and for all basis, as a capital levy to repay a substantial proportion of the National

---

[1] J. A. Venn, *Foundations of Agricultural Economics*, Chapter 6, CUP 1933.
For a brief history of the Land Tax, see William Phillips 'No Flowers by Request', *British Tax Review*, July-August 1963, pp. 285-293. Phillips disputes the historical importance of the 1692 Act and sees that of 1697 as more significant.

Debt[2]; but the proposals came to nought. However, two small levies have been imposed since the Second World War, one by Sir Stafford Cripps in 1948 called a 'Special Contribution', the other by Mr. Roy Jenkins as a 'Special Charge' in 1968. Both were at a level which necessitated some disposal of assets by the wealthy and both were levied for a single year and described by their authors as expedients which could only be repeated at long intervals for, to quote Mr. Jenkins, they 'would otherwise militate against the employment of capital so as to produce investment income'.[3] Although these 'once and for all' levies were called wealth taxes by some commentators, this was a misnomer, for the tax base was investment income, not wealth; they thus multiplied an existing income charge.

6.3 Interest in a regular annual wealth tax in the United Kingdom appears to date from the 'sixties, though one outstanding British economist, Nicholas Kaldor, was advising some developing countries to adopt one in the 'fifties.[4] Mr. James Callaghan was the first major politician to give the idea an airing, shortly before the 1964 General Election; but the Labour Party did not include it in their Manifesto and when he became Chancellor Mr. Callaghan shelved the idea in favour of other reforms, notably the capital gains tax and corporation tax. His successor at the Exchequer, Mr. Jenkins, soon indicated his interest in 'the further exploration of the ways in which the taxable capacity of those who possess wealth should be differentiated from those who depend primarily on wages and salaries';[5] but congestion in the Inland Revenue precluded any bold new ventures in taxation and Mr. Jenkins had to be content with the special charge on investment income.

6.4 It was not only the Labour Party and its supporters who were giving some thought to an annual wealth tax. In 1963, an NEDC publication[6] suggested examining the possibilities of replacing top rates of tax on income by a wealth tax which might 'have a useful role in any major review of taxation related to a programme of growth'. An industrialist, Mr. Joe Hyman, in a letter to *The Times*,[7] argued for a shift in taxation from income to capital to promote efficiency in resource use: 'A $1\frac{1}{2}\%$ annual tax on personal capital above £50,000, accompanied by a maximum total taxation charge of 50% on earned or unearned income would provide us with the managerial incentive which is so inhibited in the £5,000 to £10,000 a year bracket . . .' A wealth tax of this kind also seems to have had a passing attraction for Mr. Iain Macleod when Shadow Chancellor.[8]

---

[2] See, for example, H. Dalton, *The Capital Levy Explained*, Labour Publishing Company, 1923.
[3] *Budget Speech*, 19 March 1968.
[4] See Chapter 16, especially paragraph 16.37.
[5] *Budget Speech*, 1968
[6] *Conditions Favourable to Faster Growth*, HMSO 1963, p. 42.
[7] 18 September 1968.
[8] Nigel (now Sir Nigel) Fisher, *Iain Macleod*, Andre Deutsch, 1973, pp. 263-5.

6.5 But, whilst NEDC, Mr. Hyman and Mr. Macleod were all thinking of substitutive wealth taxes, and possibly Mr. Callaghan and Mr. Jenkins like-wise, Labour thinking and policy statements suggest that the Party was being increasingly drawn to the additive variety, a tax which the wealthy could only meet by disposing of assets. In this it was backed by the TUC, which regularly advocated a wealth tax of varying degrees of severity in its annual economic reviews. *Labour's Economic Strategy* (August 1969), contained specific proposals for a wealth tax 'with a starting point of £50,000, and with progressive rates of 1% through to 5% on wealth above £400,000'. Even so, the Party's Manifesto for the 1970 General Election, although emphasising the need to reduce inequalities of wealth by taxation, contained no explicit under-taking to introduce an annual wealth tax. However, the proposal continued to harden. *Labour's Programme for Britain*[9] declared the intention of the Party to 'introduce a wealth tax, consisting of an annual levy on the largest concentrations of private wealth . . . progressive on net personal wealth holdings in excess of £50,000 at present values'. As the same document promised an increase in income tax on very high incomes and a reduction of the threshold for the investment income surcharge, an additive wealth tax was clearly implied. In the February 1974 General Election, the wealth tax at last made the Labour Party Manifesto in the unadorned and unelaborated phrase: 'We shall introduce an annual wealth tax on the rich'.

6.6 When Labour became the Government in February 1974 and Mr. Denis Healey introduced his first budget a few weeks later, he announced the same cryptic message as the Manifesto, 'This Government intends to introduce an annual wealth tax on the rich'. He continued, 'Such a tax is an accepted feature of many other countries' taxation systems. But it will be a new departure in this country, and I believe it should be introduced only after a thorough public discussion about the precise form it should take, the rate at which it is levied, and its relationship with other forms of taxation. My first step towards this reform will, therefore, be the publication of a Green Paper during the summer'.[10] The Green Paper, *Wealth Tax*, Cmnd. 5704, duly appeared on 8 August 1974. In the October election of 1974, the Labour Party re-affirmed the commitment in its Manifesto and indicated that the threshold would be £100,000.

An Outline of The Green Paper

6.7 Details of the proposals in the Green Paper are included as part of the comparative summary of wealth taxes set out in tabular form in Appendix C, and the Green Paper's proposed treatment for specific problems is considered in Part IV of this volume. Our main purpose in this chapter, having indicated

---

[9] Published in *Labour Weekly*, 8 June 1973.
[10] *Budget Speech*, 26 March 1974.

the background of the Green Paper, is to outline its main features as a basis
for exploring some of its macro implications such as the weight of taxation
implied, the differences in its scope from the investment income surcharge, the
revenue and demand effects.

Purpose

6.8 In his Foreword, the Chancellor sets out the purpose of the tax 'to
promote greater social and economic equality'. He continues with a statement
of the horizontal equity argument. 'Income by itself is not an adequate
measure of taxable capacity. The ownership of wealth, whether it produces
income or not, adds to the economic resources of a taxpayer so that the
person who has wealth as well as income of a given size necessarily has a
greater taxable capacity than one who has only income of that size'. He then
links this with the argument for reducing inequality, for he continues:
'Because our present tax system takes no account of this fact, although we
have a highly progressive system of income tax, the bulk of privately owned
wealth is still concentrated in relatively few hands'. Finally, this paragraph
ends with just a hint of a substitutive element in the tax, perhaps with
efficiency in resource use in mind: 'Once the additional taxable capacity
represented by ownership of wealth is adequately brought into charge, excessive inequalities of wealth will in time be eroded, and it will be possible to
reduce the high rates of tax on earned income'. (p. iii)

Rates of Tax

6.9 Two possible scales of rates of wealth tax have been assumed in the
Green Paper *for illustrative purposes,* as follows:

Tax A			Tax B		
£100,000 – £500,000	1%		£100,000 – £300,000	1%	
£500,000 – £2,000,000	1½%		£300,000 – £500,000	2%	
£2,000,000 – £5,000,000	2%		£500,000 – £2,000,000	3%	
Over £5,000,000	2½%		£2,000,000 – £5,000,000	4%	
			Over £5,000,000	5%	

Yield

6.10 Because of difficulties in establishing accurately the distribution of
personal wealth, the Green Paper could not estimate yield with precision, but
suggested the probability that had the tax been operating in 1972, tax A
would have yielded between £200m and £275m and Tax B between £350m
and £425m. These figures, however, take no account of various possible
offsets, notably the effect of a ceiling provision or of the partial displacement
of the investment income surcharge (paragraph 4).

6.11 Well under 1% of the adult population would be subject to the charge
(paragraph 5).

General Scope

6.12 It was proposed that the tax should be levied on individuals, and possibly the wealth of husband and wife would be aggregated (in which case there would be a higher threshold and a less steeply progressive scale). In any case, the wealth of minor children would be combined with that of their parents, (or, if the tax unit was the individual, the parent from whose side of the family the wealth derived). Those domiciled and resident in the United Kingdom would be fully liable on their world wide assets. In other cases of residence or non-residence, the charge would have a narrower scope. Elaborate provisions were suggested for dealing with trusts (paragraphs 16-24). Estates in administration would be subject to tax as though they had been distributed; but the beneficiaries would only be required to pay after they had received their legacies (paragraph 25).

Treatment of Particular Assets

6.13 It was proposed that *owner-occupied houses* should be included within the charge (paragraph 28). *Household and personal goods* might benefit from an exemption up to a certain value sufficient to cover normal household contents. The exemption might also cover *cars* used primarily for private purposes or perhaps one car per person might be exempt (paragraph 29).

6.14 *Copyrights and patent rights* should count as net wealth, but where sold the wealth tax should be allowed as an offset against income tax (paragraph 40). *Pension rights*, within broad limits, and *retirement annuity contracts* should be excluded. *Life assurance policies* should be included (paragraphs 40-44).

6.15 *Deductions* would be allowed against gross wealth except for debts related to exempt assets (paragraph 45).

Interaction with Other Taxes

6.16 Because of the high threshold proposed, the Government took the view that the wealth tax could not replace the *investment income surcharge* completely, but they would consider limiting liability to whichever was the higher (paragraph 31). Also a *ceiling provision* might be considered (paragraph 32).

Productive Assets

6.17 The abatement of investment income surcharge would not help the owner of an unincorporated business (whose assets might also lack marketability) nor the tenant farmer or owner-occupier in agriculture; but a ceiling provision would help them. Further, the Green Paper suggested that they might be allowed to defer payment (subject to interest at a commercial rate which might also be deferred) until sale, retirement or death. Any such provision would also be extended, as appropriate, to cover shares in unquoted trading companies (paragraphs 33-35).

The National Heritage

6.18 The Government were sympathetic to easing the difficulties the tax would cause in respect of works of art, collections of books, and other objects of national, scientific, historic or artistic importance. The Green Paper suggested that different treatment might be granted according to the degree of public access. Similarly with historic houses. A possible solution was the deferment of tax, which for some categories of work of art might extend to exemption of interest on the deferred charge. 'This could be combined with arrangements to take the works into public ownership in satisfaction of accrued wealth tax liabilities' (paragraphs 36-39).

Valuation

6.19 The proposed basis was, in principle, open market valuation; it was proposed that holdings in property would be aggregated if they were owned by connected persons (paragraphs 46-48).

6.20 To ease valuation problems with *owner-occupied houses*, it might be possible to value at a multiple of their annual value for rating purposes (paragraph 49).

6.21 *Quoted securities* would be valued at their Stock Exchange valuation in line with the rules for capital gains tax. *Unquoted securities* would be valued on an open market basis; an assets valuation might not be necessary for a majority holding. Businesses owned by *sole proprietors* would be valued as a going concern on normal open market principles with the balance sheet as the basis. *Goodwill* would normally be valued according to the custom of the business. *Partnerships* would be valued in a similar manner to businesses owned by sole proprietors (paragraphs 50-54).

6.22 *Life insurance policies* would be valued at net realisable value (normally surrender value). *Rights to annuities* (other than pension annuities) acquired by purchase, would be charged at market value (paragraphs 55-56).

Administration

6.23 A regional organisation was proposed with 'very close links with existing Inland Revenue offices'. Returns would be required from persons who estimated that their wealth exceeded a prescribed fraction of the exemption limit, and from trusts (paragraphs 58-60).

6.24 The Government proposed a system of self-assessment with sample checks by the Inland Revenue. Taxpayers would be responsible for listing their property, valuing it, totalling their gross wealth, subtracting allowable deductions, and calculating and paying over the tax due. Either taxpayer or Revenue would have the right to reopen, in the light of later information, such as a sale or professional valuation, previous values which had been accepted. On any reassessment, interest at normal commercial rates would be paid or allowed. 'Penalties might be imposed, but only where it was shown that the taxpayer had deliberately and wilfully understated the value of his asset' (paragraphs 61-64).

6.25 All valuations would be on the basis of a given valuation day, probably either 31 December or 31 March. Returns might be due six months later, with interest at normal commercial rates on delayed payments (paragraph 66).

6.26 The Green Paper stated that the Inland Revenue would need additional powers to acquire information and there would be the usual rights of appeal (paragraphs 69-70).

Introduction of the Tax

6.27 The Government intended to recommend the setting up of a Select Committee of the House of Commons to examine the proposals. The Government hoped to legislate in 1976; in that case, the first valuation would be 31 December 1976 or 31 March 1977 (paragraphs 71-73).

Related Taxes

6.28 The wealth tax proposals can only be properly appreciated against the background of other related taxes in the United Kingdom. These can be summarised as follows:

6.29 *Income Tax on Investment Income.* The scale of income tax rates 1974-5 on taxable income is as follows:

Bands of Taxable Income

£	%	£	%
0 – 4,500	33	8,000 – 10,000	58
4,500 – 5,000	38	10,000 – 12,000	63
5,000 – 6,000	43	12,000 – 15,000	68
6,000 – 7,000	48	15,000 – 20,000	73
7,000 – 8,000	53	Over 20,000	83

6.30 In addition, there is a 15% surcharge on investment income in excess of £2,000.[11]

6.31 The single person's tax free allowance was fixed at £625 for 1974-5 and the married allowance at £865.

---

[11] In his Budget on 12 November 1974, the Chancellor of the Exchequer proposed to levy a surcharge of 10% on the first £1,000-£2,000 of investment income except for taxpayers over 65 for whom the starting point would be £1,500. This additional surcharge was to apply from and including the tax year 1974-5. The proposal came just as this report was going to print. Rather than delay publication by altering all the calculations of investment income surcharge for a proposal that still lacked the force of law, it was considered best to leave the calculations unchanged. All calculations of investment income surcharge throughout this report therefore assume it to be at 15% on investment income over £2,000 and take no account of the lowering of the starting point and of the reduced rate.

Capital Transfer Tax

6.32 The capital transfer tax is charged on the cumulative total of gifts made during a person's lifetime with the further final cumulation of property passing on death. The proposed rates (to come into effect in 1974[12]) are:

Capital Transfer Tax

Slice of chargeable transfers £'000s								*Rate* %
0 – 15	...	...	...	...	...	...	...	0
15 – 20	...	...	...	...	...	...	...	10
20 – 25	...	...	...	...	...	...	...	15
25 – 30	...	...	...	...	...	...	...	20
30 – 40	...	...	...	...	...	...	...	25
40 – 50	...	...	...	...	...	...	...	30
50 – 60	...	...	...	...	...	...	...	35
60 – 80	...	...	...	...	...	...	...	40
80 – 100	...	...	...	...	...	...	...	45
100 – 120	...	...	...	...	...	...	...	50
120 – 150	...	...	...	...	...	...	...	55
150 – 500	...	...	...	...	...	...	...	60
500 – 1,000	...	...	...	...	...	...	...	65
1,000 – 2,000	...	...	...	...	...	...	...	70
Over 2,000	...	...	...	...	...	...	...	75

6.33 Gifts between husband and wife and property left at death to a surviving spouse are wholly exempt.

6.34 The White Paper proposing the Capital Transfer Tax (Cmnd. 5705) stated that the special 45% reduction for Estate Duty accorded to agricultural land and certain business assets and the favourable treatment of woodlands would be discontinued, but the Government were 'considering the possibility of continuing some relief for full-time working farmers and businessmen in respect of agricultural land and business assets'.[13]

Capital Gains Tax

6.35 The tax is levied at a rate of 30%, except that as a concession to those with smaller incomes, income tax at marginal rates can be charged on a fraction of the net gain: for net gains under £5,000 the fraction is one half; for net gains over £5,000, tax is charged on the sum of £2,500 plus the excess of the net gain over £5,000.

---

[12] The tax came into effect for gifts as from 26 March 1974. It comes into effect for deaths (replacing estate duty) from the date at which the Autumn Finance Bill receives the Royal Assent.

[13] The 1974 Autumn Budget provided for a relief for 'full-time working farmers' by which, subject to certain limits, the value of a farm was to be reduced for purposes of capital transfer tax to 20 times the gross rental obtainable on an open market letting of the land. (See Chapter 13, especially paragraphs 13.24 and 13.38).

Some Implications of The Green Paper

6.36 In this section of the chapter, we seek to draw out some of the broad economic implications of the Green Paper. In attempting this task, we face two main difficulties. First, the Green Paper itself leaves many vital questions open (and the options are not costed) so in some cases, the best we can do is to illustrate several alternatives corresponding to the major options. Second, there is a lack of data, published and unpublished, so that parts of our analysis can only be qualitative when it would be much more useful if we could assign quantities.

The Weight of the Wealth Tax

6.37 In Table 6.1, we attempt to indicate the possible increase in taxation resulting from the introduction of a wealth tax by comparing the current income tax on investment income with what the combined weight of income tax and wealth tax would be on different amounts of wealth at different rates of return on alternative assumptions about the scale of wealth tax and the continuation of the investment income surcharge. Table 6.1a assumes a single person with minimum allowances and no earned income; table 6.1b looks at the same situation where the single person has £10,000 earned income. If wealth tax, especially at scale A, were to replace investment income surcharge completely, then there would be some situations where the total tax burden would be less than at present, even at high levels of wealth such as £1m, provided the rate of return was high; but there would be many others, especially if the wealth tax were unaccompanied by a reduction in income tax, where the combined income tax and wealth tax would approach or exceed 100% of income.

6.38 Particularly relevant to decision-making are the returns to the marginal increment of saving and investment. Marginal tax rates are therefore shown in Tables 6.2a and 6.2b. The marginal rate of wealth tax is defined as the tax on that amount of wealth required to generate an additional £100 of income. In the tables of marginal rates we have taken some situations offering a higher rate of return (for reasons set out in paragraph 3.31). In a large number of the situations indicated in the two tables, the combined marginal rate of tax is over 100% and often well above it.

6.39 The Green Paper indicated that the Government would 'consider' limiting the taxpayer's liability to whichever of wealth tax or investment income surcharge was the higher (paragraph 31). Table 6.3 sets out, for the two illustrative wealth tax scales, tax as a percentage of investment income if this suggestion were implemented. These figures are then compared with the corresponding situation for Germany and Sweden (Table 6.3).

6.40 Whilst at the lower end of the scale for the lowest rates of return, the United Kingdom figures are low by comparison (mainly because of the

Table 6.1 (a)

United Kingdom Income Tax (IT) and Wealth Tax (WT) as a Percentage of Investment Income at different rates of return for different levels of net wealth (Single person with minimum allowances and no earned income)

Wealth £'000	IT only (including IIS) %	IT + WT on Scale A		IT + WT on Scale B	
		Including IIS %	Without IIS %	Including IIS %	Without IIS %
2% rate of return					
100	23	23	23	23	23
200	35	60	53	60	53
5% rate of return					
100	38	38	29	38	29
200	51	61	49	61	49
500	73	89	75	97	83
1,000	86	109	94	128	113
5,000	96	130	115	164	142
10% rate of return					
500	86	94	79	98	86
1,000	92	103	89	113	98
5,000	97	114	99	131	116

NOTES:
IIS=Investment Income Surcharge—taken as 15 per cent on investment income over £2,000.
IT rates as UK 1974-5 (except for investment income surcharge on investment incomes of £1,000-£2,000).
WT rates as illustrative scales in Green Paper.
For more comprehensive tables see Appendix D7-D12.

Table 6.1 (b)

United Kingdom Income Tax (IT) and Wealth Tax (WT) as a Percentage of Income at different rates of return for different levels of net wealth, assuming £10,000 Earned Income (Single person with minimum allowances)

Wealth £'000	IT only (including IIS) %	IT + WT on Scale A		IT + WT on Scale B	
		Including IIS %	Without IIS %	Including IIS %	Without IIS %
2% rate of return					
100	43	43	43	43	43
200	48	56	53	56	53
5% rate of return					
100	51	51	48	51	48
200	60	65	59	65	59
500	76	87	78	93	83
1,000	85	104	92	120	108
5,000	95	128	114	161	147
10% rate of return					
500	85	92	80	95	83
1,000	91	102	88	110	97
5,000	97	114	99	130	115

NOTES: as table 6.1a.

H

Table 6.2 (a)

United Kingdom Marginal Rates of Income Tax (IT) and Wealth Tax (WT) at different rates of return for different levels of net wealth (Single person with minimum allowances and no earned income)

Wealth £'000	IT only (including IIS) %	IT + WT on Scale A		IT + WT on Scale B	
		Including IIS %	Without IIS %	Including IIS %	Without IIS %
5% rate of return					
100	48	68	53	73	53
200	73	93	78	93	78
10% rate of return					
100	73	83	68	83	68
200	88	98	83	98	83
500	98	113	98	128	113
1,000	98	113	98	128	113
5,000	98	123	108	148	133
15% rate of return					
500	98	108	93	118	103
1,000	98	108	93	118	103
5,000	98	115	100	131	116

NOTES:
As table 6.1a.
The marginal rate of wealth tax is the tax on that amount of wealth required to generate an additional £100 of income.

Table 6.2 (b)

United Kingdom Marginal Rates of Income Tax (IT) and Wealth Tax (WT) at different rates of return for different levels of net wealth, assuming £10,000 earned income (Single person with minimum allowances)

Wealth £'000	IT only (including IIS) %	IT + WT on Scale A Including IIS %	IT + WT on Scale A Without IIS %	IT + WT on Scale B Including IIS %	IT + WT on Scale B Without IIS %
5% rate of return					
100	83	103	88	103	88
200	98	108	93	108	93
10% rate of return					
100	88	98	83	98	83
200	98	108	93	108	93
500	98	113	98	128	113
1,000	98	113	98	128	113
5,000	98	123	108	148	133
15% rate of return					
500	98	108	93	118	103
1,000	98	108	93	118	103
5,000	98	115	100	131	116

NOTES: as table 6.2a.

Table 6.3 Comparison of Combined Wealth Tax (WT) and investment Income Tax (IT) expressed as a Percentage of Investment Income at different rates of return and different levels of net wealth (Single person with minimum allowances and no earned income)

Wealth	United Kingdom		Germany	Sweden
£'000	IT + WT (Scale A) or IIS whichever is the higher %	IT + WT (Scale B) or IIS whichever is the higher %	IT + WT %	IT + WT (including local IT at average rates) %
2% rate of return				
100	23*	23*	48	80ᶜ
200	53	53	57	80ᶜ
5% rate of return				
100	38 (IIS)	38 (IIS)	39	73
200	51 (IIS)	51 (IIS)	50	80ᶜ
500	75	83	61	81ᶜ
1,000	94	113	66	83ᶜ
5,000	115	149	69	85ᶜ
10% rate of return				
500	86 (IIS)	86 (IIS)	59	83ᶜ
1,000	92 (IIS)	98	61	84ᶜ
5,000	99	116	63	85ᶜ

NOTES:
UK tax rates 1974-5; Swedish rates 1974; German rates 1975; investment income surcharge (IIS) taken at 15 per cent on investment income in excess of £2,000.
(IIS) indicates investment income surcharge higher than wealth tax.
* neither investment income surcharge nor wealth tax applies.
ᶜ ceiling provision operative (see paragraph 4.18).

proposed high threshold for wealth tax), on the largest wealth holdings the tax level in the United Kingdom is substantially above that of Sweden—which probably ranks as the highest in Europe (the United Kingdom apart)—and some 50% higher than that of Germany even on scale A.

6.41 One significant point of comparison with Sweden is how frequently the Swedish ceiling provisions are called into play. This raises the question of the possibility of a ceiling provision in the United Kingdom. The Green Paper commented: 'One possibility is that there should be some ceiling on a tax-payer's total tax liability along the lines of that to be found in the tax system in Sweden and in some other European countries. However such a ceiling would benefit most those whose assets produce a low income yield and it might be preferable to give relief on total liabilities so as to benefit most those who receive a high taxable return on their assets' (paragraph 32). Unfortunately, this suggestion is not developed further.[14] Clearly, if a ceiling such as that of the Swedes or the Dutch was introduced in the United Kingdom along with the wealth tax, it would make a big difference to the weight of taxation; indeed, applying the ceiling of any Continental country would reduce the total tax on some of the rich below its current levels with the investment income surcharge and no wealth tax.

6.42 Before leaving this section on the weight of a wealth tax, we need to explore a little further some of the efficiency implications.

6.43 Consider first the incentive to save. Tables 6.2a and 6.2b indicated the wide number of possible situations where the combined marginal rate of income tax and wealth tax would exceed 100% of income. In such a situation (paragraph 2.11), the incentive to save must be very seriously impaired. Anyone who saves (or fails to consume an addition to their capital by gift or legacy) is actually worse off in terms of income. There is a positive incentive to dissave.

6.44 The introduction of a Continental type ceiling, say at 90 or 95%, would reduce the disincentive to save for those whose tax liability was restricted by the ceiling provision. But if, as on the Continent, the ceiling restricted the proportion of *total* income taken in tax, it would have the unintended effect of raising the marginal rate of income tax on earned income. Anyone with liability restricted, say, by a 90% ceiling, who then earned an additional £100 would effectively be taxed on it at a marginal rate of 90%, substantially higher than the current 83% on earned income—with corresponding danger of increased disincentive effects on effort and enterprise.

6.45 What of the possibility that a wealth tax might increase efficiency by encouraging investment in higher yielding assets? It may, indeed, have some effect in this direction—but at best it would be very small. The Green Paper proposal to charge the higher of wealth tax or investment income surcharge removes some of the incentive to go for high yield: a taxpayer might minimise wealth tax as a proportion of income by holding high-yielding assets only to find his 'diminished' wealth tax replaced by an extra 15% on his income tax. But there is an even stronger reason why the proposals (whichever of the possible options is adopted) would have little effect. The return on an asset can be measured not only in terms of income but also in terms of capital gain. As long as income tax remained at its present high levels (with or without surcharge) and capital gains tax at its relatively low levels (and avoidable by holding assets until death) a wealth tax would do relatively little

---

[14] We explore the possibilities and make recommendations for a suitable form of ceiling in Chapter 9.

Table 6.4 (a)

Calculation to compare Annual Capital Gain Required to Compensate for a 2% income yield as against 5%, under present United Kingdom Investment Income Tax and Capital Gains Tax and Various Wealth Tax Alternatives.

	IT only (including IIS)	IT + WT on Scale A (including IIS)	IT + WT on Scale A (without IIS)	IT + WT on Scale B (including IIS)	IT + WT on Scale B (without IIS)
Comparison at £200,000 level, earning 5% or 2%.					
5%					
Gross Income	£10,000	£10,000	£10,000	£10,000	£10,000
Tax	5,000	6,000	4,900	6,000	4,900
(a) Net Income	£5,000	£4,000	£5,100	£4,000	£5,100
2%					
Gross Income	£4,000	£4,000	£4,000	£4,000	£4,000
Tax	1,320	2,320	2,120	2,320	2,120
(b) Net Income	£2,680	£1,680	£1,880	£1,680	£1,880
(c) (a - b)	£2,320	£2,320	£3,220	£2,320	£3,220
(d) Add C.G.T. 3/7 X (c) *	994	994	1,380	994	1,380
(e) Gross gain required to make good shortfall of income	£3,314	£3,314	£4,600	£3,314	£4,600
(f) Percentage of capital	1.65%	1.65%	2.3%	1.65%	2.3%

* ignoring alternative basis of assessment (paragraph 6. 35).

to offset the attractions of capital growth as against income yield. This point is illustrated in Table 6.4. Table 6.4a explores what percentage increase in annual capital growth would be necessary at £200,000 wealth holding to compensate for a yield of 2% instead of 5%; tables 6.4b and 6.4c consider for higher wealth holdings what capital growth would compensate for a 5% instead of a 10% yield. To illustrate by reference to some of the answers: at the £200,000 level, a wealth tax imposed on top of the investment income surcharge would not affect the level of capital growth required at all; whilst one which replaced the surcharge would only raise the necessary annual

Table 6.4 (b)

Calculation to compare Annual Capital Gain Required to Compensate for a 5% income yield as against 10%, under present United Kingdom Investment Income Tax and Capital Gains Tax and Various Wealth Tax Alternatives.

	IT only (including IIS)	IT + WT on Scale A (including IIS)	IT + WT on Scale A (without IIS)	IT + WT on Scale B (including IIS)	IT + WT on Scale B (without IIS)
Comparison at £500,000 level earning 10% or 5%.					
10%					
Gross Income	£50,000	£50,000	£50,000	£50,000	£50,000
Tax	42,500	46,500	39,500	48,500	41,500
(a) Net Income	£7,500	£3,500	£10,500	£1,500	£8,500
5%					
Gross Income	£25,000	£25,000	£25,000	£25,000	£25,000
Tax	18,250	22,250	18,750	24,750	20,750
(b) Net Income	£6,750	£2,750	£6,250	£250	£4,250
(c) (a - b)	£750	£750	£4,250	£1,250	£4,250
(d) Add C.G.T. 3/7 × (c)	321	321	1,821	536	1,821
(e) Gross gain required	£1,071	£1,071	£6,071	£1,786	£6,071
(f) Percentage	.21	.21	1.21	.36	1.21

growth by 0.65% (2.3%–1.65%). At the higher levels, the difference is rather larger, but it is still doubtful if the imposition of a wealth tax would have much effect—especially in view of the possibility of postponing capital gains tax indefinitely and avoiding it ultimately. For a wealth tax to be effective in promoting a search for high yield, it is necessary for income tax to be significantly reduced or capital gains tax increased and tightened up, or both.

6.46 In short, it is difficult to see how the proposals of the Green Paper can fail to reduce the incentive to save amongst the wealthy and replace it by a strong motive for dissaving; a ceiling provision along Continental lines would modify this only at the cost of a disincentive to effort; the proposal to apply the higher of the investment income surcharge or the wealth tax will diminish whatever benefit the wealth tax might have had in promoting investment in

Table 6.4 (c)

Calculation to compare Annual Capital Gain Required to Compensate for a 5% income yield as against 10%, under present United Kingdom Investment Income Tax and Capital Gains Tax and Various Wealth Tax Alternatives.

Comparison at £5,000,000 level earning 10% or 5%.

	IT only (including IIS)	IT + WT on Scale A (including IIS)	IT + WT on Scale A (without IIS)	IT + WT on Scale B (including IIS)	IT + WT on Scale B (without IIS)
10%					
Gross Income	£500,000	£500,000	£500,000	£500,000	£500,000
Tax	485,000	570,000	495,000	655,000	580,000
(a) Net Income	£15,000	£(-70,000)	£5,000	£(-155,000)	£(-80,000)
5%					
Gross Income	£250,000	£250,000	£250,000	£250,000	£250,000
Tax	237,500	325,000	287,500	410,000	372,500
(b) Net Income	£12,500	£(-75,000)	£(-37,500)	£(-160,000)	£(-122,500)
(c) (a - b)	£2,500	£5,000	£42,500	£5,000	£42,500
(d) Add C.G.T. 3/7 X (c)	1,071	2,143	18,214	2,143	18,214
(e) Gross gain required	£3,571	£7,143	£60,714	£7,153	£60,714
(f) Percentage	.07	.14	1.21	.14	1.21

high yielding assets; and in any case, the incentive to invest for yield rather than capital growth must remain small without a more significant reduction in income tax (or some increase in capital gains tax) than anything proposed in the Green Paper. By the standards of economic efficiency, the proposals are hardly attractive.

Assets Brought Into Tax

6.47 The point of a wealth tax, as compared with an investment income surcharge, is that it brings nil-yielding assets into the tax net and it taxes low-yielding capital more heavily. The significance of its heavier taxation of low-yielding assets is difficult to assess; but we can do more to assess quantitatively the importance of including nil-yielding assets.

Table 6.5: Distribution of Personal Assets by Type of Asset, Great Britain, 1971 as per cent (a) of total gross wealth, and (b) of gross wealth in estates over and under £100,000.

	All Estates	Estates Under £100,000	Estates Over £100,000
1. Government and Municipal Securities	4.6	4.3	6.6
2. Shares and Debentures in Companies, unquoted	2.5	1.9	6.7
3. Total quoted shares and debentures including unit trusts	14.2	9.7	44.4
4. Shares and deposits in Building Societies	7.2	8.0	1.8
5. Money on various bonds and securities	2.7	2.7	2.6
6. Household goods, pictures, china, etc.	3.3	3.4	2.5
7. Policies of life insurance	14.8	16.6	2.6
8. Cash and bank deposits	9.4	9.7	7.5
9. Trade, business and professional assets	2.5	2.6	1.7
10. Other personalty	7.0	7.2	5.9
11. Land freehold and leasehold	2.8	1.7	10.3
12. Buildings—residential	28.2	31.4	6.7
13. Other land and buildings	0.7	0.7	0.8
TOTAL GROSS WEALTH	100.0	100.0	100.0

NOTE:
Deductions to obtain net wealth amount to just over 10 per cent of gross wealth.
SOURCE:
Inland Revenue Statistics 1973.

6.48 Table 6.5 summarises the information on the distribution of assets derived from the latest published *Inland Revenue Statistics*, distinguishing estates above and below the proposed wealth tax threshold. The data is derived from estate duty returns in the manner described in Appendix B. For the reasons given there (basically because the assets people hold at death, and the value of these assets, are not wholly representative of the living), the data almost certainly understates the value of household goods and possibly the value of residential accommodation; it understates cash held in the house (part of item 9); it overstates the value of life insurance; but it understates other insurance such as endowment insurance. Estate duty figures also understate the values of high quality works of art. The information in the table is thus a less than perfect indicator of the proportion of wealth held in different forms of asset, though it is some guide.

6.49 The main nil-yielding assets in the table consist of all or part of items 6 (household goods, etc.), 8 (cash and bank deposits), and 12 (residential buildings). In addition, life insurance policies are not subject to income tax in the hands of the policy holder (although income from invested premiums is subject to corporation tax in the hands of the company); and the income of unincorporated businesses is treated as earned income and does not rank for investment income surcharge.

6.50 In total, the first three items constitute just over 40% of the total value of estates under £100,000 in size, but only about 16% of those over that figure. But this overstates the total assets which would incur liability to wealth tax. Although we indicated that household goods were undervalued for death duties, it seems doubtful if any higher values will be obtained for wealth tax and much of the sum indicated in the table is likely to disappear into an exemption: the Green Paper suggests a general exemption up to a certain value for all personal and domestic property held primarily for current use.

6.51 Of cash and bank deposits, less than one half represents cash in the house and drawing deposits; the rest is deposit accounts which currently yield a high interest and are fully taxable.

6.52 When these deductions have been made, the nil-yielding assets newly brought into charge, which did not previously pay income tax and surcharge, are likely to amount only to about 10% for estates over £100,000. These assets remain much more significant for small estates, which consist of residential buildings to the extent of over 30%.

6.53 Life insurance, despite its over-valuation, also figures only to a very small extent in estates over £100,000 (in marked contrast to the estates below this figure). No precise statement is possible from this data covering un-incorporated business assets (including the land of owner-occupiers). But the inclusion of these assets within the tax base is a dubious economic advantage and creates serious problems (see Chapters 12 and 13).

6.54 All in all, with a threshold of £100,000, the value of the assets brought into charge under wealth tax which are not liable to income tax, will be only a small proportion of the total.

6.55 It is, of course, only putting the same point in another way to say that the larger estates possess a much larger proportion of income-earning assets—notably over 50% of estates over £100,000 consisted of quoted and unquoted shares and debentures as against not much more than 10% in estates under £100,000. Our table, however, gives no guide to the proportion of low yielding assets amongst the shares and debentures of the wealthy.

The Net Yield

6.56 The Green Paper suggests that, if the wealth tax had been operating in 1972, the gross yield might have been £200-£275m for tax A and £350-

£425m for tax B (paragraph 4). This would have represented something of the order of 1.5% (scale A) or 2.5% (scale B) of the total central government revenue from taxation in that year. The document recognises that the yield will vary from year to year according to changes in the value of assets. An estimate for 1971 or 1974 would certainly have had to put the gross yield much lower than for 1972 because of the changes in house values, land values and stock market prices.

6.57 The figure of gross yield in the Green Paper makes no allowance for offsets of any kind. It is important to try to assess the net revenue from the tax (which is some measure of its effect on the distribution of wealth) and also to try to measure its effect on the demand for resources.

6.58 To obtain the net revenue, we have to deduct from the gross yield an offset for exemptions and for any valuation methods which result in lower than open market values. We have further to allow for the possibility that where wealth tax is higher than investment income surcharge, the surcharge will not be levied; and for the possibility of some reduction both directly in wealth tax yield and conceivably also in income tax yield, from the application of a ceiling provision. Finally, in so far as the wealth tax reduces the wealth of the rich, the yield of capital transfer tax will be lower when they come to pass on their assets. The figure of net revenue so arrived at, is some approximate indication of the effectiveness of the tax in reducing inequality.

6.59 To estimate the effect of the tax in reducing demand for current output, we must assess how far the tax is paid by a reduction in saving and by dissaving (disposal of assets) and how far by a reduction in consumption. In so far as the rich meet it by reduced saving or by dissaving, the tax does not reduce demand for current output; more accurately, it leads to a transfer of assets from the private to the public sector, increases Government income on capital account, reduces the Government's borrowing requirements and saves some expenditure on current account in the form of interest on the national debt (which the recipients might have been expected to spend on consumption).

6.60 Having arrived at the gross amount by which claims on current output are reduced, we must then deduct from this any loss of income tax which would have been paid on the debt interest saved, and also deduct the (probably considerable) operating costs—administrative and compliance costs.

6.61 The calculations can be summarised in tabular form as follows:

GROSS YIELD

minus Exemptions proposed in Green Paper.

minus Any other exemptions, e.g. works of art, (Chapter 14) and deductions, e.g. from valuing some assets at less than open market values (Chapter 10).

minus Investment income surcharge credit (if the higher of wealth tax or investment income surcharge is taken).

minus Reduction in tax yield if a ceiling provision is introduced.

minus Reduction in revenue from capital transfer tax.

NET REVENUE

minus Extent to which tax paid by disposal of assets (less reduction in Government expenditure on debt interest).

GROSS REDUCTION IN CLAIMS ON CURRENT OUTPUT

minus Reduction in income tax yield from saving on debt interest.

minus Administrative costs.

minus Compliance costs.

NET REDUCTION IN CLAIMS ON CURRENT OUTPUT (OR NET DEMAND EFFECT)

6.62 Unfortunately, it is hardly possible to do more than guess at the size of the items in the table. But on some not implausible assumptions, it is possible that the final figure of net demand effect could be very small or even negative. This is important to know, but if the intention of the tax is to reduce inequality of wealth, the net demand effect is not particularly relevant. A more valid measurement of its effectiveness for that purpose is the figure of net revenue.

Summary and Conclusions

6.63 The idea of a wealth tax is not new in the United Kingdom, and several possibilities have been suggested over the past 10 or 15 years. The Labour Party has appeared to move increasingly towards an additive tax to reduce inequalities of wealth although, because of the range of choices left open, the Green Paper would be compatible with a largely substitutive or an additive tax. On almost any combination of the main possibilities suggested in the Green Paper, the rich in the United Kingdom would be taxed considerably more heavily than in Germany or Sweden. Marginal rates of combined income and wealth tax in excess of 100% would be very likely and carry serious threats to the incentive to save amongst the wealthy and possibly also to incentives to effort and enterprise. The Green Paper proposals are unlikely to do much to promote a movement into higher yielding investments. With a threshold of £100,000, the nil yielding assets which currently escape income tax (and the investment income surcharge) and would be brought into charge by a wealth tax are only a relatively small proportion of the assets of their owners; the proportion would be much higher if the wealth tax threshold were reduced. No attempt is made in the Green Paper to estimate a net yield from a wealth tax or to assess its demand effects.

Part IV
Particular Problems of a Wealth Tax

Chapter 7

Persons Chargeable

7.1 It seems *prima facie* reasonable that the scope of an annual wealth tax should be broadly the same as that of an income tax. That is to say, a resident of the taxing country should be chargeable to the tax on the total value of all his assets, wherever situated, except such assets as may be specifically exempted, while a non-resident should be chargeable only on assets situated in the taxing country. It is, however, necessary to consider what constitutes residence for the purposes of the tax, and whether a non-resident (as defined) should be charged on all, or only on certain specified kinds of, assets in the taxing country; and also whether the tax should apply to both individuals and companies, or to individuals only. The treatment of the family—husband, wife and minor children—has to be decided, and, particularly in the United Kingdom situation, special provisions may be required for the taxation of trusts.

Residents and Non-Residents

7.2 The general rule in our five European countries is that an individual who is resident for income tax purposes and so taxable on his world income is also resident for wealth tax purposes and taxable on his world assets. The British concept of legal domicile, as distinct from residence, is not found in these countries, where liability on world assets accordingly turns exclusively on the facts of residence. In Norway, as in the United Kingdom, an individual is resident for tax purposes if he is in the country for a period of six months or more. In Germany, similarly, a six months stay strictly constitutes residence and an individual may also become resident as a result of regular annual visits of significant length; but in practice a certain amount of discretion is exercised in the application of the six months rule (paragraph 5.6). In Sweden, on the other hand, there is no specific six months rule, and an individual may be able to spend considerable periods in the country without becoming taxable as a resident on world assets (paragraph 4.10). In the Republic of Ireland the concept of legal domicile exists, and it is proposed to charge the world assets where the individual is both domiciled and ordinarily resident in the Republic.

7.3 In the UK situation it seems clear that, in order to attach liability to wealth tax on the individual's world assets, some more regular connexion with this country should be required than mere residence in the relevant year (i.e. presence in the country for six months, or for any period if a place of abode is maintained here). A person who is resident and ordinarily resident and domiciled in the UK should clearly be liable on his total wealth, including property situated overseas; but the following cases in particular have to be considered:

(a) The individual is domiciled and ordinarily resident in the UK, but not resident for the particular year of assessment. Such a person is not charged to income tax on foreign investment income for that year, though he remains liable to capital gains tax. The connexion with the UK might be thought sufficiently firm to justify maintenance of the charge on foreign wealth (as proposed in the Irish Republic); but the closer parallel is with the income tax rather than the capital gains tax, since the wealth tax is an annual tax and is in a sense an extension of the income tax. This suggests that foreign wealth should not be charged in this case.

The Green Paper (paragraph 13) similarly proposes that foreign wealth should not be charged unless the individual is resident (and domiciled) in the year of assessment. The case for aligning the charge with the income tax treatment will be reinforced if payment of investment income surcharge is treated as satisfying *pro tanto* the wealth tax charge, or if a ceiling is placed on aggregate income tax and wealth tax liability.

(b) The individual is domiciled, and resident for the particular year, but not ordinarily resident. In this case a British subject is entitled to the remittance basis for purposes of income tax on foreign investment income. He has not entirely severed his connexion with the United Kingdom but his visits are occasional and of relatively short duration. We suggest that he should be chargeable on all his United Kingdom wealth in the relevant year, but not on his foreign wealth.

The Green Paper proposes, however, to charge wealth tax on the world assets; but it would seem unduly harsh to charge the foreign wealth if a person who is following a career abroad happens to be resident for a particular year, e.g. while on leave.

(c) The individual is resident and ordinarily resident, but not domiciled. Here again the remittance basis applies for income tax purposes, and so long as this treatment of foreign investment income continues it would seem that foreign wealth should not be charged. (The remittance basis has no place in a wealth tax; if foreign property is transferred to the United Kingdom it automatically forms part of the taxpayer's UK wealth at the end of the year; while if it is transferred and spent during the year on current consumption or on the purchase of exempt assets there is no more reason for taxing it in this case than in the case of a person who also has United Kingdom domicile).

The Green Paper suggests that an individual who is resident but not domiciled in the United Kingdom should be chargeable on foreign as well as United Kingdom assets if he has lived here for a considerable period. This appears to echo the proposals put forward by the Government in connexion with the 1974 Finance Bill for imposing income tax on the foreign investment income, whether remitted or not, of a person not domiciled here who had been resident for nine out of the last ten years. If those proposals had become law it would be consistent and defensible to impose liability to wealth tax on foreign assets, though the rule might be considered rather severe where the United Kingdom is only a secondary home, visited for only part of the year, and the principal home is abroad. So long as the income tax law remains unchanged, however, exemption of the foreign assets is to be preferred.

7.4 On the basis suggested above, foreign wealth would only be charged in the case of a person who is resident *and* ordinarily resident *and* domiciled here. In all other cases, liability would not extend beyond United Kingdom property. Where the individual is resident but not ordinarily resident or domiciled in this country it would be defensible to charge him on all his United Kingdom assets, though enforcement of the liability might be more difficult than for income tax in the case of a person becoming liable by reason of an isolated visit of over six months; but we would not dissent from the Green Paper proposal to treat such persons as if they were non-resident. A charge on all United Kingdom assets would, however, be appropriate in the case of a person who, though not domiciled here, is ordinarily resident as well as resident.

7.5 There is a fundamental problem of enforcement in connexion with the taxation of persons who have no sort of residential connexion with the United Kingdom. Unless the non-resident has someone in this country representing him, there is no means of forcing a return of his wealth or otherwise obtaining particulars of it. He may, for example, hold shares in a number of United Kingdom companies, but companies are not required to make returns to the Inland Revenue of the dividends paid to individual shareholders, and, even if they were, a non-resident's liability, if any, to wealth tax could not be determined unless all his shareholdings were collated at a central point. The share registers could of course be examined, and the details extracted and collated, but the process would be extremely laborious; and in the great majority of cases it is probable that no liability would arise. Further, the non-resident's shares might be registered in the name of a nominee; particulars of beneficial owners can be obtained from a resident nominee but not from a non-resident one.

7.6 It may be partly because of this kind of difficulty that in several European countries (e.g. Sweden, the Netherlands) the wealth tax charge in the case of non-residents applies only to such fixed and visible assets as real property and business enterprises carried on in the country by the non-resident. Other considerations may point the same way. In Sweden (paragraph 4.9) the purpose was to limit the charge on the non-resident to productive assets in Sweden; but shares in a Swedish company continue to be excluded, partly at least because of the practical difficulties of enforcement. In the United Kingdom situation there would be obvious objections to imposing a charge on, for example, the London deposits of non-residents or generally discouraging portfolio investment by non-residents in United Kingdom securities. On all counts therefore, the best course appears to be to limit the charge to (broadly) real property in the United Kingdom and United Kingdom permanent business establishments, as proposed in the Green Paper (paragraph 14)—a course which, as the Green Paper points out, would be in line with the relevant article[1] in the OECD Fiscal Committee's model double taxation agreement.

7.7 It may be noted that it appears to be the intention in the Irish Republic to include within the scope of the wealth tax all assets situated in the Republic and held by non-residents, and not to limit the charge in the manner proposed in the United Kingdom. The practical problem is less severe in the case of a flat-rate tax as distinct from a progressive tax, as is now proposed in the Republic, but enforcement would appear to require that the tax should be deducted by the payer out of any payment made to the non-resident. Thus a company paying a dividend to a foreign address, or a bank crediting a dividend to a non-resident customer, could be required to calculate the value of the shareholding at the valuation date and deduct the appropriate amount of flat-rate tax from the dividend. This seems to imply either that the tax should be charged without any initial exemption, which might be considered unduly severe treatment of the non-resident in the context of a tax which in the case of residents applies only above a high threshold, or alternatively that the onus should be on the taxpayer to claim any repayment appropriate to his circumstances.

---

[1] *Draft Double Taxation Convention on Income and Capital*, 1963

Conclusions

7.8 Our conclusions may be summarised as follows:

Residence status	*Charge on*
Resident, ordinarily resident and domiciled.	World-wide assets.
Resident and ordinarily resident but not domiciled.	All United Kingdom assets.
Resident and domiciled but not ordinarily resident.	All United Kingdom assets.
Resident but neither ordinarily resident nor domiciled.	Real property in United Kingdom and United Kingdom permanent establishments.
Not resident (irrespective of ordinary residence and domicile).	Real property in United Kingdom and United Kingdom permanent establishments.

Companies

7.9 Companies as well as individuals are subject to the wealth tax in Germany, Norway, Finland, Switzerland and Luxembourg. In Sweden, and also in Sri Lanka, foreign companies are chargeable, but not domestic companies. In Denmark and the Netherlands, and in India and Pakistan, the tax applies to individuals only.

7.10 The charge on companies, as well as on the individual shareholders in respect of their holdings, has been criticised in Germany as double taxation, but the double charge remains in being.[2] In Norway the national (though not the local) wealth tax on companies was abolished in 1970; but it was reintroduced in 1972.

7.11 The Swedish charge on foreign companies doing business in Sweden is justified as a substitute for a charge on the shareholders.[3] There is some logic in this, though the charge is hardly consistent with the freedom from tax of the non-resident shareholder in a Swedish company.

7.12 Whether companies should be charged turns ultimately on the purpose for which the tax is imposed. In the United Kingdom the stated objective is not merely to adjust taxation more precisely to taxable capacity, but to bring about, over time, a reduction of the existing inequality of distribution of private wealth, that is, of the wealth of individuals. In this context there is no reason to impose a separate charge on companies, whose wealth will, as the Green Paper says (paragraph 11), be taxed indirectly in the hands of those shareholders whose individual wealth is such as to render them liable to the

---

[2] Paragraph 5.8
[3] Paragraph 4.11

tax. If companies were charged, the burden would in effect fall on shareholders of modest means as well as on the wealthy.

7.13 As regards non-resident companies, a case could perhaps be made on Swedish lines for charging them on real property and permanent establishments in the United Kingdom; but it will probably be sufficient as suggested in the Green Paper (paragraph 15) to confine any such charge to closely held companies, so far as may be necessary to protect the charge on non-resident individuals and partnerships owning such assets.

Conclusion

7.14 In general, companies should not come within the scope of the wealth tax.

The Family

7.15 The principal question to be considered here is whether the capital of husband and wife should be aggregated for wealth tax purposes or whether each spouse should be taxed separately on his or her wealth.

7.16 Aggregation appears to be the universal rule in the existing European wealth taxes. In Sweden and Denmark the aggregate is taxed exactly as if it belonged to a single person; the threshold of liability is the same for both single persons and married couples. In Norway the threshold for the married couple (and generally for persons with dependants) is one-third higher than the single person's threshold; in the Netherlands the addition is rather more than a third, and in Finland one-fifth. In Germany the single threshold is doubled for the married couple. In all these countries the wealth tax is viewed essentially as a supplement to the income tax and it is natural that the general rule of aggregation of spouses' income for income tax purposes should be followed in the wealth tax.

7.17 Aggregation is also proposed in the Republic of Ireland, with a married threshold of £100,000 compared with £70,000 for the single person.

7.18 If the wealth tax were to be imposed in the UK as a straightforward substitute for the investment income surcharge, intended like the surcharge to be met out of income, the natural course would again be to follow the income tax pattern and treat the capital of husband and wife as a single aggregate, with a higher threshold than for single persons. The broad justification for aggregating spouses' incomes for income tax purposes is that 'two can live cheaper than one'; husband and wife have a greater taxable capacity[4] than two separate single persons with the same aggregate income—though not so great as one single person with that income (for which reason they receive a

---

[4] A consideration which is, however, pushed into the background where the wife is earning.

higher personal allowance). There is an underlying assumption, which is probably true enough in most cases, that the spouses regard their incomes as forming a common pool, available to meet the joint living expenses. True as this may be of income, it is not so evidently true in regard to their capital; but with a substitutive tax generally it is reasonable to make the same assumption, namely that the capital resources are available for their joint purposes and that they therefore have a greater taxable capacity than two single persons. As with income tax, there is also the point that if they were taxed as separate individuals on their respective capitals the burden of wealth tax on the household would vary arbitrarily between different couples with the same aggregate wealth according to the distribution of the capital between the two of them: which would be inconsistent with the idea of the substitutive wealth tax as an extension of the income tax.

7.19 With an additive tax the issue is less clear-cut. By definition the weight of the tax is such that at any rate some taxpayers are unable to meet it out of income and are obliged to dispose of assets. Such a tax might be entirely divorced from the income tax. In that situation it would not be essential to follow the income tax rule; the spouses could be treated as two separate single persons. The argument for such treatment would be that husband and wife do not regard their respective capitals as in effect jointly owned, or at any rate not so commonly or not to the same degree as in the case of income, and that, hard as it may be for (say) a wife with little income of her own to have it taxed at a rate determined by her husband's large income, it would be even harder to have her correspondingly small capital eroded by aggregation with her husband's large fortune.

7.20 The argument is hardly conclusive. It can be replied that, however much a spouse may regard his or her capital as his or her own and not as part of a common pool, husband and wife do in fact live together as one, and that the fairest way to measure their taxable capacity—both in the particular case and on a comparison with other couples with the same aggregate wealth, however it may be distributed between them—is by reference to their combined capital resources. Separate taxation would provide an incentive to transfer capital between them so as to equalise their respective wealths and so minimise liability; and the fact of doing so would itself be an indication that they regard, or are prepared to regard, their respective fortunes as a common fund. Nor should it be overlooked that aggregation with a higher threshold would be more favourable than separate taxation in some cases, i.e. where one spouse's wealth exceeds the single threshold but their aggregate wealth is below the married one.

7.21 A wealth tax as described in the Green Paper might be either additive or substitutive or a mixture of the two. The material question for present purposes is whether there is to be a link with the income tax. The Green

Paper appears to look sympathetically at the proposition that the wealth tax and the investment income surcharge should be treated as alternatives, only the higher of the two being payable. It also envisages that, at any rate in some situations, there should be a ceiling on total tax liability related to the taxpayer's income. Both these suggestions create a link between the wealth tax and the income tax. If either is adopted the logical solution for married couples is aggregation, though separate taxation is not excluded if it were thought preferable on other grounds (the surcharge paid, for example, could be attributed to the spouses in proportion to their respective investment incomes).

7.22 Leaving aside considerations of taxable capacity and logical structure, probably the main argument for separate taxation is the growing desire to promote the financial independence of married women. Many people, without necessarily advocating complete community of property for married couples, consider that capital accumulated during marriage, normally by the business activities of the husband, ought to be regarded as created by the joint efforts of the spouses and as belonging to the wife as much as the husband, since she in her own sphere will also have contributed to the success. She ought, it may be argued, to be treated as legally owning the half of it (it is note-worthy that when a married couple buy a house it is nowadays commonly bought in both their names),[5] and her independence should be recognised for tax purposes by treating her as a separate individual from her husband.

7.23 Such treatment is no doubt perfectly practicable, whether or not part of the husband's wealth is treated as belonging to the wife, though (as already indicated) it is not necessarily as favourable as aggregation with a higher threshold. That particular difficulty could be got over by allowing the spouses to choose aggregation or separate taxation, whichever paid them better; but options are administratively troublesome and should be avoided if possible. There is also the solution of 'twice the tax on half the wealth', i.e. deeming the aggregate wealth to belong half to each spouse and taxing each half as if it belonged to a single person. But this is a form of aggregation, although in its practical results it gives the most favourable treatment possible and entirely discards the view that a married couple have a greater taxable capacity than two single persons.

7.24 Our own conclusion is that, for a wealth tax with the structure outlined in the Green Paper, aggregation with a higher threshold (and perhaps lower rates—see paragraph 8 of the Green Paper) is to be preferred. Our view is reinforced by the proposal to exempt interspousal transfers, whether by gift

---

[5] The Law Commission has recommended that a matrimonial home should be shared equally between husband and wife unless they agree otherwise; but the Commission did not favour a system of 'deferred community' under which other assets acquired during the marriage would be shared on its termination by death or otherwise. (*First Report on Family Property: a New Approach,* Law Comm. No. 52, 1973).

inter vivos or on death, from the capital transfer tax (Cmnd. 5705, paragraph 9); in effect, husband and wife are to be treated as one person, so that inter-spousal gifts leave the 'person's' wealth unchanged. It would be inconsistent with this proposal to treat them as two persons for wealth tax purposes and to vary the wealth tax liability in consequence of such gifts.

7.25 How much higher the married couple's threshold should be than the single person's is obviously a question on which different views can be held. In principle, even double the single threshold is defensible; but it might be considered excessive with a single threshold as high as £100,000. Perhaps 40-50% above the single threshold would be appropriate.

Conclusion

7.26 The wealth of married couples should be aggregated for wealth tax purposes, with a higher threshold than for single persons and perhaps a more favourable scale of rates.

Minor Children

7.27 In Sweden, Norway and Germany the wealth of minor children is aggregated with the parents' wealth. In Denmark only wealth derived from the parents themselves is aggregated. In the Netherlands there is no aggregation, although a minor's income is aggregated with its parents' incomes for income tax purposes. Aggregation is proposed in the Irish Republic.

7.28 It seems right that capital of a minor child which is derived directly or indirectly from its parent, and whether in trust or otherwise, should be aggregated with the parents' capital for wealth tax purposes. A transfer of capital from a parent to a minor child is essentially artificial since the control of the capital remains with the parent during the child's minority, unless he has voluntarily surrendered it to independent trustees. There is not, however, the same case as with interspousal gifts for exempting the parent's gift from capital transfer tax. Logic and consistency no doubt point to exemption; but if the gift were exempted, parents would have a strong incentive to give capital to their children while still minors, instead of waiting until the child comes of age when liability to capital transfer tax would be incurred.

7.29 Where the child's capital is derived from someone other than the parent the proper treatment for wealth tax is rather more debatable. If the capital is the child's absolutely (subject to his legal disability) the control of it is again with the parent, but the parents may not consider it so freely available to the family as their own capital, or as the child's income from the capital; often it will be the intention that the capital shall be preserved untouched until the child is of age. In that situation it is arguable that, at any rate for the purposes of an additive wealth tax, the child should be treated as a separate person from his parents. On the other hand, there is no legal barrier against touching the capital, and in many cases part or even all of it may be spent—spent of course for the benefit of the child, but the parent is saved from using his own resources. On the whole, and so long as the child's income is aggregated with the parents' for income tax purposes, aggregation with the parents' capital, as proposed in the Green Paper, seems the right course.

7.30 Aggregation of the child's capital in effect presupposes that the two parents' capital is aggregated. If the parents were treated separately there would be no rational basis for allocating the child's capital to one or the other parent, except as respects capital derived from a parent. The Green Paper, indeed, suggests (paragraph 10) that it should be allocated to the parent from whose side of the family the wealth derived—no doubt as good a rule as any, but quite arbitrary. The case for parent/child aggregation is thus an additional argument in favour of husband/wife aggregation.

7.31 In Sweden no additional exemption (higher threshold) is given in respect of minor children, whether or not the children have capital of their own to be aggregated with the parents. In Norway the higher threshold for persons with dependants is the same whatever the number of dependants. In the Netherlands there is an additional exemption for each child of about the same amount as the addition for the wife. In Germany, each child brings an exemption of the same amount as the single person's. In the Irish Republic only a small addition is proposed, one-twelfth of that proposed for the wife.

7.32 Given that a child's capital is to be aggregated, it seems right that there should be a higher threshold where there are children; the addition must of course be given whether the child has capital of its own or not. As to the amount of the addition, the income tax allowance for a child under 11 is at present (1974-75) exactly equal to the difference between the single and married allowance. For the wealth tax a more modest allowance might be appropriate.

Conclusion

7.33 Minor children's capital should be aggregated with the parents' capital. Some allowance in respect of children should be given.

Estates in Administration and Trusts

7.34 Estates of deceased persons in course of administration clearly could not be allowed to escape wealth tax by indefinite deferment of the final winding-up of the estate. A number of countries provide specifically for their taxation. In Sweden, for example, the estate is treated for the first four years after the death as if it were a single person; thereafter, if it is of significant size, the capital is attributed to the various beneficiaries and taxed as theirs.

7.35 For the UK the Green Paper proposes (paragraph 25) to attribute the property to the beneficiaries from the beginning—as, for example, in the Netherlands—subject to possible exemption for the first twelve months, with payment of tax deferred until the property is transferred to them (unless the transfer is unduly delayed). This seems satisfactory.

7.36 The treatment of trusts present special problems in the UK such as do not arise in the Continental countries. These problems are considered in Chapter 11.

Note on paragraph 7.3(c). The Autumn Finance Bill 1974—which was published when this book was already in proof—proposes that, for the purposes of the capital transfer tax, a person who has been resident in the UK in 17 out of the 20 years ending with the year of assessment shall be treated as domiciled in the UK.

Chapter 8

Threshold and Exemptions

Threshold

8.1 The precise level of wealth at which liability to the wealth tax should begin is ultimately a matter for political judgement, but it also depends on the purpose for which the tax is introduced. Thus it may be conceived primarily as a means of promoting horizontal equity. On that approach there is no reason why it should not begin at a level roughly comparable with the income tax threshold. In Sweden, for example, where the exemption limit for the income tax is Skr 4,500 (£429), the wealth tax threshold until quite recently was Skr 100,000 (£9,524) (it is now Skr 200,000 (£19,048)). If in the past the taxpayer's overall yield on his capital was $4\frac{1}{2}\%$, the point at which his capital attracted wealth tax corresponded precisely with the point at which his income became liable to income tax. The pattern of the income tax structure in the United Kingdom was similar, before the introduction of the unified income tax in 1973/74; the person living on investment income began to pay tax at a lower level than the earner and paid it at a considerably higher rate (e.g. 41.25% against just over 32% in 1970/71).

8.2 If the principal object of the tax is to encourage efficiency in the use of resources, it would seem right to encourage the search for higher yields at all levels; briefly, therefore, the threshold should be fairly low.

8.3 Different considerations arise if the primary object is to reduce the capital wealth of the richer or richest people with a view to bringing about a more even distribution of wealth. Essentially this involves making a judgement about the amount of wealth which anybody may reasonably be allowed to possess; that in effect fixes a minimum figure for the wealth tax threshold. Whether the threshold should be set at that figure or at a higher level depends on a variety of considerations. In the United Kingdom, for example, the greater taxable capacity of capital is already partly recognised in the investment income surcharge. In the social climate of the time it may not be thought desirable or politically viable to exact a contribution from everybody with more than the minimum. A gradual process may be preferred of starting at a relatively high figure and reducing it as time goes by (or leaving it unchanged despite the inroads of inflation).

8.4 Finally, the objective may be to improve administrative control. It seems highly unlikely that any country would introduce a wealth tax primarily for this purpose; but, if it did, the point at which actual liability to the tax began would be of no great significance. The important thing would be secure information about people's wealth. Probably everyone within the income tax field should be required to make a wealth tax return. This is the position in Sweden and Denmark where a return of wealth has to be made along with the income tax return, although in Sweden less than 300,000 out of several million income tax payers are actually liable to wealth tax and in Denmark, with its relatively high wealth tax threshold (Table 8.1), the proportion is probably lower still.

The Threshold in Other Countries

8.5 The five European wealth taxes which we have studied have been in force, in one form or another, for many years, but it appears that all were originally introduced primarily in order to supplement the income tax, i.e. to exact a higher contribution from investment income than from earned income. They are intended to be met out of income and are regarded as in the main fulfilling the function performed in the United Kingdom by the investment income surcharge, and formerly by the earned income relief. It is recognised, however, that they have some part to play in the reduction of inequality—in 'offsetting social imbalance', as it was expressed to us on one occasion.

8.6 Table 8.1 compares the wealth tax threshold in the five countries with the income tax threshold, for both single persons and married couples. The figures are given in the local currency in each case. The two right-hand columns show the level of income at which differentiation between earned and investment income begins if the overall yield on net wealth is 5%. It should be noted that until quite recently the wealth tax threshold in Sweden was only Skr 100,000 (£9,524); even more striking, the threshold in Germany, now DM 70,000 (£11,447), was only DM 10,000 (£1,635) before 1974.

The Threshold in the United Kingdom

8.7 The stated objective of the proposed wealth tax in the United Kingdom is to reduce inequalities of wealth. The mention in past statements of Labour Party policy of a specific figure of £50,000 (paragraph 6.5) implied a political judgement that the possession by an individual of that amount of wealth was acceptable but that wealth in excess of that amount ought to be reduced. The

Table 8.1 Comparison of Income Tax and Wealth Tax Thresholds

	Wealth Tax Threshold		Income Tax Threshold		Differentiation At Income Over	
	Single	Married	Single	Married	Single	Married
Denmark	450,000	450,000	5,800	11,600	22,500	22,500
	(£31,469)	(£31,469)	(£406)	(£811)	(£1,573)	(£1,573)
Germany	70,000	140,000	1,680	3,360	3,500	7,000
	(£11,447)	(£22,895)	(£275)	(£549)	(£572)	(£1,145)
Netherlands	43,000	59,000	4,300	7,412	2,150	2,950
	(£6,766)	(£9,284)	(£676)	(£1,166)	(£338)	(£464)
Norway (a)	75,000	100,000	18,000	27,000	3,750	5,000
	(£5,765)	(£7,686)	(£1,384)	(£2,075)	(£288)	(£384)
Sweden	200,000	200,000	4,500	(b)	10,000	10,000
	(£19,048)	(£19,048)	(£429)		(£952)	(£952)

(a) There is, however, no liability to national wealth tax if income does not exceed Nkr 18,000 (£1,384).
(b) No fixed figure. Relief for the spouse, where due, is given by means of a credit in terms of tax.

tax in view was clearly an additive tax. On the other hand the Chancellor's Foreword to the Green Paper lays stress on the promotion of horizontal equity, apparently envisaging this as the means by which 'excessive inequalities of wealth will in time be eroded' (paragraph 6.8). The implication here is a gradual process and a tax which is at least partly substitutive.

8.8 If the instrument for reducing inequality is to be the promotion of horizontal equity it would be justifiable in principle to set the threshold at a level broadly corresponding to the income tax threshold (paragraph 8.1). The income tax thresholds for single and married persons respectively are £625 and £865. On the basis of a 5% overall yield on capital the corresponding wealth tax thresholds would be £12,500 and £17,300 (assuming married couples to be treated as one person). Figures of this order would be appropriate if the income tax structure differentiated against investment income at all levels, as it did before 1973. In 1973/74 however, the system was changed, and differentiation did not begin until £2,000 of investment income. The corresponding wealth tax threshold, on the 5% basis, would be £40,000 (single). But for 1974/75 the figure falls to £20,000 consequent on the decision to apply the surcharge at £1,000 investment income. (As the surcharge begins at the same level for both single and married no separate threshold for married couples emerges automatically.)

8.9 If therefore it remains the policy not to differentiate against investment income below £1,000, a wealth tax threshold not lower than £20,000 would be indicated. Comparing this figure with the wealth tax thresholds in other countries (Table 8.1), it will be seen that in Germany and Sweden the thresholds correspond, on the 5% basis, to investment incomes which are more than twice the basic income tax personal allowance. In Denmark the corresponding income is four times the personal allowance. A £20,000 threshold in the United Kingdom would be less generous, the presumed income of £1,000 being less than twice the single personal allowance (£625). It would, however, be more generous than in the Netherlands, where it is possible to be liable to wealth tax without also being liable to income tax. And the picture in Germany and Sweden would have looked very different in the recent past, when the thresholds were much lower (paragraph 8.6). But the increases to present figures in those countries may in part reflect a judgement that differentiation in respect of capital should not begin until the likely income is significantly above the income tax threshold; which would be an endorsement of the existing United Kingdom policy on differentiation.

8.10 The comparison with the starting point for the surcharge, however, does not take account of the fact that a considerable proportion of a person's capital, and particularly that of the less wealthy, may produce no money income. An individual with income-producing capital of £20,000 is more likely than not to own his own home, the value of which (if it is unencumbered) may well be another £20,000. Assuming there to be no exemption for the owner-occupied house, the payment of wealth tax on £20,000 would be a heavy burden to be met out of an income of £1,000—less than half the average industrial wage and already reduced by income tax to about £875.

8.11 It can be fairly argued that horizontal equity requires that in such a case the tax should nevertheless be charged. The house is charged in the Continental countries—and the notional income from it is charged to income tax. Nevertheless, in considering the United Kingdom situation one must take the facts as one finds them, and one of the facts is that at the lower levels of wealth a high proportion of the total is commonly represented by the individual's house. It would seem, therefore, that the threshold ought to be considerably higher than £20,000.

8.12 It would be fairer, then, to assume say a 3% rather than a 5% overall return on capital for the purpose of arriving at a threshold comparable to the threshold for the surcharge. This suggests a threshold in the region of £35,000 with the surcharge starting at £1,000 investment income—and of course double that figure if the comparison is with a £2,000 surcharge threshold.

8.13 Turning now to the threshold for a tax designed for radical reduction of inequalities of wealth, it is, as already said, a question of deciding what constitutes an acceptable amount of wealth for an individual to possess. The Labour Party's figure (which in 1973 was expressly stated to take account of the owner-occupier's situation) was £50,000 (paragraph 6.5). If, however, the tax were added on top of the surcharge, even at £50,000 the burden would be severe. Suppose the individual's capital is £50,000 and produces an income of £2,500, rather more than the average industrial wage at the time of writing. The marginal rate of income tax at that point, including surcharge, is 48%;

wealth tax at 1%, which is equivalent to 20% of a 5% yield, would increase the total tax to 68%. If £20,000 of the capital was represented by the individual's house, his money income would be only £1,500; but the total marginal rate above that point, with surcharge starting (at a rate of 10%) at £1,000, would be no less than 63% (53% if the surcharge started at £2,000).

8.14 Nevertheless, if the tax was founded on the view that nobody ought to have more than £50,000 of capital, even a £50,000 threshold would be defensible in principle; it would act powerfully to cause people above, even a little above, that level to sell capital in order that they might both pay their taxes and live tolerably. But the effects for such people might be unduly harsh and the economic consequences undesirable, and the political judgement might well be that £50,000 was too low.

8.15 To sum up at this point, we have suggested that, if the policy is (as it appears to be in the Green Paper) to reduce inequality of wealth gradually by promotion of horizontal equity, the threshold should be in the region of £35,000 if £1,000 is considered to be the appropriate starting point for differentiation through the surcharge (or £70,000 if the surcharge figure is £2,000). In making this suggestion we have assumed that wealth tax and surcharge would be alternatives (if the surcharge cannot be abolished) and that the situation of the owner-occupier would be allowed for by taking 3% instead of 5% as a reasonable overall yield. For a radical tax, we have suggested that £50,000 would be defensible but on the low side.

8.16 But in either case the administrative task must be taken into account. In 1971 there were, according to the Inland Revenue estimates, 233,000 individuals with property in excess of £50,000,[1] but (in 1971-72) only 6,167 estate duty cases above that figure. The latter represented about one-fifth of the total number of estate duty cases over £15,000, but it is, of course, the bigger cases which cause most work and make the biggest demands on expert staff. A wealth tax case is the equivalent of an estate duty case—it is as if every liable person died every year—but it is inconceivable, at any rate in the short term and if estate duty standards of administration were adopted, that the Inland Revenue could handle some thirty-eight times the number of cases over £50,000 that it handles now. It is true that if the wealth of husband and wife is aggregated the actual number of cases would be considerably less than 233,000, but the number of items of property to be dealt with would not be affected. It is also true that a system of self-assessment is proposed in the Green Paper, which would enable the Inland Revenue to adjust the work it does to the resources available to do it. But this does not help the taxpayer or his professional advisers—lawyers, accountants, surveyors—who would have a very substantial additional burden

---

[1] *Inland Revenue Statistics 1973*, Tables 92 and 75.

thrust upon them. On administrative grounds alone, therefore, a £50,000, let alone a £35,000, threshold seems out of the question at the present time.

8.17 The Green Paper (paragraph 30) recognises the case for applying the tax at a relatively low figure, as on the Continent, and abolishing the surcharge, but discards the possibility on administrative grounds. We accept that it may not be possible in 1976/77, the target date for introduction of the tax. With the threshold fixed at £100,000, as now proposed, the number of individuals affected (counting husband and wife as two) falls to 75,000 and the administrative problem becomes much more manageable. But we are in no doubt that the objective should be to abolish the surcharge as soon as possible and make the wealth tax, with a lower threshold, the sole instrument for achieving horizontal equity.

8.18 The question of higher thresholds for a married couple and in respect of children has been discussed in Chapter 7. In Germany an additional exemption is given where the taxpayer is over 60 or incapacitated (paragraph 5.12); and there is a similar addition of fl 38,000 (£5,980) in the Netherlands for aged (over 65) or incapacitated persons. These exemptions correspond in both countries to an additional personal allowance which is given for income tax purposes on account of age. With a £100,000 threshold there would seem no reason to propose special relief for aged (or incapacitated) persons by analogy with the existing (1974/75) income tax age exemption, which only applies at relatively low levels of income. In 1975/76, however, it is proposed to replace that exemption by an extra personal allowance for all persons over 65 with up to £3,000 income (the allowance tapering off above that figure). Further, the new starting point for the investment income surcharge is to be £1,500, not £1,000, in the case of persons over 65. Given these two changes, there is a reasonable case for a higher wealth tax threshold for the over-65s; the case would be reinforced if the wealth tax, with a lower threshold, entirely replaced the investment income surcharge. And, irrespective of the level of the threshold, a case can be made for an allowance which would recognise the additional advantage which persons at work have over retired persons as a result of excluding from the wealth tax base the capitalised value of future earnings and pension rights (Appendix A).

Conclusion

8.19 The appropriate threshold for the wealth tax is ultimately a matter of political judgement; but if, in the context of a tax to promote horizontal equity, it is to correspond broadly to the threshold for differentiation against investment income by means of the surcharge, a figure in the region of £35,000 is indicated if the threshold for the surcharge is £1,000 investment income (£70,000 on the basis of the 1973/74 surcharge threshold of £2,000). These figures allow for the fact that, particularly at the lower levels of chargeable wealth, a considerable proportion of total wealth consists of an owner-occupied house. For radical reduction of inequality, a threshold of £50,000 is defensible but too low. It must probably be accepted, however, that administrative considerations make it impossible to fix a threshold as low as £50,000 at the present time. On this basis, the proposed threshold of £100,000 is acceptable. In the longer term, however, the surcharge should be abolished and the wealth tax, with a lower threshold, should be the sole instrument for promoting horizontal equity. Proposed new income tax reliefs for persons over 65, and also theoretical considerations, suggest that a higher wealth tax threshold might reasonably be fixed for such persons.

Exemptions

8.20 In principle there should be no exemption from wealth tax of particular classes of asset, least of all assets which produce no income. If all assets were income-producing, and the rate of return on capital were the same in all cases, there would be no occasion for a separate wealth tax; the taxable capacity referable to any asset could be fully and fairly tapped through the income tax, with top rates exceeding 100% if it was desired to bring about a steady reduction in the wealth of the richest people. The wealth tax, however, makes it possible to adjust taxation by reference to overall taxable capacity, and to achieve a better balance between the burdens falling on high-yielding and low-yielding assets respectively. The asset which yields no income is the extreme case; the taxable capacity which it represents cannot be touched by the income tax, and it is therefore in relation to such assets that the case for the wealth tax is at its strongest. Nevertheless the imposition of wealth tax on certain classes of assets and particularly non-income-producing assets can be questioned, either on practical grounds or on grounds of policy.

Owner-Occupied Houses

8.21 The prime instance of the non-income-producing asset is the owner-occupied house. All our five European wealth taxes include it within the charge (and also attribute a notional income to it for income tax purposes), though exemption is given in Finland and in Pakistan and a first slice of Rs 100,000 (£5,345) is exempted in India. The Republic of Ireland also now intends, contrary to what was originally proposed, to provide for exemption in its wealth tax. The absence of exemption in other countries does not preclude benevolent treatment of real property. Thus in Sweden the value to be adopted for wealth tax purposes is fixed by law at 75% of the value of the property as determined at the quinquennial revaluations; in Norway it appears that the values fixed by the local tax boards represent a comparable reduction from open market value, though there is no statutory provision to that effect; and it is understood that in Germany the new values which took effect in 1974 (derived from 1964 valuations, increased by 40%) will still be substantially

K

below market value in the case of residential property. But these benevolent valuations apply to residential property generally; there is no concession in favour of the owner-occupier as such.

8.22 The position in the Netherlands is slightly different. Where property is vacant the value for wealth tax purposes is the full open market vacant possession value. Where it is let, a reduction of about one-third is made in order to arrive at the price which the house would fetch if sold in the existing circumstances, i.e. subject to the tenancy; and a similar reduction is allowed to the owner-occupier. The owner-occupier's reduction is thus not presented as a matter of benevolence, although in fact of course he is able to realise the full vacant possession value if he sells, which the owner of let property is not.

8.23 In the United Kingdom the owner-occupied house already enjoys substantial tax privileges; since 1963 it has gone free of income tax (in Continental countries generally the annual value of the house is taxable as income) and it also enjoys exemption from capital gains tax. In addition the owner-occupier receives income tax relief for mortgage interest in respect of his house (subject now to the exclusion of any excess of the mortgage debt over £25,000), as an exception to the general disallowance of payments of non-business interest.

8.24 The owner-occupier is thus very favourably treated for tax purposes compared with the person who chooses, or is obliged, to rent the living accommodation which everyone must have. It is strongly arguable that the existing reliefs already go too far and that any change should be in the direction of narrowing rather than extending the owner-occupier's privileges. The Green Paper dismisses the case for exemption from wealth tax in three lines (paragraph 28) on the grounds that it would be unfair to taxpayers living in rented accommodation. Certainly the incidence of the wealth tax will be more equitable if it applies to owner-occupied houses as to other assets. At the same time one cannot ignore the fact that the owner-occupier cannot sell off a bit of his house to pay the tax; he must find it out of his other resources. The enormous rise in house values in recent years relative to other assets accentuates his problem. This, however, as has been suggested above, is a factor which is best taken into account in deciding the threshold for the tax; to set the threshold at a higher level than might be otherwise considered appropriate will both relieve the owner-occupier's difficulties to some extent and give parity of treatment to the person living in rented accommodation.

8.25 If, contrary to the view expressed here and in the Green Paper, it was considered that the owner-occupier ought to have some specific relief, the simple course would be to exempt the first £X of the value of the house; this would of course still add to the existing tax privileges of the owner-occupier as compared with the renter.

Conclusion

8.26 No exemption should be given for the owner-occupied house.

Chattels

8.27 After owner-occupied houses, chattels are the most obvious class of non-income-producing asset, covering furniture and other household and personal effects, jewellery, works of art, cars, boats, etc. Some exemption for furniture and household and personal effects appears to be universal in wealth tax codes.

8.28 In Sweden, furniture and other movables for use in the home are exempt, however valuable any individual article may be. Works of art and collections of books, paintings, etc. are also exempt. Jewellery, however, is chargeable, as are assets for outdoor use, such as cars and boats; there is exemption if the value of all these classes does not exceed Skr 1,000 (£95), but such a low limit is obviously of little significance.

8.29 A similar exemption for articles inside the home, including works of art and collections, is given in Denmark. In addition, jewellery is exempt. The principle there is that the wealth tax 'stops at the door'.

8.30 In Norway the exemption is more limited. There is no specific exemption for works of art, etc. The value of indoor effects, including jewellery and works of art, is aggregated, and only the first Nkr 40,000 (£3,075) of the aggregate value is exempted. The value for wealth tax purposes is based on insurance values and is taken to be 20% of the first Nkr 100,000 (£7,686), 30% of the next Nkr 100,000 (£7,686), and 40% of any excess. The exemption of Nkr 40,000 (£3,075) is deducted from the resulting figure. As insured values will usually be replacement values some reduction of the figures is clearly justified in order to arrive at the price which the effects would fetch on a sale in the open market. Nevertheless the treatment appears to be more benevolent than the Nkr 40,000 (£3,075) exemption, taken by itself, would suggest.

8.31 In Germany, ordinary household and personal effects are exempt, as are 'ordinary' cars. 'Luxury' articles, however, and jewellery are chargeable unless their aggregate value does not exceed DM 10,000 (£1,635); in the latter event they are exempt. Works of art and collections may be exempted on grounds of artistic, etc. importance; otherwise they are exempt if their aggregate value does not exceed DM 20,000 (£3,271).

8.32 Household effects are also exempt in the Netherlands, together with objects of artistic or scientific interest.

8.33 According to the Inland Revenue statistics, chattels account for about 2½% of the total net wealth of persons in the UK with wealth in excess of £100,000 as compared with under 7% under the heading 'residential' buildings (for wealth in excess of £50,000 the figures are approximately 2½% and 10%).[2]

---

[2] *Inland Revenue Statistics 1973*, Table 94. See table 6.5, paragraph 6.48.

They are therefore a considerably less important item than houses. No doubt the values for chattels which are accepted for estate duty purposes are conservative and the figure of $2\frac{1}{2}\%$ may understate their real importance; but it is obvious that, whatever administrative machinery were adopted for wealth tax purposes, the valuation of chattels would not be any closer to true market values than it is for estate duty. It should be noted, also, that works of art, etc. which are exempt from estate duty are not reflected in the estimates of wealth.[3]

8.34 The total exemption of furniture and other household and personal effects is tempting. Every household must have furniture and there is some case for exempting a necessity which cannot yield income. On the other hand, the amount invested in furniture may vary widely according to the taste and interests of the owner. One man's dining table may be worth twenty times another's, even at comparable levels of total wealth; there is no reason of principle for giving the former a wealth tax preference merely because he chooses to indulge a taste for beautiful things (or regards them as good investments), while the other is content with ordinary things and prefers to make his money earn an income. Nor, despite the Danish precedent, is it easy to see any case for the exemption of jewellery, apart from items of small value.

8.35 There is, however, the practical problem of valuation. It is true that the contents of the house will be insured, but probably most people make their own guesses at value for insurance purposes and tend to put the figure high in order to be on the safe side. For wealth tax purposes it is likely that they would need to pay for a professional valuation—though they may already have done so for insurance purposes in the case of jewellery and the more valuable articles of furniture. And, as already noted in relation to Norway (paragraph 8.30), insured values, although no doubt a guide, do not necessarily represent the open market value of the articles in question.

8.36 The Green Paper (paragraph 29) accepts the case for some exemption of household effects but is reluctant to go the whole way, as in Denmark. It appears to favour the Norwegian solution of exempting the first £X of aggregate value, the figure being set high enough to cover 'normal household contents'. This course would largely solve the valuation difficulty, which the Green Paper evidently considers the important aspect, provided that the figure were set so high that most taxpayers could see at once that their effects were well covered; where they could not, it is a defect of the proposal that the entire contents of the house would have to be valued.

8.37 The Green Paper rather surprisingly suggests that the exemption might cover cars or that one car per person might be exempt. The latter alternative would apparently exempt a Rolls-Royce equally with a Mini, which seems difficult to justify. The three Scandinavian countries and the Netherlands all

---

[3] See Appendix paragraphs B.10-11.

charge cars; in Germany an 'ordinary' car is exempt but a 'luxury' one would be taxed. The valuation of cars would present no difficulty in the UK since up-to-date figures are available for the prices fetched by second-hand cars according to make, age and condition.

8.38 An alternative to exempting the first £X of normal household contents would be to follow the capital gains tax precedent and exempt articles below a certain value. This alternative could be applied to chattels generally. The capital gains tax figure of £1,000 would perhaps be on the high side but a figure of £500 would not be unreasonable. (It might not be unreasonable for capital gains tax either and there would be a certain convenience in having the same figure for both taxes.) Such an exemption would be rather like the German system of charging 'luxury' articles, but without the need for administrative definitions which the German provision requires. It would admittedly add to the attractions of investment in chattels but it would substantially reduce the practical problems. On the whole, this is the solution we prefer.

Conclusion

8.39 Some exemption should be provided for household and personal effects. One possible course would be to exempt the first £X of the total value of such effects. An alternative, which could apply to chattels generally and which we prefer, would be to exempt any individual article (including a car) if its value does not exceed, say, £500.

Insurance Policies

8.40 In Sweden, life insurance policies are exempt from wealth tax without limit of amount, though it appears that the extent of the relief has given rise to misgivings. The position is the same in Denmark. In the Netherlands, general exemption is also given provided that premiums are payable for five years or more. A limited exemption is given in Norway and Germany, in Norway for the first Nkr 22,500 (£1,729) and in Germany for the first DM 10,000 (£1,635).

8.41 Saving by means of life insurance is encouraged in the UK by income tax reliefs on the ground that it is socially desirable that people should make provision for their old age or for their dependants after their death. The argument for exempting insurance policies from wealth tax is that they produce no current income for the insured which he could use to meet tax liability (though of course the tax is intended to apply to non-income-producing assets generally); that to encroach on the capital to pay the tax (e.g. by borrowing on the policy) would frustrate *pro tanto* the essential purpose of insurance; and that saving for the future in this desirable form would be discouraged if tax were charged. The Green Paper (paragraph 44), however, rejects exemption on the ground that since insurance policies can be assigned or used as security they cannot be distinguished from savings generally. Nor can it be said that the argument in favour has much force in the context of a wealth tax which only affects people with substantial assets. Life insurance is particularly important for people relying on their earnings who would otherwise have little or no capital to fall back on in the future; people with substantial capital have not the same need to secure provision for the future.

8.42 In recent years the attractions of insurance as a form of investment, rather than as provision for future emergencies, have come to the fore, and it is probably this aspect of insurance which has most appeal for the better-off.

8.43 In comparing the position under the Continental taxes it must be remembered that in general they apply at relatively low levels of wealth where insurance is important; it is no doubt for this reason that in Norway and Germany there is also an exemption for small savings in cash—the first Nkr 10,000 (£769) of savings deposits in Norway and the first DM 10,000 (£1,635) in Germany. There would be a case for allowing some exemption for insurance in the United Kingdom if the threshold were low; even then the exemption ought to be limited in amount and to apply only to 'genuine' life assurance, i.e. to policies which rank as 'qualifying' policies for income tax purposes. But with a £100,000 threshold no exemption should be allowed.

Conclusion

8.44 There should be no exemption for life insurance policies.

Pensions and Annuities

8.45 The exemption of pensions and pension rights is general in the Continental taxes and is proposed in the Republic of Ireland. In Sweden, there is no limit on the exemption, which applies equally to annuities which the individual may purchase for himself, notwithstanding the opportunities thus offered for reduction of wealth tax liability. The position is similar in Norway and Denmark. In Germany, genuine pensions are exempt whether provided by an employer or by the taxpayer himself, the test being broadly that the pension becomes payable at age 60 or in the event of incapacity; the value of other pensions or annuities is taxable, subject to the exemption (which also covers insurance policies) of the first DM 10,000 (£1,635). Pension rights are also exempt in the Netherlands. Rights to privately purchased deferred annuities are exempt during the build-up period but are taxable when in course of payment. In the case, however, of annuities which became payable at age 65 or on account of disability the first fl 8,000 (£1,259) of capital value is exempt (fl 12,000 (£1,888) where the recipient is the widow of the person who provided the annuity), with an additional fl 2,000 (£315) for each minor child (fl 4,000 (£629) where one parent is dead).

8.46 Pensions and pension rights are a valuable possession and are commonly taken into account by economists in estimates of the distribution of wealth. It is undeniable that a pensioner, or a person whose future pension is assured, is better-off in a general sense than his apparent capital resources indicate, and in particular (as the Green Paper points out) better off than a man with the same apparent resources who has no pension rights. It is also true that a capital value could be placed on the pension by reference to his current expectation of life. It does not follow, however, that pension rights are a proper subject for taxation by a wealth tax. During working life the individual cannot realise the value of his future pension (although he may get a return of his contributions if he leaves the particular employment). At retirement he may be able to take part of the pension in lump sum form; in that event the lump sum becomes part of his taxable wealth. But the pension itself when in course of payment is non-commutable and non-assignable. All the pensioner has or can have from it is income. Consequently, in the context of a tax which is in general limited to realisable assets (Green Paper paragraph 42) his taxable capacity in respect of his pension rights is exhausted by income taxation of the pension when in payment. The Green Paper makes the further points that pensions amount to a form of deferred pay and that it is well established practice in the UK to give fiscal encouragement to savings for retirement. The conclusion is that pensions and pension rights should be exempt as the Green Paper proposes, whether they arise under the national scheme, a statutory scheme or an approved private scheme.

8.47 Similar exemption, as again proposed in the Green Paper (paragraph 43), should be given in respect of the retirement annuities provided for themselves by self-employed persons and non-pensionable employees, where the conditions for income tax relief are satisfied.

8.48 It may be said that, although the individual cannot be made liable to wealth tax, the pension is produced by a capital fund held by trustees and that the fund is in principle taxable like the funds of private trusts. The result of so taxing it would, however, be a steady diminution of the amount available for the pensioners; it is clear that the fund also must be granted specific exemption, corresponding to its existing exemption from income tax and capital gains tax (see Green Paper, paragraph 17).

8.49 Private annuities, other than approved retirement annuities, are on a different footing. If the annuity is payable under a trust, tax should be charged on the same basis as in the case of a life tenant. In the case of a purchased annuity the taxpayer has voluntarily surrendered his capital and ought not to be able to reduce his wealth tax liability as a result. It is relevant here that the capital element of the annuity is not subject to income tax, so that the annuitant already enjoys some tax advantage. It is true that he may be reluctant to realise the capital represented by his annuity in order to pay the wealth tax, but his position does not appear to differ greatly from that of the holder of an insurance policy. The full value of the annuity ought therefore to be charged.

8.50 In the case of annual payments under covenant the beneficiary has no possibility of access to capital. The proper course here, as indicated in the Green Paper (paragraph 56), will be to ignore the value of the covenant in computing the beneficiary's wealth but to allow no deduction to the covenantor for his liability to make the payments.

Conclusion

8.51 (1) Pensions and pension rights should be exempt, as should the approved retirement annuities of the self-employed, etc. Approved funds which provide the pensions or annuities should also be exempt.

(2) Purchased annuities should be chargeable.

(3) Covenants should be exempt in the hands of the beneficiary but no deduction should be allowed to the covenantor.

Goodwill, Patents and Copyrights

8.52 Goodwill created by the owner of a business, and patents and copyrights in the hands of the inventor or author, are excluded from the wealth tax charge in a number of the Continental systems. The Green Paper rejects exemption of patents and copyrights (paragraph 40) and does not consider the exemption of created goodwill (paragraphs 52 and 54). We think there is a case for both exemptions, but defer consideration of the subject to Chapter 10 (paragraphs 10.33 ff. and 10.75-6).

Chapter 9
Relationship to Other Taxes

The Link with Investment Income Surcharge

9.1 As a means of differentiating between earned and investment income, the wealth tax duplicates the investment income surcharge. On this basis, the surcharge should be abolished on the introduction of the wealth tax. Alternatively, if it is to remain operative at a level of capital wealth below the wealth tax threshold it ought to be allowed as a credit against wealth tax where the latter is chargeable.

9.2 If the surcharge is to be retained alongside the wealth tax, without any offset for the double charge, it must be justified on some other grounds than differentiation. The original argument for differentiation was that earned income is 'precarious'; but that is only another way of saying that investment income has capital behind it. It has also been pointed out that earning income involves expenses, in travelling to work and so forth, which are not allowed in computing the income for tax purposes; but this is a relatively minor factor which could not justify differentiation on the scale which applied under the old earned income relief, or which applies today above the level at which the investment income surcharge begins. Finally it is said that, quite apart from considerations of taxable capacity, the preferential taxation of earnings is an incentive to personal effort which is in the national interest on economic grounds. The incentive is not so apparent as it was in the days of the earned income relief, but, such as it is, it appears to be the only possible ground—and uncertain ground at that—for retaining the surcharge without offset against wealth tax, though no doubt it would be generally felt that it is socially more virtuous to go out and earn than to sit at home and draw dividends.

9.3 The Green Paper recognises (paragraphs 30 and 31) that the wealth tax performs much the same function as the surcharge in so far as property generates income and that in theory it would be possible to replace the latter by a wealth tax which, broadly, applied to all those taxpayers who at present incur liability to surcharge. As it points out, the Continental wealth taxes apply at a considerably lower level of wealth than is contemplated in the UK (or the Republic of Ireland); but it rules out a low threshold for the UK on administrative grounds and concludes that the surcharge must remain as the instrument for differentiation in the case of persons of moderate wealth. On this basis it acknowledges the case for treating the wealth tax and the surcharge as alternatives and limiting the taxpayer's liability to whichever of them is the higher. We accept that, given a threshold of £100,000, there is a case for retaining investment income surcharge to deal with taxpayers below and just above the threshold (paragraph 8.17).

9.4 However, the effect of levying surcharge or wealth tax, whichever is greater, would be that at any given level of wealth there would be a yield below which wealth tax would be the operative tax and above which surcharge would take over. This is demonstrated in the form of a graph in table 9.1. From an inspection of that graph it can be seen that with wealth of £1.0m at yields of less than 7.87%, wealth tax on Scale A will exceed surcharge and at yields above that figure the reverse is true.

9.5 At the lower yield levels at which wealth tax is the operative tax, additional investment income bears only basic and higher rate tax; at the higher yields where investment income surcharge takes over, additional investment income bears basic and higher rate tax and surcharge. The point of change-over from wealth tax to investment income surcharge for selected levels of wealth is shown below.

Amount of wealth	Level below which wealth tax on Scale A is the operative tax and above which investment income surcharge is the operative tax			
£m	Amount of investment income	Marginal rate of income tax		Yield %
		Below this level %	Above this level %	
	£			
0.25	12,000	68.0	83.0	4.80
0.50	28,667	83.0	98.0	5.73
0.75	53,667	83.0	98.0	7.16
1.00	78,667	83.0	98.0	7.87
2.00	178,667	83.0	98.0	8.93
5.00	578,666	83.0	98.0	11.57

Whilst it is no doubt true that the greater the wealth the greater the opportunity to obtain high yield, there is evidence that, because of the high rates of tax on income as compared with capital gains, wealthy taxpayers deliberately seek low yielding assets. Hence it is perhaps unlikely that a taxpayer with net

Table 9.1

Taxpayer with wealth of £1m.

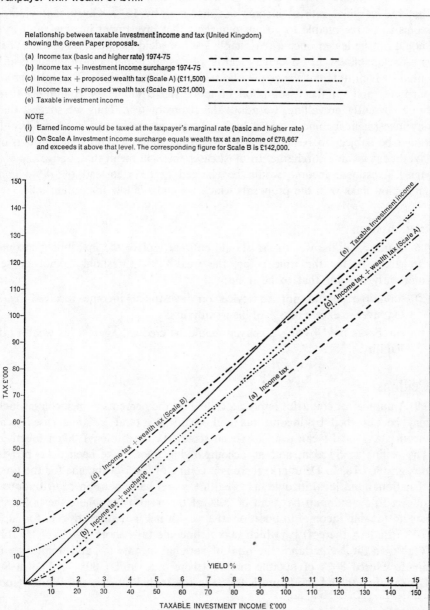

Relationship between taxable investment income and tax (United Kingdom) showing the Green Paper proposals.

(a) Income tax (basic and higher rate) 1974-75

(b) Income tax + investment income surcharge 1974-75

(c) Income tax + proposed wealth tax (Scale A) (£11,500)

(d) Income tax + proposed wealth tax (Scale B) (£21,000)

(e) Taxable investment income

NOTE

(i) Earned income would be taxed at the taxpayer's marginal rate (basic and higher rate)

(ii) On Scale A investment income surcharge equals wealth tax at an income of £78,667 and exceeds it above that level. The corresponding figure for Scale B is £142,000.

wealth of £5m will obtain an average taxable yield in excess of 11.57% and so find that his marginal rate of income tax increases from 83.0% to 98.0%. But at lower levels it is surely undesirable that a taxpayer with wealth of £0.5m who manages to increase his average yield above 5.73% should find that his marginal rate of income tax increases by 15%. Given that view it seems to us reasonable to go on to suggest that investment income surcharge should not be levied once a reasonable level of yield has been obtained. What is a reasonable level of average yield is, of course, a matter of judgement and one on which different views may be taken at different times. But for present purposes, and on the assumption of more stable monetary conditions than those currently prevailing, we adopt the figure of 6%. Thus we suggest that any investment income received by a taxpayer in excess of 6% of his wealth would be subject to basic and higher rate tax alone without the addition of investment income surcharge. In most cases this will mean that, above the 6% yield, investment income would be charged at 83% instead of 98%. This suggestion links with the proposals which we make below for ceiling relief.

Conclusions

9.6 In principle, the wealth tax should entirely replace the investment income surcharge. If, for the time being, the wealth tax threshold cannot be set sufficiently low for that to be done:

(a) surcharge should not be levied on investment income received by a taxpayer in excess of 6% of his wealth; and

(b) surcharge paid by the taxpayer should be credited against his wealth tax liability.

Ceilings

9.7 A number of countries impose a ceiling on the percentage of income which may be absorbed by income tax and wealth tax (and in some cases local income tax, local wealth tax or social security contributions) taken together. The ceiling in Sweden, and its accompanying floor, have been described in paragraph 4.18. In Denmark, there is a ceiling of 70% of income for the total of national and local income tax, wealth tax and basic pension contributions,[1] subject to a minimum payment of 20% of the wealth tax where the taxpayer has no taxable income. In addition, the wealth tax is reduced by 5% for each 0.4% (or part thereof) by which taxable income falls short of 6% of taxable wealth. In the Netherlands the total of national income tax and wealth tax is not to exceed 80% of taxable income (there is a similar 80% ceiling in Sri Lanka). In Finland the figure is 90%. In the Irish Republic the White Paper

---

[1] Contributions of 2% to a special pension fund and of 1% to a sickness fund raise the effective ceiling to 73%.

containing the Government's proposals indicated that there would be no ceiling but that there would be some reduction in the top rates of income tax. Subsequently a figure was put on the proposed reduction, and it was also announced that the question of a ceiling was being further examined, since otherwise income tax and wealth tax might together 'absorb an unacceptably high proportion of total income'.

9.8 There is no ceiling provision in Germany. In Norway, a ceiling (relating to national and local income tax and national and local wealth tax) formerly applied but it was abolished in 1973. It has now been decided to reintroduce a ceiling for the income year 1974 so that total assessed tax cannot exceed 90% of income as assessed for national tax. In 1972 the ceiling was 80%.

9.9 If the principal object of a wealth tax is to bring about a reduction of inequalities in the distribution of wealth (regardless of the economic effects) there is in principle no call for a ceiling; nothing could be more effective for the purpose than an annual tax burden exceeding 100% of income.

9.10 However, a ceiling related to taxable income is understandable where the primary purpose of a wealth tax is to impose some additional tax on investment income without, in the words of the Irish Minister of Finance, absorbing 'an unacceptably high proportion of total income'. Even so, it is essentially anomalous in so far as the object, or one object, of the tax is to tap the taxable capacity of capital as such, whether or not it yields income; in principle the tax bill ought not to be limited merely because the yield is low. With a ceiling in operation, a person who has an earned income sufficient to provide for his needs, or whose wealth is so large that income on only a part of it is enough to live on, or who is prepared to live on capital could, with a tax ceiling directly related to income, protect his assets from the tax by holding all or part of them in the form of jewellery or other non-income-producing forms. The Swedish law guards against this to some extent by the provision that total tax liability is not to be reduced below the sum of the local income tax (which averaged 24% in 1974) plus the amount of wealth tax which would be payable if the taxpayer's wealth were half its actual amount. The Danish provision preserving a minimum liability of 20% of the wealth tax gives similar protection.

9.11 If the ceiling is related to total income, including earned income (as is the case in the Continental systems), there can be some anomalous effects. In Sweden, for example, the highest rate of income tax (national and local) applies to taxable income over Skr 150,000 (£14,286); it is about 78% but, if the ceiling provision is in operation, 85% of any additional earnings may go in tax. A similar situation may arise under the Danish relief, which reduces the wealth tax where income is less than 6% of wealth. Suppose that the taxpayer has wealth of Dkr 1 million (£69,930), the tax on which is Dkr 4,950 (£346). If he has no earned income and his investment income is Dkr 50,000 (£3,496) (5%

of Dkr 1 million) his wealth tax bill is reduced by 15% (Dkr 742) to Dkr 4,208. But if the taxpayer then earns Dkr 10,000, bringing his income up to 6% of wealth, he loses the relief; his tax bill is increased not only by the income tax on the additional earnings, but by the Dkr 742 wealth tax which he was previously excused—equivalent to an additional rate of 7.4% on the earnings on top of the tax of about 60% which applies at this level of income. In the Netherlands the situation can be even more anomalous. A taxpayer with wealth but no taxable income (perhaps because most of his wealth is in a loss-making family business) will find that any income which he then earns from a second source is taxed at 80%. These anomalies can be defended on the view that a taxpayer whose assets produce a low income cannot complain if his earned income is highly taxed; but sometimes low yields are due to causes over which the taxpayer may have little control (e.g. losses in closely owned businesses) and also the high marginal rates of tax on earned income may have an unintended and undesirable disincentive effect on work effort.

9.12 There is a more fundamental point in relation to ceilings which are expressed as a fixed percentage of income and which are above any floor of the kind used in Sweden and Denmark. For example, the graph in table 9.2 shows that the ceiling provisions in Sweden operate over a very wide band of income. If a taxpayer is affected by the ceiling provisions, at any particular level of income he pays the same tax whatever his net wealth may be unless his total income is so low that the floor comes into operation (typically if his total income including earned income is less than about 2% of his wealth). Thus in Sweden a taxpayer with an income equivalent to £25,000 will pay the same aggregate amount of tax whether his wealth is £170,000 or £1.2m. We do not think that this is satisfactory.

9.13 If there is to be ceiling relief in the proposed United Kingdom tax, we therefore suggest that, at any particular level of investment income, the ceiling should be directly related to the taxpayer's wealth, i.e. a higher percentage of investment income for a taxpayer with large wealth and a lower percentage for a taxpayer with little wealth.

9.14 The level of any ceiling is essentially a matter of political judgement, but it is likely to be influenced by the level of income taxation. If the proposal made by us in paragraph 9.5 with regard to investment income surcharge on yields in excess of 6% is not adopted, there would at some levels of income be little scope for ceiling relief. For example, the marginal rate of basic and higher rate tax and investment income surcharge on investment income in excess of £2,000 when taxable income is in excess of £20,000 is 98% and the average rate on taxable investment income (with no earned income) at representative levels is:

Amount of investment income £	Average rate of income tax as a % of income
30,000	79.08
50,000	86.65
70,000	89.89
100,000	92.33

Adoption of our suggestion to abolish investment income surcharge on yields in excess of 6% would provide rather more room for manoeuvre.

9.15 The suggestion we now put forward for ceiling relief is meant to do no more than illustrate an appropriate shape for the relief, given the Green Paper proposals and assuming that it is decided to give ceiling relief notwithstanding the object of the tax as expressed in the Chancellor's Foreword and in paragraph 71 of the Green Paper. Appropriate formulae for ceiling relief could, no doubt, take many forms, but we think that our suggestions highlight most of the main issues. We have assumed that our proposal for abolition of investment income surcharge on yields in excess of 6% has been adopted and our illustrations are confined to Scale A. Relief under Scale B would, of course, be greater than under Scale A given the same ceiling rules.

9.16 Our proposal is that for any given level of wealth there should be an 'appropriate percentage' of investment income which should act as a ceiling on total tax liability. In calculating the ceiling:

(a) earned income would be ignored so that it would not be affected by the ceiling;

(b) there would be no abatement of surcharge (if it remains applicable) when basic and higher rate tax plus surcharge exceeds the ceiling;

(c) personal allowances would be ignored. (This is favourable to the taxpayer but it is done for reasons of simplicity and on the footing that most taxpayers have earned income against which personal allowances are normally given.)

Our solution to the problem of fixing the appropriate percentage is to use at any given level of wealth the percentage of income which is absorbed by basic and higher rate tax and surcharge if there is no earned income and investment income is taken as equivalent to 6% of wealth. This links the ceiling relief with our proposal to exempt income in excess of 6% from investment income surcharge. But we again emphasise that this is no more than an illustrative method designed to exemplify our approach to a problem which must ulti-mately be dealt with on a political level and does not imply our endorsement

Table 9.2

Swedish taxpayer with wealth of £1m.

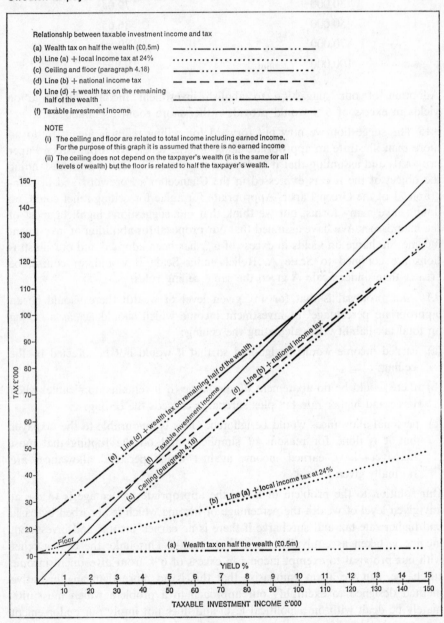

Relationship between taxable investment income and tax

(a) Wealth tax on half the wealth (£0.5m)

(b) Line (a) + local income tax at 24%

(c) Ceiling and floor (paragraph 4.18)

(d) Line (b) + national income tax

(e) Line (d) + wealth tax on the remaining half of the wealth

(f) Taxable investment income

NOTE

(i) The ceiling and floor are related to total income including earned income. For the purpose of this graph it is assumed that there is no earned income

(ii) The ceiling does not depend on the taxpayer's wealth (it is the same for all levels of wealth) but the floor is related to half the taxpayer's wealth.

of the resulting aggregate tax burden. Thus, if a taxpayer has wealth of £1.0m the calculation would be:

	£	£
Notional income—6% of £1.0m		60,000
Basic and higher rate tax on £60,000	44,425	
Surcharge on £60,000—£2,000	8,700	
		53,125
Percentage		88.54%

9.17 Clearly it would be an administrative burden to do this computation for every taxpayer based on his exact wealth, so that bands are likely to be used. The bands should be small so that the change on passing from one band to the next is also small; less acceptably, some form of marginal relief could be used. This problem is inherent in our view that the appropriate percentage must be related to the taxpayer's wealth. At representative levels of wealth the percentages on this basis would be as follows (but the bands should be smaller than those shown below):

Net wealth £m	Appropriate percentage
0.25	63.50
0.50	79.08
0.75	85.39
1.00	88.54
2.00	93.27
3.00	94.85
4.00	95.64
5.00	96.11

9.18 We have no doubt that as well as a ceiling there ought to be a floor, otherwise a taxpayer with no income would pay no income tax and no wealth tax. Our proposal to divorce the computation of the ceiling from earned income makes this all the more necessary. As with the ceiling, the level of the floor is a matter of political judgement, but we put forward suggestions to illustrate the way in which the problem could be tackled. One solution would be to enact that, as yields fall below say 3%, there should be no further reduction in wealth tax. For example, with wealth of £1.0m and income of £30,000 wealth tax becomes £7,037 (£11,500—£4,463) (table 9.3). Wealth tax could remain at that level down to zero yield. The difficulty of this approach is that at, for example, wealth of £0.5m and income of £15,000 (i.e. a 3% yield) there is no ceiling relief—wealth tax remains unabated at £4,000[2] so that at zero income, 100% of the wealth tax would be payable, whereas with zero income

---

[2] £15,000 × .7908 (paragraph 9.17) = £11,862. Income tax on £15,000 = £7,575. Ceiling £4,287. But wealth tax on £0.5m = £4,000.

and wealth of £1.0m only 61.2% (£7,037) of the wealth tax would be payable. The percentage would get lower still as wealth increases.

9.19 An alternative which appeals to us as giving a reasonable answer is to say that the floor at zero income is half the total wealth tax (not wealth tax on half the wealth as in Sweden) and that two-thirds of investment income should be added to this until the ceiling coincides with the floor! (See the graph in table 9.4.) At selected levels of wealth this happens at the level of income and yield shown below:

Wealth	Income at which floor = ceiling	Yield
£m	£	%
0.25[3]	—	—
0.5	16,116	3.22
0.75	20,700	2.76
1.0	26,292	2.63
2.0	49,812	2.49
3.0	82,505	2.75
4.0	114,774	2.87
5.0	146,909	2.94

Thus the yield level at which the ceiling takes over displays a reasonably consistent pattern.

9.20 In table 9.3 we have set out by way of example the tax liability based on our ceiling and floor proposals and Scale A of the Green Paper for a taxpayer with wealth of £1.0m and varying investment yields. It should be noted that:

(a) on the 6% line the ceiling relief cancels out the extra wealth tax (i.e. the excess over surcharge); and

(b) if it were not for our proposed exemption from surcharge of yields in excess of 6%, wealth tax would cease to be the effective tax when income exceeds £78,667 (a yield of 7.87%). The marginal rate of tax would become 98% instead of 83% and the average rate of tax would increase from 88.54% at £60,000, to 90.79% at £78,667, to 94.22% at £150,000 and go on increasing. (Admittedly yields of this order are not very likely.)

It can be seen that our proposals are in line with the Green Paper suggestion (paragraph 32) that a ceiling should benefit a taxpayer whose capital produces a high yield, but of course it would be possible to go further in that direction than we have done.

---

[3] The floor ceases to be effective at an income of £2,228, at which point unabated wealth tax of £1,500 becomes payable.

Table 9.3   Ceiling Relief. Taxpayer with Wealth of £1.0m and Varying Yields[1]

Yield (1) %	Income (2) £	Basic and higher rate tax[2] (3) £	Investment income surcharge (4) £	Total income tax (5) £	Extra wealth tax[3] (6) £	Total tax before ceiling relief (7) £	Ceiling relief[4] (8) £	Total tax after ceiling relief[5] (9) £	Tax after ceiling relief as a % of income (10) %
0	—	—	—	—	11,500	11,500	5,750	5,750	—
1	10,000	4,275	1,200	5,475	10,300	15,775	3,358	12,417	124.17
2	20,000	11,225	2,700	13,925	8,800	22,725	3,642	19,083	95.41
3	30,000	19,525	4,200	23,725	7,300	31,025	4,463	26,562	88.54
4	40,000	27,825	5,700	33,525	5,800	39,325	3,909	35,416	88.54
5	50,000	36,125	7,200	43,325	4,300	47,625	3,355	44,270	88.54
6	60,000	44,425	8,700	53,125	2,800	55,925	2,800	53,125	88.54
7	70,000	52,725	8,700[6]	61,425	2,800	64,225	2,247	61,978	88.54
8	80,000	61,025	8,700	69,725	2,800	72,525	1,693	70,832	88.54
9	90,000	69,325	8,700	78,025	2,800	80,825	1,139	79,686	88.54
10	100,000	77,625	8,700	86,325	2,800	89,125	585	88,540	88.54
11	110,000	85,925	8,700	94,625	2,800	97,425	31	97,394	88.54
12	120,000	94,225	8,700	102,925	2,800	105,725	—	105,725	88.10
13	130,000	102,525	8,700	111,225	2,800	114,025	—	114,025	87.71
14	140,000	110,825	8,700	119,525	2,800	122,325	—	122,325	87.38
15	150,000	119,125	8,700	127,825	2,800	130,625	—	130,625	87.08

NOTES:
1 See paragraph 9.20 and table 9.4.
2 Ignoring personal allowances on the basis that they are given against earned income. But if there is no earned income we suggest that ceiling relief should not be affected by personal allowances.
3 Extra wealth tax, ie wealth tax on Scale A on £1m (£11,500) less investment income surcharge set-off.
4 Ceiling relief is not to be given against surcharge. (If surcharge is levied on yields over 6% column 4 can, at certain yields and levels of wealth, exceed column 8.)
5 The ceiling is 88.54% of income but the floor (which operates on the first three lines) is ¼ × 11,500 + ⅜ of income.
6 Restricted from this point to investment income surcharge due at the 6% level.

Any earned income would be taxed to basic and higher rate tax only on a top slicing basis (less personal allowances).

9.21 This table is set out in the form of a graph in table 9.4, where the effect of levying surcharge on yields in excess of 6% is also shown. In table 9.5 we have compared the floor and ceiling under our proposals at various levels of wealth with the Swedish floor and ceiling. It should, however, be remembered that the Swedish floor and ceiling are based on total income. This will usually cause earned income of Swedish taxpayers affected by the ceiling provisions to be taxed at 80% or 85% instead of at their marginal income tax rate (which typically goes up to 78%) whereas, under our proposals, earned income is not affected by ceiling calculations and will frequently be taxed at a marginal rate lower than the ceiling rate.

9.22 We deal in Chapter 12 with the special problem of ceiling relief for closely owned businesses.

Conclusion

9.23 A ceiling is anomalous if a wealth tax is intended to be additive and has as its main objective the reduction of inequality of wealth. It is also anomalous with a well designed substitutive wealth tax, since it would conflict with the objectives of horizontal equity and efficiency in resource use. There are special problems, however, with closely owned businesses (Chapter 12). If there are to be general ceiling provisions we think that tax as a percentage of income should be differentiated by reference to the taxpayer's wealth: high percentages for taxpayers with large wealth and lower percentages for taxpayers with less wealth. There should be a floor below which liability does not fall; this should be designed so that at zero income half the wealth tax is payable. Earned income should not be affected by ceiling relief.

Deduction of Tax Liabilities

9.24 A wealth tax based on a valuation of wealth at the end of the year automatically allows a deduction for other taxes paid during the year, including wealth tax paid for earlier years. It is arguable that it should also take account of taxes payable in respect of income arising or events occurring during the year which have still to be assessed (e.g. capital gains tax) or, if already assessed, have not yet been paid. If, however, such items (with the exception, of course, of the wealth tax itself) were deductible as debts, it would follow that the wealth tax liability could not be finally determined until all the other tax liabilities had been settled. The consequence would be considerable delay in finalising wealth tax assessments; and revision would be necessary where other tax liabilities were subsequently revised. Further, if prospective tax liabilities which had not yet been quantified were deductible the same treatment should apply to other, non-tax, liabilities where goods or services had been supplied to the taxpayer but the bill had not been presented by the valuation

Table 9.4

Taxpayer with wealth of £1m.

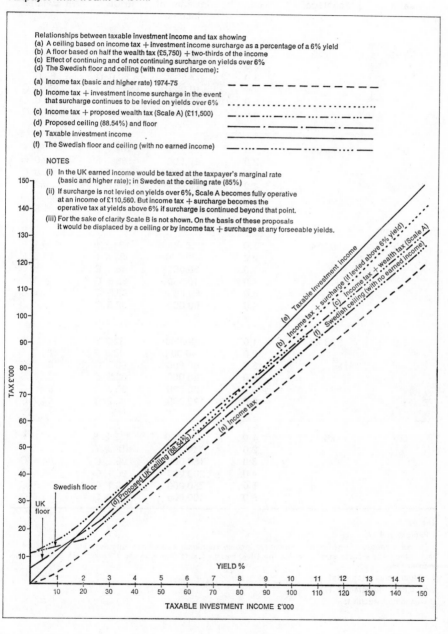

Relationships between taxable investment income and tax showing
(a) A ceiling based on income tax + investment income surcharge as a percentage of a 6% yield
(b) A floor based on half the wealth tax (£5,750) + two-thirds of the income
(c) Effect of continuing and of not continuing surcharge on yields over 6%
(d) The Swedish floor and ceiling (with no earned income):

(a) Income tax (basic and higher rate) 1974-75

(b) Income tax + investment income surcharge in the event
    that surcharge continues to be levied on yields over 6%

(c) Income tax + proposed wealth tax (Scale A) (£11,500)

(d) Proposed ceiling (88.54%) and floor

(e) Taxable investment income

(f) The Swedish floor and ceiling (with no earned income)

NOTES

(i) In the UK earned income would be taxed at the taxpayer's marginal rate
    (basic and higher rate); in Sweden at the ceiling rate (85%)

(ii) If surcharge is not levied on yields over 6%, Scale A becomes fully operative
     at an income of £110,560. But income tax + surcharge becomes the
     operative tax at yields above 6% if surcharge is continued beyond that point.

(iii) For the sake of clarity Scale B is not shown. On the basis of these proposals
      it would be displaced by a ceiling or by income tax + surcharge at any forseeable yields.

AN ANNUAL WEALTH TAX

Table 9.5 Proposed ceiling and floor (UK) compared with Swedish ceiling and floor at selected levels of wealth and yield.

Net wealth £m	Appropriate percentage[1] %	Yield %	Taxable investment income £	Tax payable in UK[2] %	Tax payable in Sweden[2] %
0.25	63.50	1.0	2,500	93.0 U	109.5 F
		2.0	5,000	63.0 U	80.0 C
		3.0	7,500	58.0 U	80.0 C
		4.0	10,000	57.8 U	80.0 C
		5.0	12,500	59.6 U	80.0 C
		6.0	15,000	63.5 C	80.0 C
0.5	79.08	1.0	5,000	106.7 F	129.2 F
		2.0	10,000	86.7 F	80.0 C
		3.0	15,000	77.2 U	80.0 C
		4.0	20,000	76.1 U	80.2 C
		5.0	25,000	77.5 U	81.2 C
		6.0	30,000	79.1 C	81.8 C
1.0	88.54	1.0	10,000	124.2 F	139.1 F
		2.0	20,000	95.4 F	81.6 F
		3.0	30,000	88.5 C	81.8 C
		4.0	40,000	88.5 C	82.6 C
		5.0	50,000	88.5 C	83.1 C
		6.0	60,000	88.5 C	83.4 C
2.0	93.27	1.0	20,000	132.9 F	144.1 F
		2.0	40,000	99.8 F	84.0 F
		3.0	60,000	93.3 C	83.4 C
		4.0	80,000	93.3 C	83.8 C
		5.0	100,000	93.3 C	84.1 C
		6.0	120,000	93.3 C	84.2 C
5.0	96.11	1.0	50,000	153.2 F	147.0 F
		2.0	100,000	109.9 F	85.5 F
		3.0	150,000	96.1 C	84.4 C
		4.0	200,000	96.1 C	84.5 C
		5.0	250,000	96.1 C	84.6 C
		6.0	300,000	96.1 C	84.7 C

NOTES:

1 Paragraph 9.17.

2 Tax as a percentage of taxable investment income (personal allowances ignored). Tax includes income tax, investment income surcharge (in the UK), wealth tax (Scale A in the UK) and (in Sweden) local income tax.

F=Floor (paragraph 9.19).

C=Ceiling (paragraph 9.17).

U=Unabated wealth tax.

date. To allow a deduction for such liabilities would complicate matters still further.

9.25 As a practical matter therefore the deduction for taxes should in any case be limited to established liabilities, i.e. where the tax has been assessed and is due and payable at the valuation date but has not been paid. The same rule would apply to non-tax debts. There would then be no deduction where tax had been assessed but the assessment was under appeal or the due date for payment had not arrived. It would, however, be open to the taxpayer, in so far as he accepted that tax would ultimately become payable, to pay it in advance and reduce his wealth accordingly.

9.26 Even this limited deduction, however, is open to objection. To allow the deduction, although correct in principle, would be to acquiesce in the non-payment of taxes which are due and payable. To prohibit deduction, on the other hand, would be a positive encouragement to prompt payment. On the whole, therefore, we think that no deduction at all should be allowed for unpaid taxes other than those which have been the subject of formal defer-ment. Non-tax debts, however, which are due and payable (e.g. to tradesmen) should be allowed, since the Revenue is not directly concerned.

9.27 There appears to be no general case for allowing wealth tax as a deduc-tion for the purpose of other taxes (though in paragraphs 12.20 to 12.24 we suggest some relaxation in the case of closely owned businesses). In Germany, the wealth tax was formerly allowed to be deducted in computing income for income tax purposes, but the relief has now been discontinued, concurrently with the reduction of the rate of tax from 1% to 0.7%. The defect of the relief was that, being allowed in effect at the individual's marginal rate of income tax, it gave most relief (i.e. the biggest reduction in effective wealth tax liability) to the wealthiest people. The new arrangement is more equitable.

Conclusion

9.28 No deduction should be allowed for unpaid taxes or other tax liabilities unless they have been the subject of formal deferment. Wealth tax paid should not normally be allowed as a deduction in computing income for income tax purposes.

Double Taxation

9.29 The usual credit provisions will be required where property situated in another country and belonging to a UK resident who is liable to wealth tax on world assets has been subject to wealth tax in the other country. Subject to one point, double taxation agreements should present no difficulty, as the Green Paper proposes (paragraph 15) to limit the charge on non-residents along the lines recommended by the Fiscal Committee of the OECD[4] (paragraph 7.6).

---

[4] *Draft Double Taxation Convention on Income and Capital 1963.*

9.30 The point of difficulty is that the OECD Convention also provides that the individuals and companies of one country shall enjoy the same tax treatment in the other country as the individuals and companies of that other country. It is in accordance with this principle of 'national' treatment that UK companies with a permanent establishment in Sweden are exempted from wealth tax in Sweden under the double taxation agreement between the two countries, since the tax does not apply to Swedish, but only to foreign, companies (paragraph 4.11). The Green Paper proposes, however (paragraph 15), that non-resident companies shall be brought within the charge in certain circumstances in order that non-resident individuals owning chargeable UK assets shall not be able to escape tax by interposing a corporate screen. To charge non-resident companies, however, would be a denial of national treatment, since UK companies are not to be subject to the tax. In negotiating double taxation agreements the UK will need to secure a waiver of national treatment in these special cases if it is to retain its power to charge a company belonging to the other country.

The Link with Capital Gains Tax

9.31 There is a link between the wealth tax and the capital gains tax which deserves consideration. The wealth tax taxes all wealth annually, including increases in wealth due to the appreciation of assets. In these circumstances is there room for an additional tax on increases which are realised by the sale or other disposal of particular assets?

9.32 One view of capital gains is that when realised, but not before, they are a form of income; they are available for spending even if they are not actually spent but reinvested. In the United States, capital gains rank as income, though they are taxed at a lower rate than ordinary income. On this view there is no more reason in principle to abolish the capital gains tax, or to reduce its rate, than there is to abolish or reduce the income tax.

9.33 It is, however, often argued that ideally, capital appreciation should be taxed annually, whether realised or not and that the taxation of realised gains is no more than a substitute for the ideal, adopted because it is reasonably practicable. Unrealised appreciation is not so obviously akin to income as a realised gain, but the additional command over resources which appreciation confers is the same whether it is realised or not. This appreciation is in fact taxed by the wealth tax annually. However, it does not follow that the appreciation should not be taxed more heavily than the taxpayer's previously existing wealth. This result will be achieved automatically in a progressive wealth tax if the addition attracts a higher rate of tax, but the result is not peculiar to increases in wealth; the same bands and rates apply to a person with the same total wealth which has remained unchanged in value during the year; the increase is not more heavily taxed as such.

9.34 To tax the increase, although unrealised, more heavily would be somewhat easier with a wealth tax in operation; given that the taxpayer must list all his assets and place values on them every year, it would simply be a matter of comparing the changes in value from one year to another. But it would be laborious to do so (much more work than taxing the whole gain at the time of disposal); a separate account would have to be kept for each asset, in order to allow for falls in value occurring during the period of ownership of the asset; otherwise the taxpayer might suffer the heavier charge on more than the total appreciation during the period. Further, if cadastral values were adopted for land, the charge could not be imposed every year, but only after each revaluation, when the appreciation of several years would be swept up. From a practical point of view this might be an advantage, but it would add to the disparity of treatment between land and assets such as quoted securities which can be revalued every year. (The simple course of imposing the additional charge on the increase in total net wealth during the year would not be satisfactory, since it would tax savings out of income as well as appreciation of assets.)

9.35 It would seem, therefore, that gains should continue to be taxed on realisation. However, it remains true that to a limited extent the wealth tax is a partial substitute for the capital gains tax since all appreciation, realised or not, comes under charge; and therefore that in principle the rate of capital gains tax, if appropriate before the introduction of the wealth tax, should be reduced somewhat when the latter is in force. But what is the appropriate rate for realised gains is a matter for political judgement.

Conclusion

9.36 The introduction of a wealth tax does not entail the abolition of capital gains tax on realised gains.

Chapter 10

Valuation

The Theoretical Basis

10.1 Most commentators are agreed that the basis of valuation for wealth tax should be open market value; i.e. the price which an asset would fetch as between a willing buyer and a willing seller in a market open to all comers. The tax is regarded as a tax on resources and market value is the natural measure of those resources. This is the basis used for estate duty and capital gains tax and—at least in principle—is the basis of wealth tax in many other countries.

10.2 It is claimed that open market value is the value which least distorts resource allocation, that any higher value would be regarded as unfair and that any lower value will create a locked in effect similar to that which now obtains in relation to capital gains tax (because selling the undervalued asset will cause the taxpayer's wealth tax base to increase by the difference between the proceeds of sale and the valuation unless another undervalued asset is acquired).

10.3 Market value may be the best measure we have of resources but it has many defects. It can be influenced by the form in which assets are held; for example an unquoted company as compared with a quoted company of the same size and profitability. Stock Exchange quotations represent the price at which jobbers are prepared to buy or sell comparatively small quantities of a share. It is common experience to find that the existence of a buyer or seller of a relatively small quantity of the shares of a particular company will move the price up or down respectively by what seems a disproportionate amount. An owner of a substantial minority interest in a quoted company will rarely be able to sell all his shares at the bid price, let alone at the conventional 'one quarter up' price (i.e. at the bid price plus one quarter of the difference between the bid and offer price as published in the Stock Exchange Daily Official List). On the other hand the holder of a very large block of quoted shares may, in some circumstances, be able to sell above the offer price. If the holder of a large block is gradually unloading his shares on to an unreceptive market, he may depress the quoted price of those shares over quite a long period and thus artificially lower the wealth tax base of other holders of those shares. Quotations can be affected by rumours, which may be totally unfounded and may even be maliciously inspired. In none of these cases does the conventional market price give a fair measure of a taxpayer's resources. Nor are market prices necessarily a measure of actual resources since the price of shares may exceed the value of the underlying tangible assets (the difference being goodwill) or be less than that value. In the latter case the difference may be because the rate of return on the company's assets is too low; that may indicate the need for a change of use of those assets but such a change of use, whether involving liquidation or not, is likely to cause losses which would reduce their value.

10.4 The 'one quarter up' convention which applies to quoted securities is presumably intended to arrive at the price at which a sale, rather than a purchase, can take place (but even so only of a marginal quantity) since actual quotations tend to be narrower than those shown in the Daily Official List. Yet, in relation to other assets, no account is taken of the difference between the price at which a taxpayer can buy and that at which he can sell a particular asset. The Stock Exchange may be an imperfect market but it is a great deal better than some other markets where it makes all the difference whether one is a seller who is finding it difficult to trace a buyer or a buyer who is finding it difficult to trace a seller. Theory requires that the willing buyer and willing seller meet; in practice they do not always do so. Or, put in another way, the willingness is frequently greater on one side than another so that, in effect, there is a very big difference between the price at which a taxpayer can sell an asset and that at which he can acquire it. Sometimes this is because the taxpayer can, in practice, only buy in one market (e.g. retail shops) and sell in another (e.g. through advertisements in the newspaper). And, particularly in relation to assets which are in some measure unique, the price at which they can be bought at auction one day may be very different from that at which the new owner could sell them the following day. This can apply, for example, to houses which have special characteristics or location, to pictures and even to shares in unquoted companies. It even applies to jewels, as the Consumers' Association found when they bought a diamond for £2,595, including VAT at £236, and tried to sell it the following week when they could only get two offers—one for £550 and another for £1,000[1]. The loss of

---

[1] *Money Which?* September 1974 p. 160

the VAT is understandable but, even apart from that, there was a loss of £1,359 on an asset costing £2,595.

10.5 We think that the existence of this gap should be explicitly recognised and that legislation should clearly state what point in the gap is to be taken as the value for wealth tax purposes. In relation to assets which were received as gifts or bequests we see much merit in using the bottom end of the range, which is in effect the price at which an auctioneer would recommend that the object should be withdrawn from an auction sale on the view that he felt that the owner's interests would be better served by a sale on another occasion or in another way. For assets which are purchased the wealth tax value should certainly not, in our view, be higher than half way between the highest and lowest values even though, when an asset such as a picture has been bought at the top end of the range, this might mean a fairly substantial reduction below purchase price. We contemplate that these methods would only be applied to a comparatively narrow range of assets in view of the suggestions which we make below for valuation of land, trade assets and unquoted companies.

Valuation in practice

10.6 In our view the choice of valuation methods must be influenced by two major considerations; the need to keep down administrative and compliance costs and to have methods which reduce as much as possible uncertainty about, and delay in arriving at, valuations. Administrative and compliance costs use real resources and may thus have a greater effect on the economy than distortions of resource allocation caused by the use of a value other than market value. There are three reasons why it is important to avoid uncertainty and delay. Firstly because they always increase administrative and compliance costs. Secondly, taxpayers are entitled to know the extent of their tax liabilities with certainty and without delay and thus be able to plan their personal and business finances accordingly; it is no reply to say that a wealth tax is directed at people whose resources are adequate to enable them to live with uncertainty without great inconvenience. That is not true of taxpayers whose resources are largely committed to their business and, even to those of whom it is true, society has a duty to make its demands known without delay. Thirdly, if there is uncertainty, it is bound to lead taxpayers (other than the most sensitive and conscientious minority) to put forward figures which are right at the bottom end of any possible range of figures. Apart from the resulting inequity, there is a risk that the Revenue will lack the resources to challenge the figures and, because they are not challenged, taxpayers will be tempted to put forward yet lower ones. Once habits of this kind are established, they will be difficult to eradicate and could spill over to cause lower tax morality in other areas; they could cause a marked increase in enforcement costs (paragraph 16.22).

10.7 In terms of the monetary amounts involved and the number of taxpayers affected, the areas of greatest uncertainty are in the valuation of land and buildings and of sole traders, partnerships and unquoted companies. Four of the five Continental systems which we have examined (the exception being the Netherlands) have dealt with the valuation of these assets in a similar way. There are official procedures for arriving at the capital value of all land and buildings. These values are used for several purposes; wealth tax, imputed income of owner occupiers, gift tax, inheritance tax and local taxes. In all four countries there are stylised methods of computing the value of businesses, partnerships and unquoted companies. In Sweden (and, in practice, to a considerable extent in Norway) the value is related to net assets (other than created goodwill) and the values placed on individual assets are, broadly speaking, the same as those used for income tax. This value is referred to as the 'intrinsic value'. In Denmark and Germany, when valuing unquoted companies, earnings and dividends are also taken into account. In Denmark an average of intrinsic value, earnings value and dividend value is taken. Germany uses a formula which adds to 85% of the intrinsic value the excess of the distributable profits of the past five years over 10% per annum of the value of the shares (paragraph 5.26). In all four countries the value thus arrived at can be displaced if there is evidence to support a different value, e.g. if shares are actively traded at arms length. We have the impression that this does not happen to any great extent in Denmark, Germany and Sweden, but perhaps rather more often in Norway. In none of these countries did the valuation of businesses and companies appear to be burdensome or a matter of controversy. No doubt this is partly because these methods have been in use for a long time and partly because, in their different ways, they arrive at values which are conservative.

10.8 In the Netherlands, however, no stylised methods or procedures are laid down for any class of asset; it is for the taxpayer to put forward his own valuation and for the tax authorities to challenge it if they disagree.

10.9 The Green Paper proposes that methods similar to those used in the Netherlands should be used in the United Kingdom; that is to say, that primary responsibility for valuations should rest with taxpayers who would have to use subjective judgement or professional advice rather than a cadastral value, formula or process of computation. We are uneasy about this proposal. In principle, the methods which are used in the Netherlands are those which now apply in the United Kingdom for estate duty and for capital gains tax, but the practice is very different. In the United Kingdom delays of up to three years in agreeing the value of unquoted shares are quite common. There are also considerable delays in settling the value of land and buildings. At present, share valuation is centralised in London. Rates of estate duty are high so that the cost of negotiations is offset by savings in tax payable. In the Netherlands decentralised administration, with experienced Revenue officials who carry full responsibility, permits informal discussion to take place readily. The rate of wealth tax is 0.8% per annum so that there is little to be gained on either side from extended negotiations. The appeal procedure in the Netherlands is simple and effective whereas here it is costly and time consuming. In our view, the success of Dutch methods depends on the fact that they have been long established, the decentralised administration and the willingness of taxpayers and Revenue authorities not to press the valuation procedure to the limit. It is true that the Green Paper proposes regional administration for the UK but this is very different from local administration. And we think that it will require considerable time and effort to displace present attitudes and practices amongst both the Revenue and those advising taxpayers. We, therefore, prefer something closer to the methods used in the other four countries.

Frequency of valuation

10.10 In Germany returns are required from most taxpayers only once in three years, but with rights on both sides to file returns in the intermediate years if the change exceeds specified percentages of the opening valuation. The other countries which we visited require annual returns and they are, of course, essential if wealth tax information is used, as it is in some of those countries, as a check on declarations of income. On the whole we think that annual returns are more satisfactory, although it could be that less frequent returns would enable more careful examination of those returns, particularly if neither side could seek any variation in the intermediate years. No doubt, if values fall, that may be thought to be harsh; but it should be remembered that the Continental systems are based on valuation on a specific date with instalment payments during the year, which is no different in principle from valuation once in three years with annual instalments during the triennium.

10.11 But, at least in relation to assets which are difficult to value, we think that there is much to be said for values remaining unchanged for a fixed period of, say, five years. Since such assets would often be a comparatively small part of total wealth, it may be reasonable to provide that values will only be revised during the quinquennium if the revision causes a change of more than £X or Y%, whichever is greater, in the taxpayer's liability for wealth tax.

Professional valuation

10.12 Under the Green Paper proposals for self assessment of value (paragraph 62) it will be nervous or conscientious taxpayers who take the initiative in employing professional valuers. Others will wait until the values which they have put forward are challenged by the Inland Revenue. The proposals which are made in this chapter are intended to reduce the number of occasions on which professional valuation is required and to simplify the task of the professional valuer when he is called in. In paragraph 15.35 proposals are made for a credit to be given towards the cost of professional valuations required by the Revenue or, given self assessment, by the taxpayer for his own protection.

10.13 We wonder if it is possible to distinguish two situations. Firstly, when a valuer is acting as an advocate on behalf of his client, in which case his initial valuation is likely to be as low as credulity will permit. Secondly, when a valuer is acting as an expert rather as he would do on receiving joint instructions from two parties whose interests are divergent. If so, it may not be unreasonable to restrict the circumstances when credit is given for professional costs to the second case. The wording of a valuer's opinion would, of course, be different in the two different situations and in the second case he should be required to include an assertion that he had no link with the taxpayer which put him under a conflict of interest. Would it then be reasonable for the Inland Revenue to establish a practice of not challenging professional valuations of the second type except as a matter of last resort, and then only through the disciplinary procedure of the professional organisation concerned, without attempting to disturb past assessments on affected taxpayers? If so, we think that this could have a beneficial effect in preventing delay and uncertainty and in reducing compliance costs. Given arrangements of this kind, we think it would be reasonable for the Revenue to have power to call for a professional valuation; the taxpayer could choose whether that was done on an 'advocate' basis at his own expense or on an 'expert' basis partly at Revenue expense.

10.14 We think also it may be desirable for the professional associations to consider giving guidance to their members as to their responsibilities when giving their professional opinion on values for taxation purposes. Is there a limit of advocacy or negotiation beyond which they should not go and, if so, where is it? Are professional people in giving an opinion on value for taxation purposes entitled to put forward an opening opinion of value which is unrealistically low in order to influence subsequent negotiations? Still more, should they do so in the context of a self assessed wealth tax when many valuations may not be challenged because of pressure of work?

10.15 Paragraph 64 of the Green Paper speaks of penalties where a taxpayer has deliberately and wilfully understated the value of an asset. Except in such areas as quoted shares, we think that it will be difficult under the procedures outlined in the Green Paper to prove deliberate and wilful understatement and that those procedures may easily lead to substantial understatement because of their lack of precision. We feel that some apparent sacrifice of equity is justified in order to achieve a higher degree of certainty. If the bases of valuation are fully spelt out they will be observed by most people and, when they are not, penalties can be imposed. If they are left vague they will be stretched to the limit.

10.16 Suggestions have been made that, in order to check on undervaluations, the Revenue should have the right to buy in any asset, such as a picture, at say 10% above its declared value. Presumably it would then be put up for auction and the taxpayer could buy it in. If the price at auction was low the Revenue would lose; if high they would gain; and the article, if bought in by the owner, would have to be brought in to subsequent wealth tax assessments at the auction price. Although ingenious, we do not see powers of this kind being used. There would be anxiety that the auction sale was rigged.

Valuation of particular assets

Land and buildings generally

10.17 Denmark and Sweden arrive at the capital value of all land by periodic assessments, every four years in Denmark and every five years in Sweden. Both start from open market value but, in Sweden, a deduction of 25% is then made. In Denmark the values in the valuation year approximate very closely to, and may indeed influence, actual sale prices. In Norway established capital values are periodically revised by indices to take account of inflation. New properties are in theory assessed at open market value, but in practice these values are conservative. Germany arrives at its wealth tax values by capitalising assessed rental values. The multipliers are derived from tables which take account of the age of the property, the bracket within which the rental falls, the location, type of construction, etc. By way of contrast, in the Netherlands the value of occupied property is taken as two-thirds of its open market vacant possession value as declared by the taxpayer (but subject to challenge by the Revenue). If it is vacant, it is taken at 100% of that value. We were impressed by the extent to which, in Germany and Sweden in particular, assessed capital values were used as the basis for a number of different taxes.

10.18 It is often argued that, in the United Kingdom, the concept of basing the rates payable by occupiers to local authorities on open market rents is no longer valid for domestic property. Approximately one-half of all houses are owner occupied and, of the remainder, two-thirds are owned by local authorities and let at subsidised rents, so that only one-sixth of all houses are privately let and most of those are rent controlled. This leads to a situation where there is little evidence of true open market rents. On the other hand there is a great deal of evidence of prices obtained on sale in the open market. There can be little doubt, therefore, that—both for wealth tax and local rates—quinquennial valuations based on sales statistics are likely to be a better

M

measure of ability to pay than notional rents, or notional capital values derived from notional rents.

10.19 The return made by property owners to the assessing authority in Sweden gives a great deal more information about a property than is given in the corresponding returns used for rating valuation purposes in this country. This information, used in conjunction with detailed statistics about property sales, must greatly speed up the revaluation process. In principle it would seem that most of this information is capable of being held in computerised form; in which case much of the work of revaluation could be done by the use of suitable indices which take account of size, age, mode of construction, standard of construction, location, etc.

10.20 Whilst it is a matter for regret that the quinquennial rating revaluation due in 1978 is to be postponed, it does provide an opportunity to change to a capital value basis. If this is done, we would be in favour of making information about ownership and sale prices freely accessible to any enquirer and of the publication of regular statistics about land transactions. This would facilitate appeal procedures and should help to keep assessments in line with actual values ruling at the basis date for any particular quinquennium or other fixed period. Property erected during a quinquennium would then be valued initially at the value which would have been placed on it had it been in existence at the basis date for the quinquennium. Existing property purchased during a quinquennium would be taken at its assessed value, not at its purchase price, nor would the purchase price be conclusive as to the next valuation; that would depend on values in the district generally.

10.21 Recent experience in this country has shown that property values can fall fairly dramatically. It is true that a fall is most likely to come after an exceptional rise and that an exceptional rise is not likely to be allowed to exert its full influence on a periodic revaluation. However, this suggests that periodic revaluations should be somewhat below prevailing values to allow for the possibility of a fall during the quinquennium or other fixed period. This involves the risk that, by the end of the fixed period, the gap between assessed and actual values may be fairly large. For this reason care should be taken to ensure that the initial gap is no more than is justified. Alternatively, increasing computerisation of valuation records and of the rate collection process could make it possible to have a rolling revaluation; that is to say, one in which one-fifth of all property has a full scale re-assessment each year whilst the other four-fifths are revalued by the application of indices.

10.22 We discuss the problem of hope value and marriage value in paragraphs 10.31 and 10.32.

Owner occupied houses

10.23 If a capital value basis is introduced for rates, it would clearly be used in arriving at the wealth tax base of owner occupiers. Since the existing fiscal bias in favour of owner occupation is so great there seems to us to be little case for a favourable valuation basis for owner occupied houses.

10.24 However, a change to a capital value basis is not likely to be made in time for the planned introduction of wealth tax at 31 December 1976 or 31 March 1977. It is, therefore, necessary to consider alternative methods. The Green Paper says in paragraph 49 that, in principle, owner occupied houses will be valued at their market value but that it might be possible, to ease valuation difficulties, to provide that houses (except perhaps very expensive ones) should be valued at a multiple of the annual value on which the rateable value is based. Because of our preference for certainty, we believe that, until a complete revaluation can be done on a capital value basis, the multiplier method should be used to the exclusion of any other method for owner occupied houses (even expensive ones). The figure to which the multiplier is applied should, we think, be the rateable value rather than the annual value from which the former is derived. (The difference between the two is an allowance for repairs which proportionately is larger for low values than for high ones.) We also think that consideration may need to be given to the use of different multipliers for different parts of the country, for different types of construction and for different ranges of rateable value. (This is distinct from the need, to which the Green Paper refers, to have different multipliers in Scotland and Northern Ireland because of their different rating systems.)

Houses which are let

10.25 Even in the absence of rent control and with only minimum security of tenure for tenants, the capital value of tenanted property would usually be less than that of property with vacant possession (unless there was an excess supply of property for letting). With rent control and security of tenure, that difference will be greater depending on the extent to which the rent of a particular property is depressed below its open market rental. If the capital value basis is adopted for rating, the lower capital value of rent controlled property would presumably be ignored for rating purposes since the benefit derived from *occupation* of the property is the same for both tenant and owner occupier. But it would not then be right to use the assessed capital value for the purpose of arriving at the wealth tax base of the owner. In the absence of rent control and unlimited security of tenure a percentage deduction would take care of the difference between the two values, but this would not be sufficient for rent controlled property. If rateable values are still in operation, it may be a sufficient expedient to apply suitable multipliers (different from those used for owner occupied property) to rateable values, since those values should be a fair representation of actual rent. Again, no one multiplier is likely to be fair. But if rateable values based on rents have been abolished then there seems to be no alternative but either to apply a multiplier to actual rents, less an allowance for repairs, or to have professional valuation—a formidable task.

Industrial and commercial property (owned and occupied)

10.26 If assessed capital values are available these would be used; if not, then the choice is between the application of a multiplier to rateable value or professional valuation. The multipliers should be specific to this kind of property. Because much industrial and commercial property, whether owner occupied or let, is owned by quoted companies, the valuation problem for wealth tax is reduced but valuation will still be required for other purposes. This also applies in some measure to houses which are let and to farms.

Industrial and commercial properties which are let

10.27 If assessed capital values are in force, it would probably be right to allow a percentage deduction to take care of the difference between tenanted and vacant possession value. But that reduced value may then have to be divided between the occupier and the owner in accordance with their respective rights. Typically this would have to be done when the rent payable is below currently prevailing rents and there are some years to go before the rent can be revised. It may often be possible for this division to be done on the basis of conventions and tables agreed between the surveying profession and the Inland Revenue. But, if there are cases which require individual negotiation, it may put the interests of landlord and tenant in opposition unless one is liable to wealth tax and the other is not. Nor can the Inland Revenue be indifferent as to the allocation. It should be remembered that there may be a number of intermediate lessors between the freeholder and the actual occupier.

10.28 If the change to an assessed capital value system has not been made, then the choice is between the application of a multiplier to rateable value (which should reflect rental value) or professional valuation; and then division between freehold and leasehold interests as suggested in the preceding paragraph.

Farms—owned and occupied

10.29 At present there are no rateable values for farms, as distinct from farmhouses, as they are not liable for local rates. If assessed capital values are available they would be used unless special relief is to be given to farmers (paragraph 13.37.4). But, in their absence, we feel particularly uneasy about the Green Paper emphasis on self assessment. The subject is beyond our sphere of competence, but we believe that it may be better to require that, in the first instance, values for a quinquennium are based on tables published by the Inland Revenue and agreed in advance with the surveying profession, showing values per acre of broad categories of farm land in various parts of the country, perhaps with a further adjustment based on the size of the holding. The value of farmhouses could be fixed by the same methods as domestic property. It could then be open to an owner of a farm to appeal on the grounds that there were particular circumstances affecting his farm for which no allowance or inadequate allowance was made in the tables. In the absence of such a method we see no alternative to professional valuation[2].

Farms which are let

10.30 Similar considerations arise except that there is the added problem of the difference between tenanted and vacant possession value. We doubt if a single percentage deduction would deal with this problem, but it may be feasible to prescribe different percentages for different types of farm and different parts of the country.

Hope and marriage values

10.31 'Hope value' derives from the hope that planning permission will be given for a change of use of land; it is the excess of open market value over existing use value. If the proposals contained in the White Paper *'Land'* (Cmnd 5730) are enacted, hope value will in time largely disappear. However, we think that we should record the view which we formed before the issue of the White Paper as to the proper treatment of hope value for wealth tax. (In the remainder of this paragraph hope value is taken as being net of development gains tax.) The view which we have formed is that hope value should be ignored except where land was bought at a price above existing use value. It is important to be clear that a difference between assessed capital values (if such are in force) and actual prices does not necessarily refer to hope value. At the beginning of a quinquennium it may do so, but later in the period it may be due to a general movement in prices. We formed our view of this problem by considering the position of a farmer who owns land with hope value which he bought some time ago at existing use value. So long as he does not sell the land the hope value is of no use to him; he can only use the land in its existing use. Once planning permission (even if only in outline form) has been given for a change of use, whether on his application or as a result of an application by someone else, the community is indicating that it is prepared to see the land put to that different use and it seems reasonable to assess the owner on that enhanced value. That may add to the pressures on the farmer to sell his land for development, but that, it seems to us, is as it should be, even though the application for planning permission was made by someone else. It is clearly fair that the farmer who buys land without planning permission at a price above its maximum agricultural value should include the excess in his wealth tax base. The hope value should probably be

---

[2] For the purpose of capital transfer tax it is proposed in the November 1974 Finance Bill that land transferred by or on the death of an owner-occupier shall, if certain conditions are fulfilled, be valued at twenty times its agricultural rental value. The estimation of that value will frequently require professional assistance.

re-assessed every five years by professional valuers, but there is a case for saying that the hope value should not exceed:

$$\frac{\text{Hope value at date of acquisition}}{\text{Purchase price}} \times \frac{\text{Existing use value + hope value at valuation date}}{1}$$

We have used farming as an example because it is the common one; but, since farming carries emotional overtones, we should say explicitly that we believe the same argument applies to other land and building.

10.32 'Marriage value' is the additional price which would be paid by the owner of land in order to acquire ownership of land contiguous with his own, over and above that which would be paid by other persons who did not own contiguous land. When the owner of the land in question is a reluctant seller or a good negotiator the difference may be considerable if the additional land would enable the would-be purchaser to put the combined land to better use than can be achieved with the separate plots. We think that this additional value should be ignored, except perhaps in the case of vacant land, on the view that its realisation depends on a change of use and that meanwhile its marriage value is very uncertain.

Goodwill generally

10.33 Before examining the valuation of various forms of business enterprises, we think that we should first consider the treatment of goodwill. Because there is a good deal of misunderstanding on the subject, and also because we are taking a different view from the Green Paper, we think it necessary to consider this in some detail. For this purpose it is sufficient if we define goodwill as the price which is paid, on purchasing a business or a share in a business, in excess of the price which would be paid for the net tangible assets as such (treating monetary assets such as debtors as tangible for this purpose). It should be noted that this definition is apt to embrace that element in the price of shares which is not backed by net tangible assets. There are problems in defining or in arriving at the price which would be paid for the net tangible assets, but they need not concern us here. Goodwill is sometimes spoken of as the capitalised value of the super profit which the purchaser expects to make; that is, the excess of the anticipated profit over the aggregate of interest on the amount invested (at a rate which has regard to the risk) plus arms length remuneration for any work done by the new proprietor. That definition will not do for our purpose because amounts are frequently paid for goodwill when there is no such excess.

10.34 It is easy to see why a payment is made for goodwill when there is a super profit. Businesses acquire their own momentum and there is a probability that the old customers will continue to patronise the old business even if there is a change in management (and a change in ownership does not necessarily require a change in management or, at least, a change in management that is discernible to customers). However, sometimes payments which purport to be for goodwill really relate to premises rather than to a business. Consider the village shop which has a monopoly position because planning permission would not be given for another shop or because the village could not support two shops. The owner of such a shop could let it at a rent which would eliminate entirely any super profit goodwill value of the business (paragraph 53 of the Green Paper). But if there is no super profit a payment may still be made for goodwill, usually because the incoming person wishes to work in a particular place, profession or trade and is willing to pay a price for the satisfaction he gets from so doing.

10.35 Should a value be attributed for wealth tax purposes to goodwill which has been created by the existing owner of a business? It is exempt in Germany, the Netherlands, Norway and Sweden except to the extent that the German formulae for valuing shares in unquoted companies attaches some weight to earnings and dividend. For the purpose of wealth tax payable by German companies as distinct from individuals, created goodwill is exempt. There is a strong practical reason for the exemption; goodwill is often very difficult to value and liable to fluctuate in value. The market in which goodwill of this kind is traded is an imperfect one with comparatively infrequent arms length transactions and those which take place do so at widely different values, sometimes affected by psychic considerations. Paragraph 53 of the Green Paper speaks of valuing 'according to the custom of the trade, such as a multiple of recent annual earnings'. There are comparatively few trades where there are such customs, those where they exist are usually small and, even so, the range of multiples which is used may be quite large. Our proposals reduce the number of occasions when goodwill has to be valued. Such valuations are rarely easy and frequently require a valuation of the business as a whole. It may therefore be worth considering the use of a formula similar to the Stuttgart formula (paragraph 5.26) where, by implication, goodwill (or negative goodwill in appropriate cases) is the difference between net tangible assets and the price which emerges from the application of the formula. But such a formula will give rise to dissatisfaction unless the resulting valuations tend to be on the low side.

10.36 There are other reasons why it is reasonable to exempt created goodwill. Firstly, the act of creating it makes no demand on resources; the creation of super profit may involve expense, but that expense has been recovered against revenue and resulted in larger than normal profit. Secondly, goodwill is a recognition of the fact that an owner of a successful business gives it a momentum which goes on after he retires; in some ways it is akin to an inventor who receives payment from his rights after the act of invention is over. (We argue in paragraphs 10.75 and 10.76 that an inventor or author should be exempt on the value of his patent rights or copyright respectively.) Thirdly, it may not be a bad thing to give favourable treatment to owners of businesses which make a high return on the net tangible assets which they use. Fourthly, if it is decided not to exempt created goodwill it will result in some very anomalous situations. Fifthly, it is a way of giving some help to closely owned businesses without breaching the basic principle of the tax.

10.37 The main argument against exemption is that it may cause some owners of a business to continue in it longer than is good for them or the business; but if they do that they may find that the value of their goodwill drops as a result.

Goodwill—sole proprietors

10.38 Paragraph 53 of the Green Paper indicates that goodwill is to be liable to wealth tax. We see no objection to that in the case of purchased goodwill. But, if purchased goodwill is to be liable and, as we advocate above, created goodwill is to be exempt, what is to happen in years subsequent to the year of purchase? Usually purchased goodwill cannot then be separately valued because it will merge with created goodwill. In Denmark at least this is dealt with by giving a writing down allowance on purchased goodwill similar to capital allowances on plant and machinery for income tax and using the written down value for wealth tax (as well as exempting created goodwill). In Germany no writing off of purchased goodwill is permitted for either tax unless it can be proved that the value has dropped, which in practice it is difficult to do. We think the Danish practice should be followed in this country (both for income tax and wealth tax—but if not for income tax then certainly for wealth tax).

Goodwill—partnerships

10.39 Most partnership deeds prescribe how goodwill is to be dealt with when a partner is admitted to or leaves the partnership. If a capital payment is made, it is often fixed by reference to profit, sales or some other feature of the business. Sometimes no capital payment is made but the partnership pays a pension to retired partners or their dependants. In other cases no capital sum or pension is paid. These differing treatments, which occur in large as well as small partnerships, are inevitably affected by the treatment accorded to goodwill in the past as well as by the view which is taken about the recruitment of new partners. It is sometimes argued that goodwill exists (and by implication has a value) even in those cases where no payment whatsoever for goodwill is made to partners when they retire or die and, in support of that view, it is said that partners receive a super profit as defined in paragraph 10.33. Partners who work in such firms are likely to deny that they receive a super profit! But, at least in those firms where partners are not related, there can only be two reasons for making no payment for goodwill. Either partners think that it has no value; or, alternatively, the dominant consideration is to put no obstacle in the way of recruiting partners by reference to their professional or managerial ability rather than by reference to their ability or willingness to pay for goodwill. It is often felt that under present day conditions many of the ablest young professional people can find an attractive career without making any payment for goodwill. This last consideration has led to a considerable reduction in the number of firms that put a capital value on goodwill.

10.40 Paragraph 54 of the Green Paper can be read as indicating that wealth tax is to be levied on partnership goodwill, even in those cases where a partner is to receive no goodwill payment on retirement or death. This is in contrast to estate duty and capital gains tax practice where in these circumstances no attempt is made to levy tax on notional values (unless most partners are related, in which case it may be argued that there is a gift—for example, from father to son). We think the same practice should be applied for wealth tax.

10.41 As stated above there are partnerships which pay pensions to partners out of post retirement profits in partial or complete substitution for capital payments for goodwill. These pensions are nonetheless a payment for goodwill, but it would be illogical to charge the capitalised value of such pensions to wealth tax if the capital value of pensions paid to employees are to be exempt from wealth tax. And if they were to be charged then there should be a corresponding deduction of the capitalised liability from the wealth tax base of those partners who will pay the pensions (and at any one time it would be impossible to discover who they would be!) Exemption of partnership pensions would, of course, hasten the demise of arrangements which involve capital payments for goodwill.

10.42 If a partner makes a capital payment for goodwill that should clearly form part of his wealth tax base. But if, at a later date, the amount which would be paid to him on retirement or death has gone up, should that increased amount be subjected to wealth tax even though the partner hopes to go on working for some years? The increase represents created goodwill, but the situation can be distinguished from that of the sole proprietor in two ways. In the first place there is usually no valuation problem; the formula in the partnership deed fixes the amount. In the second place there is an *entitlement* to receive the payment albeit at some future date. On the whole we think that the right course, in spite of our advocacy of the exemption of created goodwill, is to bring the capital amount, if any, which would be payable on retirement or death into the wealth tax base of the partners, whether that value has gone up or down, whether created or purchased and whether partners are related or not. (Perhaps the amount should be discounted to its present value but this would be very complex.) The capital cost of goodwill purchased by a partnership from third parties should be written off on purchase, except to the extent that it alters the amount payable to partners on retirement; or alternatively it could be included in the wealth tax base but be written down year by year.

10.43 The Green Paper (paragraph 54) is uncertain about the way in which the capital value of goodwill should be divided among partners and, indeed, some partnership deeds are not very clear about it. Goodwill not recorded in the books of a partnership is frequently, but not necessarily, owned in profit sharing ratios. It may be owned in capital account ratios (which may differ from profit sharing ratios) or partly in one way and partly in another. But, of course, there is no need for any uncertainty if the current value of goodwill is recorded in the books of the partnership and thus reflected in the capital accounts of the partners.

Goodwill—companies

10.44 The value of many shares exceeds the value of attributable net tangible assets; the excess is akin to goodwill. The proposals which we make in paragraph 10.57 would, in effect, exempt such goodwill in so far as it relates to shares in smaller unquoted companies. We do not think that there is any case for exempting the goodwill element in the value of shares in quoted and the larger unquoted companies.

Gifted goodwill

10.45 Logic would require that this should be dealt with in the same way as purchased goodwill, i.e. brought into the wealth tax base of the owner at the value on acquisition less whatever writing down allowance may be given. However, on emotional grounds, we think that there is much to be said for exempting owners who acquire goodwill by gift or bequest and who work full time in the business. That is the treatment in Germany, at least as between father and son, and perhaps also elsewhere on the Continent. That exemption would in any case apply to partnerships which place no value on goodwill if our suggestion in paragraph 10.42 is adopted.

Plant and machinery (sole proprietors and partnerships)

10.46 All five European countries which we have visited value plant and machinery for wealth tax purposes at the same written down value as used for computing capital allowances for income tax. In none of these countries are the allowances so high and the written down values so low as they are at present in this country, where there is a 100% allowance in the year of acquisition for plant and machinery other than cars. In principle we do not think that wealthy taxpayers should have greater investment incentives than those of more modest means, which would suggest that higher values should be used for wealth tax than for income tax. The difficulty is to find a simple alternative. The diminishing balance method involves a large write off in early years and less in later years and never reduces the asset to nil. We prefer the straight line method, but it requires slightly more detailed records. Our choice would be straight line method over ten years or, alternatively, diminishing balance method at 25% which would reduce the asset to 5.6% of cost at the end of ten years, compared with nil by the straight line method. (The diminishing balance would need a 36.9% rate to reduce an asset to 1% of cost at the end of ten years.)

Stock and work in progress (sole proprietors and partnerships)

10.47 We think that stock and work in progress of trading concerns should be taken at the same value as used for income tax; that is, at the lower of cost or net realisable value. The Continental countries also use income tax values which are broadly the same as our cost or net realisable value, except that Sweden now permits a deduction of 60% from cost or net realisable value both for income tax and wealth tax. (In fact there are in some circumstances other permissible deductions for Swedish income tax which can even give rise to a negative value (paragraph 4.48).) There seems no doubt that in the United Kingdom the only practical course is to take the same value for income determination and wealth tax.

10.48 The Green Paper draws a distinction in paragraph 53 between the treatment of manufacturing work in progress which is to be valued at the lower of cost or net realisable value and professional work in progress which is to be valued at cost. We know of no valid reason for this distinction. If professional work in progress is brought into account for the purpose of income determination, it is at the lower of cost or net realisable value. We think the same rule should apply for wealth tax. It cannot be right to tax an amount which is not going to be received.

10.49 But there is a further point. Some professional partnerships do not bring work in progress into account for the purpose of determining a partner's share of income and the income tax which is based on it, nor for the purpose of fixing the amount which is to be paid to him on his retirement. Admittedly it may, but not necessarily, be a factor which indirectly influences the amount of goodwill payment or pension which he is to receive. Again, we think that wealth tax should not be levied on an amount which is not going to be received. The Green Paper evidently takes a different view because its discussion in paragraph 54 of the way in which work in progress should be divided among partners can only arise if it is not taken into account for the purpose of income determination.

10.50 Work in progress of a professional person in practice on his own is something for which the practitioner may or may not receive payment when he retires. He may die, in which case it probably has little value, or he may find that he can only take in a partner on terms which give him no credit for work in progress. It is frequently left out of account for income tax purposes and we think that the wealth tax treatment should follow that for income tax.

Aggregate value of trade assets (sole proprietors and partnerships)

10.51 Trade assets other than those separately dealt with in this chapter, and trade liabilities should be taken at the values used for income tax (e.g. trade debtors). Investments should be valued on the same basis as personal investments. It can be argued that a deduction should be allowed for unfunded pension liabilities (as in Sweden). We think that this should be resisted as a further inducement to the funding of pension liabilities as they accrue. The net aggregate value of a business carried on by a sole proprietor or partnership can then, in the first instance, be taken as the aggregate of the value of the trade assets, arrived at by the methods described in this chapter, less trade liabilities. We do not think that any relief should be given against that value, other than the special ceiling relief mentioned in paragraph 12.27 and 12.30, if the particular business is making low profits or incurring losses. But at those times when many quoted companies have a market capitalisation less than the value of their net tangible assets (on bases which approximate to those suggested in this chapter) there is a case for making a prescribed percentage deduction from the net aggregate value of unincorporated businesses in order to bring the valuation of those businesses into line with quoted companies.

Unquoted companies

10.52 In valuing unquoted shares, United Kingdom practice requires that the following are taken into account:

(a) The rights and restrictions attaching to the shares, e.g. as to dividend, votes, surplus on winding up, etc.

(b) The dividends declared on the shares.

(c) The earnings cover for the dividend.

(d) The amount and trend of past profits and estimates of future profits, involving consideration of the general economic and political climate and prospects for the particular trade. This may involve considering whether remuneration payable to directors etc. has been fixed at arms length.

(e) The net tangible assets per share and the nature of those assets.

(f) The possibility of liquidation or take-over bid (either as biddee or bidder).

(g) The dividend yield, price earnings ratio, asset cover of comparable quoted companies (often difficult to find).

(h) Consideration of the difference in those factors which is appropriate between those quoted companies and the company to be valued.

(i) Recent transactions in the company's shares and an attempt to assess whether they took place at arms length or were influenced by other factors.

(j) The size of the holding and the size and disposition of other shareholdings.

(k) The possible existence of buyers who may be particularly anxious to acquire the shares.

10.53 When selling shares in unquoted companies at arms length, it is quite common to find a big gap between the ideas of the seller and of the buyer, so big sometimes that no sale takes place. This is reflected in the large gap which often exists during negotiations with the Share Valuation Division of the Revenue between the opening value put forward by taxpayers and the opening value put forward by the Revenue. This gap can also be seen in the views of expert witnesses called in the few cases which have been heard in the UK courts affecting share valuations. The general experience is that taxpayers and Revenue move by slow stages from their starting points to a point somewhere in the middle. (In probate practice the agreed figure may tend to be nearer the Revenue's opening figure than to the taxpayer's because the figure put into the initial probate papers is often a nominal one for the purpose of getting probate as quickly as possible.) This process often takes three years.

10.54 We recognise that after a time the process of setting values for unquoted companies year by year would tend to speed up and make easier the process of reaching agreement between taxpayer and Revenue. However, in view of traditions in this country, we think that it would take some time for this to happen and, in relation to smaller companies, there is always the basic problem of lack of evidence in the form of arms length sales and of the wide range within which even arms length sales can take place. These considerations, our preference for certainty, our desire to reduce administrative and compliance costs and the extent to which stylised methods seem to us to have been generally accepted on the Continent, lead us to suggest that, in the first instance, all shareholdings in unquoted companies should be valued by some predetermined arithmetical process. However, we think that the Revenue should, in relation to companies which exceed a certain size, (defined by reference to turnover, net tangible assets or profits) be able to give notice that *for the future* they would require that shares of that company be valued on an open market value basis.

10.55 Before discussing the arithmetical process which might be appropriate we consider whether there should be changes in the method of arriving at open market value either in the event that that method is used for all unquoted companies or if it is to be used, as suggested by us, only for larger companies as to which the Revenue give notice. Paragraph 47 of the Green Paper refers to the fact that the aggregate of the values of a number of interests in an asset held by different people is normally less than the value of that asset as a whole and goes on to say that the general rule will be to recognise the situation as it exists. It then says, however, that—for anti-avoidance reasons—holdings by connected persons (husband, wife, brothers, sisters, ancestors, lineal descendants and the trustees of a trust set up by any of them or in which they have an interest in possession) will be aggregated for the purpose of valuation. This rule is to be applied to holdings of unquoted securities but not of quoted securities. The reason for the rule is, of course, the big gap between the value of a small holding in an unquoted company (probably based on or influenced by dividend yield—the dividend being small or non existent) and that of a substantial holding (particularly one exceeding 50%) which will be influenced by earnings and assets and the psychic satisfaction to be derived from control. We think that this approach is unsatisfactory. It is true that the negotiated value of small holdings is often below their true value except in the sense that they could not be sold at arms length at any higher value to a person who was not related or not working in the company. There are, of course, not infrequent cases where minority holders in unquoted companies are being oppressed by the payment of excessive salaries to majority shareholders or other means, but the remedy for that situation must be in improved protection for minority shareholders (paragraph 12.10). But a value based on aggregated holdings is also not satisfactory; there is not always amity between generations or among siblings and, even if there is, it is unsatisfactory to impose tax on a value which can only be realised by agreement on joint action between a number of people who have no intention whatsoever of taking that action, nor any possibility of doing so as separate individuals. The dissatisfaction will be heightened if the different treatment of partnerships would have resulted in a lower value had the business been organised as a partnership rather than as a company.

10.56 We are inclined to approach the problem in this way:

(a) Estimate the price per share at which the shares would be quoted if it were a quoted company paying the kind of dividends which it would be expected to pay if it was such a company. If the company is not big enough to be quoted, make the further assumption that it is big enough for that purpose. (This may not be an easy judgement but it is less difficult than that implied by the considerations listed in paragraph 10.52.)

(b) Reduce the price by a prescribed percentage because it is not quoted.

(c) In the case of companies which are not big enough to be quoted, further reduce the price by a percentage derived from a scale which prescribes a larger deduction for those companies which have a small capitalised value than for those which have a higher capitalised value.

The resulting price could be applied to shareholdings of all sizes, the negotiations could be conducted by the company on behalf of all shareholders (though not all of them are necessarily liable to wealth tax) and the judgement which has to be made (paragraph (a)) can be based on a wider range of comparisons than is normally available of arms length transactions in the shares of unquoted companies. It does not and cannot remove the judgement which has to be made about management remuneration paid to shareholders who work in the company, but that is one of the reasons why we believe that the open market valuation process should only be applied to the larger unquoted companies. Admittedly, if the company is responsible for the negotiations, it is not likely to be unbiased about management remuneration but in practice the company would be involved under any method of negotiation. Perhaps an individual shareholder would have to have the right to appeal against a value negotiated by the company but only on the ground that it is not the right value for the shares at large, not by reference to his own holding. We think that the administrative and compliance costs of the suggested process would be a good deal less than those of negotiations between individual shareholders and the Inland Revenue on traditional lines.

10.57 We turn now to discuss the kind of arithmetical process which we had in mind in paragraph 10.54 and which we suggest should be applied to all unquoted companies, except those as to which the Revenue gives notice. The Danish formula takes an average of 80% of net tangible asset value, a multiple of dividend and a multiple of earnings. In Danish circumstances that is satisfactory because there are rules or conventions which govern management remuneration. It would not do in the United Kingdom unless we get similar rules or conventions. The German formula adds to 85% of net tangible assets the excess of the distributable profits of the past five years over 10% per annum of the value of the shares (distributable profits being taken by convention as 70% of profit after tax). Norway and Sweden base their valuations (with exceptions) on net tangible assets in much the same way as if they were the assets of a sole trader or partnership so that, for example, in Sweden created goodwill is ignored and stocks and work in progress are written down to 40% of the lower of cost or net realisable value. We believe that valuation by reference to net tangible assets is also the right basis for use in the United Kingdom. As with the proposal made in paragraph 10.56, it can be applied to all shareholders and be negotiated by the company on their behalf. Valuation by reference to net tangible assets would thus lead to the same value as if the business was carried on in unincorporated form. We referred in paragraph 10.51 to the possibility of a prescribed percentage deduction from the net value of trade assets of unincorporated businesses at those times when the market capitalisation of many quoted companies exceeds the value of their net tangible assets. The same concession would be appropriate for unquoted companies which were valued on a net tangible asset basis. It is a matter for consideration whether minority holdings should be valued on a dividend yield basis rather than a net tangible asset basis. Some of the Continental tax systems make the distinction (for example, in Germany the Stuttgart formula is modified—paragraph 5.26). On the whole we think it better to apply the same value to all shareholders but to improve the protection for minority holders.

10.58 With the wealth tax threshold at £100,000 there should not be many cases where delay in submitting accounts would lead to delay in agreeing net tangible assets for wealth tax purposes. The problem could be more acute if the threshold is lowered, but if that increases the pressure from the Revenue on taxpayers for prompt submission of accounts that cannot be regarded as unreasonable. It may be wise to set the time-table in such a way that the valuation of unquoted shares at 1 January 1977 is based on the balance sheet for the company's year end during the year to (say) 31 March 1976. This value may require some adjustment if, for example, there has been a bonus issue or the subscription of new shares between the balance sheet date and the formal valuation date. We notice, incidentally, the proposal in paragraph 66 of the Green Paper that businesses will have to draw up a balance sheet on the date which is selected as the formal valuation date (31 December or 31 March). It seems to us that that will cause intolerable and unnecessary pressure in accountants' and Inland Revenue offices as well as causing delay in establishing the amount of a taxpayer's liability. There would be more virtue in encouraging a trend away from those dates. It is true that the use of the formal valuation date for non business assets and of other dates for trade assets and closely owned companies could open avoidance routes (particularly if there are several such businesses largely owned by one taxpayer and using different dates). We think that forcing all businesses and closely owned companies to make up accounts on the formal valuation date is too big a price to pay for closing those routes; some other method should be found.

10.59 However, we think that the net tangible assets basis should be displaced in those few cases where the articles of association of a company or agreements between shareholders prescribe a price or a formula for arriving at a price at which share transactions are to be undertaken, provided however that that figure is higher than the value derived from net tangible assets. This follows from the argument which we used in paragraph 10.42 dealing with partnerships, namely that there is an established right to a stated value.

10.60 In both Norway and Sweden there is a deduction in arriving at net tangible assets of an amount which is related to the capital gains tax which would be payable on reduction of share capital or on liquidation of the company. This is, of course, very generous as in most cases the liability to capital gains tax is so far away in time that its discounted present value must be small. We are not inclined to suggest such a deduction in the United Kingdom until a company passes a resolution for winding up.

10.61 The Continental arrangements for unquoted companies involve one anomaly which we do not think has been corrected in any way. The position of a shareholder who buys shares at or below their wealth tax value is straight forward enough. But should the person who buys shares at a price in excess of their wealth tax value put that lower value in his next wealth tax return? It would be possible to value the new shareholder's shares at the price he paid for them and other shareholders' shares at net tangible asset value. This may be reasonable in the year of purchase but could cause difficulties in later years. If that is not the treatment, then it has to be said that the excess of the price over the wealth tax value is in effect a payment for goodwill. Unless purchased goodwill is exempt, logic would appear to require that the difference remains part of the shareholder's wealth tax base less whatever writing down allowance may be given. In practice we think that the net tangible asset value should displace purchase price.

Quoted shares

10.62 The Green Paper (paragraph 50) proposes that the same methods should be used as those now used for capital gains tax, i.e. at whichever is the lower of (a) the bid price plus one quarter of the difference between bid and offer price or (b) the mid point between the highest and lowest prices at which bargains (other than those at special prices) were done on the relevant day. This is the method in general use on the Continent and it has obvious advantages. However, we think that the use of an average price during a stipulated period may be worth considering, partly because it is not difficult to manipulate the price of the shares of a good many companies over quite a number of days and partly because recent experience has shown that there can be, within quite short periods, large fluctuations in the aggregate value of all shares. Wealth tax is not based on the proposition that a taxpayer is going to realise the whole of his wealth on or near a stipulated date; wealth is simply a measure of resources. With the aid of a computer it would be easy to arrange for the publication, say in December, of the average price of all listed shares during the year to 30 November. No doubt this would be readily accepted when values are rising but not so readily when they are falling (particularly if a taxpayer buys shares late in the year and the price drops sharply after they are purchased). Even so it can be argued that average values over a period of time are a better measure of resources and hence of ability to pay than values on a particular date. The case for using average values (perhaps even a three year average) is strengthened if the wealth tax is regarded as a tax which is in partial substitution for income tax and so is intended to be paid from income. The case is even stronger if the wealth tax is payable by instalments during the year as in the Continental system. The use of average values would also do something to ensure a more even yield year by year and prevent the big fluctuations in the number of taxpayers liable to wealth tax which will otherwise occur when there are big variations in Stock Exchange values (with consequent administrative problems).

N

Cash and cash equivalent

10.63 This should present no problem. The valuation of national savings certificates will be slightly awkward unless it is decided to ignore accrued interest. (We assume that accruals, for example of dividends and rents, will not be brought in although they are for estate duty.)

Debts and loans

10.64 These should not be included to the extent that they are bad or doubtful (even although they are not trade debts). A more difficult question is whether debts which will not bear interest and will not be paid for some time, or loans at a fixed rate of interest below the now prevailing rate, should be discounted to their present value. On the whole, for reasons of simplicity, we think not and that, therefore, the corresponding liability should be deducted at face value. There is, of course, an illogicality here because the prices of government securities do reflect such a discount; and there may need to be anti-avoidance measures since interest free loans could be used to mitigate the burden of capital transfer tax.

Cars

10.65 We think the simplest course is for the Revenue to publish lists giving prices agreed with the motoring associations by reference to model and age.

Life insurance policies

10.66 Paragraph 55 of the Green Paper refers to realisable value and says that this will normally be surrender value. We think that the complication of having to consider whether realisable value is higher than surrender value is unnecessary. It will be an added burden on insurance companies to have to notify surrender values to policyholders, but it may be no bad thing that greater emphasis is put on surrender values when policies are taken out or that insurance company law is amended to prevent insurance companies attaching artificially low surrender values to their policies.

Purchased life annuity policies

10.67 The Green Paper says that these will be charged at market value. We think it would be simpler to value them at surrender value. Alternatively, prescribed tables could be used but these would not take account of different interest levels (and hence annuity rates) prevailing at the time when different annuities were purchased.

Other annuities receivable

10.68 It is proposed in paragraph 56 of the Green Paper that, if an annuity is paid under a trust deed, the appropriate portion of the capital of the trust fund will be taxed as if the annuitant were a life tenant. Given the proposed treatment of life tenancies, it is difficult to disagree with this treatment. However, consideration will have to be given to situations where the annuity exceeds the income of the trust fund, so that part is paid out of capital. Presumably 100% of the trust fund will be added to the wealth tax base of the annuitant but no more.

Normal household chattels

10.69 If these are to be valued at all they will have to be valued by taxpayers and the imperfections of the process will have to be accepted. In Norway they are taken at a percentage of the insured value. We do not attach any great value to that as a check on the taxpayer but it may remind him of the necessity to revise the insured value! If they are not to be exempt, it is important that the basis should be clear, i.e. whether it is at what they will sell for or what it would cost to buy them in their existing state or somewhere in between (paragraph 10.5).

Pictures, jewellery, etc.

10.70 Assets in this category may be bought or retained as stores of value or for the pleasure derived from their ownership or use, or for both reasons. It includes pictures, antique furniture, jewellery, collections of old coins and other antique objects, stamps, uncut precious stones and gold coins. They are articles which, broadly speaking, do not 'wear out' but they may change in value because of changes in the esteem with which particular groups of objects or particular artists or craftsmen are held, or because they are thought to be or not to be good investments.

10.71 Gold coins are the easiest to value. There is a daily price for them.

10.72 Most of the other objects are ones which, even if their provenance and authenticity are well established, are inherently difficult to value precisely because they are in varying degrees unique and the price in the open market at any one time may lie within quite a wide range. An article may be bought at auction at a high price, but if an attempt is made to sell it the next day it may sell for a much lower figure (paragraph 10.4). In those circumstances how should such articles be valued? One possibility would be to leave it open to the taxpayer to put forward a professional valuation at any time. Alternatively, the taxpayer could be required to value them in the first five years of ownership at cost (if purchased) or at acquisition value (if a gift or bequest). At the end of five years, he would be required to increase that value by the movement in the current purchasing power index or alternatively, and at his option, to substitute a professional valuation (paragraph 10.13). The resulting figure would then remain unchanged for another five years when the process would be repeated. This would, of course, usually result in some undervaluation. Perhaps these values could also be used for capital transfer tax. The application of differential indices to various categories of antiques etc. does not appeal to us.

10.73 This is an area where we think it particularly important that the basis of valuation is clearly specified (paragraph 10.5). If there is doubt about authenticity of an object, then a professional valuation should refer to the doubt and proceed on the assumption that it is not authentic. It is then for the Revenue to displace that view if it wishes and can. There will need to be suitable rules for valuing items which have a greater value as a set or collection than they do as single items.

10.74 These suggestions are, of course, without prejudice to the proposals made in Chapter 14. In relation to articles received as bequests or gifts, or purchased a long time ago, the question of a *de minimis* limit is a difficult one. Taxpayers may genuinely not have any idea of the current value of articles which they own and thus be mistaken in believing that an article is within an exemption of the kind suggested in paragraph 8.38.

Patents, copyrights, etc.

10.75 In general the Continental systems exempt patents and copyright in the hands of the inventor or author (Appendix C). Theory might require that an inventor or author should be charged to wealth tax on the capitalised value of royalties receivable on patents or copyrights, or indeed on the capital sum for which they could be sold or licensed. This is the view taken in paragraph 40 of the Green Paper. But since both royalties and capital sums are subject to income tax, the Green Paper proposes that when the rights are sold the wealth tax paid should be allowed as an offset against any income tax falling due. The Green Paper does not indicate whether the word 'sold' includes licensing nor how the rights are to be valued; is it to be the year by year fluctuating present value of future amounts receivable less the income tax which will be paid on them, or is income tax to be ignored? Particularly if the amounts receivable take the form of royalties rather than capital payments, how is wealth tax on the capital value of royalties receivable to be set against income tax on those royalties? And what happens when there are both royalties and capital sums? If wealth tax is no more than an advance payment of income tax, we doubt if this is worth the very considerable complications involved in attempting to value these rights and in arranging the set off.

10.76 The problem can be looked at in two other ways. The capital value of such rights can be regarded as akin to created goodwill and the same argument for exemption can be advanced as we have used in paragraph 10.36. Secondly, both royalties and capital sums can be regarded as earned income (and indeed are so taxed); they are payment for work done. We refer in Appendix A to the theoretical argument for taxing the capital value of an individual's earning power. It is true that an individual's earning power is uncertain (although long term service contracts do introduce at least a measure of security) and that patents or copyrights are a form of property which confers rights on the owner even after death of the inventor or author. But it is quite clear that the capital value of future earnings from employment will not be taxed in practice and we see no reason to apply different treatment to this particular form of earnings.

10.77 It follows of course that, once the rights are acquired by other persons, either outright or by licence, and whether by gift or bequest or as a commercial transaction, that the holder of those rights should be taxed on their capital value. The valuation problems are difficult and we would favour the establishment of agreed guide lines, e.g. as to the multipliers to be used, the bases for estimating future flows and the treatment of income tax. In these circumstances, there seems to be no justification for setting wealth tax against income tax. The rights are an investment whose value will gradually drop to nil.

Overseas assets

10.78 This could include land, buildings, a share in a partnership, blocked currency, mining rights, overseas securities. Some will present considerable valuation problems.

Liabilities

10.79 In general, debts should be deductible but there may be virtue in a *de minimis* rule whereby individual household debts of less than a stated figure, and perhaps also of less than a stated aggregate, are ignored.

10.80 It will save considerable work and perhaps encourage early payment of tax if no deduction is permitted for unpaid taxes (except for wealth tax on productive assets which has formally been deferred) (paragraph 9.26). For wealthy taxpayers computation of unpaid tax can be a complex exercise; if they want the deduction they have the opportunity to pay the tax or to make payments on account before the valuation date. Tax refunds should be omitted until they are received.

10.81 Should debts incurred to buy exempt assets be disallowed? In Denmark and Sweden, and perhaps on the Continent generally, such debts are not disallowed. In spite of the contrary view taken in the Green Paper we think that no attempt should be made to disallow debts of this kind. Sophisticated taxpayers will always contrive to borrow in such a way that it is impossible to link a debt with an exempt asset.

10.82 So far as we are aware, none of the tax systems in the five Continental countries permit the deduction of any tax which would be payable on realisation of assets apart from the particular case of trade assets (paragraph 10.60). Although the case for such a deduction is strong, we do not think that it should be permitted; the task of computing the contingent liability and of checking the computations is altogether too great, even apart from the question of the method of discounting the liability and of allowing for the exemption on death.

To some extent this may offset the locked in effect which inhibits taxpayers from selling assets which are 'full of gain'.

Conclusions

10.83 The gap between a taxpayer's buying and selling prices should be recognised and the point between those prices at which value for wealth tax purposes is to be fixed should be clearly identified. Valuation methods should be chosen for certainty and avoidance of cost and delay. The value of assets which are difficult to value should, in general, remain unchanged for five years at a time. Consideration should be given to distinguishing when a professional valuer is acting as an advocate for his taxpayer client and when he is acting as an expert as if on joint instructions from taxpayer and Inland Revenue.

10.84 In general we favour a switch to a capital value basis for local rating. Those values could then also serve for wealth tax. Even given that change, a distinction will have to be made between owner occupied property and let property. In the absence of a change, appropriate multipliers of annual value or of rents should be used whenever possible, but professional valuation will be unavoidable in some cases. Farms should be valued, in the first instance, on the basis of tables of value per acre for different areas and different kinds of land. If land continues to have a value in excess of existing use value that excess should be ignored except to the extent that the owner paid a price for it in excess of existing use value. Marriage value of land should be ignored unless it is vacant.

10.85 Created goodwill should in general be exempt. Partners entitled to a capital payment on retirement or death should be liable to wealth tax on that amount, but in other circumstances partnership goodwill should not be assessed. Purchased goodwill should be liable to wealth tax but should be written down year by year. Gifted goodwill should be exempt to owners who work full time in the business. Patents and copyrights should be exempt in the hands of the inventor or author.

10.86 Plant and machinery should be valued on a writing down basis. Stock and work in progress should be valued in the same way as for income tax. Partners in professional firms who are not entitled to receive anything for work in progress when they die or retire should not be assessed on it. Other trade assets should be valued on the same basis as personal assets (e.g. land) or as for income tax (e.g. debtors). At times when Stock Exchange values are very depressed a percentage deduction should be made from the aggregate value of trade assets owned by unincorporated businesses.

10.87 Shares in unquoted companies should in general be valued in the same way as unincorporated businesses, but the Inland Revenue should have the option, if companies are more than a stipulated size, to require future valuations to be on an open market value basis. In the event open market value should start from an estimate of the value of the shares if the company was quoted; from that value a prescribed deduction should be made because the company is unquoted and a further prescribed deduction if it is less than a specified size.

10.88 Valuation of trade assets and unquoted companies should be based on their normal accounting date. To avoid delay, valuations should be based on the accounting date ending in the year ending (say) nine months before the formal valuation date.

10.89 Quoted prices of company shares on the formal valuation date are not free from objection as the basis for wealth tax valuations, but it is difficult to find a better basis. It may be worth considering average prices over a period.

10.90 Accrued dividends and rents should be ignored. Low interest or interest free loans not currently repayable should not be discounted. Lists of car values should be published. Life insurance and purchased life annuity policies should be valued at surrender value, but there should be precautions to prevent artificially low surrender values. Chattels such as antiques which are bought as stores of value and/or for the pleasure derived from ownership or use should be valued every five years, initially at cost or acquisition value and subsequently at the taxpayer's option at that figure updated by the movement in the current purchasing power index or at professional valuation.

10.91 No deduction should be permitted for unpaid taxes (except for wealth tax on productive assets which has formally been deferred). Debts incurred to buy exempt assets should not be disallowed. No deduction should be permitted for contingent capital gains tax.

Chapter 11

Trusts

Possible Methods of Treatment

11.1 It is clear that trusts must come within the scope of the wealth tax, and equally clear that the incidence of the tax should as far as possible be neutral as between trust capital and capital owned outright by individuals. The problem is to find reasonably straightforward and reasonably practicable ways of taxing them which will do justice to the great variety of trusts which can be set up under British law. The practice in Continental countries offers some guidance, but trusts in those countries are relatively uncommon compared with the UK and relatively simple; in the typical situation where the rights to income and capital respectively are divided, the capital is owned by an individual, not by trustees at all, subject to the enjoyment of the income (the 'usufruct') by another individual for the latter's life. In the three Scandinavian countries a life tenant (as he would be described in England) is taxable on the full value of the capital; in the Netherlands on 80% of that value; in Germany on the actuarial value of his interest according to a statutory formula, the balance of the value of the capital being attributed to its legal owner. Family trusts, as we know them in the United Kingdom, are comparatively rare in Germany. They appear to be found more frequently in Sweden, where the capital is attributed to the beneficiaries and taxed as theirs; discretionary trusts, with power to accumulate income, are also possible but uncommon. Where income of such a trust is accumulated the trust is taxable in respect of the corresponding capital as if it were a separate individual. In the Netherlands, if the trust income is accumulated (an unusual case) there appears to be no wealth tax charge.

11.2 This chapter first considers various possible ways of taxing trusts in a

UK wealth tax, and then compares the conclusions with the proposals in the Green Paper.

11.3 The first possibility would be to treat a trust as a separate individual, entitled to the same exemption of the first slice of the trust capital as an individual and taxable on the excess according to the same scale of rates. But this is obviously unsatisfactory, because settlors would then make a multiplicity of small settlements instead of one large one in order to get the benefit of the exemption and the graduation several times over.

11.4 Secondly, trusts might be charged at a flat rate without any exemption of the first slice. But the denial of the exemption would bear hardly where all the beneficiaries of the trust were of small means and would not be liable to tax if they were absolute owners of the capital; and, in a progressive tax, any flat rate of tax must be too high in some cases, having regard to the circumstances of the beneficiaries, and too low in others. A high flat rate (presumably the top rate) could possibly be defended in the case of discretionary and accumulator trusts, on the broad grounds that there is no occasion to bother about the beneficiaries' circumstances if it is uncertain who will be getting benefits and that discretionary and accumulator trusts are predominantly tax-avoidance devices which have no claim to protection and ought to be discouraged. But where beneficiaries have definite rights, e.g. a life tenant, such treatment seems oppressive.

11.5 Thirdly, and as an alternative to a flat rate solution, the multiple settlement device could be blocked by aggregating the capital of all trusts made by the same settlor, charging tax on the aggregate as if it all belonged to one individual, and apportioning the tax rateably between the trusts in proportion to the value of their respective funds. This, however, would still be arbitrary in the context of a tax which is aimed at the wealth of persons who have the enjoyment of capital; the source of the wealth is irrelevant. There could be no justification for taxing the 'small' beneficiaries of a small trust heavily merely because other trusts deriving from the same settlor had large funds.

11.6 Fourthly, trust capital might be attributed to the settlor as if it still belonged to him (the tax, however, being payable by the trust). This would be even stiffer than the third course; in effect it makes trusts ineffective for wealth tax purposes. It raises obvious questions about the treatment of trusts set up long before the introduction of the tax; would it be reasonable to alter the rules retrospectively (so to speak) at this juncture, and if not, how are such trusts to be dealt with? Further, attribution to the settlor is no longer possible after his death—unless he is deemed to remain alive and to possess the same amount of personal wealth as he actually possessed at the time of his death. Failing this, one is driven back again to the arbitrary flat rate—and to the unfortunate effects for beneficiaries with ascertainable rights under the settlement.

11.7 This leads to the fifth possibility, which is to calculate the liability by reference to the beneficiaries' circumstances to the greatest possible extent. With a straightforward life tenancy (or an annuity) it would be practicable to tax as if the trust capital belonged to the life tenant absolutely, as in Norway, Sweden and Denmark; in the case of concurrent life interests the capital would be attributed to the beneficiaries according to the proportion of income to which each was entitled. This seems to be the most satisfactory solution. In the case of a discretionary trust the attribution would be governed by the shares of the income distributed to the various beneficiaries in the relevant year. The fact that the beneficiaries, and their shares, may differ from year to year does not seem to raise any difficulty of principle in the context of an annual tax. As to practicality, the trustees do at least know what share they have distributed to each beneficiary, so that the process should not be unduly complicated for them, though overall it would add considerably to the volume of work for all concerned. Trustees even of a small trust would have to value their fund and make the attribution if any beneficiary was within the field of liability; and, initially at any rate, the capital position of even small beneficiaries of the trust would have to be examined, though they would not necessarily have to make a return of their wealth every year once it was established that they were well below the tax threshold. There would be a rule prescribing which part of the beneficiary's wealth should be taken to represent his interest in the trust; the simple course would be to treat it as the highest part. An additional rule would be needed where a beneficiary derived income from more than one trust.

11.8 The question of confidentiality arises here. Trustees would need to know about the beneficiary's total wealth if they were to satisfy themselves that the correct tax was being charged, which they would presumably wish to do if the tax was payable out of the trust capital. Beneficiaries might resent this, but there seems to be no escape from it—unless the tax were purely substitutive and to be borne by the beneficiary. In that case the trust could be charged at the top rate, which it would deduct from payments to the beneficiary; it would then be for the beneficiary to claim repayment from the Revenue according to his circumstances.

11.9 Should the tax fall on the beneficiary or on the trust capital? It is obviously arguable that a tax on capital should always be borne by the capital, but the answer in our view depends to some extent on the philosophy of the tax. If the tax is purely substitutive and conceived essentially as an extension of the income tax, as in the Continental systems, it seems right that the beneficiary should pay. If, however, the tax is additive and the combined income tax and wealth tax can amount to more than 100% of income, so that they cannot be paid without some recourse to capital, it is a question whether the beneficiary could reasonably be expected to pay, at any rate in the over 100% case, since he does not command the capital. It is true that a life tenant (though not a discretionary beneficiary) has the security of income which his interest in the capital confers, and in fact has a saleable asset, even if he would not normally think of selling it. It is arguable, therefore, that he should contribute some part of the tax himself. But, on the assumption that the full capital value is attributed to the beneficiary for the purpose of computing the liability, it is difficult to see any rational basis for determining his contribution; it would presumably have to be an arbitrary percentage of the income. Probably, therefore, the better view is that, unless the tax is purely substitutive, it should be borne by the capital of the trust. The income beneficiary is then affected only to the extent that the available income is reduced every year in consequence of the reduction of the trust capital. The trust, however, is put in a less favourable position than the absolute owner of capital, who has the possibility of keeping his capital intact by paying the tax (or part of it) out of income.

11.10 Where income is accumulated, the system of attribution to beneficiaries breaks down, except in the case of settlements by a parent on his minor children, when contingencies can fairly be disregarded and the capital attributed to the parent. This case apart, it would seem that the capital corresponding to the undistributed income can only be attributed to the trust itself. The question is, on what basis should it be charged? To tax at the top rate would be oppressive where the fund is small and the prospective beneficiaries have little capital of their own. Such a course would in effect ban accumulator trusts, except perhaps for the very richest families. Whether a ban is desirable as a matter of general policy may be open to debate; but, assuming such trusts to continue, the ill effects could in theory be alleviated by recomputation of the liability, and repayment of the excess tax paid, when the accumulation period ended and the capital passed to a beneficiary. It would, however, be a burdensome task at that stage to compute the beneficiary's liability for each year of the accumulation period; some short cut would have to be adopted, such as assuming that the beneficiary's total wealth (including the trust capital) had throughout the period remained constant at the figure which it had reached at the end of the period. That figure would normally be considerably higher than at the beginning through the growth of the trust capital, and very much higher where the accumulated income ranked as capital. (If it was distributed as income at the end of the period it should be subject to higher rate tax, on some 'top-slicing' basis, in the hands of the recipient.) A price would therefore be paid for accumulation, but perhaps this would not be unreasonable. In addition, of course, the trust will have lost the income from the amounts paid out for wealth tax during the accumulation period, and it is a question whether interest should be allowed by the Revenue on the amount repaid.

11.11 The same procedure could be adopted where the beneficiaries succeeding at the end of the accumulation period became entitled, not to the capital absolutely, but to the income thereafter arising from it. Safeguards might be needed to prevent avoidance, e.g. through arrangements under which beneficiaries with no wealth of their own became entitled to the income for a short period, prior to the capital (or income) passing to a person, already wealthy, for whom it was really destined. It would not, however, be possible to adopt the procedure where income arising from the relevant capital after the end of the accumulation period became distributable at the trustees' discretion; in such cases there could be no revision of the liability. A further objection is that, where accumulation continued until some time after the beneficiary came of age (e.g. accumulation until age 30), it would be open to him to minimise the liability, if he had other capital, by giving some of the other capital away before the vesting date. However, the danger of avoidance by this means would be fairly small unless his wife and minor children—the most obvious candidates for a gift—were taxable as separate individuals; with aggregation, gifts to them would not affect the wealth tax liability.

11.12 It has been assumed in the foregoing discussion that the amount of capital to be attributed to an income beneficiary should be the full amount of that proportion of the trust capital which corresponds to his share of the income. It may be objected that the only value properly attributable to (for example) a life tenant is the actuarial value of his life interest, which is all that he could realise if he sold the interest. The life tenant in Germany is taxed on the actuarial value (in contrast to Norway, Sweden and Denmark, where he is taxed as if he was absolute owner of the capital), and the argument for this basis has considerable force where the tax is a direct charge on the beneficiary, to be borne by him. Limitation of the charge on the life tenant means of course that the reversioner must also be separately taxed in respect of his interest. In the United Kingdom this would give rise to difficult problems, e.g. problems of valuation where there were a variety of reversionary interests, problems of payment for the reversioner, who has no access to the capital. More important, the principle of the scheme could not be applied where the destination of the property after the life tenant's death depended on future decisions or events. The scheme would also break down in the case of discretionary trusts, since the discretionary beneficiary has nothing on which a money value can be put. For both these situations some more or less arbitrary expedient would have to be devised.

11.13 Further, the aggregate value of the several interests would commonly be less than the full value of the trust capital. Either this result would have to be accepted as flowing inevitably from the principle of the charge—with the consequence that trusts would have some advantage over absolute owners of capital—or some deviation from principle would have to be introduced. In Germany the latter course has been adopted, the reversioner being charged on the full value of the capital less the amount charged on the life tenant.

11.14 There would thus be serious difficulties to overcome in the United Kingdom even if the tax was a direct charge on the individual beneficiary. On the footing, however, that the tax is a charge on the trust, the practical problems are less daunting and there is no reason to charge less than the full amount of the trust capital. The current beneficiaries' circumstances are taken into account as a means of measuring the charge on the trust, so as to achieve a result which compares fairly with the charge on absolute owners of capital and is at least more satisfactory than charging at some arbitrary rate.

11.15 To sum up, it is suggested that the tax on trust capital should, as far as possible, be computed by reference to the circumstances of the beneficiaries, the capital being allocated to them in proportion to the shares of the trust income to which they are entitled or which, in the case of discretionary beneficiaries, they in fact receive in the relevant year. The tax should be borne by the beneficiary in the case of a purely substitutive tax, and otherwise by the trust. Where income is accumulated, tax should normally be charged at the top rate but the liability should be re-computed, and any appropriate repayment made (perhaps with interest), at the end of the accumulation period by reference to the circumstances of the persons who then become entitled to the capital or to the income thereafter arising from it.

The Green Paper Proposals

11.16 The Green Paper proposes (paragraph 17) that trusts should *prima facie* be liable to tax at the top rate or possibly the top rate but one, apparently without any exemption of a first slice of the capital, but that there should be provision for abating the charge by reference to the circumstances of individual beneficiaries. Where a life tenant is entitled to the income of the trust the whole of the trust capital would be attributed to him, and the trust's liability would be reduced to the amount which would be payable if the trust capital formed the top slice of the life tenant's own wealth. This is the same as the solution suggested above (beginning of paragraph 11.7), assuming that it would also be adopted where there are several beneficiaries with defined rights to a share in the trust income. Where a person has an interest in more than one trust it is proposed that the combined trust assets should be treated as the top slice of his wealth and that the resulting tax should be apportioned to the several trusts, for the purposes of relief from the top rate, in proportion to the respective amounts of the trust capital.

11.17 In the case of discretionary trusts the Green Paper says (paragraph 19) that there are no beneficiaries to whom the trust capital could be attributed and proposes instead to attribute it to the settlor while he lives. It is not in fact the case that there are no such beneficiaries (unless the entire income is accumulated); as suggested in paragraph 11.7 above, the capital (or the proportion of it corresponding to the distributed income) could be attributed to the individuals who actually received the income of the trust in the relevant year (or perhaps, for convenience, the preceding year). It is true that the beneficiaries, and the amounts they receive, may change from year to year; but this does not affect the principle. The burden of work for the trustees may also be considerable; but the result in terms of tax payable is likely to be more acceptable to them than the Green Paper proposal.

11.18 Attribution to the settlor is defended on the ground that in practice the trustees are likely to exercise their discretion in accordance with the settlor's wishes. There is something in the point. Nevertheless, where the settlement was made long ago it is difficult to justify bringing the settlor back into the picture. As regards future settlements, the settlor will have paid capital transfer tax on the occasion of the settlement, and it seems doubtfully fair to treat him as having divested himself of the relevant capital for the purposes of one tax and as having retained possession of it for the purposes of another. It might be replied that the wealth tax proposal is not a charge but a relief, to save the trust from paying at the top rate; but the *prima facie* charge at the top rate is essentially a matter of presentation or procedure since it is clearly not intended to charge the top rate if it can be avoided.

11.19 The Green Paper itself has qualms about attribution to the settlor, even in his life, and acknowledges that the idea breaks down on his death. It suggests, with considerable reserve, that some relief might be given by reference to the payments of income made to discretionary beneficiaries. This appears to be the same solution as that suggested in paragraph 11.7, and in our view it should be adopted in preference to attribution to the settlor.

11.20 The Green Paper's reservations spring from fears of avoidance. If income was not needed by the trust the capital could be invested in such a way as to produce only a trifling income, which would then be distributed to discretionary beneficiaries, included in the settlement for the purpose, who had no capital of their own. In this way the trust capital could escape wealth tax altogether. The Green Paper proposes that in such a case only part of the capital should be attributed to the income beneficiaries, viz. so much of it as would have produced the income if it had been invested to yield a reasonable, instead of a trifling, rate of return. We agree that such safeguards would be needed.

11.21 As regards income which is accumulated, the Green Paper proposes (paragraph 18) that, where there is an identified beneficiary for whom income is accumulated contingently on his reaching a specified age, the contingency should be disregarded and the capital attributed to him. This is undoubtedly simpler than our own suggestion for charging at the top rate and recomputing the liability when the contingency occurs. We would therefore accept it. The charge at the top rate will still be necessary where the beneficiaries are unidentified during the accumulation period, with recomputation at the end of the period, as proposed in paragraph 11.10, if identified beneficiaries then succeed.

11.22 The Green Paper proposes (paragraph 21) that the tax on trusts should be paid out of the trust capital. This would be acceptable if the tax were additional to the investment income surcharge, but the case is different if the investment income surcharge is an offset against wealth tax. The individual beneficiary who is liable to surcharge ought not to be relieved of it merely because the wealth tax liability comes out higher; in that situation only the excess of the wealth tax over the surcharge should fall on the trust.

Non-Resident Trusts

11.23 A non-resident trust would *prima facie* be liable to wealth tax only on such assets within the UK as are chargeable in the case of a non-resident individual. A UK beneficiary of such a trust, however, if he has a defined interest, has an asset of value which ought not to be left out of account. The Green Paper (paragraph 23) proposes that in the case of a 'genuine' trust set up by a person with little or no connexion with this country, the UK beneficiary should be charged in respect of the actuarial value of his interest, whether it is in possession or reversion. A life tenant at least has the income from the trust out of which to meet the tax (and would have considerable protection against hardship if the investment income surcharge and the wealth tax were alternatives, or if there was a 'ceiling' provision). A reversioner, however, would be in a more difficult position, and might be obliged to borrow to pay the tax or even to sell his reversion. However, it would hardly be fair to load the whole burden on the life tenant, i.e. to charge the latter on the capital value of the trust fund. Presumably the reversioner would be allowed to defer payment until his reversion falls in.

11.24 It is also necessary to consider what the Green Paper (paragraph 24) calls 'artificial' overseas trusts. A United Kingdom settlor, i.e. one domiciled or ordinarily resident in the United Kingdom, might set up a non-resident trust to hold overseas assets, or United Kingdom assets which would not be chargeable if owned by a non-resident individual; or a resident trust which he had set up might transfer its residence abroad. Insofar as the beneficiaries are United Kingdom residents within the wealth tax charge, such trusts ought to be liable to tax on the same extent as if they were resident. The Green Paper proposes that they should be so liable where the settlor was within the wealth tax charge at the time of setting up the trust, and that the tax, if not paid by the trustees, should be recoverable from the settlor (if alive) or from the beneficiaries. There are obvious difficulties in securing payment of tax (or indeed in obtaining the necessary information for determining liability) from a non-resident trust; but the course proposed is probably the best that can be done. We have one reservation; we think it would be unreasonable to make the settlor liable for payment where the trust was set up before the introduction of the wealth tax.

Conclusions

11.25 (1) The tax on trusts should be computed as if the trust capital constituted the top slice of the wealth of the beneficiary or beneficiaries who are entitled to, or in the case of a discretionary trust receive, the income.

(2) Where income is accumulated for an identified beneficiary the same rule should apply, contingencies being disregarded. In other cases tax on the capital corresponding to the accumulated income should be charged at the top rate (or possibly the top rate but one), but where identified beneficiaries succeed at the end of the accumulation period the liability should be recomputed by reference to their circumstances at that time and appropriate repayment made, possibly with interest.

(3) If the wealth tax is an alternative to the investment income surcharge, only the higher of the two being charged, the surcharge should continue to be borne by the beneficiary and only the excess (if the wealth tax is the higher) should fall on the trust. Otherwise the tax should be payable out of the capital of the trust.

(4) Non-resident trusts should be dealt with on the general lines proposed in the Green Paper.

o

Chapter 12

The Closely Owned Business

12.1 This chapter deals with the impact of wealth tax on those businesses (other than quoted companies) of which the greater part is owned by a small number of individuals. (The special problems of agriculture are dealt with in the next chapter.) Such businesses are organised as unincorporated businesses, partnerships or unquoted companies. They may be owned by an individual, an individual and his wife, related persons or unrelated persons. Frequently the owners are also the managers but not necessarily so. Sometimes one owner may dominate the business because of his personal qualities or the proportion of the business which he owns; in other cases control may be more widely spread. The business may or may not constitute the principal asset of the owners.

12.2 In the United Kingdom there is a sharp distinction between the taxation treatment of unincorporated businesses and partnerships on the one hand and companies and their shareholders on the other. The whole of the profits made by the former are taxed as earned income; thus higher rate tax may be applicable but not investment income surcharge. Companies pay corporation tax on retained profits at 52% (or at rates between 42% and 52% if they are small companies). Salaries paid to shareholders reduce the profits of the company and are taxed in the hands of the recipient at his appropriate rate. Part of the corporation tax paid by the company is imputed to any dividend so that shareholders pay only the excess of higher rate tax over basic rate tax, but they also pay investment income surcharge at 15% on the excess of total investment income over £2,000.[1]

---

[1] In the November 1974 Budget it is proposed to reduce the threshold for the investment income surcharge for 1974/5 from £2,000 to £1,000, but the band of investment income from £1,000 to £2,000 will be liable to surcharge at the reduced rate of 10%. For persons over 65, however, the threshold will be £1,500, with a reduced rate band of £500. Examples in this chapter are based on the threshold of £2,000.

12.3 The effect of these different treatments, coupled with other advantages of companies, is that most closely owned businesses are carried on as companies unless (a) they are small (in which case their owners are not likely to be within the wealth tax net unless they have substantial other assets) or (b) they have to be carried on in unincorporated form because of legislation or the rules of professional organisations (and even in those cases professional firms sometimes form associated companies to provide premises, staff and other facilities and then retain profits in those companies to provide for expansion). So far as possible, we have sought to avoid suggesting different treatment for the two different forms of business organisation (incorporated and unincorporated) but the different taxation treatment of income should be borne in mind.

12.4 In this book, and in particular in this chapter, we suggest several ways in which closely owned businesses might be favourably treated. The definition of a closely owned business which we give in the opening paragraph of this chapter is not precise. Exclusions such as property and investment companies spring readily to mind. It may be suggested that favourable treatment should be restricted to close companies (as defined in S282 Income and Corporation Taxes Act 1970) and unincorporated businesses. That does not seem to us to be satisfactory. There are unquoted open companies which ought, in our view, to be eligible for these reliefs; on the other hand, if all unincorporated businesses are entitled to them, they will be used as an avoidance route. Time does not permit us to conduct the research which would be needed to evolve a satisfactory and comprehensive definition, but we think that the aim should be to give the reliefs not solely by reference to size or number of owners but by reference to the severity of the problems to which we refer below. For example, we are aware that there are some large unquoted family-controlled businesses for which an additive wealth tax, coupled with a capital transfer tax, will cause serious problems. Typically, the dividends paid by such companies are restricted, both because the rate of tax paid by their share-holders is high and because retained profits are needed to finance a high rate of expansion. These businesses are of a size where they would have no difficulty in getting a quotation so that the issue raised by an additive wealth tax for such companies and their controlling families is not so much that of finding the cash with which to pay the tax as whether the change from unquoted to quoted status would cause changes in policy or in the terms on which finance for expansion became available, which would cause them to become less efficient, less enterprising or less willing to take risks.

12.5 This is not the place to examine the function and importance of closely owned enterprises in the national economy, particularly as much of the ground has recently been covered by the Bolton Report[2] and a number of

[2] *Report of the Committee of Inquiry on Small Firms*, Cmnd. 4811, HMSO, London, 1971.

other studies, including one by Jonathan Boswell dealing with the rise and decline of small firms[3]. We accept many of the conclusions reached by Boswell in that study; thus in general we believe that it is important to create a fiscal and regulatory climate in which closely owned efficient businesses can be established and grow and in the process fulfil those functions for which they are better suited than organisations owned by the public at large. It is equally important not to make it easy for inefficient management to continue to control such businesses, particularly as Boswell has shown that they have a remarkable capacity for survival.

Special Problems of Applying Wealth Tax to Closely Owned Businesses

Finding cash to pay the tax

12.6 The first set of problems arises when the aggregate burden of taxation on the owner of a closely owned business is such that the profit after tax is not sufficient to give the owner a reasonable standard of living and to provide for additional capital needed in the business because of inflation, expansion or new ventures. Other taxpayers do not have the need to provide extra capital for their business and, if they find that they want to supplement their income, can probably do so by realising some of their wealth. Admittedly the business owner may also have some wealth in addition to his business, but he may feel that the risks of his business are such that he needs to retain that additional wealth; and provision has to be made for the man who has no material wealth except his house (probably mortgaged) and business.

12.7 In theory the taxpayer has several alternatives. He can:

(a) borrow,

(b) defer payment,

(c) sell part of the business year by year,

(d) sell a sizeable part of the business,

(e) sell or close down the whole business,

(f) give away all or part of the business.

In practice it may be difficult or impossible to do any of these things without damage to the business.

12.8 *Borrowing.* The taxpayer's ability to borrow will depend on the security which he is able to offer, the means by which he is able to provide for repayment, the rate of interest which he has to pay and whether he will get tax relief on the interest. His willingness to borrow will depend on his temperament and his view of the prospects for his business as well as his view of the other alternatives open to him. He may find that lenders insist on also having part

---

[3] Jonathan Boswell, *The Rise and Decline of Small Firms,* Allen & Unwin, 1972.

of the equity of his business or the option to convert the borrowing into equity capital. Unless other ways can be found of paying the wealth tax, or the situation alters in some way, the borrowing will increase year by year. Conditions imposed by borrowers may affect the taxpayer's freedom to manage the business or to start new ventures and, even without those conditions, his own attitude to business decisions may be affected. Current interest rates are likely to inhibit borrowing.

12.9 *Deferment*. The Green Paper (paragraph 35) says that if a business taxpayer '. . . had no assets out of which he could reasonably pay the wealth tax he might also be allowed to defer payment of the tax attributable to productive assets, subject to interest (which might also be deferred) at a commercial rate, until the owner sells the assets, retires or dies . . .' This is similar to borrowing but, since it is not borrowing on commercial terms, it raises additional questions:

(a) Commercial rates of interest are at present so high that payment of interest (if it could not be deferred) would be a heavy burden whilst, if it is deferred, the unpaid tax would grow at a frightening rate. Presumably the unpaid tax would be a deduction from wealth (paragraph 9.26) but that would not prevent the tax growing to become a high proportion of the taxpayer's net wealth. What happens when the unpaid tax exceeds a certain proportion of the taxpayer's wealth either because the wealth tax has been unpaid for a long period or because the value of the business has fallen? In what circumstances can the Inland Revenue take action to protect its debt and what kinds of action can it take? And if the Inland Revenue forces the sale of the business what happens if the proceeds of sale do not meet the tax—can the excess be claimed from the taxpayer's other assets? Is he to be made bankrupt if those other assets are insufficient? What happens if a business runs into trouble when some shareholders have deferred and others have not?

(b) If precedent is followed, the rate of interest charged on deferred tax will be a net rate on which no tax relief will be allowed. What will be the relationship between that net rate and gross interest rates on commercial loans? Over the long periods which may be involved, the rate of interest is critical, particularly if compound interest is applied. (The Inland Revenue does not at present use compound interest when calculating interest on unpaid tax.)

(c) What happens when rates of interest fluctuate? For administrative reasons the same rate is likely to be applied to the whole debt. On that basis, tax may be deferred when interest rates are low and the taxpayer then be faced a few years later with a much higher interest rate at a time when it would be impossible for him to pay off the deferred tax. The alternative is for the rate to be fixed by reference to rates prevailing in the several years in which tax is deferred.

(d) Will deferment become the method which is used by decaying management which lacks the confidence to borrow or the ability to inspire any confidence in arms length lenders or investors?

(e) Deferment is only to be allowed if the taxpayer has 'no assets out of which he could reasonably pay the wealth tax'. Will this mean that a taxpayer cannot defer tax if he has other assets which he wishes to retain as a reserve against the risks of his business?

12.10 *Sale of part of the business.* The position of minority owners of closely owned businesses, except to the extent that they can rely on family or similar ties, is an uncomfortable one. For that reason it may not be easy for controlling shareholders to find buyers for a part only of their business. Even apart from the proposed introduction of wealth tax, we think that there should be better protection for minority owners of such businesses, in the hope that that would improve the supply of capital for those businesses and, in particular, lead to greater willingness to support new ventures of which the investor has some personal knowledge. Typical complaints of minority shareholders are that:

(a) excessive management remuneration is taken;

(b) no dividend or an inadequate dividend is paid; and

(c) when a shareholder wishes to sell his shares he finds that under the Articles of Association he can only sell to existing shareholdings at a price which is influenced by the excessive remuneration and lack of dividend and gives him inadequate compensation for the profits which have been retained during his period of ownership.

Hitherto this state of affairs has suited majority shareholders and has not disturbed some minority shareholders (because the minority have, in practice, been adequately looked after by the majority) but, if a wealth tax forces majority shareholders to become sellers of some of their shares, different considerations will apply. To that extent, there could be a tendency for companies themselves to take the initiative to alter their Articles of Association so as to improve the protection for minority shareholders. However, we think that there is a case for amending company legislation so that:

(a) companies are prevented from adopting Articles of Association which give less than a stipulated level of protection to shareholders; and

(b) the procedures by which shareholders can appeal to the courts for relief from oppression are improved[4].

---

[4] The Danish Companies Act No. 37 of 13 June 1973 contains two clauses designed to protect minorities. Section 63—Directors 'shall not act in such a manner that the action taken is obviously tending to procure for certain shareholders or others an undue advantage at the cost of other shareholders or the company'. Section 80—'The general meeting shall not pass any resolution which obviously tends to procure for certain shareholders or others an undue advantage at the expense of other shareholders or the company'. There is also provision for a non mandatory committee of shareholders which may not however include managers or directors (Section 59).

There is also room for more widespread adoption of the kind of protective arrangements which are used by institutional investors when taking minority stakes in unquoted companies. On the whole, most partnership deeds give better protection to individual partners than do company Articles of Association but, in principle, similar considerations apply.

12.11 Given changes of this kind, the practice may become more widespread of controlling shareholders selling small blocks of shares to long term employees of the company. The problem is to ensure that, when the employee wishes to sell, he can do so at a fair price.

12.12 On the whole, institutional investors are not anxious to acquire minority shares in closely held companies unless the company is likely to apply for a quotation in the foreseeable future or is showing exceptional profitability. To a considerable extent, this is due to the difficulty of displacing or improving poor management when that management holds or controls a majority of a company's shares. Even if better remedies become available to oppressed minorities, it is difficult to envisage a process by which existing management could be assessed by some independent body, discharged if found wanting and better successors recruited. If, however, institutional investors, together with other investors who are at arms length from the management, hold in the aggregate upwards of (say) 35% of a company's shares, it is probable that very considerable and perhaps decisive influence could be exerted on management. It may be, therefore, that apart from exceptional situations, institutional investors will develop a practice of refusing to take minority holdings in closely held companies except:

(a) at very low prices which would admittedly influence wealth tax values downwards but would raise little cash for payment of wealth tax; or

(b) in such circumstances that they, with other arms length investors, have a powerful voting influence.

If so, controlling shareholders who lack confidence in their ability to satisfy institutional investors, instead of selling shares, may prefer to defer payment of tax until sale of the company, retirement or death, precisely in order to avoid the threat of pressure from arms length shareholders.

12.13 We have the impression that, in Europe, institutional investment in closely owned companies on a long term basis is more common and extends to smaller companies than in this country. This may be because:

(a) there are many more quoted securities in this country;

(b) investment managers dislike having investments of less than a certain size (e.g. £50,000) in their portfolio;

(c) investments of that size in small companies are difficult to supervise and represent an unacceptably large risk.

It may be that institutions will become more willing to take smaller shareholdings in closely owned companies if a number of them act together to invest on a long term basis in a stipulated company, with one of them acting as consortium leader for the purpose of maintaining contact with the company and of informing their co-investors.

12.14 Given changes of this kind, it may be reasonable to permit unit trusts to invest more freely in closely held companies, or even to permit the formation of specialised unit trusts with the express object of long term investment in such companies. It must be emphasised that a specialised unit trust of that kind would need special rules (as with property funds which usually have power to defer withdrawals in some circumstances) but, given proper safeguards, they could be a way of encouraging public participation in smaller and medium size companies. The main technical problem is that of valuing the investments held by the unit trust in such a way as to ensure that incoming, outgoing and continuing unit holders are fairly dealt with.

12.15 Given the establishment of a number of specialised unit trusts of this kind, the controlling shareholders of a closely owned company may find it attractive to sell a substantial block of shares to several such unit trusts in exchange for units (particularly if this could be done without immediate liability to capital gains tax). The taxpayer could then sell some of the units as necessary to meet wealth tax or other liabilities. It would be a disadvantage of such an exchange, unless special relief was given, that created goodwill would to that extent cease to be exempt from wealth tax because the units received in exchange would be taken at their quoted values including goodwill. It is tempting to suggest that a taxpayer would have the right to tender those units to the government in payment of wealth tax, but there would then be the prospect of the government holding the units indefinitely or, alternatively, of selling the units back to the managers of the unit trusts; in which latter case they might as well have been sold by the taxpayer. But even to have the units held indefinitely by the government may be preferable to deferment or to direct government ownership of shares in closely owned businesses.

12.16 On balance we think it is no bad thing that changes of the kind which we envisage would bring greater outside pressure to bear on controlling shareholders in their capacity as directors or managers. But we recognise that occasionally the existence of substantial minority holdings may discourage management from taking risks. For that reason, we think that directors should be required to take minority shareholders more fully into their confidence than is normal under current practice in closely owned companies.

12.17 *Sell or close down the whole business.* A decision to sell the business may not, in isolation, have adverse economic effects. The new owner may be as efficient as or more efficient than the old. The former owner may simply sell the business to a quoted company for cash or shares and himself continue as manager of it. But there are some businesses which are likely to be less efficient or enterprising under the ownership of a quoted company. In our view it would be a serious matter for the national economy if a wealth tax had the long term effect of reducing the number and scope of closely owned businesses, but it would be no loss if it hastened the demise of inefficient firms.

12.18 *Gift of all or part of the business.* The owner of a closely owned business may or may not have relatives or friends to whom he would like to give some part of the business, with a view to reducing his wealth tax base. But some of them may face the same problem of finding cash for wealth tax. Furthermore, he would still have the problem of finding cash, only now it would be for capital gains tax and capital transfer tax on any gifts. He could transfer shares to a charitable trust, free of capital gains tax and within limits, free of capital transfer tax and thus reduce his wealth, but that may introduce a fresh constraint on dividend policy because the trustees of the charitable trust may feel impelled to press for greater dividends and thus have an effect on the availability of retained profits for expansion of the business. He might consider a gift of shares to a trust for employees.

Extraction of cash for wealth tax from companies

12.19 As we implied in paragraph 12.3, above a certain level of profit, and particularly when profits are needed for expansion, the rate of personal taxation in the United Kingdom is so high that the company form of organisation is virtually mandatory except for those professions where practice through the medium of a company is prohibited by their own regulations or by statute. But how are shareholders in closely owned companies to obtain the cash needed to pay that part of their wealth tax attributable to their shareholdings (assuming that they cannot or do not wish to draw on other personal resources)? Loans to directors are prohibited by company law and loans to shareholders who are not directors involve an additional tax liability (S286 Income and Corporation Taxes Act 1970). Additional salary will attract additional personal income tax and may not be allowed as an expense for corporation tax purposes if it is regarded as excessive. Additional dividend will attract additional personal income tax and possibly investment income surcharge. If, for example, a shareholder has earned income of £10,000 and investment income of £2,000, the additional income he will need to meet wealth tax of the amounts shown below is as follows:

Wealth tax attributable to a closely owned company £	Extra salary or extra dividend (including related tax credit) £	Cost to the company	
		Of the salary £	Of the dividend £
4,000	29,941	14,372	20,060
10,000	53,235	25,553	35,667
20,000	112,059	53,788	75,080

(It is assumed that the extra salary is admitted as an expense for corporation tax although that may be questionable.)

12.20 We feel, therefore, that it is essential that some way is devised of enabling cash to be extracted from closely owned companies to pay wealth tax attributable to those companies without thereby incurring an additional personal tax liability. We suggest that:

(a) The wealth tax attributable to the closely owned company is arrived at on a top slicing basis (if a taxpayer owns shares in several such companies, the division between them may not matter greatly). If it is going too far to give relief for the whole of the attributable wealth tax, then some appropriate fraction could be taken instead.

(b) The amount thus arrived at would be grossed up by adding an amount equal to basic rate tax on the grossed up amount.

(c) Up to the amount thus arrived at, dividends and related tax credit from the company in question would not form part of the taxpayer's income and thus would not be liable to higher rate tax or investment income surcharge.

(d) This deduction would not be allowed to reduce the wealth tax below any floor which would otherwise be operative (paragraphs 9.19 and 12.27).

The result is that the amount thus relieved bears only corporation tax and no personal tax. It has to be recognised that the effect of the deduction of wealth tax from income in this way is to give more relief to taxpayers with a high marginal income tax rate, so that the taxpayer with high income will get more relief than a taxpayer with a business of the same value but with less income (whether from the business or other sources). This can be avoided by giving relief on a bottom slicing basis, but the relief would then be smaller for all taxpayers.

12.21 Relief on these lines would enable a taxpayer to borrow or defer wealth tax for several years and then, when the cash position of the company is easier, to draw a substantial dividend to pay off the borrowings or deferred tax without increasing his personal income tax. But this might cause problems in the company if there was unrelieved ACT (advance corporation tax).

12.22 In order to avoid interaction with the special ceiling relief for closely owned businesses suggested in paragraph 12.27, it would be convenient if the wealth tax of one year serves as the basis for the relief given against dividend income in the following year (see example in paragraph 12.29).

12.23 However, relief along these lines could lead to distortion of dividend policy. There is no problem if a man and wife own the whole of a company; they can take what dividend they like. But with more mixed ownership there would be yet another factor to take into account in fixing dividends; namely the level of wealth tax borne by different shareholders. Because of this, we think that there is a case for amending tax and company law so that loans can be made to shareholders (even if they are directors) without causing any tax liability. Such loans would be limited to the appropriate part of the shareholder's wealth tax liability and should only be made at the time when the tax was paid. They would have to bear interest, perhaps at a rate prescribed by the government from time to time. Even so, there could be problems of equity as between shareholders and also of security for the loans. Shareholders could be required to give the company a charge over shares having a wealth tax value not less than, say, one and a half times the loan. The security could be held on behalf of the company by an authorised depositary (as for exchange control) but there could be difficulty if the value of the shares fell. In principle, this is the same as deferring the tax with interest, but may be preferred by some taxpayers.

Corresponding relief for unincorporated businesses

12.24 We say in paragraph 9.27 that wealth tax should not, in general, be deductible in arriving at income tax but, if shareholders in closely owned companies are to get relief against dividend income for wealth tax attributable to their shares, some corresponding relief should be given to sole proprietors and partners. Since they bear personal income tax on the whole of their profit, the simple rule is probably to say that income tax on the top slice of profit shall be at a rate not higher than the corporation tax rate. The size of the slice would not exceed the attributable wealth tax grossed up by adding an amount equal to corporation tax on the grossed up amount, and for that purpose and for computing the tax payable, the applicable corporation tax rate would be taken as the rate which would be appropriate to a company with an income equal to (say) 3% of the value of the business in question.

Ceiling relief

12.25 Our discussion of ceiling relief for closely owned businesses proceeds against the background of the proposals which we made in Chapter 9 when discussing ceilings as applied to other forms of wealth. There are two features of closely owned businesses which pose problems in relation to ceiling reliefs. Firstly, if they are unincorporated businesses, there is no objective way of assessing the yield on the investment in the business as distinct from remuneration for work done; and, if they are incorporated, the remuneration paid to shareholders is probably under their own control and is not necessarily an arms length assessment of the value of services rendered. Secondly, in the case of companies, dividends are not very attractive to shareholders and if paid are frequently small in relation to the value of the enterprise. This is because distributions of profit often take the form of additional remuneration and retained profits are needed for expansion or to offset the effect of inflation. For these reasons, ceilings cannot be related to profits made by unincorporated businesses or to dividends paid by closely owned companies.

12.26 In considering the following proposals, it should be remembered that investment income surcharge does not apply to unincorporated businesses and applies to closely owned companies only to the extent that they pay dividends. If, in general, surcharge is to be set off against wealth tax, the latter tax will cause a bigger increase in tax burden to owners of closely owned businesses than to others already bearing surcharge on their general investment income.

12.27 Any method which involves attempting to make an arms length assessment of remuneration for services rendered by shareholders should be rejected; it is a very difficult administrative task. But the computation of ceiling relief cannot ignore profits made by closely owned businesses. The solution which we favour is to bring into the calculation of ceiling relief and floor a notional investment income attributable to the business which could, for purposes of illustration, be the lesser of 3% of the value of the business or shares or the actual profits. If actual dividends were higher than 3% of the value of the shares, then that higher figure would be used. We realise that in suggesting 3% we are putting forward a very low figure, but we think that this form of limit (which could, of course, be based on a higher figure than 3%) may be an acceptable way of giving some help to such businesses. To reduce, so far as possible, differences between incorporated and unincorporated businesses, we suggest that in both cases actual profits should be taken before tax and that, in the case of companies, remuneration paid to a shareholder should be added to his share of profits. The floor which we suggested in paragraph 9.19 would be reduced by the following amount:

$$\frac{\text{Wealth tax on total wealth}}{2} \times \frac{\text{Value of closely owned business}}{\text{Total wealth}}$$

12.28 Thus, to put it in extreme terms, a taxpayer whose only wealth was his closely owned business would, if the profit of the business is zero, pay no wealth tax at all. There would be no actual or notional investment income and his floor would be nil. To take another extreme example, the wealth tax (Scale A) payable by a single person whose only asset is a company valued at £1m, with a profit of £150,000, paying no dividend (because it is expanding fast) but paying a salary of £10,625 to its owner would be:

	£	£
Basic and higher rate tax on £10,625		4,275
Unabated wealth tax on £1m	11,500	
Ceiling:		
Notional investment income (3% of £1m)	30,000	
Appropriate percentage thereof (88.54%) (paragraph 9.17)	26,562	26,562

Floor:

$$\frac{11,500}{2} - \left(\frac{11,500}{2} \times \frac{\text{£1m.}}{\text{£1m.}}\right) + \frac{2 \times 30,000}{3} \quad = 20,000$$

(paragraphs 9.19 and 12.27)

	£	£
Basic and higher rate tax on £30,000	(19,525)	
Limit on wealth tax	7,037	7,037
Tax payable		11,312

This consists of income tax on the earned income plus the same wealth tax as would have been payable if there had been a dividend, including tax credit, of £30,000. It will be seen that, with no other assets than a closely owned business, the floor will only become operative at low levels of wealth (paragraph 9.17). If the circumstances were identical except that the profit of the company after paying the salary was £4,375, the calculation would be:

		£	£
Basic and higher rate on £10,625			4,275
Unabated wealth tax on £1m		11,500	
Ceiling:			
Notional investment income £10,625 + £4,375		15,000	
(being less than 3% of £1m)			
Appropriate percentage thereof (88.54%)	13,281	13,281	
Floor $\frac{2}{3} \times$ 15,000	10,000		
Basic and higher rate tax on £15,000		7,575	
Limit on wealth tax		5,706	5,706
Tax payable			9,981

A further example may be helpful. A taxpayer with a salary of £3,625 from a third party is assumed to own a company valued at £0.5m with a profit of £1,000, paying no dividend but paying a salary of £5,000. He also owns other assets of £0.5m on which dividends plus tax credit are £2,000. The liability becomes:

	£	£
Basic and higher rate tax on £10,625		4,275
Unabated wealth tax	11,500	

	£	£
Ceiling:		
Notional investment income £1,000 + £5,000 + actual investment income £2,000 = ...	8,000	
Appropriate percentage thereof (88.54%)	7,083	

Floor:

$$\frac{11,500}{2} - \left(\frac{11,500}{2} \times \frac{£0.5m.}{£1.0m.}\right) + \frac{2 \times 8,000}{3} \quad =8,208 \qquad 8,208$$

(paragraph 12.27)

	£	£
Basic and higher rate tax on £8,000	3,115	
Limit on wealth tax	5,093	5,093
Tax payable		9,368

12.29 Now consider the relief proposed in paragraph 12.20 to enable extraction of cash from the company without extra personal tax. The net wealth tax of £7,037, shown in the first example in the previous paragraph, grossed up by basic rate tax at 33% is £10,503. If, in the next year (paragraph 12.22), a dividend of £7,037 is paid, that, with its associated tax credit, would become £10,503, which would ordinarily be included in total income. But, because it is applied in payment of the previous year's wealth tax, it is not so included so that, if the circumstances remain as in the first example, the tax payable would be exactly as in the previous year.

12.30 If, however, in the second year the dividend was £33,500, which with tax credit becomes £50,000, the calculation becomes:

	£	£
Taxable income (£10,000 + £50,000 − £10,503)		49,497
Basic and higher rate tax thereon		35,708
Investment income surcharge at 15% on £50,000 − £2,000 − £10,503 = £37,497	5,625	5,625
(Since investment income does not exceed a yield of 6% there is no restriction of the surcharge of the kind suggested in paragraph 9.5)		
Unabated wealth tax on £1m	11,500	
Excess of unabated wealth tax over surcharge	5,875	

	£	£

Ceiling relief:

Use as a basis the greater of (a) actual investment income
(£50,000 – £10,503 = £39,497) or (b) notional income,
i.e. the lesser of 3% of the value of the shares (£30,000)
or the actual income of the company before tax (£150,000
+£10,625)   39,497

Appropriate percentage thereof (88.54%) 34,971*
Basic and higher rate tax on £39,497   ...   .   (27,408)
Investment income surcharge on £39,497 – £2,000   ...   (5,625)

Limit on wealth tax (relief = £3,937)   1,938   1,938

Tax payable   43,271

* The floor is clearly not operative.

This gives a net income of £13,888 (£10,625 + £50,000 – £43,271 – tax
credit on £10,503) which can be thought of as:

	£

The net income from salary as before £10,625 – £4,275   6,350
The amount drawn from the company to pay the previous year's
wealth tax   7,037
The net benefit of the dividend of £39,497 (£50,000 – £10,503)   ...   8,064
The current year's wealth tax and investment income surcharge
(£5,625 + £1,938) ...   .   (7,563)

13,888

If the taxpayer had other wealth, the actual or notional investment income
from the closely owned business would, in the ceiling calculation, be increased
by the income from the other wealth. However, it is a matter for consideration whether, if the closely owned business is loss making, the taxpayer
should be permitted in ceiling computations to deduct from actual or notional
investment income on his other wealth all or part of the loss. Our anxiety
in making that suggestion and in abandoning the concept of a floor for
closely owned businesses is whether we are doing too much to bolster the
inefficient business. To counter that possibility there could be a requirement
that in any six year period the aggregate amount of income attributed to a
closely owned business in a ceiling calculation should not be less than, say,
18% of its value (i.e. an average 3% per annum).

Newly established businesses

12.31 We think it is worth considering whether there should be a wealth tax holiday of limited duration for capital invested in new closely controlled enterprises. The difficulty is that of defining 'new' in such a way as to encourage genuine initiative and enterprise without giving relief to old businesses dressed up to look like new. The aim should be to give relief to investors who are willing to back a genuinely new venture or, in some circumstances, revive a dying one. The need for and form of such relief would be affected by the ceiling and floor provisions as applied to closely owned businesses. The case for relief is particularly strong for the taxpayer who puts virtually all his resources into a new venture which makes losses or inadequate profits in its early years.

Valuation

12.32 The valuation methods which we suggest in Chapter 10 would give some relief to closely owned businesses, in particular the exemption of created goodwill (paragraph 10.35).

Other reliefs

12.33 We are not particularly happy about other forms of relief, such as applying a percentage reduction to valuations or applying a reduced scale. To that extent we are in agreement with the view taken in paragraph 35 of the Green Paper. However, it is apparent that in other respects we do not think that the Green Paper goes far enough in recognising the particular problems of owners of closely owned businesses.

Examples

12.34 In table 12.1 we have given some indication of the effect of our proposals on the impact of wealth tax in a fairly extreme but not unknown situation. We postulate that the owner has no other assets or income, that the closely owned company is valued at £1m and, except in example 8, that its profits exceed £100,000. For ease of calculation we have ignored personal allowances. Scale A of the Green Paper is assumed throughout.

International Comparisons

12.35 In some European countries, loans can be made to directors and shareholders so that, to that extent, the problem of extracting cash from a company to pay wealth tax is eased. In Germany, although there is double taxation of company assets (on the company and on the shareholder), the total burden of tax does not appear to create overmuch difficulty in finding cash to pay wealth tax. In that country, many businesses are organised as limited partnerships which would be limited companies in the United Kingdom. As the top marginal rate of personal income taxation is 56.0%,

P

Table 12.1 Wealth Tax Applied to a Closely Owned Company[1]

Example number	Salary from company £	Dividend from company[2] £	Relief given against dividend £	Net income of owner (after tax)[3] £	Net cost to the company of salary in excess of £10,000 or of dividend £	Wealth tax + surcharge after ceiling relief (if any) £
1	Before introduction of wealth tax					
	10,000	—	—	5,725	—	—
2	Wealth tax on Scale A borrowed or deferred. No ceiling					
	10,000	—	—	(5,775)	—	11,500
3	Increased salary to provide for unabated wealth tax					
	69,706	—	—	5,725	28,659[4]	11,500
4	Dividend to provide for unabated wealth tax					
	10,000	59,706	—	5,725	40,003	11,500
5	Wealth tax ceiling based on notional income of £30,000. Tax borrowed or deferred					
	10,000			(1,312)		7,037
6	As (5) but increased salary paid					
	43,453			5,725	16,057[4]	7,037
7	As (5) but dividend paid (the ceiling is based on the dividend of £35,123 as this exceeds £30,000)					
	10,000	35,123		5,725	23,532	7,321
8	As (5) but relief given against dividend income					
	10,000	10,503	10,503	5,725	7,037	7,037
9	As (8) but profits fall to £5,000 (Ceiling based on £10,000 & £5,000)					
	10,000	8,516	8,516	5,725	5,706	5,706

NOTES:
1 See paragraph 12.34 for postulated circumstances.
2 Including related tax credit.
3 Bracketed figures indicate a cash deficit before borrowing.
4 Assuming that the salary is admitted as an expense for corporation tax purposes.

this form of organisation is attractive as it avoids double wealth tax and profits can be withdrawn from the partnership without further taxation. There is no ceiling relief in Germany and ceiling reliefs in Denmark, the Netherlands, Norway and Sweden are based on total income irrespective of source. Profits retained in companies appear to be ignored in ceiling calculations. Both Denmark and Sweden have a floor (paragraphs 4.18 and 9.7).

12.36 In the three Scandinavian countries, the valuation methods used for closely owned businesses appear to be favourable and in Germany the use until recently of 1935 valuations for land and buildings has reduced the burden of the tax. In Sweden, the basis of valuing stock is particularly favourable and created goodwill is largely exempt in most of these countries.

The Dilemma

12.37 Even in these days of large scale enterprises, there is, we believe, a case for small and medium size businesses, largely dependent on the energy, skill, initiative and leadership of one person or of a small number of people working together, using largely their own financial resources, sometimes together with those of a small number of associates. In so far as such a business is efficient, a substitutive wealth tax which permits income tax rates to be lower than they otherwise would be presents no particular problems; in fact the effect could be beneficial. But it is on efficient businesses that the effect of an additive wealth tax on saving could be particularly severe as their successful establishment and expansion requires a high rate of saving and investment. We have little doubt that some people are so strongly motivated that taxation has little adverse impact on their efforts; it is simply another obstacle to be overcome. But on others we think that the effect would be more serious. Society will have to decide whether any resulting loss of innovation and of efficiency is adequately offset by any improved social cohesiveness which may result from reducing inequalities of wealth by an additive wealth tax. This raises the further question of whether inequalities in wealth can be sufficiently reduced by other forms of taxation (e.g. an accessions tax or capital transfer tax) which may have less effect on motivation (paragraphs 17.48 and 17.52 to 17.58).

12.38 A number of large businesses have been built up to the advantage of the national economy in a single generation; will an additive wealth tax make it less likely that that will happen either because motivation is impaired, because the founder has less financial resources of his own at his command at critical stages in the development of the business, or because institutional shareholders are introduced and their presence induces more cautious policies than would be followed by a founder/owner? We think that there is a risk that a wealth tax at either of the rates suggested in the Green Paper will have those effects unless it is accompanied by ceilings or special reliefs for closely owned businesses. The danger is that those reliefs will be indiscriminate or even biased in favour of inefficient firms. But it then has to be recognised that, if reliefs are given to efficient firms, that will result in some *increase* in inequality of wealth in favour not only of owner/managers but also in favour of those who take financial risks in backing them. We believe that such an increase in inequality may be socially acceptable provided that it is confined to those who create wealth by their own skill, enterprise and risk taking, particularly if it becomes more difficult to make a fortune from manipulation of assets as distinct from the organisation of efficient manufacturing and service industries.

Summary

12.39 Closely owned businesses play an important part in the national economy. They could be adversely affected by an additive wealth tax or by one which does not have regard to their special circumstances. Interest on amounts borrowed to pay wealth tax should be deductible in computing income tax. The conditions on which wealth tax can be deferred, particularly as to rate of interest, are critical. Steps should be taken to give better protection to minority owners of closely owned businesses, and to encourage private and institutional investment in such businesses. Shareholders in closely owned companies should not incur liability to higher rate tax or surcharge on dividends applied in payment of wealth tax. Profits of unincorporated businesses applied in payment of wealth tax should not bear tax at any higher rate than the corporation tax rate. Loans by closely owned companies to shareholders to pay wealth tax attributable to those companies should be permitted without any extra tax being payable (even if they are directors). Ceilings should be related to the profit of closely owned companies, whether distributed or not, but in their case and in the case of unincorporated businesses should not be based on income in excess of 3% of the value of the shares or business (except to the extent that actual dividends exceed that level). The starting point of a floor calculation should be lower for owners of closely owned businesses. A wealth tax holiday for owners of newly established businesses should be considered.

Chapter 13
Agriculture

The Nature of the Problem

13.1 The effect of a wealth tax on agriculture is really a special case of the effect of the tax on the closely owned business considered in the previous chapter; indeed, the position of the tenant farmer is virtually identical to that of the owner of an unincorporated business, with the same problems as those set out in Chapter 12. But when we consider the agricultural industry as a whole, particular considerations apply because of four inter-related special features: the ownership structure; the economic unit; the rate of return; and the fixed stock of land. An appreciation of the problems raised by a wealth tax and the consideration of possible solutions is bound up with these special characteristics.

13.2 Whilst the distinguishing features we have listed apply in some degree to agriculture in all the countries with wealth taxes that we consider, it will be helpful to examine these features in more detail as they apply to the United Kingdom.

Characteristics of Agriculture in the United Kingdom

13.3 (1) *Ownership structure.* Agricultural land is predominantly held in individual rather than corporate ownership and often constitutes the vast majority of the wealth of its owner. There has been some institutional buying of agricultural land in recent years (for example, by large insurance companies as part of their investment portfolios) and much land is farmed by tenants of large public landlords (like the National Trust, the Church and University colleges) and still more is farmed by tenants of large private individual landlords; but the typical form of tenure is owner-occupation. This form of tenure has grown in importance during this century, and something like 50% of agricultural land is now owner-occupied.

13.4 (2) *The economic unit.* The average size of farm is generally held to be below the economic optimum and the policy of successive governments in the United Kingdom has been to raise the average size. If owner-occupiers were forced to sell land to pay wealth tax, farms would be fragmented and the size of units would be reduced below (or further below) the optimum. Because most owner-occupiers hold almost all their wealth in their farm, they are unlikely to have other resources with which to pay tax. Because all agriculturalists would be facing the same problem at the same time, it would be unrealistic to hope (as may be the case with sales of parcels of land to meet death duties) that other farmers may be able to purchase the extra land to raise their holdings to a more economic size.

13.5 (3) *Rate of return.* The likelihood that an owner-occupier would be unable to meet wealth tax from his income is increased by the very low rate of return on land. Traditionally the return on agricultural land has tended to be low because it has always been valued for reasons additional to the monetary return to be gained from its use in agriculture—for example, for reasons of prestige, for its amenity value, and for the prospect of gain from building development. But in recent years the yield in agriculture has declined further because of the enormous rise in agricultural land values[1] through the attractiveness of land as a hedge against inflation. The owner-occupier has become the beneficiary of a rise in the value of his farm which he did not seek, which he did not create and which is often an acute embarrassment to him. As a result of this rise in land values, the yield on agriculture has often fallen to a mere 1% to 2%.

13.6 (4) *Fixed stock of land.* Because land is a stock more or less fixed in total extent and because only a very small proportion of that stock, not much more than $1\frac{1}{2}\%$[2], comes onto the market each year, the price is particularly volatile in both directions.

13.7 As already mentioned, the problems of the tenant farmer are really dealt with in Chapter 12. Large public landlords are unaffected by wealth tax. Private landlords, however, may be seriously affected and, as a result of wealth tax, may fail to find the resources to make their proper contribution to agricultural capital—by not maintaining adequately the fixed capital of their agricultural

---

[1] I am indebted to Mr. F. Clive de Paula of the Agricultural Mortgage Corporation for pointing out, in a vivid way, one feature of the agricultural industry which the enormous rise in land values has greatly accentuated. Mr. de Paula writes that 'Agriculture is far more capital intensive than any other industry in the country and furthermore it is almost entirely financed by private individuals'. Whereas the 1973 accounts of ICI showed £14,000 of assets behind each person employed, the comparable figure for agriculture was about £33,000. It is not surprising therefore that the combination of wealth tax, capital gains tax and capital transfer tax is likely to have its maximum impact on those who own and finance the agricultural industry.

[2] *Constraints on Business Organisation in Agriculture* Report of a Working Party of the Country Landowners Association, January 1974. Table II, p. 8.

land. Nonetheless, the agricultural estate is not the primary production unit in agriculture and, for a time, the very large landlord can resolve his wealth tax difficulties without much economic harm by parting with a farm—though this may create problems both with and for a sitting tenant. Moreover, if wealth tax is an alternative to the investment income surcharge, the land-owner will have less additional liability than the owner-occupier who has not been chargeable with surcharge. The difficulties created by a wealth tax will be most acute for the owner-occupier and it is on the owner-occupier, therefore, that we shall mainly concentrate. With the low yield on land and with little income or wealth outside agriculture to pay wealth tax the owner-occupier may starve his farm of capital; fragment his holding; or at best, restrict desirable expansion; and a bad year, in which income drops but wealth tax is unchanged, may be disastrous. Moreover, these effects will tend to be most pronounced for the larger farm, which is the more economic unit.

13.8 The introduction of a gift tax into the United Kingdom as part of the capital transfer tax accentuates the problem because it blocks a method of death duty avoidance previously open to the owner-occupier. In the course of time, many farmers may find themselves trying to meet the instalment payments (plus interest) on capital transfer tax or servicing a debt incurred against tax at their predecessor's death, or on gifts, and at the same time trying to pay annual wealth tax.

13.9 Later in this chapter we shall examine some examples to show in more precise terms the effect of the proposals of the Green Paper. For the moment, let us look at how agriculture fares in other countries with wealth taxes.

Treatment of Agriculture in Other Countries

A Less Severe Problem

13.10 In general the problem posed by a wealth tax for agriculturalists, particularly the owner-occupier, is less acute in the other countries with wealth taxes than in the United Kingdom. Quite apart from questions of the rate of tax and of ceiling provisions, this difference arises from two features of their economies. First, the average size of farm is considerably smaller in the Continental countries and in the Republic of Ireland than in the United Kingdom, as the following figures indicate:

	Average size of farm (hectares)*
Denmark	19.2
West Germany	10.4
The Netherlands	10.8
Norway	17.7 (1970)

	(hectares)*
Sweden	20.0 (1970)
Republic of Ireland	16.4
United Kingdom	34.0

*1 hectare=2.471 acres

Note: The figures relate to 1969 except where stated; the statistics for the EEC countries are from *The Common Agricultural Policy,* 1971, EEC Information Office, London. The figure for Norway is from OECD *Observer,* No. 57, April 1972; that for Sweden from the FAO *Production Yearbook,* 1972.

13.11 Secondly, these countries have been subject to less rise in land values in recent years than the United Kingdom. This may be partly due to their greater success in keeping inflation in general under control; but it owes something in some of the countries to restrictions on the right to purchase agricultural land. Such restrictions apply in Denmark and Sweden. The Danish controls are of recent origin; in the face of the increasing number of purchases of farms by business people, legislation was passed some two years ago requiring that henceforward the purchaser of a farm must live on it, that the farm must be his main line of business, and that he must show agricultural competence (for example, appropriate training). In Sweden the restrictions are of longer standing. The acquisition of agricultural holdings in Sweden has been subject to strict control since 1925 when an Act restricted the right of joint stock companies, associations, and foundations to acquire real estate. More recent provisions have extended and tightened the controls over the transfer of farm property. County agricultural boards have been set up with the authority to acquire land themselves, to promote larger holdings and to prevent land transfers. The position is summed up in a recent publication: 'The legislation favours the ownership of farm land by full-time farmers by restricting land transfers and holding down land prices by preventing, to some degree, financially strong speculators from operating in the market. However, it does substitute some bureaucratic decision for that of the market place and reduces investment in agriculture by people outside the industry. This helps to prevent uneconomic investments that might otherwise be made for reasons relating to taxation, inflation, status and so on'.[3]

Special Relief for Agriculture

13.12 None of the five Continental countries we are considering provides explicit relief for agriculture, with the exception that controls on the purchase of agricultural land (paragraph 13.11), which have kept its price down, might be said to come into this category. But agriculture benefits in three ways. First, from the ceiling provisions which apply in Denmark, the Netherlands, Norway and Sweden. If the rate of return on land is very low, either in

---

[3] S. H. Lane, *A Comparison of Structural Policies in Agriculture,* 1970, chapter 4, p. 24.

general or because of a bad year, these provisions act as a safety net (although in Denmark and Sweden a floor also prevents liability from falling below a prescribed minimum). The one country without a ceiling provision, Germany, has the lowest wealth tax with a maximum rate of only 0.7%. Secondly, from the favourable methods of valuing unincorporated businesses in general, which is common to all countries. Valuation by reference to net tangible assets, often with substantial writing down of stock and machinery, favours the private business and agriculture benefits from this. (See Chapters 10 and 12.) Thirdly, and most important, agriculture benefits from the method of valuing land. In no case is land valued for wealth tax purposes at its open market value. In Norway local assessment boards are sympathetic to farmers (as to owner-occupiers) and valuations which approach 70% of an open market figure are generally accepted. In Sweden land is valued quinquennially, but only 75% of the value is taken for wealth tax purposes and the value remains the same for the next five years. Denmark approaches nearer to open market value at its four-yearly valuations—but is also the country with the most generous ceiling provisions. The valuation of agricultural land under the German wealth tax is particularly favourable, being based in principle on a capitalisation of the potential yield using a multiplier of 18 (paragraph 5.24); the result is a wealth tax valuation which is only a fraction of the open market value; as Gumpel puts it: 'The intention was to subsidise German farmers'.[4] In the Netherlands, unlike the other four countries, the owner-occupier himself assesses the value of his farm; whilst nominally a fair market value, the farmer is entitled to value it as if it were sold with himself as tenant, not with vacant possession. Where farms are let in the Netherlands, the value of the property of the landlord for wealth tax purposes is assessed in relation to the rental.

13.13 The Republic of Ireland envisages a specific relief for 'genuine farmers' by which only 50% of the value of land up to £200,000 will count for wealth tax purposes. 'Genuine farmers' are those who work the farm on a full-time basis and whose wealth consists mainly of the farm. The farmhouse itself will normally be exempt as the principal private residence of the owner-occupier.

The Green Paper Proposals

13.14 The Green Paper recognises that, for the owner-occupier and the agricultural landlord, the abnormally low rate of return in agriculture raises particular problems which could affect agricultural efficiency and investment; and it acknowledges the need for careful examination of the situation in consultation with the industry (paragraph 34). However, 'In the Government's view it would be wrong to exempt business assets or farms from the tax or to calculate liabilities from such assets on specially favourable terms'

---

[4] H. J. Gumpel, *Taxation in the Federal Republic of Germany*, World Tax Series, Commerce Clearing House, 2nd edition, 1969, p. 3628.

(paragraph 34). Thus valuation is intended to be on an open market basis. The Green Paper also recognises that making wealth tax an alternative to the investment income surcharge does nothing for farmers whose income for income tax purposes is treated as wholly earned. Suggestions to help farmers are restricted to a possible ceiling provision, and to the possibility that 'where a taxpayer has no assets out of which he could reasonably pay the wealth tax, he might also be allowed to defer payment of the tax attributable to productive assets, subject to interest (which might also be deferred) at a commercial rate until the owner sells the assets, retires or dies' (paragraph 35).

13.15 Especially when account is taken of the much larger average size of farm (paragraph 13.10) and the particularly rapid rise in the price of land in Britain, it is evident that this proposed treatment for agriculturalists is much harsher than that prevailing on the Continent or proposed for the Republic of Ireland.

13.16 The extent of the problem in the United Kingdom and of the Green Paper's proposals for solution, can best be seen by reference to some realistic examples.

Examples

13.17 The following examples illustrate the position of two extremes: a small dairy farmer and a large arable farmer, both owner-occupiers. Wealth tax rates are taken in accordance with the illustrative scales in the Green Paper without any ceiling provisions. In both cases it is assumed that the farm was purchased some 25 years ago (when land prices were not much more than one-tenth of the 1973 values) and that the mortgages have been completely repaid. It is also assumed that neither farmer has significant assets other than the farm and that the value of these other assets is balanced by debts.

Table 13.1

	Example 1 200 acre dairy farm	Example 2 1,000 acre arable farm
Land value 1973	(£600 per acre) £120,000	(£800 per acre) £800,000
Live and dead stock etc.	40,000	80,000
TOTAL value for WT purposes	160,000	880,000
Farmer's net income	3,000	20,000
Income tax (minimum allowances)	784	10,784
Income minus income tax	2,216	9,216
Wealth tax scale A	600	9,700
Wealth tax scale B	600	17,400
Income minus IT & WT (scale A)	1,616	−484
Income minus IT & WT (scale B)	1,616	−8,184

13.18 It would be difficult for the 200 acre dairy farmer to meet income tax and wealth tax without either parting with assets which would adversely affect the viability of the farm or accepting an option to defer. It would be impossible for the 1,000 acre arable farmer to meet his tax liabilities without selling part of his land or accepting deferment (whichever scale of wealth tax applied).

13.19 If deferment is accepted, the extent of the accumulated burden depends crucially on the rate of interest and changes in the price of agricultural land.

13.20. We have taken 3% as a reasonable 'real' rate of interest (see paragraphs 2.30 and 3.36) and assumed, for purposes of our calculations, that the gross value of the farm continues unchanged. If we postulate a higher rate of interest more appropriate to inflationary conditions, then we should allow for inflation in the value of the farm. However, the possibility cannot be ruled out that a higher rate of interest might be chosen by the Government as a proper commercial rate in a period of general inflation, but that the price of agricultural land (as at the time of writing, and for reasons discussed below) might be falling against the general trend. An owner-occupier might then be saddled with a rising debt on the value of an asset which was diminishing in gross as well as net value. That this is a real possibility is borne out by the proposals of the Chancellor of the Exchequer, in his budget of 12 November 1974, in relation to the capital transfer tax. The Chancellor proposed to carry over to the capital transfer tax the estate duty provisions by which payments due on the value of land could be paid in instalments over eight years; but he proposed to raise the rate of interest on payments due from 3 to 6% for liabilities resulting from a death and to charge 9% on payments due in respect of a gift. It is not clear at the time of writing whether the interest charges will be at simple or compound rates. But these increased charges have been proposed at a time of falling land values. It can be seen, therefore, that the assumption of a 3% rate of interest (compounded) may well under-estimate the seriousness of the problem.

13.21 Table 13.2 shows the effect, for various periods of accumulation, of wealth tax deferred at 3% compound interest on the farm of £160,000 the value of which is assumed to remain constant. The accumulated debt would amount to £19,700, or about one-eighth of the value of the farm, after 25 years. If the farmer then died or gave the farm to his son, capital transfer tax would become payable on the remaining value.
If the rate of interest were 5% (the other assumptions remaining unchanged) then accumulated debt would amount to £7,245 after 10 years and £26,085 after 25 years.

13.22 Table 13.3 shows the effect of deferring wealth tax at 3% interest on the 1,000 acre farm, valued at £880,000. On scale A, the accumulated debt would be £303,600 after 25 years, whilst on scale B for the same period it would amount to £471,800, well over half the value of the farm.

Table 13.2   Effects of Deferring Wealth Tax (at 3% interest) on a Farm of £160,000 (Example 1)

Years	WT + Interest* £	Net Estate £
5	3,100	156,900
10	6,600	153,400
15	10,500	149,500
25	19,700	140,300

Figures rounded to nearest 100.
* In calculating the accumulated debt it must be remembered that each year, assuming the gross value of the property to remain the same, the net value, on which wealth tax is assessed, falls by the amount of the wealth tax debt (excluding the interest).

Table 13.3   Effects of Deferring Wealth Tax (at 3% interest) on a Farm of £880,000 (Example 2)

Years	WT (Scale A) + Interest £	Net Estate £	WT (Scale B) + Interest £	Net Estate £
5	50,000	830,000	87,200	792,800
10	104,400	775,600	175,900	704,100
15	164,000	716,000	268,200	611,800
25	303,600	576,400	471,800	408,200

Figures rounded to nearest 100.

13.23 If the rate of interest were 5%, (other assumptions remaining unchanged) accumulated debt would amount to £115,000 after 10 years and £403,100 after 25 years on the basis of scale A, whilst the corresponding figures under scale B would be £193,900 after 10 years and £635,000 after 25 years. At 9% interest (the rate proposed for payments due on gifts under the capital transfer tax) the accumulated debt at compound interest (offsetting the wealth tax debt but not the interest payments against the estate each year) would exceed the value of the farm after 22 years.

13.24 These figures give some idea of the potential effect of the wealth tax on the larger owner-occupied farms. Nor do they take account of capital transfer tax. It is difficult to weigh up precisely the effect of the Chancellor's proposal for agricultural relief under capital transfer tax. The former estate duty relief of 45% abatement of duty disappears, but is to be replaced by a relief by which the valuation of farms of full-time working farmers (subject to a maximum of £250,000 or 1,000 acres) will be at twenty times what the gross rental would have been on an open market letting; this is instead of an open market capital value. At the time of writing full details of the concession have not been published. In assessing its value to the restricted class of beneficiaries it must be remembered that not only is the value of the farm for capital transfer tax purposes being capitalised by use of a favourable multiplier, but the value also assumes an occupied rather than an unoccupied farm. The extent of the concession at any time will depend on the price of land (which is reasonable). In comparing the position under capital transfer tax with the former estate duty it should be remembered that the rates of capital transfer tax are somewhat lower, but that the owner-occupier no longer has the opportunity to avoid tax (other than capital gains tax) by means of gifts.

What Kind of Agriculture?

13.25 Any attempt to assess the effects of the Green Paper proposals must begin with some consideration of the kind of agricultural industry we wish to see. To some extent that must be a subjective judgement. Our starting point is a concern with the efficiency of production rather than the form of ownership. In the short run and probably also in the long run, we think that this means the same forms of tenure as at present—owner-occupiers, tenant farmers with private landlords, tenant farmers with public landlords, and owners who employ farm managers—but not necessarily in the same proportions. We wish to see an agricultural industry which offers a ladder of opportunity for the able farmer, who may start as a tenant or a farm manager, but who might have the opportunity to become an owner, at first on a small scale, perhaps subsequently on a larger scale. We think it likely, but not easily capable of proof, that provided an owner-occupier can raise the necessary capital, he has a particular incentive to maintain his farm in good order and farm it in the interests of long-term efficiency, so we would wish to see owner-occupation continue as a major form of tenure.

13.26 We would not claim any special knowledge of agricultural economics, but from the more obvious indices, such as output per man, British agriculture would appear to have attained a relatively high standard of efficiency with its present structure of tenure and ownership. Nonetheless we are concerned that the enormous price rise in agricultural land in recent years has made it almost impossible for an able farmer with no initial capital to work his way to ownership. This in turn means that by far the largest proportion of owners became so by inheritance[5] or gift—but this will become more difficult under capital transfer tax. Often the son of a farmer will have the interest, and acquire the training and experience, to become an able farmer; but there is nothing in the process of selection by inheritance that guarantees that sons of owner-occupiers will always be the best farmers.

---

[5] In the year ending 31 March 1974, only 10% of the loans of the Agricultural Mortgage Corporation were for land purchase to newcomers setting up in farming and a further 6% to sitting tenants.

13.27 What effects are the Green Paper proposals likely to have? Crucial is the effect on the price of agricultural land. The abolition of the estate duty concession under the capital transfer tax and its replacement by a concession restricted to full-time working farmers and the proposal to include agricultural land in the wealth tax base at its open market valuation, can be expected to bring down the price of agricultural land. We noted (paragraph 13.6) the volatility in the price of land arising from its fixed stock; comparatively small changes in the supply coming on the market, or in the demand for land, have a large effect on price. That part of the stock of agricultural land held by non-farmers as a means of mitigating death duties will now gradually be released; at the same time the combined effect of wealth tax and capital transfer tax are bound to result in more land coming onto the market each year.

13.28 Before the announcement of wealth tax and capital transfer tax in March 1974, there were already signs of a decline in land prices from their previous peak; since then that decline has continued and possibly become more pronounced and the withdrawal of the estate duty concession and the threat of a wealth tax must be regarded as contributory factors. It must be recognised that, in this way, the new taxes could bring long term benefit to the industry. A steep fall in the price of agricultural land would take many farmers right out of the wealth tax range; and at the same time would make it much easier for the able farmer with little capital to become an owner.

13.29 There are two main difficulties about this possible solution to the problem. First we cannot rely on the price of agricultural land falling sufficiently; it would have to fall very far to remove the burden from the larger owner-occupier. As we have indicated (paragraph 13.5) agricultural land is sought after for a variety of reasons; in particular, holding land is a safeguard against the worst effects of hyper-inflation. As long as the threat of galloping or runaway inflation hangs over the economy, it is difficult to see land prices dropping as steeply as would be necessary, against the trend of prices in general.

13.30 Secondly, even if the fall in the price of agricultural land was steep and rapid enough to take many owner-occupiers below the wealth tax threshold and to reduce the wealth tax liability of the remainder to manageable proportions, such a price fall would itself create serious problems. It would mean a huge and sudden reduction in the wealth of present landowners; and whilst this would not seem unjust where the present owners had themselves been enriched by the fortuitous rise in land prices, it would be hard, perhaps catastrophic, for those, particularly those owner-occupiers, who had bought at the inflated prices of recent years. Not only would inequities result; such a price fall could lead to a succession of bankruptcies of those who had bought with borrowed money.

13.31 We must thus recognise that without a very steep and rapid fall in land prices the wealth tax threatens the fragmentation of farms and a decline in agricultural investment; whilst if prices do fall quickly and very steeply, the industry will be faced with a very difficult transitional period.

Possible Remedial Measures

13.32 In the light of this analysis, let us briefly consider some possible measures for easing the situation, including those suggested in the Green Paper.

13.33 *1. Complete exemption for agriculture.* The Green Paper is surely right in rejecting exemption for agriculture; it would create an artificial situation, encourage tax avoiding investment in land and farms and push up prices.

13.34 *2. A ceiling provision.* A ceiling on the lines of those in other Continental countries would provide some sort of safety net; the case is particularly strong on the same grounds as those by which state support to the agricultural industry has traditionally been justified: that its products often have a long gestation period (particularly in stock breeding and forestry); that the demand for agricultural products is inelastic and the price therefore volatile (witness the fluctuations in the market price of beef in the United Kingdom 1973–74); and that, even in modern times, the farmer is still heavily dependent on the weather. Whereas misfortune which reduces a farmer's income at least reduces his income tax liability, without special provision his wealth tax liability remains unchanged.

13.35 The question of ceiling relief is considered in Chapters 9 (paragraphs 9.7-9.21) and 12 (paragraphs 12.25-12.31) and we have proposed a rather different form from that on the Continent. We consider that the ceiling relief, including floor provisions, that we have proposed for the closely owned business would be appropriate for farmers.

13.36 *3. Deferred payment.* The Green Paper proposal to defer payment of wealth tax until the owner voluntarily parts with the land or dies is some help; but many farmers may not find it attractive and may prefer to sell parts of their land or to starve their farm of capital. We are also concerned about the psychological effect on the farmer who sees his annual burden of debt mounting at an increasing rate. A debt can be a spur to endeavour when the debtor can see the possibility of eliminating it by his own efforts; but the wealth tax debt is not of this kind and seems to us more likely to generate despair or recklessness, than productive effort. Deferment is probably the best solution for meeting the problems of payment posed by growing timber. In any proposal for deferment, the rate of interest charged is a critical factor.

13.37 *4. Relief through methods of valuation.* As we have seen (paragraph 13.12) low valuation is the main way in which the wealth tax is eased for farmers on the Continent. Some of the proposals of chapter 10 would do something to help all or some farmers, e.g. the method of valuing business assets and the proposal that 'hope values' should be ignored unless realised (paragraph 10.31). Apart from the level of values, for reasons of certainty there is much to be said for a cadastral value on the basis of quinquennial assessments or a valuation procedure more akin to the German, based on standardised values for different kinds of land. It would be entirely proper, in view of the volatility of land prices, for such valuations to be cautious. There is, too, a certain logic in the Dutch method of valuing an owner-occupied farm at a figure appropriate to a farm without vacant possession; some farmers might indeed wish to meet their wealth tax liability by selling their farm or part of it and remaining as tenants (paragraph 13.40.6).

13.38 Another possibility is to value the farm for wealth tax purposes on the basis of the capitalised return—not of each individual farm, but, like the German, of the potential yield (paragraph 5.24). (The method the Chancellor has proposed for providing relief for full-time working farmers under capital transfer tax is not dissimilar to this.) There would, indeed, be a certain justice in this treatment for 'genuine' farmers; to them the rise in the value of their farm is an embarrassment arising from events outside their control. Such a method, however, would be a relief of major proportions and ought therefore to be tied to a restriction i.e. that the sale of the property should be subject to a tax penalty—perhaps the difference (with accumulated interest) between the wealth tax they would have paid at an open market value and the wealth tax actually paid. In principle the farmers ought neither to gain nor lose from the effect of external factors on land prices; they cannot expect to have it both ways.

13.39 *5. Restrictions on the purchase of land.* If inflation continues to make land attractive to the non-agriculturalist, at least for a period there is a case for restricting the purchase of agricultural land to 'genuine' farmers in order to keep prices down, after the manner of the Swedes and the Danes (paragraph 13.11). But such a restriction might not be an unmixed advantage; it would exclude the industrialist or financier who has sometimes brought new capital into the industry and has tried to apply new management methods.

13.40 *6. Schemes for joint ownership.* The company form of ownership has never really caught on in agriculture; but schemes for joint ownership of land, which still left the running of the farm in a single pair of hands, would much ease the difficulties created by a wealth tax. One of the most promising is the 'co-ownership plan' being considered by the Agricultural Mortgage Corporation. Under this plan the AMC propose to set up a unit trust; it is expected that the trust would attract investments from pension funds and would use the money to purchase undivided shares in the ownership of farms, which would simultaneously be leased back to the original farmer-landowner on a full agricultural tenancy. The share purchased would normally be between 10 and 49% of the farm; the sale would be at a realistic market price but reflecting the fact that the property would thereafter be subject to a tenancy. The normal rules of joint ownership would apply and each party would have first right of purchase if the other wanted to sell. Further, the farmer would have an option to purchase the trust's share at the end of the tenth and every succeeding fifth year—giving guaranteed opportunities to revert to full land-owner status.

13.41 Such schemes (which could perhaps be extended to permit investment by private individuals as well) should be encouraged as a means of over-coming the problems of wealth tax payments in a way which does not fragment farms nor leave the farmers short of working capital. Paradoxically the various proposals for capital taxation have, if anything, increased the potential demand for the AMC scheme whilst, at the same time, making it more difficult to attract the investment which is essential to operate it.

13.42 *7. Land nationalisation.* One possibility would be that payment of wealth tax should be in kind and the state should become the joint owner and landlord of farms. At the rates of wealth tax and capital transfer tax proposed, this would be likely to mean the gradual nationalisation of agricultural land. Whilst eminent economists of the past and the present[6] have advocated land nationalisation, we consider that the case for it must be debated on its merits; it would be wrong for such a major change to be introduced as a by-product of a tax. We therefore favour the kind of purchase and leaseback arrangements which might be made through the Agricultural Mortgage Corporation and private institutions.

Summary and Conclusions

13.43 Because of the special characteristics of agriculture—the largely in-dividual ownership, the low rate of return and the fixed stock and volatile price of its most important factor of production, the application of a wealth tax raises particular problems and threatens the efficiency of the industry. The wealth tax, the capital transfer tax and the abolition of agricultural relief on death for landowners who are not full time working farmers are bound to reduce the price of agricultural land (at least relatively to what it would have been); but it is uncertain by how much. A big price reduction would benefit the industry in the long run but would cause serious transitional difficulties. Uncertainty about the extent of the price fall makes it difficult to offer firm recommendations. As a minimum we recommend that the valuation of land and farms should be 'cautious' and by standardised methods; and that schemes for joint ownership of land, like that proposed by the AMC, should be encouraged. There is also a particularly strong case in agriculture for the application of a ceiling provision. Further, the Govern-

---

[6] J. Brocklebank, N. Kaldor, J. Maynard, R. Nield and O. Stutchbury, *The Case for Nationalising Land,* The Campaign for Nationalising Land, 1973.

Q

ment should stand ready to take additional action in the light of what happens
to land prices; this might be the temporary imposition of restrictions on the
right to purchase agricultural land if its price is being kept up by demand for
non-agricultural reasons; or it might be measures to cushion the effect of a large
and rapid price fall.

Chapter 14

Works of Art and Historic Houses

Works of Art

14.1 The term, 'work of art', is taken to include pictures, prints, sculpture, ceramics, gold and silver work, and antiques of all kinds, which are of such a quality that a museum (whether national, local authority or university) might wish to display them regularly, or on occasion as part of an exhibition. Similar considerations apply to privately-owned objects of national, scientific or historic interest, including manuscripts, books, collections of pamphlets and family archives; and references to works of art in this chapter should be taken to include such objects.

The Case for Inclusion within the Wealth Tax Base

14.2 On grounds of horizontal equity, efficiency in resource use and the reduction of inequality, there is a clear case for including works of art within the wealth tax base. They are saleable assets; they thus confer on their owner the advantages associated with capital: security, independence and opportunity. They increase their owner's taxable capacity as much as the Maharajah's jewels[1]; on grounds of horizontal equity, therefore, they should equally be subject to tax. Also, works of art such as paintings may prove to be a lucrative investment offering capital gain and avoiding income tax. It can be argued that they thus attract investment away from income-yielding assets and they would prove a still more attractive form of investment if they were exempted from a wealth tax. Finally, to omit them from the tax base would reduce the effectiveness of a wealth tax in diminishing inequality (either in the

[1] See paragraph 1.13.

limited or the more radical sense). Exempting works of art would mean both that some wealthy persons would not pay wealth tax on a significant part of their wealth; and that on the remainder they would pay at a lower average rate.

14.3 It is no adequate answer to the case for inclusion to say that governments, on cultural and educational grounds, have sought to encourage art and therefore works of art should be exempt; even if we accept the premiss, it is not clear that a simple exemption would 'encourage art'. An exemption would have the effect of raising the price of works of art relatively to other forms of asset. This would do little to help living artists, for most important works of art are the products of dead artists and exempting works of art would simply put money into the pockets of present owners, many of whom have already seen a large appreciation in their value. Indeed, it could be plausibly argued that art, or at least the enjoyment of it, would be promoted by *including* works of art within the tax base and handing that part of the proceeds of the tax to public art galleries. Including them would tend to lower prices and the public galleries, with more funds at their disposal and lower market prices, could make additional purchases for public display.

The Peculiarities of Works of Art

14.4 Whilst a crude exemption has little to commend it, national concern for promoting art on educational and cultural grounds must be taken into account along with the social and economic aims of a wealth tax. It is, indeed, very doubtful if works of art should be treated as if they were identical with any other asset. The clue to an appropriate tax policy may be found from four particular characteristics they possess.

14.5 First, works of art are very inelastic in supply; they constitute a more or less fixed stock. If they are exempt and their price rises, few resources are likely to be diverted from current output into the 'art industry'; although there may be some marginal increase in the number of persons working in the industry (in selling, restoring, or perhaps even searching out 'old masters'), the number of masterpieces is more or less static and a higher price is not likely to do much to increase the number of persons trying to make a living from works of art. Artists tend to be singularly unmoved by economic considerations and artistry of the quality to produce masterpieces rests on genius and not on the working of the laws of supply and demand. Once this is realised, the argument for taxing works of art to prevent investment distortion is seen as of little importance. If Mr. 'A' buys a Picasso from Mr. 'B' for £500,000, then Mr. 'A' has half a million pounds less to invest but Mr. 'B' has half a million more. The purchase has made little or no claim on current real resources. (The situation is thus different from most other forms of investment. If 'A' buys a machine at £500,000 from 'B', that machine has used up current resources of steel, skilled labour and other machines). 'B' is as likely to use the £500,000 to invest in productive assets as was 'A'. Thus, the argument that works of art must be included in the tax base to secure efficiency in resource use is a weak one.

14.6 The characteristic of inelastic supply might seem to strengthen the argument of paragraph 14.3 that works of art should be included within the tax base and the proceeds given to the public galleries; because of the inelastic supply it might be expected that the price of works of art would fall substantially if a wealth tax was introduced; owners would be disposing of works of art to pay the tax or to hold income-yielding assets and few private buyers would be forthcoming. Then the galleries, with their additional resources, might have been expected to add handsomely to their collections. But this ignores the second characteristic: works of art are sold very much in an international market. If all countries adopted wealth taxes which included works of art within the tax base, the argument would be valid. But where one country alone does so, the forced disposal of private works of art would depress the international market price but little; the additional funds at the disposal of public galleries in one country would not go far; and, barring export restrictions, the most likely result would be a large-scale exodus of works of art from the country with the wealth tax—in short the dissipation of the national heritage.

14.7 The third characteristic of works of art is that, in economist's terms, the average cost of consumption is very low and the marginal cost of consumption is nil. Expressed in more ordinary language, the enjoyment of a work of art is derived from looking at it and, however many people look at it, the work of art is not used up. There is, of course, some cost in arranging for the public viewing of a painting or other art treasure; viewing times have to be made known, the painting has to be safeguarded, the public properly controlled and the dirt and debris, created by the presence of the public, cleared up. The fact remains that the painting itself is not used up however much it is consumed. Herein lies the main guide-line for public policy—to maximise consumption. Surely the encouragement of the consumption or enjoyment of works of art ought to be the kernel of any national policy to promote art. It might even be expected that thereby more people would come to appreciate the beauties of art who might themselves wish to possess some modest original works, thus helping living artists.

14.8 Finally, there is a fourth characteristic related to the third. The full enjoyment of some works of art rests on seeing them in the appropriate setting; this may sometimes be a museum; but it may also be the portrait gallery of an historic mansion; or antique furniture in the rooms for which it was designed; or a unique private collection seen as a collection, not as individual dispersed pieces.

Some Practical Considerations

14.9 There are further considerations to be taken into account in formulating a wealth tax policy on works of art. First is the practical problem of administration. There is a problem of disclosure—of the reluctance of owners to reveal the existence of works of art—especially if they see the tax as unjust[2]. Major works of art could probably not be hidden but minor works could easily be so. Perhaps even more serious is the problem of valuation. The most expert valuer cannot value a major work of art with precision, even when the identity of the artist is not in doubt; in other cases valuation may be complicated by queries about authenticity. There have been big discrepancies in recent months between expected and realised values at Sotheby's auctions. Mr. Denis Mahon, art historian and trustee of the National Gallery, in a letter to *The Economist*,[3] gives some telling examples. On 27 June 1974, a drawing by Sebastiano del Piombo, estimated by Sotheby's to fetch between £5,000 and £10,000, was in fact sold for £16,000. On 25 June, Sotheby's withdrew from sale a drawing, estimated to fetch £6,000 to £8,000, when it was pointed out that it was not, as they had believed, an authentic Guercino. The same letter points out not only the uncertainty of valuation but also that investment in works of art is by no means always profitable: a Paduan view by Canaletto, bought for £105,000 in 1969, could only raise a maximum bid of 90,000 guineas on 25 June 1974. Given this situation, there is an obvious risk in buying objects of art as an investment, which lessens the disadvantage of exemption; further, the uncertainty, when the experts can be a hundred per cent or more out in their valuations (even when the authenticity is not in doubt), could generate considerable inequity if works of art were included within the wealth tax base.

14.10 Secondly, there is a psychological consideration of much practical importance. Acquisitions by the public galleries have depended to no small extent on the goodwill of artists and art owners. Something like three-fifths of the pictures in the National Gallery in the United Kingdom were either given or bequeathed. Taxing works of art under a wealth tax would prejudice what the Duke of Grafton referred to as the 'whole delicately poised collaboration between private owners and the Government'.[4] It could well generate what Musgrave has called 'the spite effect'[5] of taxation. The art owner who planned to leave his collection 'to the nation' may be so enraged at what he perceives as gross injustice that he will sell abroad instead.

A Policy of Conditional Exemption

14.11 Let us sum up the considerations relevant to policy. There is an argu-

---

[2] See Chapter 16, especially paragraph 16.21.
[3] 3 August 1974.
[4] House of Lords, *Hansard*, 26 June 1974, col. 1484.
[5] R. A. Musgrave, *The Theory of Public Finance*, McGraw-Hill, 1959, p. 240.

ment for including works of art within the wealth tax base because, like other assets, they can be converted into purchasing power. But, unlike other assets, they embody a cultural heritage which governments have sought to preserve. Further, they have certain very relevant characteristics: they comprise a more or less fixed stock; the costs of consumption are nil or negligible; and often full enjoyment of works of art requires a particular setting. Added to that are the practical problems of administration and the possible loss to the nation as a result of alienating the art fraternity.

14.12 Where do these considerations lead? We suggest that they amount to a strong argument for conditional exemption—exemption conditional on public access. Works of art exist to be admired, experienced and enjoyed. For as long as the private owner meets certain conditions designed to ensure this objective he should be exempt. If not, then he should be taxed on his works of art (in accordance with the valuation principles set forth in Chapter 10). This procedure best meets the prime policy requirement of maximising consumption; provides opportunity for works of art to be shown in the most appropriate setting; is likely to meet with the understanding of the art fraternity, provided the principle of conditional exemption is reasonably interpreted; and at least reduces the size of the valuation problem by restricting it to the works of art of those unable or unwilling to meet the conditions. It also recognises the case for including works of art within the tax base, for the man who buys art simply as an investment has either to allow public access or have the work of art included as taxable wealth.

14.13 The detailed application of the policy needs careful treatment and the requirement of public access should be taken to cover a number of possible forms.

1. Public display in the house of the owner: this would usually be the best method where the owner had a substantial collection, or where the owner's house, perhaps an historic mansion, provided the appropriate setting for the work of art. To benefit from the exemption, the owner would have to undertake to abide by certain conditions such as: to open the appropriate part of his mansion to the public for a minimum number of hours per year; to take action to ensure that the information on opening times was made known to the interested public; and to meet certain regulations about entrance fees to ensure that the principle of public access was not defeated by prohibitive charges.

2. Lending the work of art to a museum: this would be appropriate for isolated works of art; or for works which could best be displayed at exhibitions or similar collections; or where the owner could not readily, or did not want, to open his house to the public. It would require rules about a maximum period per year (or perhaps per series of years, say six months in three years) during which the owner must be prepared to

lend the work of art. A willingness to lend would be sufficient to ensure exemption even though the offer was not taken up in the specified period.

3. Providing access on request to reputable scholars or experts: this would be the appropriate method for a work of art (or an object of scientific or historical interest) of an esoteric nature, where the general public would not be interested but specialists, researchers and the like, would be.

14.14 Given an acceptance of the principle, the detailed rules could be worked out between government officials and an appropriate committee representing the interests both of owners and of public galleries and museums; such a committee might also decide whether a particular work of art ought to be in category 2 or 3; and could perhaps also act as an informal appeal body. In applying the regulations under category 2 (the loan of works of art) it would be necessary to introduce a register and a central 'clearing house' which would receive requests from public museums and galleries to borrow the works of art, would keep a record of the length of time each work had been loaned, and how much unexpired loan period remained; it would also adjudicate, where necessary, between rival claimants for loans.

Practice in Other Countries

14.15 Of the five countries whose wealth taxes we have examined most closely, three, Denmark, Sweden and the Netherlands, completely exempt works of art. Denmark holds to the principle that no personal property inside the house is liable to wealth tax (unless used for business purposes). Sweden, whilst not offering such a wide exemption, specifically excludes both art objects (as household goods) and collections; the recent Swedish Capital Tax Committee considered whether works of art should be brought within the ambit of the tax, especially as the purchase of art objects was widely believed to be used for tax avoidance; the Committee decided against inclusion on administrative grounds—the difficulties of disclosure and valuation. In the Netherlands the unconditional exemption was justified on the grounds of the need to protect the national heritage and the difficulties of valuation.

14.16 In Germany, art treasures and collections up to a value of DM 20,000 (about £3,300) per person are disregarded, but if their value is in excess of this figure, then the whole value is taxable. However, works of art may escape duty altogether if they fulfil the requirements laid down for items of artistic, historical or scientific interest (paragraph 14.30). It should also be remembered that the German wealth tax is levied at a flat 0.7%. An interesting exemption in the German tax, of art objects created by German artists who were still living or who had died within the previous fifteen years, was rescinded in 1974 because of an EEC ruling.

14.17 In Norway, works of art are included with household goods. The first

Nkr 40,000 (£3,075) of household goods is exempt; thereafter they are taxable (including works of art) but the method of valuing all household goods is such that, if a work of art is insured for its full market value, not more than 40% of that value will be included in the owner's wealth for wealth tax purposes (paragraph 8.30).

14.18 In practice it is clear that in Germany and Norway the provisions for taxing works of art are difficult to enforce. We were left with the strong impression that in both countries there was much undetected under-reporting and under-valuation of works of art.

14.19 In the Republic of Ireland, the proposals for the treatment of works of art under their wealth tax would appear to coincide precisely with our own recommendations. The Irish White Paper on *Capital Taxation* records: 'Important works of art and other objects of national, scientific, historic or artistic interest would be exempt if they remain in the country and the public have reasonable access to them' (paragraph 98).

The Green Paper Proposals

14.20 In the Green Paper the Government indicate that they are 'not averse to easing the difficulties' which a wealth tax would cause for the owners of works of art; they 'recognise the danger that the wealth tax could lead to the dispersal of the national heritage' and 'intend to ensure that this does not happen'. The Government also recognise the importance of public access, and maintain that any special arrangements should be conditional on the work of art being on public display (paragraphs 37-39). Thus far they are in accord with the sentiments we have expressed. The Green Paper then concludes that one possible solution might be the deferment of the wealth tax attributable to the work of art, subject to interest at a commercial rate (which might also be deferred) until the owner sold the asset, or died, or as long as the appropriate conditions were being satisfied; further, 'For some categories of works of art there might perhaps be exemption from the interest accruing on deferment (though not from the charge itself). This could be combined with arrangements to take the works into public ownership in satisfaction of accrued wealth tax liabilities' (paragraph 39).

14.21 The proposal that those who meet the conditions about public display should benefit only from deferment of tax (with or without interest), not complete exemption as we suggest, is in practice a harsher treatment of the owners of works of art than in any of the five countries we have examined and harsher also than the proposals in the Republic of Ireland. The Green Paper proposals seem to us to be both ungenerous and unwise. First they raise practical difficulties. If tax is only to be deferred, then all works of art have to be valued whether or not the owners meet the conditions about public display. Further, deferment implies that the value of works of art is included in the net wealth of the owner in determining the rate of tax on his wealth as a whole. The Green Paper does not say what charge would be deferred in these circumstances; would it be the average rate of tax on the estate (including the work of art) multiplied by the value of the work of art, or the marginal addition to the wealth tax charge resulting from the possession of the work of art (which would be higher than the former, especially if the value of the work of art pushed total net wealth into a higher wealth tax bracket)? If it is the first method, its application would mean that some owners would be paying higher wealth tax bills by virtue of possessing works of art, even though wealth tax was deferred on the works of art themselves.

14.22 Secondly, the effect of this ungenerous treatment on art owners must be considered. How many of them, in these circumstances, would sell off some of their treasures either because they had to in order to meet their immediate wealth tax liabilities inflated by the possession of valuable works of art, or because they were not prepared to meet conditions about public display in return for nothing but the deferment of tax liability? Again, it is one thing freely to leave one's art treasures to the nation. It is another to be pressured into it. How would they react to the pistol, forcing them, in settlement of deferred liabilities, to hand over their works of art into public ownership? These questions cannot be answered with any certainty, but the Green Paper proposals could destroy the goodwill of the art fraternity and threaten to disperse the national heritage—precisely what the Government says should *not* be allowed to happen!

14.23 Finally, provided that the works of art are publicly displayed, we see no advantage in public ownership as such. It would require an expensive building programme to house the additional works of art; sometimes it would mean their display in a less appropriate setting; one suspects it would reduce the number of centres within the country at which works of art could be viewed; the new buildings would need to be staffed and maintained; and the art acquisitions would need to be protected. Moreover, the Green Paper proposals would make new private collections, if not impossible, at least unattractive. As Lord Eccles has pointed out,[6] private collections have blazed the trail for public collections. The museum director with limited money concentrates his purchases on generally well-known works. But a private collector can indulge his fancies. If he makes a mistake the public does not suffer and if he discovers talent the public will benefit. In the view of Lord Eccles the museums and libraries would be much poorer if this process had not been going on for several centuries.

14.24 In short, the Green Paper proposals seem to us to carry almost all the disadvantages which would accrue from including works of art within the wealth tax base without any exemptions or concessions. The main objective

---

[6] House of Lords, *Hansard*, 26 June 1974, col. 1519.

of public policy on works of art should be public display rather than public ownership. In our view, the state and the public would be getting a good bargain by public display in return for tax exemption. The art treasures are being privately looked after, housed and made available to the public. If an owner ceases to meet the conditions, then the exemption ceases, but there should be no deferred charge and no back charge extending into the period when the conditions on public access were being met.[7]

Conclusion

14.25 The prime object of public policy on works of art should be to maximise consumption or enjoyment. Works of art should be exempt from wealth tax provided the owners meet appropriate conditions about public access. We would reject the Green Paper's proposals by which, even when the owner meets conditions about public access, the wealth tax charge is simply deferred.

Historic Houses

14.26 Much the same considerations apply to historic houses as to works of art, so that we can deal with historic houses more briefly. They share the characteristics of works of art in the fixed stock available, the low marginal cost of enjoyment from viewing them and in the importance of an appropriate setting to full enjoyment. They do not readily sell in an international market, however, and this has two consequences: their inclusion in a wealth tax base could be expected to reduce, perhaps substantially, the open market value of the buildings themselves; secondly, the danger to the cultural heritage of including historic houses in the wealth tax base is not their sale abroad (although this may happen to their contents) but their decay and demolition. This is a more serious result in that the masterpiece is lost to the world, not just to the country.

14.27 The treatment for historic houses ought, therefore, in principle, to be much the same as for works of art—exemption conditional upon reasonable public access (subject, perhaps, to maintaining a partial charge on that part of the property in which the owners live). In the rare cases that their owners have succeeded in converting their stately home and grounds into a profitable business, then it might be necessary to tax it as such or, perhaps more appropriately, to levy wealth tax on a capitalised value of the net profit. Where the income from opening up house and grounds and from introducing entertainments to attract the public raised only enough to cover outgoings, no account should be taken of the income. Special rules would be needed to determine the treatment of the grounds of an historic mansion; but the prime criterion should be public access (assuming the character and quality of the grounds to be appropriate).

---

[7] We do consider, however, that there is a case for tightening up the conditions relating to the reliefs for works of art under death duties.

Practice in Other Countries

14.28 The United Kingdom is probably richer than most other countries in its heritage of historic mansions. Thus the size of the problem may be bigger in the United Kingdom; to that extent practice elsewhere may be an inadequate precedent.

14.29 In several countries (Denmark, the Netherlands, Sweden) whilst there is no specific wealth tax concession for historic buildings, they are valued 'sympathetically' and the values are low even by comparison with values for other real property (which in general is assessed at a figure well below open market value[8]). In the Netherlands, historic houses may be designated national monuments and the owner may receive a subsidy for maintenance conditional on not changing the appearance of the house; this condition itself reduces the market value, which in turn reduces the wealth tax value. Although not giving any specific exemption for historic houses, the Netherlands does provide partial exemptions for estates designated by law as preservation areas. Where such estates are not open to the public, the value taken for wealth tax purposes is two-thirds of their value as *parkland* (i.e. not their value for any other purpose). Where they are open to the public, the value for wealth tax purposes is one-quarter of their value as parkland.

14.30 The most comprehensive provisions for the taxation of historic mansions and castles are to be found in Germany. Complete exemption of houses, and of art objects also, is granted for objects important for art, history or science in which there is a public interest and which are useful for purposes of research and education; provided also that they have been at least twenty years in the ownership of the family or registered in a special list of national monuments; and that the owner agrees to the controls laid down for national monuments.

14.31 There is a further provision by which real estate and other personal private chattels are taxable on only 40% of their value if they are of public interest on account of their historical, artistic or scientific importance.

14.32 There is also an exemption for properties which are open to the public where their maintenance is regarded as being for the public benefit.

14.33 Where historic houses or estates (as mentioned in paragraphs 14.30-32) yield revenue which is normally bigger than the expenditure, they are liable to tax. Expenses connected with such property are fully deductible.

14.34 Under the proposals for the Republic of Ireland, historic houses will often benefit from the exemption of a principal private residence and the one acre of land surrounding it.

---

[8] See Appendix C for a summary of methods of valuing real property.

The Green Paper Proposals

14.35 The Green Paper proposes to treat historic houses in the same way as works of art: if the owner allows public access he can gain deferment but not complete exemption. For the same reasons as with works of art, with which the historic mansions are often indissolubly linked, we recommend complete exemption from wealth tax relating to an historic house (and appropriate grounds), provided that the quality and interest of the house are such that the public might wish to visit it, and subject to the owner meeting requirements about public access.

Conclusions

14.36 Historic houses should be treated in the same way as works of art. They should be completely exempt if their owners meet specified requirements to provide reasonable public access.

Chapter 15

Administration and Operating Costs

Administrative Pattern and Returns

15.1 The natural place for the administration of an annual wealth tax is the office which deals with the taxpayer's income tax liability. The administration of wealth tax and income tax can thus be closely integrated and the same officer can handle the taxpayer's affairs in relation to both taxes. Income and wealth can be reported on the same return. Information which is required for the purposes of both taxes need only be given once, and consistency between the information given for the purpose of each tax is assured almost automatically so far as income-producing assets are concerned.

15.2 In all the five countries whose systems we have examined, the wealth tax is dealt with in the same local office as the income tax. In four of them the taxpayer makes a combined return. In the Scandinavian countries every taxpayer who makes an income tax return has to give details of his wealth whether or not he is above the threshold for wealth tax liability. In the Netherlands the composite return form is only issued to persons who are or may be liable to wealth tax. In Germany, however, the wealth tax return is separate, since in general wealth tax assessments stand unchanged for three years and returns are only required at three-year intervals.

15.3 A combined return form need not be a massive affair. The separate wealth tax return in Germany is relatively elaborate; but in Sweden, for example, the standard form provides only about half a page for the details of net wealth. In this small space, wealth is returned under separate headings for real property; chattels (subdivided into cars, boats, other chattels and jewellery); bank balances; stocks and shares—quoted or unquoted; cash and claims on others; deductible debts (subdivided into mortgage debts, other debts and taxes due and unpaid); and the total net wealth. Chattels and debts in the various subdivisions do not have to be individually listed (in Germany, on the other hand, a list of chattels over a certain value has to be appended, so that the tax authorities can decide whether any are taxable as 'luxury' items). A separate form, however, has to be completed for a business carried on by the taxpayer.

15.4 For the UK, in contrast with the practice elsewhere, the Green Paper (paragraph 58) proposes a regional organisation, i.e. neither local nor central. With the high threshold that is envisaged, much higher than in other countries, a relatively small number, and a very small proportion, of income tax payers will be liable to wealth tax, and it may be considered that it would be uneconomic to require all the local tax offices to master the wealth tax when each office would have comparatively few cases to deal with. Further, under the thorough-going system of self-valuation and self-assessment which is proposed, it may be that greater expertise will be needed in judging whether or how to challenge the taxpayer's figures. Nor, as things stand, are the tax offices equipped to receive tax payments.

15.5 There are, however, considerable disadvantages in divorcing wealth tax administration from income tax and capital gains tax. The present tax return contains, or should contain, a description of every income-producing asset; it also gives details of all acquisitions and disposals of assets which come within the scope of the capital gains tax. Records of assets acquired are maintained in the tax office. The tax office holds particulars of the taxpayer's liability to investment income surcharge, which may be an alternative to wealth tax, and of his total income and total income tax liability, which may be required for the purposes of a ceiling provision. All this information would be necessary or useful to wealth tax offices, but with a regional organisation it will have to be sent to them specially. The Green Paper is evidently conscious of the disadvantages since it emphasises that the regional organisation will have close links and exchange information with other Inland Revenue offices (including no doubt the Estate Duty Office or other office or offices handling the new capital transfer tax, as well as the local tax offices).

15.6 The taxpayer will also suffer inconvenience. Probably the worst feature will be the need to correspond with two offices instead of one, sometimes perhaps on matters in which both offices are interested. Two returns, however, ought to be avoided if at all possible. In a combined return income-producing assets would only have to be listed once, the income and the capital value being entered in adjoining columns. Space would of course have to be provided for non-income-producing assets such as owner-occupied houses and chattels and for debts; how much space would depend on the amount of detailed description which it is decided to demand. At all events, even if the wealth tax part of the return cannot be so compact as in Sweden, there is nothing essentially impracticable about a combined return. The return would be made to the income tax office, which would send a copy of it to the wealth tax office.

15.7 There appear to be two obstacles in the way of the combined return. The Green Paper (paragraphs 66-7) suggests that the valuation date for wealth tax should be either 31 December or 31 March, and that six months from the valuation date should be allowed for making the return and paying the tax. If 31 March were chosen, a combined return would be out of the question, since clearly the receipt of income tax returns could not be delayed until the end of September. Nor, in principle, should they be delayed until the end of June if the date was 31 December; but in practice the thirty-days time limit for making income tax returns is not rigidly enforced and it is probable that a relatively high proportion of the more complicated returns, which will be the returns of wealthier people—that is to say, people within the wealth tax field —are not rendered until well after the expiry of the time-limit. Delay until the end of June might therefore not be too serious a matter in practice. But apart from that it is a question whether it is really necessary to allow six months to produce the return. It is not so in other countries. Clearly, extra time must be allowed in the first year, as the Green Paper suggests, but after that four months should be enough; the wealth tax and income tax time-limits would then expire at approximately the same time.

15.8 The second obstacle is the proposed self-assessment system. Judging by American experience with the income tax, self-assessment in the full sense requires a detailed and rather complicated form, which might not be readily combined with an income tax return made with a view to assessment by the Revenue. Secondly, the system is not tolerant about time limits; if return and payment are late it is usual to charge interest (Green Paper, paragraph 68). Thirdly, there might be difficulties for the Revenue if the payment were to be sent, along with the combined return, to the income tax office; however, the difficulty would disappear if the return and the tax went first to the wealth tax office, which then sent it (or a copy) on to the income tax office.

Conclusion

15.9 Ideally, wealth tax liabilities should be dealt with in the same office as the taxpayer's income tax liability on the basis of a single return for both taxes. If in the UK they have to be dealt with in a different office a single return is still desirable in the interests of taxpayers and their advisers.

Assessment and Self-Assessment

15.10 None of the five Continental countries has adopted a system of full self-assessment, under which the taxpayer not only returns details of all his chargeable assets and their value but also totals his net wealth, calculates the tax due and sends his cheque in with his return. In all the countries the assessment is made by the tax authorities. The Swedish system is regarded as approaching self-assessment in that the taxpayer calculates and enters his total net wealth (and his total income); but he does not enter the tax payable. Denmark adds this further stage and is nearest to full self-assessment. In Germany, the taxpayer gives full details of his assets but does not total them.

15.11 Assessments in Germany are made every third year, the assessments remaining unchanged for the two succeeding years unless the taxpayer's wealth has changed significantly (paragraph 5.33). This arrangement obviously keeps down administrative costs, but it has to be remembered that the rate of tax in Germany is only 0.7%; it would be less satisfactory with a progressive tax rising to $2\frac{1}{2}$% or even 5%.

15.12 Payment of tax is a separate matter, being made in all five countries by instalments during the course of the year. In Sweden, the tax authorities issue a provisional assessment, based on the previous year's figures, and the taxpayer pays the amount shown in six two-monthly instalments. Provisional assessment is also the rule in Denmark, Norway and the Netherlands, the provisional tax being payable by ten monthly instalments in Denmark and by quarterly instalments in Norway and the Netherlands. In Germany, where assessments stand for three years, quarterly instalments are paid on the basis of the current assessment. In the other countries the tax authorities proceed to a final assessment in the course of the following year.

15.13 For the UK the Green Paper proposes self-assessment in the full sense, the tax as calculated by the taxpayer being sent in with his return. In principle there is nothing difficult about self-assessment. Any wealth tax involves a return by the taxpayer of his assets and their value and of his liabilities; to proceed from this to calculate the total net wealth will normally be an easy matter—easier probably than calculating total income—while a simple table will enable the tax payable to be ascertained. (A ceiling provision, however, may give rise to difficulties.) It is likely that, even if the taxpayer were merely required to detail his assets and liabilities, his accountant—and most people liable to wealth tax (on the basis of a £100,000 threshold) are likely to be professionally advised—would carry out the remaining stages for his own and his client's satisfaction.

15.14 The benefits of self-assessment accrue entirely to the tax authorities. In the United States, which operates what is claimed to be a very successful self-assessment system for income tax purposes, the percentage cost of administration is only one-third of the UK figure. Part of the difference arises because the tax authorities are saved the work of computing liabilities and issuing notices of assessment and demands for payments. But probably only a small part. Undoubtedly the major factor is the very limited scale of 'audit'—scrutiny of taxpayers' returns. In the vast majority of cases only the taxpayer's arithmetic is checked, and no further action is taken. It is the deliberate policy of the United States authorities to audit only enough returns to keep every taxpayer constantly aware of the possibility that his own return may be audited. And the audit, if it comes, is thorough. The authorities believe that this policy has secured a very satisfactory standard of compliance by taxpayers.

15.15 In the UK the traditional policy has been different. It has been the practice to examine all returns, more or less intensively according to circumstances, in order that both the Revenue and the public may be assured that so far as possible each taxpayer pays the correct amount due from him under the law. The Green Paper proposes a change of policy in regard to the wealth tax—to accept the taxpayer's return, including his valuations, in the general case but to check 'a proportion of the returns . . . at a later date' (paragraph 62). Broadly it proposes to adopt the policy of the United States. Given that policy, it is sensible to go for a full-blown self-assessment system.

15.16 One may question whether this new departure is due to a conviction that it will be as effective as the traditional arrangements. It may well have been virtually forced on the authorities by lack of the resources to operate according to the old system. A wealth tax case is broadly equivalent to an estate duty case; in 1971 there were under 2,000 estate duty cases over £100,000 but an estimated 75,000 individuals with wealth above that figure. Big cases require skilled staff, and obviously the staff is not there. Current standards for estate duty could not be achieved over a wide range of wealth tax cases, at any rate for a long time. In the early stages, examination must inevitably be highly selective. From the Revenue's standpoint therefore the policy proposed is reasonable.

15.17 But it is necessary to consider it also from the taxpayer's standpoint. The Revenue saves work which it could not cope with, but there is no saving for the taxpayer; for him the work may be heavier than it would be under a traditional system. More important is the uncertainty which the policy implies. A wealth tax is a very different thing from an income tax. Income is to a large extent a matter of fact, but capital value over a wide area is a matter of opinion. Quoted securities are the only important class of assets for which there is an established market value at any given time. For practically everything else (except possibly owner-occupied houses) the taxpayer is to make his own valuation, apparently with the possibility that his values may be challenged several years later; and if they are successfully challenged he will have to pay the back tax, and, even if his own valuation was an honest attempt, with interest as well.

15.18 The taxpayer's situation in regard to values will be quite different from what it is in the Scandinavian countries and Germany. There the value of land is fixed by periodical valuations; the value of unquoted shares is fixed by the revenue authorities or (as in Germany) according to a formula; there are rules for the valuation of businesses. To a considerable extent values become a matter of fact. Virtually the only class of assets for which the taxpayer makes his own valuation is chattels; and here the authorities are generally content to take what they are offered. Consequently the taxpayer is not exposed, as he would be in the UK, to the risk that his liability will be reopened at some unknown time in the future.

15.19 It is true that in the Netherlands the tax appears to work smoothly without either cadastral values or prescribed methods of valuation. The tax-payer makes his own valuation for every class of asset, and it is left to the tax office, with little or no guidance from the centre, to accept or challenge the values. But the tax office makes the assessment and the taxpayer knows whether his valuations are accepted or not. He is not left in a state of uncertainty.

15.20 We have considerable misgivings about the adoption of a system of self-assessment unless it is combined with cadastral values for land and prescribed methods, such as have been discussed in Chapter 10, of valuing other important classes of asset. Certainly, if general self-valuation is to be the rule in the UK, a tolerant attitude on the part of the Revenue seems essential. If the taxpayer cannot get an assurance year by year that his values are accepted he ought not to be at risk of later reopening unless negligence can be proved against him. In the nature of things his valuations will be on the low side; but, in the absence of set rules to guide him, the Revenue must be prepared to acquiesce in a reasonable measure of undervaluation.

Appeals

15.21 The Green Paper proposes (paragraph 70) that the Special Commis-sioners of Income Tax shall be the tribunal for determining all appeals on wealth tax matters, including valuation, other than questions relating to the valuation of interests in land, which will go to the Lands Tribunal. We think that the present arrangements for appeals relating to the value of personal property for tax purposes are not satisfactory. The Special Commissioners have joint jurisdiction with the General Commissioners for capital gains tax purposes, except that appeals over the value of unquoted shares go to the General Commissioners exclusively. For estate duty there is no intermediate tribunal; the only avenue of appeal on any estate duty matter except the valuation of land is direct to the High Court. We suggest that the introduction of the capital transfer tax and the wealth tax makes it desirable to rationalise and co-ordinate the appeal provisions, particularly in regard to appeals on the valuation of personal property. In general, all such appeals, whether on the new taxes or on existing Inland Revenue taxes, should go to the same tribunal, which should probably have equal status with the Lands Tribunal.

15.22 We propose that the role of the Special Commissioners should be enlarged accordingly. They would then handle all wealth tax appeals, whether on valuation or other matters, and capital transfer tax appeals on valuation of personal property (indeed we think they should become an intermediate tribunal for capital transfer tax appeals generally). They would also take over valuation of unquoted shares for capital gains tax purposes from the General Commissioners; but the latter bodies could continue to share jurisdiction on the valuation of other personal property. It would be for consideration, in view of their enlarged functions, whether the membership of the Special Commissioners should include persons expert in the valuation of personal property, especially private businesses and unquoted shares. (An alternative would be to establish a separate expert tribunal to deal with appeals on the value of all property other than land.)

Conclusion

15.23 Assessment by the tax authorities is the rule on the Continent. A self-valuation, self-assessment system, as proposed for the UK in the Green Paper, enables the authorities to tailor their audit work to the available resources, but leaves the taxpayer uncertain of his position if, as suggested, assessments may be re-opened at a later date. They should not be re-opened unless the Revenue can prove negligence. Self-assessment is satisfactory if combined with cadastral values and set rules for valuing other assets; without them, a measure of undervaluation must be accepted in the interests of the smooth working of the tax. It is desirable that the functions of the Special Commissioners should be enlarged to include, not only all wealth tax appeals (except on the valuation of land), but also appeals on the valuation of personal property for the purpose of any Inland Revenue tax. Alternatively, a separate valuation tribunal for personal property might be set up.

Other Administrative Matters

15.24 It is sometimes said that a wealth tax acts by its mere existence as a check on the correctness of income tax returns and a deterrent to evasion. This seems an overstatement; a person who is minded to evade income tax on the income from a particular asset will keep silent about the asset as well. There can, however, be useful cross checks in relation particularly to a gift or death tax. We found varying attitudes to the value of a wealth tax as a control. In Norway and Denmark considerable importance is attached to it, even in relation to income tax, but it appears to be regarded as of less consequence in Sweden. In Germany, wealth tax information is cross checked against income tax and gift and inheritance tax information and is regarded as a useful instrument for encouraging correct returns. In the Netherlands the authorities find it of some value in the control of other taxes, but not highly important.

15.25 More significant, from the standpoint of administrative cost, is the possible use of valuations for the purposes of more than one tax. The values fixed for real property in Sweden, for example, are not used for wealth tax only; they also apply where a charge to gift or inheritance tax arises, as well as being the base for calculating rental value for national and local income tax purposes. In Germany, the real property valuations are used in addition for various other purposes: the local real property tax, the 7% tax on transfers of real property, coastal protection rates, notary's fees on conveyancing, contributions towards the cost of the commercial register. Even in the Netherlands, where there is no cadastral valuation, the wealth tax value forms the base for the income tax value and may also serve for gift and inheritance tax purposes.

15.26 In the United Kingdom, similarly, the same values for land and buildings would be used for both wealth tax and local rates if, as we have recommended in Chapter 10, capital valuation is adopted for rating purposes, with quinquennial revaluation. They could also be used for the purpose of other taxes. There would of course be a loss of precision if the value set on a property at a revaluation were to be used as the value for, e.g., capital transfer tax three or four years later; but this must be balanced against the saving in time, trouble and expense for both the Revenue and the taxpayer. Other countries have chosen the saving.

15.27 In other areas too, there are savings to be made. Wealth tax values for business assets may be derived from income tax figures. The values given to unquoted shares for wealth tax can be used for capital transfer tax and other taxes; but if they are to be so used they must have been arrived at by some recognised process or formula (Chapter 10).

Conclusion

15.28 Wealth tax information is of some service in the control of other taxes, and *vice versa*. The use of wealth tax values for the purpose of other taxes offers important savings in administrative and compliance costs; but their use depends on their having been fixed either officially or by some recognised process.

Administrative and Compliance Costs

15.29 None of the five Continental countries was able to put a figure on the administrative cost of the wealth tax, but the general impression we received was that the cost was nothing out of the way. The close integration of wealth tax with income tax administration, the adoption of cadastral or conventionally calculated values (mostly below true open market value), the acceptance on trust of returns and values which there is no ready means of challenging, all combine to keep the cost within acceptable bounds.

15.30 For the UK, under a self-assessment system, there will be the inescapable cost of a machine to issue and receive returns, receive and account for payments, etc.; but beyond the bare machinery the cost will largely depend on the amount of effort put into the examination and checking of returns. Audit will require highly skilled staff, since all wealth tax cases will (by estate duty standards) be big cases. American experience indicates that it is the limited audit that accounts for the low cost of their tax administration. How the administrative cost of the wealth tax, expressed as a percentage of the yield, will compare with the cost of other Inland Revenue taxes will, of course, depend not only on the number and proportion of highly skilled staff engaged in the work, but also on the extent to which the net yield of the tax (e.g. under the illustrative scales in the Green Paper) is reduced by exemptions or by reliefs such as credit for investment income surcharge or ceiling provisions. There is, however, one offsetting saving which assessment by the Revenue would bring but self-assessment will not. With annual Revenue assessment, and particularly if accompanied by cadastral and conventional valuations, the administrative cost of the capital transfer tax would be reduced in the case of persons liable to wealth tax because values would already be available for their property. With wealth tax self-assessment, on the contrary, a gift or death will probably be an occasion for fairly full examination of the taxpayer's wealth tax figures on accustomed lines.

15.31 As to compliance costs, we found no serious concern in the five countries. Generally, wealth tax costs were considered to be less important than income tax costs. In the Netherlands, compliance costs for wealth tax would appear to be rather higher than elsewhere because of the self-valuation system; even so, it is apparently uncommon to employ a professional valuer, e.g. to value real property. The general lack of complaint in the five countries is probably due partly to the conventional and conservative values placed on many classes of assets where this is the responsibility of the tax authorities, so that there is relatively little ground for dispute; partly to the generally tolerant attitude of the authorities in not seeking to extract the last penny; and partly perhaps to familiarity with an old-established tax.

15.32 For the UK taxpayer, nevertheless, compliance will appear a heavy burden, at any rate in the early years. Every year he must draw up a detailed statement of his assets and put values on them, an unfamiliar task. For his own protection, in case of a later challenge by the Revenue, he may want to have his real property professionally valued from time to time; similarly if he has chargeable chattels of significant value. In some circumstances the Revenue may require a professional valuation (paragraph 10.13). If he has his own business his accountant will have to estimate its value. Valuation of unquoted shares can be an expensive and time-consuming affair, though it will be less so if a formula is laid down (paragraph 10.56); in any event, the same value, when arrived at, will apply for all or most of the shareholders in the same company. But, whatever the rules, the statement of assets and values has to be produced and, if produced professionally, paid for. Compliance costs are likely to be particularly heavy for trustees, especially of discretionary trusts.

15.33 The burden must not be exaggerated. Often it will be simply a matter of making minor adjustments to last year's figures (though the values of quoted securities will rarely remain unchanged). In most years there will be no correspondence or discussion with the Revenue. It will not be as difficult for the professional adviser as drawing up a statement of assets for death duty purposes; the taxpayer is alive and can be consulted as necessary. On the other hand, the cost may be greater than in the death duty case, since on a death the estate has to be valued anyway for the purposes of distribution to the beneficiaries and only a part of the cost is properly allocable to the death duty requirements.

15.34 Compliance costs may nevertheless be considerable. They will be especially so, in relation to net wealth, for those who are not much above the wealth tax threshold—or indeed are below it, since the Green Paper proposes (paragraph 59) that returns shall be required from everyone whose wealth exceeds a prescribed fraction of the exemption limit. In this respect the wealth tax has some resemblance to the capital gains tax. It may cost as much to value assets which in the event are put at say £105,000 for a person whose total wealth they represent as for a millionaire; the cost of valuing the large slice below the threshold has to be paid for as well as the small slice above which actually bears tax.[1]

15.35 The question arises whether some tax relief should be given for compliance costs. Their deduction from the taxpayer's wealth next year (which will be automatic) will be little help since the percentage rate of tax is small. To give significant relief they would have to be deducted from income for income tax purposes as in Germany (paragraph 5.39). Successive governments have however resisted claims for income tax relief for professional assistance in connexion with income tax liability, and also capital gains tax liability except as respects valuation, etc. expenses in connexion with the acquisition or disposal of an asset, which are part of the cost of obtaining the gain. Resistance may equally be expected in regard to wealth tax costs. Nevertheless an exception would seem justified for the cost of professional valuations which either the Revenue required the taxpayer to produce or which, given self-assessment, he obtained for his own protection. The relief might however, be best given as a credit against the wealth tax itself rather than as an income tax deduction. The credit should not extend to the full amount of the costs; that would tempt the taxpayer to put money in the pockets of valuers rather than let the Revenue have it. A possibility might be to allow the credit to the extent that the costs exceeded a specified percentage of the wealth tax liability, for example 1%. If

---

[1] On the regressiveness of compliance costs generally, see C. T. Sandford, *Hidden Costs of Taxation*, IFS, 1973, pp. 146-7.

the taxpayer's net wealth was £120,000, the tax £200, and the valuation expenses £100, he would get a credit of £98, practically the whole cost. If, however, his wealth was £400,000, tax £3,000 and the expenses again £100, the credit would be only £70, the excess over 1% of £3,000. There could of course also be a maximum credit. It has to be admitted, however, that a credit system would be no help to a person who incurred valuation expenses but in the result was not liable to tax.

Conclusion

15.36 With self-assessment, administrative costs will largely depend on the amount of resources devoted to audit. Compliance costs however may be considerable, and perhaps heavier with self-assessment than with Revenue assessment. While tax relief for compliance costs generally may be resisted, there is a case for allowing some limited relief for the cost of professional valuations in the form of a credit against wealth tax liability.

Note on paragraph 15.22. The Autumn Finance Bill 1974—which was published when this book was already in proof—introduces a right of appeal to the Special Commissioners on capital transfer tax matters generally (except on the value of land). It also transfers capital gains tax appeals on the value of unquoted shares from the General to the Special Commissioners.

Chapter 16

Avoidance and Evasion

Definitions and General Consequences

16.1 Very little study has been done on the circumstances which generate evasion and avoidance and on their economic and social consequences. Hence there is little theoretical and still less empirical data on which to draw and much that is said in this chapter must be tentative.

Problems of Definition

16.2 We must begin by defining our terms. The usual distinction between evasion and avoidance is that the evasion is illegal tax dodging whilst avoidance is the adoption of entirely legal ways of reducing one's tax liability. However, whilst the legality or illegality of the action is a vital distinction, it is not sufficient to define the terms meaningfully; each must be refined.

16.3 We need to distinguish behaviour stemming from ignorance or quasi-ignorance from evasion knowingly entered into from deliberate intent. This distinction is important in relation to the penalties which taxing authorities impose. The omission of a major asset from a tax return could hardly be regarded as other than deliberate intent, but under-valuation could be intentional or unintentional.

16.4 Avoidance is more complex. It is unhelpful to regard avoidance as simply any method of legally reducing a tax bill. I can legally reduce my wealth tax bill in any country by spending in excess of my income; if I am a German resident, I can reduce wealth tax liability by marrying and having children; or if I am an unmarried Dutch resident I can reduce wealth tax simply by staying alive beyond the age of thirty-five. In looking at avoidance, we must ask whether the action which reduces the tax bill is something (a) which the government specifically seeks to encourage, such as exemptions for charitable covenants; or if we take a wealth tax example, like the proposed Dutch additional exemption from wealth tax for investment in productive enterprise; or (b) whether it is something about which the State is neutral, such as concessions for a wife or dependent children, where the tax relief acknowledges a welfare obligation; or (c) a method of tax reduction which takes advantage of a loop-hole because the law is incompletely framed (like the circumvention of the dividend-stripping legislation in the UK in the late 1950s) or of a concession which the State might have reluctantly granted for purely administrative reasons (like the exemption of household goods, jewellery or pictures).

16.5 We have used the term avoidance to describe the third of these possibilities. Thus the purchase of unmounted diamonds in Sweden (paragraph 4.27) is avoidance by means of a legal loophole. Further, if household goods are wholly exempt from wealth tax, it constitutes avoidance in our sense if people take advantage of the concession to add to household chattels in excess of what they would otherwise have acquired; or if a United Kingdom wealth tax exempts a motor car, it is avoidance if people buy bigger and better cars than they otherwise would; or if all debts are deductible it is avoidance if people deliberately incur debts to invest in exempt assets; or if people buy property which, for practical reasons, carries a low value for wealth tax purposes.

16.6 There are bound to be some cases in which it is not clear whether an action which reduces wealth tax liability does fall into our category of avoidance or whether it is a matter on which the government is neutral or even towards which it is favourably disposed. We are then left with nothing but a subjective judgement.

General Economic and Social Consequences

16.7 Avoidance and evasion have a number of undesirable consequences. They both result in loss of revenue to the State at given tax rates. If we assume that governments first determine their expenditure and then raise the revenue to meet it, evasion and avoidance mean higher tax rates. If we make the alternative and less plausible assumption that governments can spend only what they raise, then avoidance and evasion mean less government expenditure for given tax rates. Either way they affect the distribution of income. If the government imposes higher taxes to make good the revenue lost, then in effect there is a redistribution of income or wealth from the non-evaders to the evaders (from the honest to the dishonest) and from the non-avoiders to the avoiders (from the unsophisticated to the sophisticated). If the effect of evasion and avoidance is to curtail government expenditure, then the transfer of income or wealth is, in effect, to the evaders and avoiders from those who would have benefited from the extra expenditure. If we assume the benefit of such expenditure to have been evenly spread throughout the community, then again the transfer is to the evaders and avoiders from the rest of the community.

16.8 Evasion and more particularly avoidance also involve resource costs. The evader will spend time planning his evasion and perhaps spend money (i.e. use resources) in implementing it. The avoider may give up leisure time to plan avoidance or be diverted from his business activities to this end. More important, he is likely to consult expensive tax advisers; not infrequently some of the ablest minds in accountancy, law firms, insurance companies as well as in other professions are taken up with tax avoidance, usually referred to by the euphemism of 'tax planning' or 'tax mitigation'. The resource costs taken up with this kind of tax consultancy are difficult to measure but may well be considerable.[1]

16.9 Further, there are resource costs of another kind arising from evasion and avoidance. Either or both may lead to investment distortion. The tax evader may seek to hide his un-taxed income or wealth by placing it in unproductive but easily concealable forms of investment like jewellery or Swiss bank accounts. Avoidance generates investment distortion in the form of the purchase of assets exempt from wealth tax or under-valued for wealth tax purposes. Thus in Sweden, avoidance takes the form of investment in art collections, or insurance, or under-valued real property, sometimes with loans which can be set against wealth tax (paragraphs 4.93-4.100). At its most extreme, avoidance takes the form of the emigration of persons and capital.

16.10 Avoidance may also adversely affect the form of a business organisation. Thus if an unincorporated business is valued relatively favourably for wealth tax purposes compared with shares in a closely owned company, the company form of organisation may be discouraged; if shares in a closely owned company are favourably valued, the directors may be deterred from going public.

16.11 Finally, there is an effect on tax morality. Evasion creates horizontal inequities and generates resentment amongst the honest at the thought that other people are 'getting away with it'. Evasion generates a contempt for law and tends to feed on itself. Avoidance, though legal, may have similar consequences. It creates horizontal inequities because some people are better placed than others to take advantage of avoidance opportunities. Moreover, many unsophisticated people find it difficult to distinguish one from the other, avoidance from evasion.

16.12 Thus tax policy should aim to minimise both evasion and avoidance. For this reason it is important to examine the circumstances which generate them and how these circumstances relate to a wealth tax.

---

[1] C. T. Sandford, *Hidden Costs of Taxation*, IFS, July 1973, especially Chapter 4.

Evasion and a Wealth Tax

Economists' approach

16.13 The economists' approach to the circumstances generating evasion is to argue that evasion will increase in accordance with its profitability—an approach resting on the assumption that the individual's behaviour is determined by the desire to maximise income or wealth. The amount of evasion is thus seen as a function of four circumstances: (i) the level of tax rates; (ii) the evasion opportunities; (iii) the likelihood of discovery; and (iv) the penalties if discovered. The higher are tax rates, especially marginal tax rates, the more is evasion worth while; the more the opportunities, the easier it is to evade; the less the chance of discovery and the lower the penalties of discovery, the more worth while it is to take the risk.

16.14 How do these considerations relate to a wealth tax? On the level of tax rates we must distinguish once more between a substitutive and an additive tax; the much higher average and marginal tax rates of an additive wealth tax will stimulate evasion more than a substitutive. Opportunities for evasion in part depend on the methods of assessment and valuation adopted. If assets are valued strictly in accordance with set rules and in many cases the value is worked out by the authorities, then opportunities for evasion by under-valuation will be much less than if the taxpayer is required to assess himself and to provide his own valuations for a wide range of assets. The likelihood of discovery depends in large measure on the coverage of the tax; a tax which attempts to be comprehensive will include within its base assets which are easy to conceal and where evasion will be difficult to discover. This is strongly borne out by the experience of the five countries whose wealth taxes have been examined. Take jewellery for example: in four of these countries, jewellery in excess of a specified exemption limit is included within the tax base. In practice, it is accepted that under-reporting of jewellery is widespread. The same is true of works of art which are included within the tax base in Norway and Germany. One can see the argument for the Danish practice of completely excluding such items and adopting the realistic principle that 'the tax stops short at the doors'.

16.15 Stiffer penalties may help to counteract the additional likelihood of evasion from a wealth tax, but it will be difficult to prove intent with some forms of evasion; how can the authorities distinguish under-valuation that is deliberate from under-valuation based on ignorance of the market?

16.16 One counter argument to the view that a wealth tax increases evasion is that it acts as an instrument of control to reveal and hence reduce evasion in the tax system as a whole by increasing the possibilities for the Revenue authorities to cross-check; income and capital gains can be cross-checked with wealth and wealth with death and gift tax returns. As we have seen (paragraph

15.24), countries differ in the importance they attach to this function of a wealth tax. But those particular ways in which a wealth tax most readily lends itself to evasion—the omission and under-valuation of personal assets—offer little scope for cross-checking. The link with income tax is no use for nil-yielding assets, nor is it much help in identifying under-valuation. Potentially there is more opportunity for cross-checking the existence and value of these assets against gift tax and death duty returns, but where the information is filed at different times and on different forms with different branches of the Revenue co-ordination in practice is much less than perfect.[2] Another reason for doubting the efficiency of the cross-check of income and wealth is that it would seem likely that any reasonably intelligent evader in filling in a joint return would cheat consistently on both; and the introduction of a wealth tax which can be cross-checked against death and gift taxes may serve to encourage the evasion of both. Nevertheless, one must accept the possibility that although a wealth tax may itself be widely evaded, its presence may do something to reveal evasion elsewhere in the system and perhaps, by revealing it, reduce it.

16.17 Where the tax authorities introduce stiffer penalties to reduce evasion, it can be counter-productive. Especially if the penalties are imposed where there is some doubt about the intention to evade, they will be strongly resented, and the attitude engendered will be unfavourable to taxpayer compliance; but at this point, in speaking of 'attitudes' we are adopting a wider approach than that of the economist.

The Behavioural Approach

16.18 The economists' approach suggests that even a substitutive wealth tax would be likely to generate evasion because of the wide opportunities most wealth taxes offer for evading successfully. With an additive wealth tax, evasion is further encouraged by the high marginal rates.

16.19 The economists' approach is useful but limited. Like Marxism it is not so much wrong as too simple. We must recognise the contribution of the other social sciences, especially psychology and sociology, to an understanding of the circumstances generating evasion. The economists' approach takes no account of social climate nor of how tax morality may change with changing perceptions of equity and under the influence of peer groups. How may a wealth tax affect these attitudes?

16.20 One observer in a European country with one of the lowest rates of wealth tax held that wealth tax was resented more than other taxes, partly because it was seen as an addition to an already high income tax and partly because people felt it unfair that they should be charged tax on assets which yield no income with which to pay it.

---

[2] E.g., the position in Sweden, see paragraph 4.103.

16.21 If this is true of a substitutive wealth tax, it is likely to be much more true of an additive tax where, however much people cut their consumption, or seek high-yielding investments, they can only meet their tax liability by parting with assets. In circumstances of national emergency in which the need is clearly recognised, such a tax may be accepted as necessary and fair. In other circumstances, it is likely to be perceived as grossly unfair and to be bitterly resented by individual taxpayers. Because it is widely shared by peer groups, this antagonism will feed on itself and grow. In these circumstances, methods of evasion are likely to be widely adopted.

16.22 It is a weakness of the economists' approach that, because it ignores tax morality, it implies a symmetrical pattern of behaviour in relation to evasion. Given the opportunities, the likelihood of discovery and the penalties, the economists' approach implies that there is a unique quantity of evasion associated with each level of marginal tax rates. Whilst, in the absence of empirical evidence, it can be no more than hypothesis, it seems to us unlikely that this is so. Tax morality is a tender plant which once damaged will not readily grow again. Many people will have a strong reluctance to break the law and this reluctance constitutes an important barrier to evasion. But if, under what they regard as extreme provocation, that reluctance is overcome and they resort to evasion, then the barriers may well be down for all time. Reducing tax rates then may not reduce evasion, or at any rate, not reduce it to the level formerly associated with those rates. If this hypothesis is correct, then the taxpayer's propensity to evade is asymmetrical with respect to tax rates. Generating evasion by very high rates may do irreparable harm to tax morality.

Avoidance and a Wealth Tax

16.23 High marginal tax rates which stimulate evasion also encourage avoidance, and tax avoiders do not have to overcome the same scruples as law breakers nor worry about discovery or penalties (save in so far as a new law blocking a previous loophole renders nugatory the costs they have incurred in implementing an avoidance scheme). Easy opportunities will likewise encourage avoidance. The obvious forms it takes, believed to be widely used in those countries with wealth taxes, are the purchase of exempt assets and of assets which carry a low value for wealth tax purposes.

16.24 There is here a somewhat subtle inter-relationship between avoidance and evasion. On the one hand, if assets which lend themselves to tax evasion, like jewellery, pictures, collections of stamps or coins, are exempt from wealth tax, then the opportunity for tax evasion is reduced; but the opportunity for avoidance is correspondingly increased. On the other hand, the fewer the avenues for avoidance, the more will taxpayers who regard themselves as unfairly treated be inclined to step over the legal line and move from avoidance to evasion.

16.25 Also the higher the marginal rates of wealth tax, the fewer the opportunities for simple avoidance and the more taxpayers perceive a levy as unfair, the more they will be attracted to extreme forms of avoidance, most notably the emigration of themselves and their capital.

The Dangers of an Additive Wealth Tax
The Green Paper Proposals

16.26 The proposals for a wealth tax in the United Kingdom as set out in the Green Paper are compatible with a largely substitutive or a largely additive tax (paragraphs 6.37 ff).

16.27 Even if the tax which ultimately results is largely substitutive the form proposed in the Green Paper is bound to stimulate evasion. The general impression from the Green Paper is that an attempt is to be made at a comprehensive coverage which will bring within the tax net assets of a kind easy to conceal from the Revenue. Moreover, the adoption of a full-scale system of self-assessment, in which the taxpayer is expected to value all his own assets with very little precise guidance, will combine evasion possibilities by under-valuation with strong temptation. The compliance cost which this system imposes on the taxpayer is likely to add to resentment. Penalties for 'negligence, fraud or wilful default' would be the same as for income tax, but the Green Paper recognises the difficulty of imposing penalties for under-valuation when it states: 'there would be no question of imposing a penalty on a taxpayer who had understated the value of his assets provided he had valued them according to the best of his knowledge and judgement' (paragraph 64). Some people may prove distinctly lacking in knowledge and market judgement!

16.28 Checking is to be on a sample basis only. Moreover, the tax is to be administered separately from income tax or capital transfer tax in regional offices. Although the Green Paper stresses that this organisation 'will have very close links with existing Inland Revenue offices' and that there will be cross-checking, it is hard to believe that such checks would be very consistent or complete.

16.29 If the wealth tax turns out to be substantially additive, then high marginal rates and taxpayer resentment will feed the urge to evade. But the most serious danger from an additive tax is likely to be the emigration not only of some of those who currently come within its scope, but of the bright executives and professional men who, whilst below the wealth tax threshold, see themselves rising above it in a few years' time. It would probably be wrong to suggest that a wealth tax alone would be responsible for emigration; but it

S

might well be one, and perhaps the culminating influence which, with high marginal tax rates generally, and an uncongenial economic and social climate, leads to a decision to emigrate. Increasing contacts with other countries in a shrinking world make emigration a less formidable prospect than once it was. To be outside the scope of the tax, emigrants must not only give up their United Kingdom residence, but also move out of United Kingdom assets taxable in the hands of non-residents, i.e. land and business assets. But if they emigrate they are likely to wish to transfer out of United Kingdom assets altogether. Should this happen on any scale, then thought might have to be taken to restrict further the movement of capital. To put severe restrictions on capital movements in effect restricts the movement of persons too, for a man can hardly emigrate if he must leave most of his possessions behind. Thus, severe capital restrictions would gainsay a fundamental human freedom. Rather than this, it might be preferable to impose some sort of emigration tax in lieu of wealth tax. But the emigration of persons and capital on any scale would represent a serious loss of enterprise and be detrimental to the balance of payments.

Foreign Precedents

16.30 Any attempt to assess the consequences for evasion and avoidance of an additive wealth tax must be extremely tentative for there is no entirely appropriate experience on which to go. All the European countries have wealth taxes which are simply supplements to income taxes, so it is not possible to draw on their experience. The few precedents of additive wealth taxes are to be found outside Europe in developing countries and therefore of limited value.

16.31 Ceylon, now Sri Lanka, introduced a wealth tax in 1960 at modest rates, only to raise them shortly afterwards to a maximum of 5%, at which level it became impossible for the wealthy to meet the tax from income. However, in 1965 the Finance Minister, the Hon. U. B. Wanninayake, repudiated the concept of a tax that had necessarily to be paid from wealth. Pointing out the implications of a 5% rate, he went on to say: 'This is not the concept underlying the wealth tax. Wealth tax provides for a measure of differentiation of the burden of tax between earned and unearned income. It is in effect an additional income tax payable out of income.' He announced a reduction in rates to a maximum of 2%, which is the present level.[3] Thus Sri Lanka, after a flirtation with an additive wealth tax, had second thoughts.

16.32 Not so India, as yet. Adopting a wealth tax at rates of $\frac{1}{2}$ to $1\frac{1}{2}\%$ in 1957, by 1970-1, after five increases, the rates had become 1% at the minimum

---

[3] See H. W. T. Pepper, 'The Taxation of Wealth', *Bulletin of the International Bureau of Fiscal Documentation*, July 1967.

on wealth holdings over 1 R lakh to 5% on holdings over 20 Rs lakh.[4] Dr. M. H. Gopal,[5] analysing the effects of wealth tax at that time, concluded that there were many cases where combined income tax and wealth tax could be expected to exceed 100% of income—and, indeed, this view was accepted by the Indian Prime Minister and Minister of Finance in her Budget Speech in 1970.

16.33 From a comparison of pre- and post-wealth tax situations, Dr. Gopal could find little evidence of any decline in aggregate capital formation or personal saving as a result of the tax. His main conclusion, however, was that it generated evasion and black money. Whilst the amount of it was uncertain he argued that data collected about *detected* income that had been concealed strongly suggested that the amount of income that evaded tax was growing rapidly and that a major part of this evasion was concentrated in the higher income groups comprising the wealth tax and higher income tax assessees. Concealed income could not come into the open and be used as capital for normal operations. Hence it tended to be used in unsocial, less productive and more wasteful ways, e.g. bank deposits in fictitious names, the purchase of gold and jewellery for secret hoarding, the acquisition of foreign currency, and so on. High tax rates, in Dr. Gopal's view, were not the only cause of evasion, but were one cause, and he believed that a reduction in the top rates of tax on income and wealth would bring out a large portion of unaccounted money and divert it into more productive channels. He consequently recommended a reduction in income tax and wealth tax combined to 90% of income in the immediate future and subsequently to 80%.

16.34 His recommendations appear to have been ignored. Wealth tax rates in India (in 1974-5) reached a maximum of 8% on 15 Rs lakh and the indications are that evasion continues rife.[6]

16.35 There are many relevant differences between India and the United Kingdom and it would be quite wrong to suggest that the Indian experience of evasion would be repeated if an additive wealth tax were introduced into the United Kingdom. Not least the general attitude to tax evasion is different in the two countries. But attitudes can change. The United Kingdom could be expected to move nearer to the Indian position if a tax was introduced which was perceived by taxpayers to be uniquely unfair and which at the same time offered wide opportunities for evasion with comparative safety from penalties. Alternatively, the reaction of United Kingdom taxpayers could be increasing avoidance, taking the form of emigration.

16.36 The real point is that an annual tax which had to be paid out of capital

---

[4] 1 lakh is 100,000; 20 Rs lakh (2,000,000 rupees) was at that time equivalent to about £150,000.

[5] *Wealth Tax in India*, Economic & Scientific Research Foundation, New Delhi, 1970.

[6] See, for example, 'Only Thirty Lakh Indians Pay Income Tax', *Blitz,* 20 July 1974.

would create an entirely new situation. We just do not know how the wealthy would react to the prospect of a year by year reduction in their wealth.

16.37 In introducing such high wealth tax rates, Ceylon (temporarily) and India were diverging from the precepts of the author of their wealth taxes, Professor Lord Kaldor. As he wrote in his Report to the Indian Government[7]: 'From every point of view, it is far better to have a foolproof system of taxation with a moderate rate schedule, than a system which has the appearance of high progressivity, but which cannot be effectively or impartially administered' (p. 1). And again, 'India like most Western countries has been in the grip of a vicious circle as far as progressive taxation is concerned—evasion and avoidance by cutting down potential revenue led to higher nominal rates of taxation and this in turn to further evasion and avoidance and still higher rates. It is a vicious circle of charging more and more on less and less' (p. 5). And finally, 'The incentive to evade taxes depends on the marginal rates of taxation, since these govern the gains from evasion as a percentage of the sums so evaded. The actual extent of evasion depends on those incentives as well as on the ease with which evasion can be accomplished. Since different taxpayers are very differently situated as regards facilities for evading taxation, anything that makes tax evasion easy is bound to be the source of great social inequities' (p. 6).

Summary and Conclusions

16.38 A wealth tax, especially one which attempts to be comprehensive and which puts the responsibility for valuation on the taxpayer as proposed in the Green Paper, offers considerable scope for evasion which it is not easy to detect or punish. If the wealth tax is additive, high marginal tax rates and taxpayer resentment increase the likelihood both of evasion and of avoidance in the extreme form of the emigration of the wealthy and the potentially wealthy with their capital. There are no precedents for an additive tax in Western Europe, but the experience of India is not auspicious.

---

[7] *Indian Tax Reform*, Ministry of Finance, Government of India, New Delhi, 1956.

Part V
Conclusions and Recommendations

Chapter 17

A Wealth Tax for the United Kingdom?

17.1 Any wealth tax in the United Kingdom, whether substitutive or additive, will give rise to some difficult problems. We begin this final chapter by giving our views on some of the main points on which opinion was invited in the Green Paper and summarising the main ways in which our proposals differ from those of the Green Paper. We then turn to consider in more detail the purpose a wealth tax might serve in the United Kingdom, how this would affect its structure and what effects the alternative forms of wealth tax might have. Finally we ask the question whether there might not be better ways of achieving the same objectives.

The Detail of a Wealth Tax
17.2 Our own recommendations on the details of a wealth tax differ in important respects from those of the Green Paper. The main differences together with our views on some of the options suggested in the Green Paper are summarised as follows:

Scope of the Charge

17.3 *Persons Chargeable.* So long as the remittance basis applies for income tax on foreign investment income in the case of persons not domiciled in the United Kingdom, an individual should only be liable to wealth tax on world-wide assets if he is resident and ordinarily resident and also domiciled in the United Kingdom (paragraphs 7.1-7.7).

17.4 The wealth of married couples should be aggregated for wealth tax purposes, with a higher threshold than for single persons (paragraphs 7.15-7.25). There is also a case for an age or retirement relief (paragraph 8.18 and Appendix A).

17.5 *Trusts.* Trust assets should be attributed to the greatest possible extent to the individuals, including discretionary beneficiaries, who enjoy the income. We do not favour a charge related to the wealth of the settlor. With accumulation trusts liability should be revised at the end of the accumulation period by reference to the circumstances of the beneficiary or beneficiaries if then identified (Chapter 11).

Exemptions

17.6 *Household and personal effects.* We suggest that the exemption for household and personal effects should take the form of excluding from charge any article of less than a specified value, say £500, as being more convenient than the exemption of the first £X of the aggregate value of the effects. We see no virtue in the Green Paper proposal to exempt cars irrespective of value; but under our proposal they could be treated in the same way as other personal effects, i.e. exempt if less than a prescribed value (paragraphs 8.27-8.39).

17.7 *Patents and copyrights.* Contrary to the view in the Green Paper, we consider that there is a good case on theoretical as well as practical grounds for exempting patent rights and copyrights in the hands of the inventor or author (paragraphs 10.75-10.77).

Productive Assets

17.8 *Closely owned business.* We have made several suggestions which would benefit closely owned businesses (whether unincorporated businesses, partnerships or companies):

(a) Created goodwill should be exempt in line with the treatment of patents and copyrights (paragraphs 10.33-10.45).

(b) Valuations should normally be based on net tangible assets but, at times when quoted shares are depressed, should be at a prescribed percentage below that amount. Net tangible assets should be computed. by methods which arrive at a cautious value.

(c) On applying general ceiling provisions to closely owned businesses, the income attributed to them should be the lesser of 3% of the value of the business or shares or the actual profits unless actual dividends from a closely owned company are greater. Floor provisions for such businesses should be less onerous than for other assets.

(d) The Green Paper proposal to allow deferment of tax (with accumulated interest) in suitable cases raises doubts as to the appropriateness of taxing a business to an annual wealth tax at all. Leaving that aside, we fear that a mounting debt will sap enterprise whilst encouraging the owners to remain locked in to postpone payment. To reduce deferment to a minimum we suggest that the owners of a closely owned company should be able to draw a dividend for payment of wealth tax without incurring income tax liability on the dividend; and that in the case of unincorporated businesses that part of the profits which is required for payment of wealth tax shall be charged at the corporation tax rate. If the proposal for deferment of tax is adopted we consider it vital that the rate of interest should be kept low.

(e) Minority shareholders in closely owned companies should be better protected and other steps should be taken to encourage participation in such companies.

(f) A wealth tax holiday of limited duration should be considered for newly established businesses (Chapter 12).

17.9 *Agriculture.* Similar considerations apply to the tenant farmer as to the closely owned business; with the owner-occupier there is the additional problem of the current high value of land and the consequent low rate of return. We suggest that valuation of land should be cautious and by stand-ardised methods. Hope value should not be taxed unless it has entered the purchase price. Schemes for joint ownership of land like that proposed by the Agricultural Mortgage Corporation should be encouraged. There is also a particularly strong case for a ceiling provision in agriculture because of its dependence on the vagaries of the weather (Chapter 13).

The National Heritage

17.10 *Works of art.* Where the owners of works of art or other objects of national, historical or scientific interest agree to suitable provisions for public access, we recommend complete exemption from wealth tax, not simply the deferment proposed in the Green Paper. Otherwise, works of art etc. should be included within the tax base (paragraphs 14.1-14.25).

17.11 *Historic houses.* Similarly, historic houses should be completely exempt, conditional on reasonable public access (paragraphs 14.26-14.36).

Relationship with Other Taxes

17.12 *Investment income surcharge.* The Green Paper looks sympathetically on the proposition that investment income surcharge and wealth tax should be alternatives, only the higher of the two being charged. In our view the case for offsetting the surcharge is unanswerable; indeed, in principle the surcharge ought to be abolished and we do not agree with the Green Paper view that abolition should be ruled out for 'the foreseeable future'. In the meantime investment income surcharge should not be levied on investment income in excess of 6% of the taxpayer's net wealth (paragraph 9.5).

17.13 *Ceiling relief.* The general case for and against a ceiling is considered in paragraphs 17.21-17.23 in relation to the purpose of a wealth tax. But if a ceiling is necessary, we suggest that, at any particular level of wealth, it should be that percentage of income which would be taken by income tax and investment income surcharge if the taxpayer's only income were investment income equal to 6% of his net wealth. The relevant percentage should then be applied to investment income only; earned income should not be affected. There should also be a floor, below which tax liability should not be reduced, which should be half the taxpayer's (unabated) wealth tax liability plus two-thirds of his investment income.

Administration and Valuation

17.14 We consider that, in the interests of the taxpayer, the best arrangement would be for wealth tax and income tax liabilities to be dealt with in the same office. At the least the same return should be used for both (paragraphs 15.1-15.8). There is also a case for allowing some limited credit against wealth tax for valuation expenses (paragraph 15.35).

17.15 We have major reservations on the Green Paper proposals for self-valuation and self-assessment. Even if Revenue assessment were proposed we should think it highly desirable, for ease of administration, to adopt cadastral or conventional valuation methods. These methods are more necessary under the proposed system of self-assessment and sample checking, for the taxpayer will not know whether his valuations are acceptable to the Revenue unless and until his case is selected for audit; and then, if they are not acceptable, the Revenue may reopen past years. We think this is wrong; if the Revenue is not prepared to agree liabilities year by year as they arise it ought not to be entitled to reopen the past unless it can at least prove negligence on the part of the taxpayer (paragraphs 15.10-15.22).

17.16 We have therefore proposed that there should be periodical official valuations of land and buildings, which would normally stand for say five years. (The Green Paper appears to accept the need for cadastral valuation of land and buildings by suggesting valuation at a multiple of annual value for rating purposes. This may serve as an interim measure, but we consider that as soon as possible there should be an official capital valuation, which would be used for rating purposes, followed by quinquennial revaluation.)

17.17 Further, we consider that definite rules should be laid down for the valuation of businesses and unquoted shares which should normally be based on the net tangible assets, ignoring created goodwill; so far as possible income tax figures should be used also for wealth tax purposes.

17.18 We have, however, suggested that the value of the shares of larger unquoted companies could, at the option of the Inland Revenue, be the price at which they might be expected to be quoted if the company was a quoted company paying the kind of dividend which would be expected in that situation. The price so estimated would then be reduced by a prescribed percentage to take account of the fact that the shares are not quoted, and by a further prescribed percentage in the case of companies not big enough to be quoted. The figure per share so arrived at would be adopted irrespective of the size of the holding.

17.19 The Green Paper envisages that businesses will have to draw up a balance sheet on the prescribed valuation date, whether or not that is their normal accounting date. We consider that this requirement would prove highly unsatisfactory to both the Revenue and the taxpayer; the valuation should be as at the normal accounting date, adjusted where necessary, and subject to any safeguards that may be required to counter avoidance.

What Kind of Wealth Tax?

17.20 The proposals just outlined would be relevant to whatever form of wealth tax the United Kingdom might adopt. But the major issues which the Green Paper left open—the threshold, rate structure and form of ceiling provision, if any—depend very much on what purpose the tax is primarily intended to serve. (Chapter 1). The possible objectives of a wealth tax, with their implications for structure, can be summarised as follows:

Table 17.1   Purpose and Structure of a Wealth Tax

Purpose	Appropriate Threshold	Appropriate Rates	Ceiling	Additive or Substitutive
Horizontal equity (paragraphs 1.11-1.19)	Low	Low: proportional or mildly progressive	None or 'notional'	Substitutive
Efficiency (paragraphs 1.20-1.24)	Low	Low: proportional or mildly progressive	None or 'notional'	Substitutive
Reduction in Inequality				
(a) Limited (paragraphs 1.31-1.32)	Could be high	Mildly progressive	High	Substitutive
(b) Radical (paragraphs 1.33-1.36)	Could be high	Progressive	None or 'restricted'	Additive
Control (paragraphs 1.37-1.39)	Low	Immaterial	Immaterial	Immaterial

17.21 Presentation in tabular form oversimplifies (for example 'substitutive' might mean largely or wholly), but it highlights the policy choices. One feature of the table needs explanation—the reference to 'notional' and 'restricted' ceiling provisions. In general our view would be that if the purpose of a wealth tax is any other than the radical reduction of inequality, rates of wealth tax, taken together with income tax, ought to be low enough to make a ceiling unnecessary; in that situation combined wealth tax and income tax would only approach or exceed 100% of income for those very wealthy persons who chose to hold assets with an extremely low rate of return—and we do not consider such persons merit relief, for they hold the remedy in their own hands. If, however, the objective is to bring about an immediate reduction in inequality, then any general ceiling provision is equally inappropriate, for it would run directly counter to that purpose.

17.22 However, as we have seen (paragraphs 3.23-3.47), both average and marginal rates of taxation on the wealth and investment income of the very wealthy in the United Kingdom are already the highest in Western Europe even without a wealth tax; and in our view (as elaborated below) top marginal rates of income tax on earned and investment income are already so high as to be prejudicial to efficiency. In these circumstances it might seem wise to provide for a ceiling provision even with a substitutive wealth tax. In that case, on grounds of efficiency and horizontal equity, the need is to avoid a form of ceiling which favours low yield: where two people have the same investment income from different amounts of capital we must ensure that the one with the higher capital pays more tax. We therefore reject the form of ceiling of the Continental countries which simply limits the total burden of income tax and wealth tax to X% of total income. Instead we recommend a ceiling related to investment income alone (so that earned income is unaffected) and which rises as a proportion of income as wealth increases. A suggested method of arriving at the appropriate percentages is summarised in paragraph 17.13. Furthermore, there should be a floor which tapers the ceiling relief in such a way that at zero income half the unabated wealth tax is payable. As notional yields are used to compute the appropriate percentages, such a ceiling is designated by the shorthand 'notional' in table 17.1.

17.23 Further, whilst we can see no logic in a general ceiling provision as part of a wealth tax aiming at a radical reduction in inequality, it would be wise, if such a tax were introduced, to limit the damage to enterprise by providing for a special ceiling which applied exclusively to private businesses (including agriculture). Such a ceiling should take a similar form to the 'notional' ceiling but the income to which the ceiling calculation is applied should be specially restricted. Such a ceiling is designated a 'restricted' ceiling in the table.

17.24 Let us return to the question, 'what kind of wealth tax?' It is fairly clear from our study of Continental wealth taxes and from the summary in table 17.1 that the choice lies between the following two categories of tax:

(a) A substitutive wealth tax with horizontal equity as prime aim, but possibly bringing some supplementary advantages in terms of control, efficiency and reduction in inequality in the limited sense. In other words, a wealth tax on Continental lines.

(b) An additive wealth tax aiming at a radical reduction in inequality, which the rich can only meet by disposing annually of some of their assets.

17.25 The statements in Labour Party policy documents in the five or so years preceding the Green Paper (paragraphs 6.5-6.6) imply the intention to introduce an additive wealth tax to reduce inequality. But the Green Paper itself is less clear in its statement of aims. In his foreword the Chancellor states that the tax is intended 'to promote greater social and economic equality'. He then formulates the horizontal equity argument: 'Income by itself is not an adequate measure of taxable capacity . . .' and continues that 'Because our present tax system takes no account of this fact, although we have a highly progressive system of income tax, the bulk of privately owned wealth is still concentrated in relatively few hands.' He appears to conclude that the improvement of horizontal equity resulting from a wealth tax will necessarily reduce inequality of wealth. This would only be so if the wealthy held a large proportion of their wealth in non-income-yielding, or possibly very low-yielding, assets. The statistical evidence suggests that at any rate the proposition is not true in so far as it relates to nil-yielding assets (paragraphs 6.47-6.55). Whilst the horizontal equity argument and the reduction in inequality argument are not entirely divorced, they are essentially different. The horizontal equity argument is concerned with the additional taxable capacity conferred by capital (over and above any income derived from it) at all levels of wealth holding. Its logic is a low threshold and the replacement of the investment income surcharge all down the scale, as, indeed, the Green Paper explicitly recognises, but rules out on administrative grounds 'for the foreseeable future'. (Paragraph 30.) Further, the horizontal equity argument logically implies rates which are low, roughly equivalent to the investment income surcharge, and like many of the Continental wealth taxes, could be proportional. The reduction in inequality argument is compatible with a high threshold; its concern is not so much the additional taxable capacity which capital confers over and above income, but the overall rates of income tax and wealth tax combined. (Indeed, a government could go a long way to reduce inequalities of wealth by means of annual taxes without a wealth tax, if it was prepared to levy income tax rates exceeding 100% of investment income.) A wealth tax radically to reduce inequality implies progressive rates and, as already stressed, is incompatible with a general ceiling provision.

17.26 If the Green Paper is unclear in its aim it is not surprising that there is no consistent attempt to match structure to objectives. The Green Paper proposes a high threshold (of £100,000); it suggests two scales as illustrations, both progressive, one with a maximum rate of $2\frac{1}{2}\%$ (and with a rate of 1% up to £500,000 wealth) and the other with a top rate of 5%; it indicates that the investment surcharge will be retained, but that the taxpayer might be charged wealth tax or surcharge whichever was the larger; and it contemplates the possibility of a general ceiling provision. Besides the decisions on these major alternatives, the effective burden of a wealth tax depends also on conclusions reached about exemptions, special reliefs and methods of valuation.

17.27 According to the decision taken on each of these issues, so the wealth tax would move closer to one or other of the two categories we postulated. Partial replacement of the investment income surcharge, the lower scale and a general ceiling provision would bring the tax nearer to alternative (a) the substitutive tax for horizontal equity; the higher scale, with no set off of the investment income surcharge and no ceiling provision would turn it into (b), an additive wealth tax to reduce inequality. Let us examine more fully the case for each of these forms of wealth tax in the United Kingdom.

The Case for a Substitutive Wealth Tax

17.28 The Continental countries which we have studied adopted wealth taxes half a century or more ago to improve the horizontal equity of their tax systems by recognising the additional taxable capacity conferred by capital. None of them levies an investment income surcharge or (what amounts to the same thing) gives earned income relief, which was the method the United Kingdom adopted in the first decade of this century to secure similar ends— to tax income from property more heavily than income from work, because of the greater permanence of the former. The question we must seek to answer, therefore, is which is the better method and by how much?

17.29 There is no doubt that the theoretically perfect wealth tax is a superior instrument for attaining horizontal equity than the perfect investment income surcharge. This is so because a wealth tax comprehends nil-yielding assets which increase the spending power of their owner but are untouched by an investment income surcharge; and because a wealth tax takes account of the different taxable capacities conferred by different values of capital yielding the same income. In principle, therefore, a wealth tax is to be preferred.

17.30 In practice, however, the advantages of a wealth tax start to fade away, for the perfect wealth tax would provide fully comprehensive coverage and uniform and precise valuation and these are not attainable in practice. The investment income surcharge, on the other hand, does not raise the same practical difficulties.

17.31 The experience of the Continental countries is instructive. Every wealth tax, in practice, reflects a compromise. The wider the coverage the more fully, in theory, the tax promotes horizontal equity; but the wider the coverage the more difficult it is to prevent evasion by under-reporting and the more difficult to secure uniform valuation. Of the wealth taxes we studied that of Denmark is at one extreme, excluding all assets within the house regardless of value—jewels, works of art, and furniture. At the other extreme is perhaps Norway, which (apart from an aggregate exemption for all household goods) seeks to tax pictures and jewellery but probably has difficulty in enforcing the provision—with the result that inequity results between the more honest and the less honest taxpayers.

17.32 When we examine the United Kingdom position more precisely (paragraphs 6.47-6.55) the non-income-yielding assets fall into some four categories:

1. Household goods (including furniture, china, less valuable works of art, jewellery, cars and boats).
2. Works of art of museum quality.
3. Cash in the house or in drawing accounts.
4. Residential accommodation.

17.33 On the basis of the (admittedly imperfect) estate duty statistics, items 1 and 3 combined represented just over 6% of all assets in 1971 and rather under 6% in the case of those persons with assets over £100,000. An exemption for household goods, as proposed in the Green Paper, would reduce the size of this component of a wealth tax base.

17.34 Estate duty figures offer no guide to the amount of wealth held in the form of works of art of museum quality; but we have argued that there is a very strong case for their exemption where the owner meets conditions about public access.

17.35 The most important asset not yielding a money income is residential buildings, comprising 28% of all assets but under 7% of the assets of those with over £100,000 in 1971.

17.36 Additionally the wealth tax would bring into charge the value of the assets of the unincorporated business, including the land of the owner-occupier in agriculture, which currently escape investment income surcharge because the return is treated as earned income. Similarly, with the closely owned company where director's remuneration may, in reality, include part of the return on capital. But the inclusion of private business assets in this way must be regarded as a dubious advantage creating serious liquidity and efficiency problems and requiring special treatment, as the Green Paper recognises.

17.37 Apart from the inclusion of nil-yielding assets, the advantage of a wealth tax is its heavier taxation of low-yielding assets. But, at the time of writing, this advantage has diminished because of the drop in share values and the consequent increase in yields. Furthermore, if low yields lead to capital gains, as things currently stand they will be taxed to capital gains tax on realisation with no allowance for inflation. (We suggest below, paragraph 17.55, that the provision by which death counts as realisation should be re-introduced.) Finally, as compared with two taxpayers with equal investment income, the capital transfer tax will impinge more heavily on the one whose wealth has the lower yield.

17.38 Against the theoretical superiority of a wealth tax over an investment income surcharge have to be set the higher cost of administration, the high compliance costs, the special problems created for agriculture and industry and, especially under the self-assessment and taxpayer valuation proposals of the Green Paper, the danger of a new set of inequities between taxpayers of different degrees of honesty.

17.39 Before deciding if a wealth tax aiming at horizontal equity is worth while, it is at any rate worth considering whether the assets brought into charge, or more fully into charge, by a wealth tax, could not be taxed in some simpler alternative way.

17.40 Remembering that we are talking of a wealth tax to secure horizontal equity, where the threshold would be low and a proportional rate would be appropriate, consumer durables like cars, boats and jewellery might be taxed by an excise duty on purchase. The amount of excise duty could be fixed at a figure which would approximately equal the discounted present value of the sum of the wealth tax payments which would otherwise have been paid over the life of the asset. (Indeed, if a wealth tax were introduced, it might be fairer and simpler to tax in this way some assets which are difficult to value and easy to hide.) However, the limitations and disadvantages of this procedure must be recognised. To introduce an excise duty on purchase would not catch such assets already in the hands of the taxpayer; and it would tax all purchasers of these assets, irrespective of whether their total wealth would have brought them above the wealth tax threshold. As for houses, the simplest procedure would be to bring them back into the income tax net by attributing a notional income and reintroducing a Schedule A tax on owner-occupiers (but not on the real property of corporations or on let property); if that happened it would be best to express the notional income as a comparatively low percentage of the capital value of the property (as do several of the Continental countries) and not to give relief for expenditure on repairs and maintenance. This would obviate the defects of the previous system which was administratively burdensome, based on out-dated values and benefited the sophisticated compared with the unsophisticated taxpayer.[1]

17.41 If the purpose is horizontal equity, given the existence of an investment income surcharge, the general disadvantages of a wealth tax and alternative ways of taxing nil-yielding assets, it is a finely balanced issue whether a switch

---

[1] The case for bringing the value of owner-occupied houses back within the tax net is increased by the significance of house-ownership in the distribution of wealth. (See Appendix B, paragraph B30.)

from investment income surcharge to a wealth tax is worth while in the United Kingdom, unless associated with a re-structuring of income tax rates as discussed in paragraph 17.43.

17.42 It might be argued that the incidental advantages of replacing an investment income surcharge by a wealth tax, in the form of administrative control and efficiency in resource use, tip the balance in favour of its adoption. However, we do not find these arguments strong. The control argument breaks down just where control is most needed—in identifying nil-yielding assets. As for the efficiency argument, it is perhaps significant that in none of the Continental countries was it suggested to us as an argument for a wealth tax. Because of its inevitably uneven coverage of assets and lack of a uniform valuation, a wealth tax creates its own investment distortions. Most seriously, there are many circumstances, especially connected with agriculture and the private business, where a low yield is not necessarily a sign of inefficiency and a wealth tax may consequently do more economic damage than good. Moreover, even where high yield does reflect an efficient use of resources, as long as income tax rates remain at their present high level and capital gains tax is much lower and avoidable by holding an asset until death, capital growth will remain attractive despite a wealth tax.

17.43 The position would, however, be different if the introduction of a wealth tax was associated with modifications in income tax designed significantly to reduce the present high marginal rates (currently amounting to 83% on earned income and 98% on investment income). If these rates were lowered, not only would the detrimental effects of a wealth tax be eased, but the combination of lower income tax and a wealth tax would provide a dual incentive to investment in high yielding assets; attractions of capital growth (and nil or low yield) would be substantially reduced.

17.44 The United Kingdom has maximum rates of income tax which are much higher than those of any other country we studied. Whilst there is little evidence to suggest that, at low rates, income tax acts as a net disincentive, research does point to a restrictive effect on work effort from rates of 70% or more.[2] Although there is a general lack of empirical evidence, we should also expect rates above 70% seriously to diminish the incentives to enterprise and accumulation; and we should expect them to encourage evasion and stimulate an unproductive search for methods of avoidance. If the introduction of a modest wealth tax were a means of getting rid of the investment income surcharge and reducing top marginal rates of income tax on earned and investment income to, say, 70% (still well above the German maximum of 56%) then we would welcome the innovation. There is just a hint of recogni-

---

[2] See especially G. F. Break, 'Effects of Taxation on Incentives', *British Tax Review,* June 1957; and D. B. Fields and W. T. Stanbury, 'Incentives, Disincentives and the Income Tax' *Public Finance,* No. 3, 1970.

T

tion in the Green Paper that rates of income tax in the United Kingdom are too high and of the possibility that the introduction of a wealth tax might be a means of reducing them: 'Once the additional taxable capacity represented by ownership of wealth is adequately brought into charge, excessive inequalities of wealth will in time be eroded, and it will be possible to reduce the high rates of tax on earned income.' (Foreword).

17.45 If a wealth tax, the prime purpose of which was horizontal equity, were to be introduced, then it should differ from the Green Paper proposals in various ways. The threshold should be brought down to a level sufficiently low to eliminate the investment income surcharge; the rates should be low— perhaps a flat 1% would be appropriate, like the current Irish proposal —but the exact rate structure should depend on the concurrent adjustment to income tax. Further, formalised valuation methods should be adopted more in line with the majority of the Continental countries, to give the taxpayer more certainty; and the costs of administration minimised by applying the same valuation to other taxes, notably death duties, gift tax and local rates, which should be levied on capital values.

17.46 We recognise that such methods could not be introduced in 1976-77 when the Government hopes to introduce its wealth tax; but, if the starting date is a matter of importance for the Government, we see no serious objection to commencing in 1976-77 at the high threshold, with the partial replacement of the investment income surcharge, and with formalised valuation methods where possible, and thereafter working on a definite plan (by stages if necessary) to reduce the threshold, replace the surcharge and widen the area of formalised valuation.

The Case for an Additive Wealth Tax

17.47 The case for a wholly or largely additive wealth tax is its direct and more or less immediate effect in reducing inequality of wealth. How far this objective is regarded as desirable, if at all, is a personal value judgement and we should make our own position plain. We wish to see a reduction in the inequalities of wealth in the United Kingdom. Further, we consider that taxes on capital have an important part to play in bringing about a redistribution of wealth. But this objective cannot be pursued without regard to other considerations. The full consequences of using an additive annual wealth tax to reduce inequalities must be conjectural; no European country uses a wealth tax for this purpose, so there is no directly comparable experience on which to rely. But our theoretical analysis, and such empirical evidence as we have examined, suggests that the social gain from a reduction in equality would be bought at a very high price. The main detrimental consequences can be summarised as follows:

1. Incentives to saving and enterprise can hardly fail to be damaged by

marginal rates of income tax and wealth tax combined which would exceed 100% of income (paragraphs 6.37-6.46).

2. An additive wealth tax would pose a serious threat to the growing points of new enterprise by its effects on the closely owned business (Chapter 12).

3. Whilst the wealth tax might aid agriculture in the long run by bringing down the value of agricultural land, at best the industry would face a difficult transition period and debilitating uncertainty, at worst its efficiency would be seriously impaired; whilst any wealth tax would cause difficulties for agriculture, they would be most severe with an additive tax (Chapter 13).

4. An additive wealth tax creates all the conditions favouring an increase of evasion and a decline in tax morality (Chapter 16).

5. Avoidance of wealth tax by the emigration of the rich with their wealth is virtually certain—only the scale is in doubt. Perhaps more serious, the tax would encourage the emigration of the enterprising and potentially wealthy (paragraph 16.29).

6. With any wealth tax operating costs would be likely to be high. Compliance costs would be particularly large if the methods of self-assessment and taxpayer valuation proposed in the Green Paper were adopted; and these methods would also introduce a new uncertainty and inequity into the tax system (Chapter 15).

7. An additive tax increases the danger to our national heritage of works of art and historic houses (the former being sold abroad and the latter decaying) if the treatment proposed in the Green Paper is implemented (Chapter 14).

17.48 There are two further considerations, of a general and less specific nature, which must give cause for disquiet. The first is the cumulative effects of the economic detriments we have listed taken in conjunction with some of the possibilities of the Green Paper. The application of an additive wealth tax could undermine the private enterprise sector of the mixed economy. It could sap the incentives to private saving and enterprise and lead to the emigration of the enterprising. The closely owned business (including agriculture) which should be the growing point of private enterprise, could be smothered by the wealth tax proposals. Moreover the Green Paper proposals for deferment of wealth tax plus accumulated interest at a commercial rate could be lethal. We hardly think it an exaggeration to say that if an additive wealth tax were introduced with no other 'concessions' for the private business than the option of deferment, and the Chancellor then decided that a 'commercial rate' of interest was 10 or 12% compound, (especially if there was a fall in asset prices) the death knell of private enterprise would have been sounded; the balance of the mixed economy would have been destroyed.

17.49 This links with the second general consideration, that of timing. An additive wealth tax could hardly be brought forward at a worse time. A high rate of inflation increases valuation problems, upsets the relationship between values of different forms of wealth, makes it more difficult to design a stable and meaningful rate structure for a wealth tax (paragraph 2.27) and brings the threat of a rapid reduction in the threshold and increase in tax rates in real terms. The current stock exchange slump both means that the yield from a wealth tax would be much less than that suggested in the Green Paper, based on 1972 values, and makes the tax less necessary to reduce inequalities. Finally, and most important, the psychological effect of an additive wealth tax would accentuate the current lack of confidence in the British economy, increasing the likelihood of a major slump.

17.50 Already, without a wealth tax, at the level at which the proposed wealth tax would bite, it is a fair generalisation that large wealth owners in the United Kingdom are the most heavily taxed in Europe. There is no doubt therefore that an additive wealth tax would reduce inequality in the distribution of wealth. It would do so partly by reducing the wealth of the rich and partly by prompting the emigration of the rich and potentially rich. But even as an instrument for reducing inequality an additive wealth tax has major deficiencies, of which there is no recognition in the Green Paper which, regrettably, lacks any clear philosophy of wealth. A wealth tax is indiscriminate as to the source of wealth: we believe that inequalities which result from hard work and enterprise combined with saving are not unfair and are not resented as unfair by the majority of the community; what seems unfair to most people is fortuitous capital gains and large inheritances. If the Chancellor seeks a fairer society, it is not clear that an additive wealth tax will achieve that, for justice and equality are not synonymous. Further, in some ways an additive wealth tax could be counter-productive in the promotion of the social cohesion which is one of its underlying objectives. A possible outcome of an additive wealth tax is dissaving and increased consumption by the rich. The visible signs of wealth might then add to social bitterness, especially if the increased share in current output which the rich were appropriating coincided with a period of national austerity. (The contrast can be painted in an extreme form. At present a large farmer who owns his farm might be worth £250,000 or £500,000, mainly in land which he has no intention of selling; he works hard and he lives frugally. An additive wealth tax might lead the same man, in frustration and desperation, to abandon independent farming, sell his land, doubtless for less than its pre-wealth tax value, and proceed to live in a much more extravagant way.) Finally an additive wealth tax operates on inequality at one end only; it reduces the wealth of the 'rich' whilst doing virtually nothing to increase that of the 'poor'. The wealth taken from the rich is not transferred to the poor but in the main increases the total wealth of the public sector of the economy and reduces that of the private sector.[3]

17.51 We believe, therefore, that an additive wealth tax could have disastrous effects on the economy. On the assumption that there is to be a wealth tax in the United Kingdom we have no doubt that it should be a substitutive tax, aimed primarily at horizontal equity on the lines indicated in paragraphs 17.45 and 17.46. On this basis the scale should not exceed Scale A of the Green Paper.

An Alternative Route to Reducing Inequality

17.52 Having rejected an additive wealth tax which would certainly reduce inequality but at a cost we find unacceptable, we think it worth considering briefly whether there are better ways of reducing inequality. We believe that any policy for the reduction of inequality of wealth ought to look more to the source of the inequality. Its emphasis should be placed on taxing wealth acquired fortuitously, that is, in particular wealth derived from capital appreciation and from inheritances.

17.53 The keynote would be a remodelled death duty. The capital transfer tax of the present Government is superior to estate duty as a means of reducing inequality from inherited wealth because it comprehends gifts and is cumulative. But it is deficient both in terms of horizontal equity and as a means of reducing inequality because it is based on the estate duty principle of taxing what is left by the deceased, irrespective of its disposition, rather than the inheritance tax principle of taxing what is received. Instead of a capital transfer tax the United Kingdom should adopt an accessions tax—a tax levied on the recipient of gifts and legacies, the rate of tax on any accession being determined by the total of previous accessions of gifts and legacies (regardless of source). Such a tax is superior to the capital transfer tax because it is more logical (and in accordance with the actual incidence of a death duty) to tax the beneficiary rather than pretending to tax the deceased (which is an impossibility). It has the advantage that because the tax is imposed on the beneficiary it becomes possible to take account of his particular circumstances (for example to give a concession to a dependent or handicapped child inheriting from a deceased parent). Most significant from our point of view, an accessions tax is more effective in reducing inequality. It is large inheritances not large estates as such which perpetuate inequality and an accessions tax falls heavily on the person who receives most by way of gifts and legacies. Further, although it is impossible to judge how strong the effect will be, an accessions tax does provide some encouragement to the wealthy to give and bequeath their wealth to those who have received least by way of earlier gifts and legacies, for by so doing the donors reduce the total tax paid.

17.54 Besides this benefit in reducing inequality an accessions tax largely

---

[3] For the way in which this happens, see Appendix A of *An Accessions Tax*, by the same authors, IFS 1973.

avoids the detrimental effects of the additive wealth tax. Valuation and administrative problems are more readily containable; taxpayer resentment is less and evasion and avoidance far less likely; and the tax may do economic good rather than harm.[4]

17.55 The second instrument for promoting equality, which would take account of the source of the wealth, would be a remodelled capital gains tax. Briefly, the rates should be increased to approach more nearly income tax rates, the scope might be widened to include major lottery and football pool winnings and there is a strong case on grounds of horizontal equity, reducing inequality and minimising the 'lock-in' effect, for reintroducing the provision by which death counts as a deemed realisation for capital gains tax purposes. But at the same time as the severity of the capital gains tax was increased, it would be essential to index the tax, so that only real and not just monetary gains were charged. Perhaps the simplest way (which the Swedes adopt in relation to gains on real property) would be to allow the acquisition price of an asset to be increased by the same percentage as a general price index.

17.56 Finally, research should be undertaken on more positive measures to increase the wealth of those with little or none, for example the idea of a negative wealth tax—lump sum bounties to all members of the community at coming of age and possibly at retirement—which might replace some of the income benefits of the welfare state; but we recognise that such a measure requires further study before it can be accepted as practical.[5]

17.57 There are other alternative possibilities for tax reform which may offer advantages. Thus Mr. J. S. Flemming and Professor I. M. D. Little have proposed a heavy wealth tax and an accessions tax which would supersede not only the investment income surcharge but also all income tax on investment income, capital gains taxation and the capital transfer tax;[6] and Professor J. E. Meade has recently advocated a combination of accessions tax and expenditure tax with a substitutive wealth tax.[7] These possibilities deserve study. It is particularly interesting that all three sets of proposals include an accessions tax. Our own suggestions for an accessions tax and a strengthened capital gains tax place more emphasis on taxing wealth according to its source than the others. Further, our proposals have the practical merit of being more easily implemented; nor would the adoption of our own proposals hamper the acceptance of the others if further study showed them to be preferable, nor prevent the introduction of a substitutive tax as outlined in paragraphs 17.43-17.45.

---

[4] For the full argument see *An Accessions Tax* by the same authors, IFS 1973.

[5] See C. T. Sandford, *Taxing Personal Wealth*, George Allen & Unwin, 1971, pp 249-254. For other ideas see A. B. Atkinson *Unequal Shares: Wealth in Britain*, Allen Lane, The Penguin Press 1972, and M. Forsyth, *Property and Property Distribution Policy*, PEP 1971.

[6] J. S. Flemming & I. M. D. Little, *Why We Need a Wealth Tax*, Methuen 1974.

[7] J. E. Meade, *The Intelligent Radical's Guide to Economic Policy*, Allen & Unwin, 1975.

17.58 The existence of alternative ways of reducing inequality in the distribution of wealth strengthens the argument for not rushing into an additive wealth tax which might do irreparable harm to the mixed economy.

Conclusion

17.59 A substitutive wealth tax to promote horizontal equity, which merely replaced the investment income surcharge, would be a doubtful improvement. Much more attractive is a substitutive wealth tax associated with significant reductions in the maximum rates of income tax on both earned and investment income. An additive wealth tax would reduce inequalities of wealth but at the price of economic consequences which could threaten the continuance of the mixed economy. There are alternative ways of reducing inequality which do not carry the same detrimental effects and which recognise the virtue of taxing wealth differently according to its derivation.

Appendices

Appendix A

The Capitalised Value of Future Earning Power

A.1 Should the capitalised value of future earning power be included within a wealth tax base? The question resolves itself into one of principle and one of practice.

A.2 The argument in principle for including the capitalised value of a person's future earning power can be summarised as follows. An adult, as a result of inherent ability, investment in education and training, and application, has skills which provide the basis for future earning power. This earning power is equivalent to personal wealth and should be regarded as such. The parallel can be seen most clearly with that part of future earning power which is a product of education. Imagine two brothers of the same natural ability. Let us say a father spends £10,000 on the education of son 'A' and gives son 'B' £10,000 of income-earning assets. Because of the education, 'A' will receive higher life-time earned income than 'B', but 'B' has more income from property than 'A' because of his father's gift. Is it right that a wealth tax should comprehend the capital value of B's assets from his father, but not the capitalised value of the father's equal investment in human capital—A's education? The question becomes still more pertinent if it is the community rather than the individual or his family which has financed the education which has created A's additional earning power.

A.3 It may be argued in reply to the case for including the capitalised value of future earnings that they have a greater uncertainty and a shorter life than the capital value of other investments like holdings of stocks and shares or land, because they are limited to the length of working life of the human being and this might itself be brought to an untimely end by ill health or premature decease. But uncertainties of obsolescence or unforeseen destruction can apply to many assets. This kind of risk can usually be insured against and constitutes an argument not for omitting human capital from the wealth tax base but for discounting its value by a risk factor.

A.4 A more serious argument of principle for exempting the capitalised value of future earnings is that they suffer from two restrictions: unlike other assets they are not freely exchangeable into cash; further, by their very nature they are inseparable from their present owner. Their non-convertibility into cash should not be pressed too far. A person can borrow on the strength of future earning power, and often does, most notably from building societies for house purchase, where the size of the loan is specifically related to the size of present income and the expectation of future income. Further there have been instances of celebrities selling their future earning capacity for a present capital sum. But the characteristic of the asset, that it is indissolubly and uniquely linked to a particular person, does mark it out from other assets and may justify different treatment. Also, since part of the case for a wealth tax (like that for a surcharge on investment income) under the horizontal equity argument has rested on the case for taxing earned income less heavily than income from property, it seems somewhat odd and contradictory to include the capitalised value of future earnings as wealth.

A.5 If the argument of principle does not give an entirely clear answer, the argument of practice points wholly in one direction—to the exclusion of capitalised future earnings from the wealth tax base. To include them would be a difficult exercise only possible by arbitrary simplification. What we seek is the present value of the individual's future income stream from work. There are three unknowns—the future income stream itself, the appropriate rate of discount to apply and the risk factor to write into it (which would vary between persons according to their state of health). The most difficult of these is the future income stream, which could only be assessed on the basis of averages—average earnings for each occupation and average promotion prospects. Any attempt to apply the formula to individuals, few of whom would coincide precisely with the average, would necessarily be arbitrary and inequitable. In fact no country with a wealth tax attempts to include the capitalised value of future earnings and its inclusion must be ruled out on practical grounds. But the exclusion does mean that those well endowed with education and intellect are favoured as compared with those whose wealth lies in physical assets which come within the wealth tax base.

A.6 Our consideration of this issue, however, is not solely academic; it may help in determining certain practical policy issues, in particular the treatment of goodwill, patents and copyrights; and the question of age relief.

A.7 If we are to exclude the capitalised value of future earnings then there is a case also for some exclusion of assets which, though saleable, are essentially a product of personal effort and ability and related to future earnings—which is the situation with some forms of goodwill and with patents and copyrights. A reasonable policy, consistent with the general exclusion of capitalised earning power, would be to exclude the value of goodwill, copyrights and patents in the hands of the creator, author or inventor. If, however, he sells these rights, then the sale value would automatically enter his wealth tax base and there is no reason why the value of the purchased goodwill, patent or copyright, written down as appropriate, should not enter the wealth tax base of the purchaser.[1]

A.8 In principle, besides the capitalised value of future earnings there is an even stronger case for including the capitalised value of future pension rights within the wealth tax base. As a person advanced through working life, the value of the former would decline and that of the latter increase, up to the point of retirement; at that point of time the capitalised value of future earnings would have fallen to zero and the capital value of pension rights would be at a maximum. From then on, the capital value of future pension rights would decline, whilst the value of future earnings would of course remain at zero (assuming no further employment was taken up). This would mean that, if both the capitalised value of future earnings and the value of pension rights entered into the wealth tax base and if the value of other assets remained the same, the amount of wealth subject to tax would decline gradually throughout a man's working life and quite rapidly once he reached retirement. In fact, of course, there would in most cases be a build up of other assets throughout life up to the point of retirement, but probably not beyond.

A.9 However, Governments in general are sympathetic towards pension rights and invariably exclude them, though sometimes with limitations; and exclude the capitalised value of future earnings on practical grounds. Consequently the wealth tax is relatively harder on older people, and especially on retired people, than if they had been included. This provides a theoretical basis for providing some age relief, as indeed is done in some wealth taxes, most notably the German (though not necessarily for this reason).

A.10 The procedure of including the capitalised value of pension rights is also in principle fairer to the private businessman who puts building up his business before providing for his own pension. (It is also more conducive to enterprise). As his business assets are liable to tax, his wealth tax liability is higher throughout his working life than if he had applied some of his resources to building up pension rights. Whilst it is unlikely that Governments would include the capitalised value of pension rights within the wealth tax base, at least an age relief, especially one applying at retirement age, would help such a man who was dependent on the sale of his business assets to provide for his retirement.

---

[1] For a full discussion of the proposed treatment, see paragraphs 10.33-10.45.

Appendix B

The Distribution of Personal Wealth in the United Kingdom

B.1 This Appendix seeks to clarify what must be to many a confusing controversy on the distribution of wealth in the United Kingdom.

B.2 The problems raised by a study of inequalities of wealth are both conceptual and practical and they range from 'what is wealth?' to 'what is a reduction in inequality?'

What is Wealth?

B.3 In ordinary speech we might describe a man as 'wealthy' who had a very large income even if he had few possessions (because he regularly spent most of his income on consumption); and we might describe someone as wealthy who had valuable possessions but not much income (like the Maharajah, with lots of gold and jewels but with no earning assets). To clarify our subject we must be more precise and distinguish between wealth, net worth or capital, on the one hand, and income on the other. By wealth we mean a stock of net assets, which can be catalogued and valued at a point of time; income is a flow generated by earnings from labour or by a return to assets, and income only has meaning in relation to a period of time. Personal wealth consists of an individual's stock of assets of all kinds, physical assets like a house, car and washing machine and financial assets such as cash, bank balances, bonds, shares and insurance policies. From the value of a person's assets has to be deducted the value of liabilities (e.g. the mortgage on his house) to arrive at the figure of an individual's net wealth or net worth.

B.4 There are some difficult borderline cases in defining personal wealth and some difficult problems of valuing individual items which will emerge as we proceed. For the moment let us move on to distinguish between personal wealth and national wealth.

National Wealth

B.5 National wealth is the sum total of the value of the net assets of individuals and institutions in the community wherever those assets are situated.[1] In an economy like ours, national wealth largely consists of personal wealth. But there are two or three ways in which national wealth may differ from the sum of personal wealth:

(i) A small amount of wealth is owned by institutions like charities—but this is negligible as a proportion of total wealth.

(ii) The public sector (the state and nationalised industries) has assets (like schools, roads, offices and the equipment of the nationalised industries as well as some financial assets) which may be greater or less in value than its debts to foreigners and to its citizens in the form of bonds, national savings certificates and the like. The UK public sector has varied between positive and negative net assets.

(iii) Some economists argue that there the differences between personal and national wealth end. The net assets of companies, they maintain, are nil, because the companies are wholly the property of the shareholders and therefore are part of personal wealth held in the form of financial assets which constitute claims to the physical assets. Others point out a valuation difficulty. The value of his shares to the individual shareholder is what he can sell them for in the market. This is what he can get for them if he has to part with them. But the market price is determined by the sales of the marginal shareholder. The vast majority of the shareholders of a public company presumably put a higher value on their shares than that because they do not sell at that price. You thus have the paradox that for shareholders as a whole the value of the company is more than the market value of shares multiplied by their total number. You could still argue that this 'extra' value is part of personal wealth; but it is not a part which has any meaning to the individual in assessing the total of his personal net assets. Hence some economists prefer to adopt the solution of attributing to the company sector a net wealth equal to this extra value.

How is Personal Wealth Distributed?

B.6 The data available on the distribution of personal wealth was not designed for the purpose of the social scientist, but consists of statistics which have emerged as a by-product of administration. Herein lies the big rub. The main source of our information on this subject is data collected by the Inland Revenue from the estate duty returns. We can 'gross-up' the figures of the

---

[1] For a recent analysis of the composition of national wealth see J. Rothman, *The Wealth of the United Kingdom*, Sandelson and Co., November 1974; also 'The Changing Face of Wealth', *The Times*, 18 November 1974.

wealth left by those dying in a particular year to obtain an estimate of the distribution of all personal wealth in that year (and of the types of assets held). The procedure is to extract from estates assessed for estate duty the number and value of estates in each property range for each age-sex group. Then this sample is multiplied by the reciprocal of the mortality rate for that age-sex group. Suppose, for example, that in the year in question, five estates in the range £100,000-£200,000 totalling £800,000 owned by women aged 85 to 86 became liable to death duty. If the mortality rates for that year for women of that age were 200 per 1,000 (1 in 5), then it is assumed that in that year there were 25 (5 × 5) estates in the population as a whole amongst women aged 85 to 86 of a size £100,000-£200,000 and that these estates together totalled £4 million (£800,000 × 5). These calculations, carried out for each age-sex group, can then be totalled for each property range.

B.7 The validity of the picture of the distribution of personal wealth so derived rests on the assumption that the sample of estates assessed to death duty in any one year is representative of all estates. In fact there are a number of recognised deficiencies in this method of estimation, some of which tend to exaggerate and some tend to under-state the degree of inequality, whilst others lead to errors which could work in either direction.

B.8 The main difficulties fall within three broad categories. First, problems associated with the 'grossing-up' process; secondly omissions; thirdly valuation problems. Let us consider these in turn.

B.9 The method used is liable to give rise to sampling errors; for example the total number of very large estates is small and those large estates falling liable to death duty in any one year may not be representative; in particular large estates possessed by those dying young may be unrepresentative for their age and sex group (for which the mortality rates are low and therefore the reciprocals, used as multipliers, are high). As Professor Atkinson vividly put it: 'A wealthy young man crashing his sports car could add one thousand to the estimate of the number of people with wealth over £200,000'. Another problem is that the use of different mortality rates obviously affects the outcome, but mortality rates vary between occupations. In practice the Inland Revenue in estimating the distribution of wealth use two different sets of death rates, those relating to social classes 1 and 2 of the population (broadly the professional and managerial) for estates over £5,000 in 1971 and rates mid-way between them and those relating to the whole population for estates under £5,000 in 1971. But clearly it is a matter of judgement which are most appropriate.

B.10 The omissions represent a serious deficiency. First, the information collected by the Estate Duty Office covers rather less than half of total deaths in a year; it excludes deaths where no property has been left or where the property left was small in amount or of a kind where transfer can take place

U

without a grant of representation (usually for amounts of less than £500). Consequently, the estate duty method estimates the number of people with any wealth in 1971 (the latest year for which full figures have been published) as 18.6 million, about one-third of the population; of the remainder who have no wealth or only small amounts, about 60 per cent are below the age of twenty-five. If the omission of small wealth-holdings biases the figures to suggest more inequality than actually exists, the other omissions probably work mainly in the opposite direction. Thus assets in a form which are not liable or only partly liable to estate duty are not covered or only incompletely covered in the figures. These assets include settled property on the death of a surviving spouse who had no power to dispose of capital; assets held in discretionary trusts; and pictures and other items benefiting from the estate duty relief on objects of national, artistic, historic or scientific interest.

B.11 The third category of deficiency is in valuation. The valuation of some assets recorded at the death of the owner is unrealistic as a measure of value to the living. The value of life assurance at death is a maturity value plus any bonuses, whereas to the living their life assurance has a much lower value— possibly a surrender value being most appropriate. As table 6.5 (paragraph 6.48) shows, life assurance is a much higher proportion of the estates of the smaller wealth owners than of the larger; its exaggerated value in the statistics therefore creates a bias to under-stating the degree of inequality. On the other hand the value of household durables is likely to be under-valued for estate duty purposes and probably houses as well. As these figures are a larger proportion of small estates than of large, then this creates a bias towards over-stating inequality.

B.12 Besides statistical difficulties there are others of a more conceptual nature. First, the unit for estate duty purposes, and therefore for the figures of the distribution of wealth as a whole, is the individual; a family unit might be more meaningful. Secondly, the figures obtained in the way outlined provide a snapshot of the distribution of wealth at a point of time. Many people will be shown as possessing little wealth who twenty years later may be quite large wealth holders. In other words there is a life cycle of saving and some part of the inequality in the distribution of wealth at a point of time simply reflects the differences of wealth associated with differences of age. Thirdly, there is the problem of what to include within personal wealth. It can be argued that private pension rights should be included and the argument is particularly strong where it is possible to realise a capital sum in exchange for part of those rights. More difficult is the problem of *state* pensions. A person contributing to a state retirement pension will not need to save as much for his retirement and the state pension can therefore be regarded as an equivalent addition to his wealth. On the other hand, a state pension right is not an asset which he is able to realise for a capital sum.

More doubtfully still, it is sometimes argued that we should add to personal wealth a sum to allow for the benefits of the national health service and other state insurance benefits, and indeed that we ought to include a value to the Council house dweller which represents the advantage he possesses from his Council house tenure at subsidised rents.[2]

B.13 Whilst there may be no wholly conclusive argument which rules out this treatment, there does seem to the authors a distinct advantage in restricting the concept of personal wealth to those assets which are capable of being realised in the market. If they cannot be so realised, they lack the attribute generally associated with personal wealth and they are almost impossible to value. Benefits like those provided by the national health service or by the tenancy of a Council house are best thought of as income benefits which, because not realisable, do not add to personal wealth even though they may reduce the need for it.

B.14 It is clear from the practical and conceptual problems that measuring the distribution of personal wealth provides almost unending scope for differences of views. Various attempts have been made to remedy the deficiencies of the statistics and various interpretations are taken of what should constitute personal wealth. Unfortunately, because the subject is so politically charged, many of those who dabble in it are like the drunken man against the lamp-post, seeking support rather than illumination.

B.15 Figures of the distribution of wealth amongst persons are usually presented in the form of proportions of persons holding proportions of wealth, e.g. the wealthiest 1% own 25% of the wealth. Confusion can arise from differences in base. Four bases are quite commonly used:

 (i) Wealth-holders—the number of people who emerge as 'wealth-holders' from employing the estate duty method of estimation (i.e. omitting those with small wealth not covered by the statistics).

 (ii) The population over the age of 25.

 (iii) The population over the age of 15.

 (iv) The total population.

B.16 Obviously the percentages will differ according to which base is used and a 'political' selection of base can give the appearance of more or less inequality.

B.17 Table B1 presents the Inland Revenue data without modification; it relates to the numbers of wealth-holders; it does not attempt to correct for inadequacies of coverage or valuation.

---

[2] Appendix A considers whether the capitalised value of future earning power should be counted as wealth.

Table B1 Distribution of Personal Wealth by Groups of Owners, Great Britain
(Estate Duty Method Unmodified)

Percentage of wealth owned by:	1961	1965	1966	1970	1971
Most wealthy 1 per cent	28.4	24.4	23.6	20.7	20.4
2	37.1	32.7	31.0	28.0	27.7
3	42.7	38.4	35.9	33.0	32.8
4	47.0	42.8	40.2	37.0	36.8
5	50.6	46.4	43.7	40.9	40.1
10	62.5	58.6	56.0	51.9	51.6
25	79.2	77.7	75.1	72.5	72.1
50	92.5	92.5	90.9	90.2	90.2
All owners	100.0	100.0	100.0	100.0	100.0
Total wealth (£ thousand million)	54.9	74.3	76.8	96.8	112.7
Total owners of wealth—thousands	18,257	18,560	17,921	17,094	18,632
—as percentage of home population aged 15 and over	46.3	45.6	43.9	41.4	46.0

Source: *Social Trends 1973,* based on *Inland Revenue Statistics 1973.*

B.18 Table B2 is an extract from the Green Paper on Wealth Tax. It relates to the population aged 15 and over and it offers a 'likely range' for the concentration of wealth in the hands of the wealthy. The figures attempt to allow for small wealth holders excluded from the estate duty statistics and for wealth held in non-dutiable settlements; and to correct real property and household goods to a full market valuation. No attempt is made to estimate and include the current value of pension rights, private or state.

Table B2 Distribution of Wealth, Great Britain,
Total Adult Population Aged 15 and over
(Wealth Tax Green Paper)

	Range of property held per cent		
	1960	1965	1970
Most wealthy 1 per cent of population	31–38	28–34	(24)–30
Most wealthy 5 per cent of population	53–64	50–60	(45)–56

Source: Cmnd. 5704.

Distribution of Wealth Between the Sexes

B.19 Of some interest is the distribution of wealth between the sexes, set out in table B3. The inequalities between males and females have diminished over the years, not least because the expectation of life of women has been increasing more than that of men, so that a woman, on average, now lives some six years longer than a man. Women have thus come to inherit wealth which, nominally at any rate, was the property of their husbands. Currently almost 40% of wealth is held by women.

Table B3   Distribution of Personal Wealth Between Males and Females 1971, Great Britain

	£000m	Per cent
Total net wealth of individuals	112.7	100
of which males	68.6	60.9
females	44.1	39.1

Source: *Inland Revenue Statistics 1973.*

The Decline in Inequality

B.20 Whilst the economists and politicians differ in their views of how much inequality exists and whether or not it is 'excessive', on one issue there is agreement; inequality of wealth, as usually measured by concentration ratios, has diminished during this century and is almost certainly continuing to diminish.

B.21 Unfortunately most of the earlier calculations used a different base (population over 25 in England and Wales) from the more recent figures we have quoted and also used unadjusted mortality multipliers. But we can see the trend from these earlier estimates and, though the actual figures are not comparable, observe the continuation of the trend from our tables B1 and B2.

Table B4   Changes in the Distribution of Wealth in England and Wales 1911-13 to 1960. (Population over the age of 25)

Year	Proportion of total wealth owned by top:		
	1%	5%	10%
1911–13	69	87	92
1924–30	62	84	91
1936–38	56	79	88
1954	43	71	79
1960	42	75	83

Source: J. R. S. Revell 'Changes in the Social Distribution of Property in Britain during the Twentieth Century', paper presented in 1965.

Why Has Inequality Declined?

B.22 When we come to interpret and explain this decline in inequality, then disagreement again creeps in. Measured in terms of concentration ratios at the top, there is no doubt about the decline in inequality in a statistical sense, but what has caused that decline and just how meaningful is it?

B.23 The most obvious cause would appear to be the growing affluence of a wide section of the population, mainly reflected in increasing owner-occupancy and substantial saving through insurance. Eighty years of a progressive estate duty must also have played some part.

B.24 But other factors have been at work: we have already mentioned the increased longevity of women compared with men. The inheritance by women of part of their husband's estates has had the effect of reducing inequality.

B.25 Further, one feature reflected in the estate duty statistics has been the increase in the proportion of wealth held by younger people; and evidence of the growth of gifts-inter-vivos over this period[3] suggests that some of the decline in inequality results from gifts from parents to children and grand-children to avoid estate duty.

B.26 These last two features are not what many people would normally understand by a decline in inequality; these forms of redistribution of wealth reveal the inadequacy of using the individual as our 'unit' rather than the family.

B.27 There has also been another factor potently at work during the century— changes in relative prices. As Professor Revell suggested in 1965, the decline in the price of land in the 'twenties reduced the degree of concentration of wealth; paradoxically, however, the increase in the price of land and real property in post-war years has also tended to reduce concentration because of the growth in the numbers of owner-occupiers of houses and farms, who have secured much of the benefit.

The New Face of Inequality

B.28 Tables B1 and B2 show a continued decline in the concentration of wealth holding amongst the richest. But one of the interesting features of table B1 is that, whilst between 1961 and 1971 it reveals a marked decline (of 11%) in the wealth of the richest 10% of wealth holders, the decline in wealth holding of the richest 50% has fallen by only 2%.

B.29 This raises an important conceptual problem of considerable practical significance for contemporary Britain. What constitutes a decline in inequality of wealth? There is not always an unambiguous answer. For example it is by no means clear which of the following two situations might be said to represent the less unequal society.

Situation A
Top 1% of wealth holders own 25% of property
Top 10% of wealth holders own 50% of property
Top 50% of wealth holders own 75% of property

Situation B
Top 1% of wealth holders own 20% or property
Top 10% of wealth holders own 40% or property
Top 50% of wealth holders own 90% or property

B.30 Apart from some incomplete figures in the Green Paper, official figures of wealth distribution for the years after 1971 have yet to be published.

---

[3] See, for example, C. T. Sandford, *Taxing Personal Wealth*, Allen and Unwin 1971, pp. 84-88 and Appendix B.

During these years the value of house property has soared, and risen much more than prices in general. The result, especially if the recorded figures are corrected to bring them in line with current values, is bound to be a reduction in the concentration of wealth of the top wealth holders—an effect accentuated by the Stock Exchange decline. Yet the rise in house prices may well open up a new form of inequality of wealth holding, not between the top 1 or 5 or 10% of the population and the rest, but between the half of families fortunate enough to own houses in a time of inflation and the other 50% who have not enjoyed that good fortune.[4] This raises a number of questions about the appropriateness of government policy.

B.31 There is one other issue on which serious students of the distribution of wealth are agreed: we need much more reliable figures of wealth distribution. One incidental benefit of a wealth tax is that it would help to provide them.

---

[4] James Rothman (*ibid*) estimates the proportion of personal wealth accounted for by the value of dwellings less mortgages at 13% in 1959, 23% in 1966 and 37% in March 1974.

Appendix C

Tabular Summary of some European Wealth Taxes

Feature	Denmark	Germany	Netherlands
Exchange rates: £1 = (1 July 1974)	Dkr 14.30	DM 6.11½	f 6.35½
Origin (first national wealth tax)	1904	1922 Modelled on Prussian 1893	1892
Yield (approx) as percentage of total tax revenue including social security contributions – latest year available.	0.5	1.3	0.9
Personal Tax Unit	Husband and wife aggregated. (Not minor children unless parents have transferred capital to them.)	Husband, wife and minor children aggregated. (Also children over 18 still dependent on parents.)	Husband and wife aggregated. (Not minor children)
Threshold of Liability	Dkr 450,000 (£31,469) (same for married and single)	*Residents:* DM 70,000 (£11,447) for single person; DM 70,000 for wife and each child. Higher threshold for persons over 60 or incapacitated, subject to limit of wealth. Companies: no initial exemption but companies under DM 10,000 (£1,635) are disregarded. *Non-Residents:* Companies and individuals: as resident company.	*Residents:* (1) f 43,000 (£6,800) for single persons under 35. (2) f 59,000 (£9,300) for married or single persons over 35. (3) f 15,000 (£2,400) for each child. (4) f 38,000 (£6,000) extra for persons of 65 or invalids. *Non-Residents:* None

...rway	Sweden	Republic of Ireland (proposals)	United Kingdom (Green Paper)
...r 13.01	Skr 10.50		
...1	1910	Proposed 1975	Possibly 1976
	0.7		
...sband, wife and ...or children ...regated. (Capital ...ived from parents ...tinues to be ...regated after ...ority if child not ... king.)	Husband, wife and minor children aggregated.	Husband, wife and minor children aggregated.	Minor children to be aggregated with parents.
...gle persons: ...75,000 (£5,765) ... anyone with ...endants: ...100,000 (£7,686)	Skr 200,000 (£19,048) for all save non-family trusts and associations (same for married as for single persons). Skr 15,000 (£1,428) for non-family trusts and associations.	£70,000 for single person £100,000 for married persons £2,500 for each minor child £90,000 for widowed persons No threshold for discretionary trusts or private non-trading companies.	£100,000. Higher for husband and wife if aggregated

Feature	Denmark	Germany	Netherlands
Rates of Tax	Progressive: Dkr 450,000 (£31,469) —2,000,000 (£139,860) taxed at 0.9% excess 1.1%	Proportional 0.7% (previously 1% deductible for income tax). From 1975, 1% for companies.	Proportional 0.8%
Ceiling Provisions	National IT, local IT, basic pension contribution and WT limited to 70% of income. WT is reduced by 5% for each 0.4% or portion thereof by which income is less than 6% of wealth. If taxpayer has no taxable income the WT is reduced by 80%. (The 70% ceiling is in practice increased by 3% because of special pension and sickness contributions.)	None	National IT and W limited to 80% of taxable income.
Scope of the Charge	*Residents:* Individuals and estates in course of administration liable on world wide assets.	*Residents:* Individuals, companies and other entities liable on world wide assets.	*Residents:* Individuals liable o world wide assets.
	Non-Residents: Liable on real property and business assets in Denmark	*Non-Residents:* Liable on business assets and real property (including certain debts charged on real property) in Germany and on 25% or over shareholding in German company.	*Non-Residents:* Liable on business assets, real property (and mortgages thereon) in the Netherlands and sh in Dutch partnersh

rway	Sweden	Republic of Ireland (proposals)	United Kingdom (Green Paper)

▸gressive for ividuals: ˻axable Wealth
√kr   £   %
  100,000 (7,686) 0.4
t 150,000 (11,530) 0.8
t 250,000 (19,215) 1.2
:ess   1.6
	Progressive for individuals: Taxable Wealth
	Skr £ %
	1st 75,000 (7,143) 1
	Nxt 125,000 (11,905) 1.5
	Nxt 600,000 (57,143) 2
	Excess 2½
		Proportional 1%	Illustrative scales:
			A B
			Taxable Taxable
			Wealth Wealth
			£'000s % £'000s %
			1st 400 1 200 1
			Nxt 1,500 1½ 200 2
			Nxt 3,000 2 1,500 3
			Excess 2½ 3,000 4
			  Excess 5

ˌal amount of ional and local IT ˍ WT limited to ⁵% of income.	Total amount of WT and national and local IT limited to 80% of first Skr 200,000 (£19,048) of taxable income and 85% of remainder, but the amount of tax must not fall below the sum of local IT and the tax on 50% of the taxable wealth.	Under consideration	To be considered.
ˍidents: iduals and ˌpanies liable on ·ld wide assets ˌpt foreign ˌovables and ˌign permanent ˌblishments. ˻-Residents: iduals liable on ˌperty in Norway; ˌpanies on ˌwegian ˌmanent ˌblishments.	Residents: Individuals and estates in course of administration liable on world wide assets. Non-Residents: Individuals liable on real property and business assets in Sweden. Companies – as individuals.	Residents: Individuals domiciled and ordinarily resident liable on world wide assets. Non-Residents: Those not domiciled and ordinarily resident liable on Irish property.	Resident and domiciled: Liable on world wide assets. Resident and ordinarily resident but not domiciled: Liable on UK assets; possibly on world wide assets if ordinarily resident for considerable period. Other Cases: Liable on land in UK and on assets held in connexion with UK permanent establishments.

Feature	Denmark	Germany	Netherlands
Treatment of Specific Assets Household and Personal Effects Generally	Exempt	Exempt unless "luxury"	Exempt
Jewellery	Exempt	Taxable unless total under DM 10,000 (£1,635) (multiplied by number in family unit.)	First f 5,000 (£800) of jewellery and precious metals exempt.
Works of Art (not used in business)	Exempt	Exemption or relief for important works; otherwise taxable unless total under DM 20,000 (£3,270) (multiplied by number in family unit).	Exempt
Collections (not used in business)	Exempt	As works of art and aggregated with them.	Exempt
Owner-occupied houses	Taxable	Taxable	Taxable
Cars	Taxable	Exempt if not classed as luxury.	Taxable
Boats	Taxable	As cars	Taxable

...way	Sweden	Republic of Ireland (proposals)	United Kingdom (Green Paper)
...Nkr 40,000 ...75) exempt	Exempt	Exempt	Possibly exemption to a certain aggregate value.
...ded as personal ...ts.	Taxable	Exempt in so far as 'normal contents' of residence.	
...ded as personal ...ts.	Exempt	Exempt if remain in country and public allowed 'reasonable access'	Possible deferment of payment subject to public access
...ded as personal ...ts.	Exempt	If consisting of important works of art or items of national, scientific, historic or artistic interest exempt subject to reasonable public access.	
...ble	Taxable	Principal private residence standing in grounds of up to 1 acre exempt	Taxable
...ble	Taxable	Taxable	Possibly include as personal effects (or one car exempt).
...ble	Taxable		

Feature	Denmark	Germany	Netherlands
Treatment of Specific Assets (cont.) Small Savings	Taxable	First DM 10,000 (£1,635) of bank and savings accounts and shares exempt. Additional exemption of first DM 1,000 (£163) of bank and savings accounts. Exemptions multiplied by number in family unit.	Taxable
Pension rights and pension-type annuities	Exempt	Generally exempt if related to employment and if can only be claimed after age 60 or upon incapacity.	Exempt
Other Annuities	Exempt	Taxable	Capitalised value included but only annuity becomes payable and with generous tax free amounts related t◦ family circumstan◦
Life insurance policies	Exempt	Taxable on excess over DM 10,000 (£1,635) (multiplied by number in family unit).	Exempt if regular annual premiums at least 5 years.
Patents, copyrights etc.	Exempt in hands of inventor, etc.	Exempt in hands of inventor etc. or his employer. If purchased, taxable.	Taxable
Goodwill	Taxable	Taxable if purchased; otherwise exempt.	Exempt

...way	Sweden	Republic of Ireland (proposals)	United Kingdom (Green Paper)
...t Nkr 10,000 (£769) ...single person, and ...ble for taxpayer ...dependants, ...npt	Taxable (housekeeping balances exempt)	Taxable	
...npt	Exempt	Exempt	Exempt
...npt	Taxable	Taxable	Taxable
...: Nkr 22,500 ...'29) for single ...ayers and double ...axpayers with ...ndants exempt	Exempt without limit		Taxable
...npt in hands of ...nal owner	Exempt in hands of inventor etc, if not used in a business nor licensed to a third party.	Taxable	Taxable
...npt	Exempt	Taxable	Taxable

v

Feature	Denmark	Germany	Netherlands
Trusts			
Life tenant	Taxable on value of fund.	Taxable on actuarial value of interest.	Taxable on 80% c value of fund.
Reversioner	Exempt	Taxable on value of fund minus amount chargeable on life tenant.	Exempt
Valuation Methods			
Personal chattels	Open market value (taxpayer valuation).	Open market value (taxpayer valuation) Tax authorities decide whether an item is 'luxury'.	Open market valu (taxpayer valuatio
Real Property	Four-yearly valuations generally a little below market value. Flats assessed on capitalised rental value.	Irregular valuations. Current figures based on 1964 values increased by 40%	Open market valu but occupied hou (whether by owne tenant) valued at thirds open mark Similarly farms h reduced value wh occupied (by own tenant)
Quoted Stocks and Shares	Stock Exchange value at 1 January	Stock Exchange value at 31 December	Stock Exchange v at 1 January

way	Sweden	Republic of Ireland (proposals)	United Kingdom (Green Paper)
able on value of	Taxable on value of fund	Taxable	Charge on the trust
npt	Exempt		Charge on the trust
ed en bloc by ence to fire ance value as ws: WT value is of first 100,000 (£7,686) of next 100,000 and 40% iy excess. From esulting figure the iption of 40,000 (£3,075) ducted.	Open market value (taxpayer valuation)	Open market value (taxpayer valuation)	Open market value (taxpayer valuation)
inciple open et value, but s fixed by local oards are ious'. (With ion, percentage ts have been ted.) is and owner-ied houses cularly low tions	Quinquennial valuation at 75% of market value	Open market (taxpayer valuation) but (1) principal private residence exempt, (2) agricultural land up to £200,000 assessed at 50% of market value, any excess at 100% of market value, for 'genuine' farmers	Open market (taxpayer valuation) Owner-occupied houses possibly valued at multiple of rating valuation
Exchange value anuary	Stock Exchange value at 31 December	Open market value at valuation date	Stock Exchange value at valuation date

Feature	Denmark	Germany	Netherlands
Valuation Methods (cont.)			
Unquoted shares	Price determined by formula taking into account (1) capitalised value of profits over 3 latest years; (2) capitalised value of declared dividends; (3) 80% of net assets value. (With various refinements and modifications for particular circumstances)	Valued by reference to recent sales if reliable. Otherwise by Stuttgart formula: The appropriate fraction of the net value of the company on an assets basis, with a reduction (or increase) if the dividend yield is less (or more) than 10% of the value of the shares. (10% was substituted for 7% in 1974)	Valued mainly by reference to value net assets and pro (including risk fac Weight given to e factor varies with of holding
Unincorporated business	Net assets basis	Valued by reference to net tangible assets	Valuation of sepa assets and liabiliti part of going con
Administration			
Centralised or decentralised	Partly decentralised; strong national guide lines and formulae. Local assessment committees (similar to Sweden)	Implementation decentralised to Land governments but very detailed rules for whole country	Strongly decentra few detailed guide Local inspectors possess wide discr
Link with IT	Combined return; IT payers must complete details of wealth even if not liable to WT	Separate return. WT return only every 3 years.	Combined return those liable to bo taxes.
	WT valuation used for calculation of imputed income of owner-occupiers	Same value used for WT and for imputed income for owner-occupied houses	WT valuation use for calculation of imputed income owner-occupiers

...way	Sweden	Republic of Ireland (proposals)	United Kingdom (Green Paper)
...d on estimated ...et value ...actice, particularly ...maller companies, ...aluation is mainly ...enced by net asset ...	(a) Where shares actively traded, market value (with some discount); (b) otherwise valued as percentage of value of company's net assets valued as for unincorporated business	Open market value (taxpayer valuation) with possibly some concession	Open market value (taxpayer valuation)
...assets basis	Net assets basis, with accelerated depreciation (according to set rules)	Open market value (taxpayer valuation) with possibly some concession	Open market value (balance sheet basis, but assets raised to market value where necessary)
...ntralised – with ...fic guide lines ...National Tax ...d. Local ...sment boards.	Decentralised – with specific guide lines from National Tax Board. Local assessment boards	Centralised	New regional organisation
...bined return.	Combined return.	Separate return annually. Agreed values of certain property to remain valid for 3 years.	Separate return
...valuation used for ...lation of imputed ...ne of owner-...piers	Real property valuation used for both WT and imputed income of owner-occupiers.		

Feature	Denmark	Germany	Netherlands
Administration (cont.)			
Link with other capital taxes	Common basis of valuation	Common valuation methods under Valuation Act for a large number of taxes	Common basis of valuation
Administrative costs	Inseparable from IT and other capital taxes	No separate costs: common valuation method	Inseparable from I and other capital
Degree of taxpayer valuation	Very restricted (eg car and boat). Generally determined in detail by set rules (eg specific values for livestock each year)	Very restricted; detailed rules. Taxpayer required to list out and value personal chattels over a certain sum	Very large – few detailed guidelines
Compliance costs	Probably light	Moderate. Triennial assessments. Professional valuers rarely used for personal assets. Calculations for unincorporated businesses time consuming	Moderate. For businesses basic d. required anyway f IT purposes.
Special Treatment for Private Business		Valuation methods favourable (Stuttgart formula)	An additional threshold of f 50,0 (£7,868) has been proposed for capit invested in unincorporated business

...ay	Sweden	Republic of Ireland (proposals)	United Kingdom (Green Paper)
...non basis of ...tion	Common valuations to some extent	Common basis of valuation	
...arable from IT ...ther capital taxes	Inseparable from IT and other capital taxes		
...ively small	Restricted to chattels. Otherwise valuations determined according to set rules	Almost complete taxpayer valuation	Full self-valuation and self-assessment
...bly light for WT; ...considerable for	Probably light: inseparable from IT		
...urable valuation ...ds	1971-3 a special concession for private enterprises of all kinds— but very restricted and complicated and little used. Replaced 1974 by new favourable valuation methods for unincorporated businesses and closely held companies	Possible reliefs under consideration. Livestock and bloodstock exempt	Possibly defer payment until sale, retirement or death

Feature	Denmark	Germany	Netherlands
Special Treatment for Agriculture	Real property valuation methods favourable Restriction on purchase of agricultural land	Real property valuation methods favourable	Additional thresh proposed as for private business. Real property valuation method favourable
Historic Houses and Estates	No specific WT concession but benevolent treatment by local assessment committees, eg taking account only of the part lived in as a house	Historic houses and estates open to public, tax free under certain conditions. Other estates and chattels of public interest: charged on 40% of full value. All exemptions dependent on expenditure normally exceeding income. See paragraphs 14.30-33.	No specific WT concession (but historic houses m: receive governme subsidy as nation: monuments). Concession for e designated as preservation area (eg if open to pu charged on 25% value as parkland
Related Taxes IT on investment income	*National:* Progressive. Maximum marginal rate of 40.95% at Dkr 86,200 (£6,028) taxable income. The bands are indexed. Additional 4% for social insurance.	*National:* Progressive. Maximum marginal rate of 56% at DM 130,000 (£21,262) taxable income.	*National:* Progressive. Maximum margi rate of 71% at f 132,960 (£20,92 taxable income. principle indexat
	Local: Proportional. Average rate 20% (1974) *Ceiling:* Marginal rate of national and local IT and basic pension contribution must not exceed 66⅔% (69⅔% in practice because of special pension and sickness contributions). No differentiation between earned and investment income	*Local:* None No differentiation between earned and investment income	*Local:* None No differentiatio between earned a investment incon

rway	Sweden	Republic of Ireland (proposals)	United Kingdom (Green Paper)
al property uation methods ourable	Real property valuation methods favourable Restriction on purchase of agricultural land Formerly special concession (as for private business)	Valuation concession of 50% of value of land up to £200,000 for "genuine" farmers (ie those who work the farm on a fulltime basis and whose wealth consists mainly of the farm)	Possibly defer payment until sale, retirement or death
specific WT cession for oric houses but ir WT valuation . However land is mpt if under utory protection by son of scientific historic interest.	No specific WT concession but their WT valuation low	House and one acre exempt if principal private residence	Possibly defer payment subject to public access
tional: gressive. ximum marginal of 50% at 275,000 (£21,138) al income (single son)	National: Progressive. Maximum marginal rate of 54% at Skr 150,000 (£14,286) taxable income.	National: Progressive. Maximum marginal rate of 70% at £10,350 taxable income	National: Progressive, rising from 33% on the first £4,500 of taxable income to 83% on taxable income over £20,000 with additional 10% on investment income in excess of £1,000 up to £2,000 and 15% over £2,000
al: Proportional. rage rate 21% differentiation ween earned and stment income	Local: Proportional. Average rate 24% (1974) No differentiation between earned and investment income	Local: None No differentation between earned and investment income	Local: None

Feature	Denmark	Germany	Netherlands
Related Taxes (cont.) Death and gift taxes	Inheritance tax with linked gift tax. Three classes Maximum marginal rate for child or spouse 32% at Dkr 1,000,000 (£69,930)	Inheritance tax with integrated gift tax. Four classes (five before 1974). Maximum rate (slab scale) for child or spouse 35% at DM 100m (£16.3m)	Inheritance tax with linked gift tax. Six classes. Maximum marginal rate for child or spouse 17% at f 500,000 (£78,678)
Capital gains taxes	Known as special income tax Threshold Dkr 6,000 (£420) Rate: 50%	No long term capital gains tax. Short term gains of the nature of "speculative transactions" are taxed to IT	None; but gains connected with a business (including gains from disposal of a substantial shareholding) are taxed as income
Other taxes	State and local fixed real property taxes and local land taxes	Local realty tax. Local trade tax on business capital	

·way	Sweden	Republic of Ireland (proposals)	United Kingdom (Green Paper)
·grated tax on ·ritances or ·dvances on ·ritances. ·ee classes ·imum marginal for child 35% at 200,000 (£15,373)	Inheritance tax with integrated gift tax Three classes Maximum marginal rate for child or spouse 65% at Skr 5,000,000 (£476,190)	Capital Acquisition Tax comprising linked gift and inheritance tax. Gift tax at 75% of rate of inheritance tax. Five classes Threshold of liability for members of immediate family of £150,000. Maximum marginal rate in Class I 55% on total acquisitions of over £450,000	Proposed capital transfer tax comprising integrated gift and estate duty charged on donor. First £15,000 tax free; maximum marginal rate 75% at £500,000 Transfers between spouses tax free
·ns realised within ·ars liable to ·tal gains tax at ·; thereafter zero. ·ns on land subject ·Γ but cost ·xed.	No capital gains tax as such. Gains on movable property taxed 100% as income if property held less than 2 years. Proportion chargeable tapered down to zero after 5 years, except for shares and securities which remain subject to tax on 10% (normally) of gross receipt. Gains on real property taxed 100% as income if property held less than 2 years, thereafter 75%; but indexing of acquisition value and certain deductions	Capital gains tax as from 6 April 1974 at rate of 26%	Capital gains tax at 30% (with lower rates for those with small incomes).
·l WT at ·ortional rate ·een 0.4 and 1% · in nearly all ·ities) ·shold Nkr 40,000 ·75)		Local rates	Local rates

Appendix D

Statistics of Wealth and Income Taxes in Some European Countries Including the United Kingdom

D.1 The prime purpose of this Appendix is to set out in detail the rates of income tax and wealth tax and their combined effect on investment income for taxpayers in Denmark, Germany, the Netherlands, Norway and Sweden; to show the same information in relation to the proposals of the Republic of Ireland; and on various alternative assumptions compatible with the Green Paper options, to show the possibilities in the United Kingdom. The tables D.1–D.12 enable the serious researcher to study more fully and completely the data from which most of the tables in Chapters 3 and 6 are derived.

D.2 In international comparisons of the weight of taxation in Chapter 3, we decided that, besides national income tax and national wealth taxes, we should include local income taxes where they existed, and the one local wealth tax, i.e. the Norwegian. All local realty taxes including the local rates of the United Kingdom were excluded (paragraph 3.24, section 2).

D.3 There are theoretical arguments in favour of this procedure. A local wealth tax is on a par with a national wealth tax in terms of its coverage, whereas a local realty tax is levied only on one form of property. Further, especially in the form of the United Kingdom local rates, which are levied on the occupier of real property and assessed on the annual value of that property, the realty tax is akin to an outlay tax on the use of a good or service. But beside these arguments, the case for including the Norwegian wealth tax and excluding the local rates, rests on their quantitative importance.

D.4 The Norwegian ceiling provision, which restricts the total of combined national and local income tax and national and local wealth tax to 90% of the income assessed to national tax, would in general apply at low rates of return whether the local wealth tax was included or not. In this situation, therefore, it makes no difference whether we include it or not. When we get to the higher rates of return, this is not so. For example, if we take different levels of wealth holding at a 10% rate of return, for a single person with minimum allowances and no earned income, we have the following situation:

Percentage of Investment Income Taken in Tax

Net Wealth £	$IT(L+N)+WT(N)$ %	$IT(L+N)+WT(L+N)$ %
100,000	55	65
500,000	78	88
1,000,000	79	89
5,000,000	80	90

L = Local; N = National.

In these circumstances, where the combined national and local income tax and national wealth tax falls short of the ceiling, the local wealth tax counts; and in the particular examples chosen, it counts to the full extent, a 1% local wealth tax taking 10% of income on a 10% return to capital.

D.5 The Norwegian local wealth tax is proportional; the United Kingdom local rates are regressive. Data from the *Family Expenditure Surveys (FES)* in the United Kingdom shows a falling trend for local rates as a percentage of household income as income increases.[1] If we take data relating to one person households we can derive the following table for 1972.

One Person Households

Original Income (£) ...	1,313	1,592	1,902	2,296	2,811	3,297	4,433
Rates as percent of original income	3.13	2.87	3.07	2.45	2.78	1.70	1.88

D.6 If we assume that all the income was investment income, the implied capital at different rates of return would be as follows:

Implied Capital at Different Rates of Return (r)

	£	£	£	£	£	£	£
Original Income:	1,313	1,592	1,902	2,296	2,811	3,297	4,433
r = 2%	65,650	79,600	95,100	114,800	140,550	164,850	221,650
r = 5%	26,260	31,840	38,040	45,920	56,220	65,940	88,660
r = 10%	13,130	15,920	19,020	22,960	28,110	32,970	44,330

D.7 Only at the 2% rate of return do any of the original income levels from the FES result in a level of wealth above the proposed wealth tax threshold of £100,000 for the United Kingdom; in all cases derived from the data, even at this rather unrealistic rate of return, the proportion of income which would have been taken in local rates would have been under 3%. If we extrapolate

---

[1] 'The Incidence of Taxes and Social Service Benefits, 1972', *Economic Trends*, November 1973, Appendix III, Tables 1 and 2.

the FES data, we can assume a further reduction in rates as a proportion of total income and can safely take it that, at 5% or 10% rates of return, for any wealth holding large enough to come above the wealth tax threshold, local rates are most unlikely to exceed 2% of original income and will generally be considerably less. This 2% for local rates compares with the 10% of the Norwegian local wealth tax.

TABLE D1 DENMARK: Income Tax and Wealth Tax at 1974 rates for different levels of net wealth and different rates of return.
(Income tax includes 4 per cent. for pension and social security contributions and local income tax at 20 per cent.)

Single person with minimum allowances

Net Wealth £	Income from Wealth £	Income Tax (IT) £	Rates of Income Tax Marginal %	Rates of Income Tax Average %	Wealth Tax (WT) £	Combined IT + WT £	Income after IT + WT £	IT + WT as per cent. of Marginal income %	IT + WT as per cent. of Total income %
Assuming Return of 2% to Wealth.									
50,000	1,000	240	40.4	24.0	167	323*	677	62.9*	32.3*
100,000	2,000	659	51.3	32.9	617	968*	1,032	73.8*	48.4*
200,000	4,000	1,777	60.4	44.4	1,638	2,596*	1,404	87.9*	64.9*
300,000	6,000	2,985	60.4	49.8	2,738	4,355*	1,645	87.9*	72.6*
400,000	8,000	4,264	65.0	53.3	3,839	5,840*	2,160	73.0*	73.0*
500,000	10,000	5,563	65.0	55.6	4,939	7,300*	2,700	73.0*	73.0*
600,000	12,000	6,862	65.0	57.2	6,039	8,760*	3,240	73.0*	73.0*
700,000	14,000	8,161	65.0	58.3	7,140	10,220*	3,780	73.0*	73.0*
800,000	16,000	9,460	65.0	59.1	8,240	11,680*	4,320	73.0*	73.0*
900,000	18,000	10,759	65.0	59.8	9,341	13,140*	4,860	73.0*	73.0*
1,000,000	20,000	12,058	65.0	60.3	10,441	14,600*	5,400	73.0*	73.0*
1,500,000	30,000	18,553	65.0	61.8	15,983	21,900*	8,100	73.0*	73.0*
2,000,000	40,000	25,049	65.0	62.6	21,445	29,200*	10,800	73.0*	73.0*
5,000,000	100,000	64,019	65.0	64.0	54,456	73,000*	27,000	73.0*	73.0*
Assuming Return of 5% to Wealth.									
50,000	2,500	915	51.3	36.6	167	1,057*	1,443	66.6*	42.3*
100,000	5,000	2,381	60.4	47.6	617	2,907*	2,093	75.7*	58.1*
200,000	10,000	5,563	65.0	55.6	1,638	6,957*	3,043	79.1*	69.6*
300,000	15,000	8,811	65.0	58.7	2,738	10,950*	4,050	73.0*	73.0*
400,000	20,000	12,058	65.0	60.3	3,839	14,600*	5,400	73.0*	73.0*
500,000	25,000	15,306	65.0	61.2	4,939	18,250*	6,750	73.0*	73.0*
600,000	30,000	18,553	65.0	61.8	6,039	21,900*	8,100	73.0*	73.0*
700,000	35,000	21,800	65.0	62.3	7,140	25,550*	9,450	73.0*	73.0*
800,000	40,000	25,048	65.0	62.6	8,240	29,200*	10,800	73.0*	73.0*
900,000	45,000	28,295	65.0	62.9	9,341	32,850*	12,150	73.0*	73.0*
1,000,000	50,000	31,543	65.0	63.1	10,441	36,500*	13,500	73.0*	73.0*
1,500,000	75,000	47,780	65.0	63.7	15,983	54,750*	20,250	73.0*	73.0*
2,000,000	100,000	64,018	65.0	64.0	21,445	73,000*	27,000	73.0*	73.0*
5,000,000	250,000	161,443	65.0	64.6	54,456	182,500*	67,500	73.0*	73.0*
Assuming Return of 10% to Wealth.									
50,000	5,000	2,381	60.4	47.4	167	2,548	2,452	69.4	51.0
100,000	10,000	5,563	65.0	55.6	617	6,182	3,818	74.0	61.8
200,000	20,000	12,058	65.0	60.3	1,638	13,700	6,300	76.0	68.5
300,000	30,000	18,553	65.0	61.8	2,738	21,298	8,702	76.0	71.0
400,000	40,000	25,048	65.0	62.6	3,839	28,895	11,105	76.0	72.2
500,000	50,000	31,543	65.0	63.1	4,939	36,493	13,507	76.0	73.0
600,000	60,000	38,038	65.0	63.4	6,039	43,800*	16,200	73.0*	73.0*
700,000	70,000	44,533	65.0	63.6	7,140	51,100*	18,900	73.0*	73.0*
800,000	80,000	51,028	65.0	63.8	8,240	58,400*	21,600	73.0*	73.0*
900,000	90,000	57,523	65.0	63.9	9,341	65,700*	24,300	73.0*	73.0*
1,000,000	100,000	64,018	65.0	64.0	10,441	73,000*	27,000	73.0*	73.0*
1,500,000	150,000	96,493	65.0	64.3	15,983	109,500*	40,500	73.0*	73.0*
2,000,000	200,000	128,968	65.0	64.5	21,445	146,000*	54,000	73.0*	73.0*
5,000,000	500,000	323,818	65.0	64.8	54,456	365,000*	135,000	73.0*	73.0*

NOTE: Ceiling provisions have been applied only to combined IT + WT columns and, where applicable, are indicated by *

TABLE D2   GERMANY: Income Tax and Wealth Tax at 1975 rates for different levels of net wealth and different rates of return.

Single person with minimum allowances

Net Wealth £	Income from Wealth £	Income Tax (IT) £	Rates of Income Tax Marginal %	Rates of Income Tax Average %	Wealth Tax (WT) £	Combined IT + WT £	Income after IT + WT £	IT + WT as per cent. of Marginal income %	IT + WT as per cent. of Total income %
Assuming Return of 2% to Wealth.									
50,000	1,000	111	22.0	11.1	270	381	619	57.0	38.1
100,000	2,000	331	22.0	16.6	620	951	1,049	57.0	47.5
200,000	4,000	947	39.7	23.7	1,320	2,267	1,733	74.7	56.7
300,000	6,000	1,791	44.6	29.9	2,020	3,811	2,189	79.6	63.5
400,000	8,000	2,731	47.1	34.1	2,718	5,449	2,551	82.1	68.1
500,000	10,000	3,720	49.7	37.2	3,419	7,139	2,861	84.7	71.4
600,000	12,000	4,752	51.5	39.6	4,118	8,870	3,130	86.5	73.9
700,000	14,000	5,813	52.8	41.5	4,818	10,631	3,369	87.8	75.9
800,000	16,000	6,902	54.0	43.1	5,518	12,420	3,580	89.0	77.6
900,000	18,000	8,009	54.6	44.5	6,217	14,226	3,774	89.6	79.0
1,000,000	20,000	9,126	54.8	45.6	6,917	16,043	3,957	89.8	80.2
1,500,000	30,000	14,727	56.0	49.1	10,417	25,144	4,856	91.0	83.8
2,000,000	40,000	20,327	56.0	50.8	13,917	34,244	5,756	91.0	85.6
5,000,000	100,000	53,927	56.0	53.9	34,917	88,844	11,156	91.0	88.8
Assuming Return of 5% to Wealth.									
50,000	2,500	441	22.0	17.7	270	711	1,789	36.0	28.4
100,000	5,000	1,351	41.7	27.0	620	1,971	3,029	55.7	39.4
200,000	10,000	3,720	49.7	37.2	1,320	5,040	4,960	63.7	50.4
300,000	15,000	6,355	53.5	42.4	2,020	8,375	6,625	67.5	55.8
400,000	20,000	9,126	54.8	45.6	2,718	11,844	8,156	68.8	59.2
500,000	25,000	11,927	56.0	47.7	3,419	15,346	9,654	70.0	61.4
600,000	30,000	14,727	56.0	49.1	4,118	18,845	11,155	70.0	62.8
700,000	35,000	17,527	56.0	50.1	4,818	22,345	12,655	70.0	63.8
800,000	40,000	20,327	56.0	50.8	5,518	25,845	14,155	70.0	64.6
900,000	45,000	23,127	56.0	51.4	6,217	29,334	15,666	70.0	65.2
1,000,000	50,000	25,927	56.0	51.9	6,917	32,844	17,156	70.0	65.7
1,500,000	75,000	39,927	56.0	53.2	10,417	50,344	24,656	70.0	67.1
2,000,000	100,000	53,927	56.0	53.9	13,917	67,844	32,156	70.0	67.8
5,000,000	250,000	137,927	56.0	55.2	34,917	172,844	77,156	70.0	69.1
Assuming Return of 10% to Wealth.									
50,000	5,000	1,351	41.7	27.0	270	1,621	3,379	48.7	32.4
100,000	10,000	3,720	49.7	37.2	620	4,340	5,660	56.7	43.4
200,000	20,000	9,126	54.8	45.6	1,320	10,446	9,554	61.8	52.2
300,000	30,000	14,727	56.0	49.1	2,020	16,747	13,253	63.0	55.8
400,000	40,000	20,327	56.0	50.8	2,718	23,045	16,955	63.0	57.6
500,000	50,000	25,927	56.0	51.9	3,419	29,346	20,654	63.0	58.7
600,000	60,000	31,527	56.0	52.6	4,118	35,645	24,355	63.0	59.4
700,000	70,000	37,127	56.0	53.0	4,818	41,945	28,055	63.0	59.9
800,000	80,000	42,727	56.0	53.4	5,518	48,245	31,755	63.0	60.3
900,000	90,000	48,327	56.0	53.7	6,217	54,544	35,456	63.0	60.6
1,000,000	100,000	53,927	56.0	53.9	6,917	60,844	39,156	63.0	60.8
1,500,000	150,000	81,927	56.0	54.6	10,417	92,344	57,656	63.0	61.6
2,000,000	200,000	109,927	56.0	55.0	13,917	123,844	76,156	63.0	61.9
5,000,000	500,000	277,927	56.0	55.6	34,917	312,844	187,156	63.0	62.6

W

TABLE D3 THE NETHERLANDS: Income Tax and Wealth Tax at 1974 rates (allowances as for first half of year) for different levels of net wealth and different rates of return.

Single person with minimum allowances

Net Wealth £	Income from Wealth £	Income Tax (IT) £	Rates of Income Tax Marginal %	Rates of Income Tax Average %	Wealth Tax (WT) £	Combined IT + WT £	Income after IT + WT £	IT + WT as per cent of Marginal income %	IT + WT as per cent of Total income %
Assuming Return of 2% to Wealth.									
50,000	1,000	91	25.0	9.9	346	437	563	65.0	43.7
100,000	2,000	341	25.0	17.1	746	1,087	913	65.0	54.4
200,000	4,000	1,002	39.0	25.1	1,546	2,548	1,452	79.0	63.7
300,000	6,000	1,927	49.0	32.1	2,346	4,273	1,727	89.0	71.2
400,000	8,000	3,048	58.0	38.1	3,146	5,891*	2,109	80.0*	74.8*
500,000	10,000	4,271	63.0	42.7	3,946	7,491*	2,509	80.0*	74.9*
600,000	12,000	5,549	66.0	46.2	4,746	9,091*	2,909	80.0*	75.8*
700,000	14,000	6,869	66.0	49.1	5,546	10,691*	3,309	80.0*	76.4*
800,000	16,000	8,224	69.0	51.4	6,346	12,291*	3,709	80.0*	76.8*
900,000	18,000	9,604	69.0	53.4	7,146	13,891*	4,109	80.0*	77.1*
1,000,000	20,000	10,984	69.0	54.9	7,946	15,491*	4,509	80.0*	77.5*
1,500,000	30,000	18,056	71.0	60.2	11,946	23,491*	6,509	80.0*	78.3*
2,000,000	40,000	25,156	71.0	62.9	15,946	31,491*	8,509	80.0*	78.7*
5,000,000	100,000	67,756	71.0	67.8	39,946	79,491*	20,509	80.0*	79.5*
Assuming Return of 5% to Wealth.									
50,000	2,500	481	31.0	19.2	346	827	1,673	47.0	33.1
100,000	5,000	1,437	49.0	28.7	746	2,183	2,817	65.0	43.7
200,000	10,000	4,271	63.0	42.7	1,546	5,817	4,183	79.0	58.2
300,000	15,000	7,534	69.0	50.2	2,346	9,880	5,120	85.0	65.9
400,000	20,000	10,984	69.0	54.9	3,146	14,130	5,870	85.0	70.7
500,000	25,000	14,506	71.0	58.0	3,946	18,452	6,548	87.0	73.8
600,000	30,000	18,056	71.0	60.2	4,746	22,802	7,198	87.0	76.0
700,000	35,000	21,606	71.0	61.7	5,546	27,152	7,848	87.0	77.6
800,000	40,000	25,156	71.0	62.9	6,346	31,491*	8,509	80.0*	78.7*
900,000	45,000	28,706	71.0	63.8	7,146	35,491*	9,509	80.0*	78.9*
1,000,000	50,000	32,256	71.0	64.5	7,946	39,491*	10,509	80.0*	79.0*
1,500,000	75,000	50,006	71.0	66.7	11,946	59,491*	15,509	80.0*	79.3*
2,000,000	100,000	67,756	71.0	67.8	15,946	79,491*	20,509	80.0*	79.5*
5,000,000	250,000	174,256	71.0	69.7	39,946	199,491*	50,509	80.0*	79.8*
Assuming Return of 10% to Wealth.									
50,000	5,000	1,437	49.0	28.7	346	1,783	3,217	57.0	35.7
100,000	10,000	4,271	63.0	42.7	746	5,017	4,983	71.0	50.2
200,000	20,000	10,984	69.0	54.9	1,546	12,530	7,470	77.0	62.3
300,000	30,000	18,056	71.0	60.2	2,346	20,402	9,598	79.0	68.0
400,000	40,000	25,156	71.0	62.9	3,146	28,302	11,698	79.0	70.8
500,000	50,000	32,256	71.0	64.5	3,946	36,202	13,495	79.0	72.4
600,000	60,000	39,356	71.0	65.6	4,746	44,102	15,898	79.0	73.5
700,000	70,000	46,456	71.0	66.4	5,546	52,002	17,998	79.0	74.3
800,000	80,000	53,556	71.0	66.9	6,346	59,902	20,098	79.0	74.9
900,000	90,000	60,656	71.0	67.4	7,146	67,802	22,198	79.0	75.3
1,000,000	100,000	67,756	71.0	67.8	7,946	75,702	24,298	79.0	75.7
1,500,000	150,000	103,256	71.0	68.8	11,946	115,202	34,798	79.0	76.8
2,000,000	200,000	138,756	71.0	69.4	15,946	154,702	45,298	79.0	77.4
5,000,000	500,000	351,756	71.0	70.4	39,946	391,702	108,298	79.0	78.3

NOTE: Ceiling provisions have been applied only to combined IT + WT columns and, where applicable, are indicated by *

TABLE D4 NORWAY: Income Tax and Wealth Tax at 1974 rates for different levels of net wealth and different rates of return.
(Income tax includes local income tax at 21%, local wealth tax is given in separate column.)

Single person with minimum allowances

Net Wealth £	Income from Wealth £	Income Tax (IT) £	Rates of Income Tax		Wealth Tax			Combined IT+WT £	Income after IT+WT £	IT+WT as per cent of	
			Marginal %	Average %	National £	Local £	Total WT £			Marginal income %	Total income %
Assuming Return of 2% to Wealth.											
50,000	1,000	145	21.0	14.5	446	469	916	0*	1,000	0*	0*
100,000	2,000	386	26.0	19.3	1,246	969	2,216	555*	1,445	90.0*	27.7*
200,000	4,000	1,117	41.0	27.9	2,846	1,969	4,816	2,355*	1,645	90.0*	58.9*
300,000	6,000	2,038	51.0	34.0	4,446	2,969	7,416	4,155*	1,845	90.0*	69.2*
400,000	8,000	3,097	56.0	38.7	6,046	3,969	10,016	5,955*	2,045	90.0*	74.4*
500,000	10,000	4,260	61.0	42.6	7,646	4,969	12,616	7,755*	2,245	90.0*	77.5*
600,000	12,000	5,480	61.0	45.7	9,246	5,969	15,216	9,555*	2,445	90.0*	79.6*
700,000	14,000	6,750	66.0	48.2	10,846	6,969	17,816	11,355*	2,645	90.0*	81.1*
800,000	16,000	8,070	66.0	50.4	12,446	7,969	20,416	13,155*	2,845	90.0*	82.2*
900,000	18,000	9,390	66.0	52.2	14,046	8,969	23,016	14,955*	3,045	90.0*	83.1*
1,000,000	20,000	10,710	66.0	53.6	15,646	9,969	25,616	16,755*	3,245	90.0*	83.8*
1,500,000	30,000	17,777	71.0	59.2	23,646	14,969	38,616	25,755*	4,245	90.0*	85.8*
2,000,000	40,000	24,877	71.0	62.2	31,646	19,969	51,616	34,755*	5,245	90.0*	86.9*
5,000,000	100,000	67,477	71.0	67.5	79,646	49,969	129,616	88,755*	11,245	90.0*	88.8*
Assuming Return of 5% to Wealth.											
50,000	2,500	536	36.0	21.4	446	469	916	1,005*	1,495	90.0*	40.2*
100,000	5,000	1,544	46.0	30.9	1,246	969	2,216	3,255*	1,745	90.0*	65.1*
200,000	10,000	4,260	61.0	42.6	2,846	1,969	4,816	7,755*	2,245	90.0*	77.5*
300,000	15,000	7,410	66.0	49.4	4,446	2,969	7,416	12,255*	2,745	90.0*	81.7*
400,000	20,000	10,710	66.0	53.6	6,046	3,969	10,016	16,755*	3,245	90.0*	83.7*
500,000	25,000	14,227	71.0	56.9	7,646	4,969	12,616	21,255*	3,745	90.0*	85.0*
600,000	30,000	17,777	71.0	59.3	9,246	5,969	15,216	25,755*	4,245	90.0*	85.8*
700,000	35,000	21,327	71.0	60.9	10,846	6,969	17,816	30,255*	4,745	90.0*	86.4*
800,000	40,000	24,877	71.0	62.2	12,446	7,969	20,416	34,755*	5,245	90.0*	86.9*
900,000	45,000	28,427	71.0	63.2	14,046	8,969	23,016	39,255*	5,745	90.0*	87.2*
1,000,000	50,000	31,977	71.0	64.0	15,646	9,969	25,616	43,755*	6,245	90.0*	87.5*
1,500,000	75,000	49,727	71.0	66.3	23,646	14,969	38,616	66,255*	8,745	90.0*	88.3*
2,000,000	100,000	67,477	71.0	67.5	31,646	19,969	51,616	88,755*	11,245	90.0*	88.8*
5,000,000	250,000	173,977	71.0	69.6	79,646	49,969	129,616	223,755*	26,245	90.0*	89.5*
Assuming Return of 10% to Wealth.											
50,000	5,000	1,544	46.0	30.9	446	469	915	2,459	2,541	72.0	49.2
100,000	10,000	4,260	61.0	42.6	1,246	969	2,216	6,476	3,524	87.0	64.8
200,000	20,000	10,710	66.0	53.6	2,846	1,969	4,816	15,526	4,474	92.0	77.6
300,000	30,000	17,777	71.0	59.3	4,446	2,969	7,416	25,192	4,808	97.0	84.0
400,000	40,000	24,877	71.0	62.2	6,046	3,969	10,016	34,755*	5,245	90.0*	86.9*
500,000	50,000	31,977	71.0	64.0	7,646	4,969	12,616	43,755*	6,245	90.0*	87.5*
600,000	60,000	39,077	71.0	65.1	9,246	5,969	15,216	52,755*	7,245	90.0*	87.9*
700,000	70,000	46,177	71.0	65.6	10,846	6,969	17,816	61,755*	8,245	90.0*	88.2*
800,000	80,000	53,277	71.0	66.6	12,446	7,969	20,416	70,755*	9,245	90.0*	88.4*
900,000	90,000	60,377	71.0	67.1	14,046	8,969	23,016	79,755*	10,245	90.0*	88.6*
1,000,000	100,000	67,477	71.0	67.5	15,646	9,969	25,616	88,755*	11,245	90.0*	88.8*
1,500,000	150,000	102,977	71.0	68.7	23,646	14,969	38,616	133,755*	16,245	90.0*	89.2*
2,000,000	200,000	138,477	71.0	69.2	31,646	19,969	51,616	178,755*	21,245	90.0*	89.4*
5,000,000	500,000	351,477	71.0	70.3	79,646	49,969	129,616	448,755*	51,245	90.0*	89.8*

NOTE: Ceiling provisions have been applied only to combined IT+WT columns and, where applicable, are indicated by *.

TABLE D5 SWEDEN: Income Tax and Wealth Tax at 1974 rates for different levels of net wealth at different rates of return.
(Income tax includes local income tax at 24 per cent.)

Net Wealth £	Income from Wealth £	Income Tax (IT) £	Rates of Income Tax Marginal %	Average %	Wealth Tax (WT) £	Combined IT + WT £	Income after IT + WT £	Single person with minimum allowances IT + WT as per cent of Marginal income %	Total income %
Assuming Return of 2% to Wealth.									
50,000	1,000	177	31.0	17.7	488	457*	543	80.0*	45.7*
100,000	2,000	496	37.0	24.8	1,512	1,257*	743	80.0*	62.9*
200,000	4,000	1,474	62.4	36.8	4,012	2,971*	1,029	80.0*	74.3*
300,000	6,000	2,725	62.0	45.4	6,512	4,800*	1,200	80.0*	80.0*
400,000	8,000	4,046	71.0	50.6	9,012	6,400*	1,600	80.0*	80.0*
500,000	10,000	5,467	73.0	54.7	11,512	8,000*	2,000	80.0*	80.0*
600,000	12,000	6,927	73.0	57.7	14,012	9,600*	2,400	80.0*	80.0*
700,000	14,000	8,387	73.0	59.9	16,512	11,200*	2,800	80.0*	80.3*
800,000	16,000	9,911	78.0	62.0	19,012	12,852*	3,148	86.5*	80.3*
900,000	18,000	11,471	78.0	63.7	21,512	14,582*	3,418	86.5*	81.0*
1,000,000	20,000	13,031	78.0	65.2	24,012	16,312*	3,688	86.5*	81.6*
1,500,000	30,000	20,831	78.0	69.4	36,512	24,962*	5,038	86.5*	83.2*
2,000,000	40,000	28,631	78.0	71.6	49,012	33,612*	6,388	86.5*	84.0*
5,000,000	100,000	75,431	78.0	75.4	124,012	85,512*	14,488	86.5*	85.5*
Assuming Return of 5% to Wealth.									
50,000	2,500	690	43.0	27.6	488	1,178	1,322	83.0	47.1
100,000	5,000	2,098	62.4	42.0	1,512	3,610	1,390	112.4	72.2
200,000	10,000	5,467	73.0	54.7	4,012	8,000*	2,000	80.0*	80.0*
300,000	15,000	9,131	78.0	60.9	6,512	12,000*	3,000	80.0*	80.0*
400,000	20,000	13,031	78.0	65.2	9,012	16,048*	3,952	85.0*	80.2*
500,000	25,000	16,931	78.0	67.7	11,512	20,298*	4,702	85.0*	81.2*
600,000	30,000	20,831	78.0	69.4	14,012	24,548*	5,452	85.0*	81.8*
700,000	35,000	24,731	78.0	70.7	16,512	28,798*	6,202	85.0*	82.3*
800,000	40,000	28,631	78.0	71.6	19,012	33,048*	6,952	85.0*	82.6*
900,000	45,000	32,531	78.0	72.3	21,512	37,298*	7,702	85.0*	82.9*
1,000,000	50,000	36,431	78.0	72.9	24,012	41,548*	8,452	85.0*	83.1*
1,500,000	75,000	55,931	78.0	74.6	36,512	62,798*	12,202	85.0*	83.7*
2,000,000	100,000	75,431	78.0	75.4	49,012	84,048*	15,952	85.0*	84.1*
5,000,000	250,000	192,431	78.0	77.0	124,012	211,548*	38,452	85.0*	84.6*
Assuming Return of 10% to Wealth.									
50,000	5,000	2,098	62.4	42.0	488	2,586	2,414	82.4	51.7
100,000	10,000	5,467	73.0	54.7	1,512	6,979	3,021	98.0	69.8
200,000	20,000	13,031	78.0	65.2	4,012	16,048*	3,952	85.0*	80.2*
300,000	30,000	20,831	78.0	69.4	6,512	24,548*	5,452	85.0*	81.8*
400,000	40,000	28,631	78.0	71.6	9,012	33,048*	6,952	85.0*	82.6*
500,000	50,000	36,231	78.0	72.9	11,512	41,548*	8,452	85.0*	83.1*
600,000	60,000	44,231	78.0	73.7	14,012	50,048*	9,952	85.0*	83.4*
700,000	70,000	52,031	78.0	74.3	16,512	58,548*	11,452	85.0*	83.6*
800,000	80,000	59,831	78.0	74.8	19,012	67,048*	12,952	85.0*	83.8*
900,000	90,000	67,631	78.0	75.2	21,512	75,548*	14,452	85.0*	83.9*
1,000,000	100,000	75,431	78.0	75.4	24,012	84,048*	15,962	85.0*	84.1*
1,500,000	150,000	114,431	78.0	76.3	36,512	126,548*	23,452	85.0*	84.4*
2,000,000	200,000	153,431	78.0	76.7	49,012	169,048*	30,952	85.0*	84.5*
5,000,000	500,000	387,431	78.0	77.5	124,012	424,048*	75,952	85.0*	84.8*

NOTE: Ceiling provisions have been applied only to combined IT + WT columns and, where applicable, are indicated by *.

TABLE D6 IRELAND: Income Tax and Wealth Tax (Proposals) for different levels of net wealth at different rates of return.

Single person with minimum allowances

Net Wealth £	Income from Wealth £	Income Tax (IT) £	Rates of Income Tax Marginal %	Rates of Income Tax Average %	Wealth Tax (WT) £	Combined IT + WT £	Income after IT + WT £	IT + WT as per cent of Marginal income %	IT + WT as per cent of Total income %
Assuming Return of 2% to Wealth.									
50,000	1,000	30	26.0	13.0	0	130	870	26.0	13.0
100,000	2,000	390	26.0	19.5	300	690	1,310	76.0	34.5
200,000	4,000	1,086	35.0	27.2	1,300	2,386	1,614	85.0	59.7
300,000	6,000	1,901	45.0	31.7	2,300	4,201	1,799	95.0	70.0
400,000	8,000	2,916	55.0	36.5	3,300	6,216	1,784	105.0	77.7
500,000	10,000	4,131	65.0	41.3	4,300	8,431	1,569	115.0	84.3
600,000	12,000	5,488	70.0	45.7	5,300	10,788	1,212	120.0	89.9
700,000	14,000	6,888	70.0	49.2	6,300	13,188	812	120.0	94.2
800,000	16,000	8,288	70.0	51.8	7,300	15,588	412	120.0	97.4
900,000	18,000	9,688	70.0	53.8	8,300	17,988	12	120.0	99.9
1,000,000	20,000	11,088	70.0	55.4	9,300	20,388	— 388	120.0	101.9
1,500,000	30,000	18,088	70.0	60.3	14,300	32,388	— 2,388	120.0	108.0
2,000,000	40,000	25,088	70.0	62.7	19,300	44,388	— 4,388	120.0	111.0
5,000,000	100,000	67,088	70.0	67.1	49,300	116,388	—16,388	120.0	116.4
Assuming Return of 5% to Wealth.									
50,000	2,500	561	35.0	22.4	0	561	1,939	35.0	22.4
100,000	5,000	1,451	45.0	29.0	300	1,751	3,249	65.0	35.0
200,000	10,000	4,131	65.0	41.3	1,300	5,431	4,569	85.0	54.3
300,000	15,000	7,588	70.0	50.6	2,300	9,888	5,112	90.0	65.9
400,000	20,000	11,088	70.0	55.4	3,300	14,388	5,612	90.0	71.9
500,000	25,000	14,588	70.0	58.4	4,300	18,888	6,112	90.0	75.6
600,000	30,000	18,088	70.0	60.3	5,300	23,388	6,612	90.0	78.0
700,000	35,000	21,588	70.0	61.7	6,300	27,888	7,112	90.0	79.7
800,000	40,000	25,088	70.0	62.7	7,300	32,388	7,612	90.0	81.0
900,000	45,000	28,588	70.0	63.5	8,300	36,888	8,112	90.0	82.0
1,000,000	50,000	32,088	70.0	64.2	9,300	41,388	8,612	90.0	82.8
1,500,000	75,000	49,588	70.0	66.1	14,300	63,888	11,112	90.0	85.2
2,000,000	100,000	67,088	70.0	67.1	19,300	86,388	13,612	90.0	86.4
5,000,000	250,000	172,088	70.0	68.8	49,300	221,388	28,612	90.0	88.6
Assuming Return of 10% to Wealth.									
50,000	5,000	1,451	45.0	29.0	0	1,451	3,549	45.0	29.0
100,000	10,000	4,131	65.0	41.3	300	4,431	5,569	75.0	44.3
200,000	20,000	11,088	70.0	55.4	1,300	12,388	7,612	80.0	61.9
300,000	30,000	18,088	70.0	60.3	2,300	20,388	9,612	80.0	68.0
400,000	40,000	25,088	70.0	62.7	3,300	28,388	11,612	80.0	71.0
500,000	50,000	32,088	70.0	64.2	4,300	36,388	13,612	80.0	72.8
600,000	60,000	39,088	70.0	65.1	5,300	44,388	15,612	80.0	74.0
700,000	70,000	46,088	70.0	65.8	6,300	52,388	17,612	80.0	74.8
800,000	80,000	53,088	70.0	66.4	7,300	60,388	19,612	80.0	75.5
900,000	90,000	60,088	70.0	66.8	8,300	68,388	21,612	80.0	76.0
1,000,000	100,000	67,088	70.0	67.1	9,300	76,388	23,612	80.0	76.4
1,500,000	150,000	102,088	70.0	68.1	14,300	116,388	33,612	80.0	77.6
2,000,000	200,000	137,088	70.0	68.5	19,300	156,388	43,612	80.0	78.2
5,000,000	500,000	347,088	70.0	69.4	49,300	396,388	103,612	80.0	79.3

NOTE: A ceiling provision is under consideration.

TABLE D7 UNITED KINGDOM: Income Tax at 1974–75 rates and Wealth Tax (at illustrative Scale A) for different levels of net wealth at different rates of return. The figures of combined Income Tax and Wealth Tax include Investment Income Surcharge (IIS).

Single person with minimum allowances

Net Wealth £	Income from Wealth £	(a) Basic + Higher rate IT £	(b) IIS £	(a) + (b) Total IT £	Rate of Income Tax (Total) Marginal %	Rate of Income Tax (Total) Average %	Wealth Tax (WT) £	Combined IT + WT £	Income after IT + WT £	IT + WT as per cent of Marginal income %	IT + WT as per cent of Total income %
Assuming Return of 2% to Wealth.											
50,000	1,000	124	0	124	33.0	12.4	0	124	876	33.0	12.4
100,000	2,000	454	0	454	48.0	22.7	0	454	1,546	98.0	22.7
200,000	4,000	1,114	300	1,414	48.0	35.4	1,000	2,414	1,586	98.0	60.4
300,000	6,000	1,836	600	2,436	58.0	40.6	2,000	4,436	1,564	108.0	73.9
400,000	8,000	2,784	900	3,684	68.0	46.1	3,000	6,684	1,316	118.0	83.6
500,000	10,000	3,913	1,200	5,113	73.0	51.1	4,000	9,113	887	148.0	91.1
600,000	12,000	5,141	1,500	6,641	78.0	55.3	5,500	12,141	—141	153.0	101.2
700,000	14,000	6,470	1,800	8,270	83.0	59.1	7,000	15,270	—1,270	158.0	109.1
800,000	16,000	7,830	2,100	9,930	88.0	62.1	8,500	18,430	—2,430	163.0	115.2
900,000	18,000	9,309	2,400	11,709	88.0	65.1	10,000	21,709	—3,709	163.0	120.6
1,000,000	20,000	10,769	2,700	13,469	88.0	67.4	11,500	24,969	—4,969	163.0	124.8
1,500,000	30,000	19,006	4,200	23,207	88.0	77.4	19,000	42,207	—12,207	173.0	140.7
2,000,000	40,000	27,306	5,700	33,006	98.0	82.5	26,500	59,506	—19,506	198.0	148.8
5,000,000	100,000	77,106	14,700	91,806	98.0	91.8	86,500	178,306	—78,306	223.0	178.3
Assuming Return of 5% to Wealth.											
50,000	2,500	619	75	694	48.0	27.8	0	694	1,806	48.0	27.6
100,000	5,000	1,444	450	1,894	48.0	37.9	0	1,894	3,106	68.0	37.9
200,000	10,000	3,913	1,200	5,113	73.0	51.1	1,000	6,113	3,887	93.0	61.1
300,000	15,000	7,150	1,950	9,100	73.0	60.7	2,000	11,100	3,900	93.0	74.0
400,000	20,000	10,769	2,700	13,469	88.0	67.4	3,000	16,469	3,531	108.0	82.3
500,000	25,000	14,856	3,450	18,307	88.0	73.2	4,000	22,307	2,693	118.0	89.2
600,000	30,000	19,006	4,200	23,207	98.0	77.4	5,500	28,707	1,293	128.0	95.7
700,000	35,000	23,156	4,950	28,107	98.0	80.3	7,000	35,107	—107	128.0	100.3
800,000	40,000	27,306	5,700	33,007	98.0	82.5	8,500	41,507	—1,507	128.0	103.8
900,000	45,000	31,456	6,450	37,907	98.0	84.2	10,000	47,907	—2,907	128.0	106.5
1,000,000	50,000	35,606	7,200	42,807	98.0	85.6	11,500	54,307	—4,307	128.0	108.6
1,500,000	75,000	56,356	10,950	67,307	98.0	89.7	19,000	86,307	—11,307	128.0	115.1
2,000,000	100,000	77,106	14,700	91,807	98.0	91.8	26,500	118,307	—18,307	138.0	118.3
5,000,000	250,000	201,606	37,200	238,807	98.0	95.5	86,500	325,307	—75,307	148.0	130.1
Assuming Return of 10% to Wealth.											
50,000	5,000	1,444	450	1,894	48.0	37.9	0	1,894	3,106	68.0	37.9
100,000	10,000	3,913	1,200	5,113	73.0	51.1	0	5,113	4,887	83.0	51.1
200,000	20,000	10,769	2,700	13,469	88.0	67.4	1,000	14,469	5,531	98.0	72.3
300,000	30,000	19,006	4,200	23,207	98.0	77.4	2,000	25,207	4,793	108.0	84.0
400,000	40,000	27,306	5,700	33,007	98.0	82.5	3,000	36,007	3,993	108.0	90.0
500,000	50,000	35,606	7,200	42,807	98.0	85.6	4,000	46,807	3,193	113.0	93.6
600,000	60,000	43,906	8,700	52,607	98.0	87.7	5,500	58,107	1,893	113.0	96.8
700,000	70,000	52,206	10,200	62,407	98.0	89.2	7,000	69,407	593	113.0	99.2
800,000	80,000	60,506	11,700	72,207	98.0	90.3	8,500	80,707	—707	113.0	100.9
900,000	90,000	68,806	13,200	82,007	98.0	91.1	10,000	92,007	—2,007	113.0	102.2
1,000,000	100,000	77,106	14,700	91,807	98.0	91.8	11,500	103,307	—3,307	113.0	103.3
1,500,000	150,000	118,606	22,200	140,807	98.0	93.3	19,000	159,807	—9,807	113.0	106.5
2,000,000	200,000	160,106	29,700	189,807	98.0	94.9	26,500	216,307	—16,307	118.0	108.2
5,000,000	500,000	409,106	74,700	483,807	98.0	96.8	86,500	570,307	—70,307	123.0	114.1

NOTE: Investment Income Surcharge is taken as 15 per cent. on investment incomes over £2,000. (The reduced rate on investment incomes between £1,000 and £2,000, introduced in the November 1974 Budget, has not been included.)

TABLE D8 UNITED KINGDOM: Income Tax at 1974–75 rates and Wealth Tax (at illustrative Scale A) for different levels of net wealth at different rates of return. The figures of combined Income Tax and Wealth Tax exclude Investment Income Surcharge (IIS).

Single person with minimum allowances

Net Wealth £	Income from Wealth £	(a) Basic + Higher rate IT £	(b) IIS £	(a) + (b) Total IT £	Rates of Income Tax (Total) Marginal %	Rates of Income Tax (Total) Average %	Wealth Tax (WT) £	Combined IT + WT £	Income after IT + WT £	IT + WT as per cent of Marginal income %	IT + WT as per cent of Total income %
Assuming Return of 2% to Wealth.											
50,000	1,000	124	0	124	33.0	12.4	0	124	876	33.0	12.4
100,000	2,000	454	0	454	48.0	22.7	0	454	1,546	83.0	22.7
200,000	4,000	1,114	300	1,414	48.0	35.4	1,000	2,114	1,886	83.0	52.9
300,000	6,000	1,836	600	2,436	58.0	40.6	2,000	3,836	2,164	93.0	63.9
400,000	8,000	2,784	900	3,684	68.0	46.1	3,000	5,784	2,216	103.0	72.3
500,000	10,000	3,913	1,200	5,113	73.0	51.1	4,000	7,913	2,087	103.0	79.1
600,000	12,000	5,141	1,500	6,641	78.0	55.3	5,500	10,641	1,359	133.0	88.7
700,000	14,000	6,470	1,800	8,270	83.0	59.1	7,000	13,470	530	138.0	96.2
800,000	16,000	7,830	2,100	9,930	83.0	62.1	8,500	16,330	— 330	143.0	102.1
900,000	18,000	9,309	2,400	11,709	88.0	65.1	10,000	19,309	—1,309	148.0	107.3
1,000,000	20,000	10,769	2,700	13,469	88.0	67.4	11,500	22,269	—2,269	148.0	111.3
1,500,000	30,000	19,006	4,200	23,207	98.0	77.4	19,000	38,006	—8,006	158.0	126.7
2,000,000	40,000	27,306	5,700	33,006	98.0	82.5	26,500	53,806	—13,806	183.0	134.5
5,000,000	100,000	77,106	14,700	91,806	98.0	91.8	86,500	163,606	—63,606	208.0	163.6
Assuming Return of 5% to Wealth.											
50,000	2,500	619	75	694	48.0	27.8	0	619	1,881	33.0	24.8
100,000	5,000	1,444	450	1,894	48.0	37.9	0	1,444	3,556	53.0	28.9
200,000	10,000	3,913	1,200	5,113	73.0	51.1	1,000	4,913	5,087	78.0	49.1
300,000	15,000	7,150	1,950	9,100	88.0	60.7	2,000	9,150	5,850	78.0	61.0
400,000	20,000	10,769	2,700	13,469	88.0	67.4	3,000	13,769	6,231	93.0	68.8
500,000	25,000	14,856	3,450	18,307	88.0	73.2	4,000	18,856	6,144	103.0	75.4
600,000	30,000	19,006	4,200	23,207	98.0	77.4	5,500	24,506	5,494	113.0	81.7
700,000	35,000	23,156	4,950	28,107	98.0	80.3	7,000	30,156	4,844	113.0	86.2
800,000	40,000	27,306	5,700	33,007	98.0	82.5	8,500	35,806	4,194	113.0	89.5
900,000	45,000	31,456	6,450	37,907	98.0	84.2	10,000	41,456	3,544	113.0	92.1
1,000,000	50,000	35,606	7,200	42,807	98.0	85.6	11,500	47,106	2,894	113.0	94.2
1,500,000	75,000	56,356	10,950	67,307	98.0	89.7	19,000	75,356	— 356	123.0	100.5
2,000,000	100,000	77,106	14,700	91,807	98.0	91.8	26,500	103,606	—3,606	123.0	103.6
5,000,000	250,000	201,606	37,200	238,807	98.0	95.5	86,500	288,106	—38,106	133.0	115.2
Assuming Return of 10% to Wealth.											
50,000	5,000	1,444	450	1,894	48.0	27.9	0	1,444	3,556	33.0	28.9
100,000	10,000	3,913	1,200	5,113	73.0	51.1	0	3,913	6,087	68.0	39.1
200,000	20,000	10,769	2,700	13,469	88.0	67.4	1,000	11,769	8,231	83.0	58.8
300,000	30,000	19,006	4,200	23,207	88.0	77.4	2,000	21,006	8,994	93.0	70.0
400,000	40,000	27,306	5,700	33,007	98.0	82.5	3,000	30,306	9,694	93.0	75.8
500,000	50,000	35,606	7,200	42,807	98.0	85.6	4,000	39,606	10,394	98.0	79.2
600,000	60,000	43,906	8,700	52,607	98.0	87.7	5,500	49,406	10,594	98.0	82.3
700,000	70,000	52,206	10,200	62,407	98.0	89.2	7,000	59,206	10,794	98.0	84.6
800,000	80,000	60,506	11,700	72,207	98.0	90.3	8,500	69,006	10,994	98.0	86.3
900,000	90,000	68,806	13,200	82,007	98.0	91.1	10,000	78,806	11,194	98.0	87.6
1,000,000	100,000	77,106	14,700	91,807	98.0	91.8	11,500	88,606	11,394	98.0	88.6
1,500,000	150,000	118,606	22,200	140,007	98.0	93.3	19,000	137,606	12,394	98.0	91.7
2,000,000	200,000	169,106	29,700	189,807	98.0	94.9	26,500	195,606	4,394	103.0	97.8
5,000,000	500,000	409,106	74,700	483,807	98.0	96.8	86,500	495,606	4,394	108.0	99.1

NOTE: Investment Income Surcharge is taken as 15 per cent. on investment incomes over £2,000. (The reduced rate on investment incomes between £1,000 and £2,000, introduced in the November 1974 Budget, has not been included.)

TABLE D9 UNITED KINGDOM: Income Tax at 1974–5 rates and Wealth Tax (at illustrative Scale A) for different levels of net wealth at different rates of return. The figures of combined Income Tax and Wealth Tax take the larger of Wealth Tax OR Investment Income Surcharge (IIS).

Single person with minimum allowances

Net Wealth £	Income from Wealth £	(a) Basic + Higher rate IT £	(b) IIS £	(a)+(b) Total IT £	Rate of Income Tax (Total) Marginal %	Rate of Income Tax (Total) Average %	Wealth Tax (WT) £	Combined IT+WT or IIS £	Income after IT+WT or IIS £	IT+WT or IIS as per cent of Marginal income %	IT+WT or IIS as per cent of Total income %
Assuming Return of 2% to Wealth.											
50,000	1,000	124	0	124	33.0	12.4	0	124	876	33.0	12.4
100,000	2,000	454	0	454	48.0	22.7	0	454	1,546	83.0	22.7
200,000	4,000	1,114	300	1,414	48.0	35.4	1,000	2,114(WT)	1,886	83.0	52.9
300,000	6,000	1,836	600	2,436	58.0	40.6	2,000	3,836(WT)	2,164	93.0	63.9
400,000	8,000	2,784	900	3,684	68.0	46.1	3,000	5,784(WT)	2,216	103.0	72.3
500,000	10,000	3,913	1,200	5,113	73.0	51.1	4,000	7,913(WT)	2,087	133.0	79.1
600,000	12,000	5,141	1,500	6,641	78.0	55.3	5,000	10,641(WT)	1,359	133.0	88.7
700,000	14,000	6,470	1,800	8,270	83.0	59.1	7,000	13,470(WT)	530	138.0	96.2
800,000	16,000	7,830	2,100	9,930	88.0	62.1	8,500	16,330(WT)	330	143.0	102.1
900,000	18,000	9,309	2,400	11,709	88.0	65.1	10,000	19,309(WT)	−1,309	148.0	107.3
1,000,000	20,000	10,769	2,700	13,469	88.0	67.4	11,500	22,269(WT)	−2,269	148.0	111.3
1,500,000	30,000	19,006	4,200	23,207	98.0	77.4	19,000	38,006(WT)	−8,006	158.0	126.7
2,000,000	40,000	27,306	5,700	33,006	98.0	82.5	26,500	53,806(WT)	−13,806	183.0	134.5
5,000,000	100,000	77,106	14,700	91,806	98.0	91.8	86,500	163,606(WT)	−63,606	208.0	163.6
Assuming Return of 5% to Wealth.											
50,000	2,500	619	75	694	48.0	27.8	0	694(IIS)	1,806	48.0	27.6
100,000	5,000	1,444	450	1,894	48.0	37.9	0	1,894(IIS)	3,106	48.0	37.9
200,000	10,000	3,913	1,200	5,113	73.0	51.1	1,000	5,113(IIS)	4,887	73.0	51.1
300,000	15,000	7,150	1,950	9,100	73.0	60.7	2,000	9,150(WT)	5,850	78.0	61.0
400,000	20,000	10,769	2,700	13,469	88.0	67.4	3,000	13,769(WT)	6,231	93.0	68.8
500,000	25,000	14,856	3,450	18,307	88.0	73.2	4,000	18,856(WT)	6,144	103.0	74.5
600,000	30,000	19,006	4,200	23,207	98.0	77.4	5,500	24,506(WT)	5,494	113.0	81.7
700,000	35,000	23,156	4,950	28,107	98.0	80.3	7,000	30,156(WT)	4,844	113.0	86.2
800,000	40,000	27,306	5,700	33,007	98.0	82.5	8,500	35,806(WT)	4,194	113.0	89.5
900,000	45,000	31,456	6,450	37,907	98.0	84.2	10,000	41,456(WT)	3,544	113.0	92.1
1,000,000	50,000	35,606	7,200	42,807	98.0	85.6	11,500	47,106(WT)	2,894	113.0	94.2
1,500,000	75,000	56,356	10,950	67,307	98.0	89.7	19,000	75,356(WT)	356	113.0	100.5
2,000,000	100,000	77,106	14,700	91,807	98.0	91.8	26,500	103,606(WT)	−3,606	123.0	103.6
5,000,000	250,000	201,606	37,200	238,807	98.0	95.5	86,500	288,106(WT)	−38,106	133.0	115.2
Assuming Return of 10% to Wealth.											
50,000	5,000	1,444	450	1,894	48.0	37.9	0	1,894(IIS)	3,106	68.0	37.9
100,000	10,000	3,913	1,200	5,113	73.0	51.1	0	5,113(IIS)	4,887	73.0	48.9
200,000	20,000	10,769	2,700	13,469	88.0	67.4	1,000	13,469(IIS)	6,531	88.0	67.3
300,000	30,000	19,006	4,200	23,207	98.0	77.4	2,000	23,207(IIS)	6,793	98.0	77.4
400,000	40,000	27,306	5,700	33,007	98.0	82.5	3,000	33,007(IIS)	6,993	98.0	82.5
500,000	50,000	35,606	7,200	42,807	98.0	85.6	4,000	42,807(IIS)	7,193	98.0	85.6
600,000	60,000	43,906	8,700	52,607	98.0	87.7	5,500	52,607(IIS)	7,393	98.0	87.7
700,000	70,000	52,206	10,200	62,407	98.0	89.2	7,000	62,407(IIS)	7,593	98.0	89.2
800,000	80,000	60,506	11,700	72,207	98.0	90.3	8,500	72,207(IIS)	7,793	98.0	90.3
900,000	90,000	68,806	13,200	82,007	98.0	91.1	10,000	82,007(IIS)	7,993	98.0	91.1
1,000,000	100,000	77,106	14,700	91,807	98.0	91.8	11,500	91,807(IIS)	8,193	98.0	91.8
1,500,000	150,000	118,606	22,200	140,007	98.0	93.3	19,000	140,007(IIS)	9,993	98.0	93.3
2,000,000	200,000	160,106	29,700	189,807	98.0	94.9	26,500	189,807(IIS)	10,193	98.0	94.9
5,000,000	500,000	409,106	74,700	483,807	98.0	96.8	86,500	495,606(WT)	4,393	108.0	99.1

NOTE: Investment Income Surcharge is taken as 15 per cent. on investment incomes over £2,000. (The reduced rate on investment incomes between £1,000 and £2,000, introduced in the November 1974 Budget, has not been included.)

TABLE D10 UNITED KINGDOM: Income Tax at 1974–75 rates and Wealth Tax (at illustrative Scale B) for different levels of net wealth at different rates of return. The figures of combined Income Tax and Wealth Tax include Investment Income Surcharge (IIS).

Net Wealth £	Income from Wealth £	(a) Basic + Higher rate IT £	(b) IIS £	(a)+(b) Total IT £	Rates of Income Tax (Total) Marginal %	Rates of Income Tax (Total) Average %	Wealth Tax (WT) £	Combined IT+WT £	Income after IT+WT £	IT+WT as per cent of Total — Marginal income %	IT+WT as per cent of Total — Total income %
Assuming Return of 2% to Wealth.											
50,000	1,000	124	0	124	33.0	12.4	0	124	876	33.0	12.4
100,000	2,000	454	0	454	48.0	22.7	0	454	1,546	98.0	22.7
200,000	4,000	1,114	300	1,414	48.0	35.4	1,000	2,414	1,586	98.0	60.4
300,000	6,000	1,836	600	2,436	58.0	40.6	2,000	4,436	1,564	158.0	73.9
400,000	8,000	2,784	900	3,684	68.0	46.1	4,000	7,684	316	168.0	96.1
500,000	10,000	3,913	1,200	5,113	73.0	51.1	6,000	11,113	−1,113	223.0	111.1
600,000	12,000	5,141	1,500	6,641	78.0	55.3	9,000	15,641	−3,641	228.0	130.3
700,000	14,000	6,470	1,800	8,270	83.0	59.1	12,000	20,270	−6,270	233.0	144.8
800,000	16,000	7,830	2,100	9,930	88.0	62.1	15,000	24,930	−8,930	238.0	155.8
900,000	18,000	9,309	2,400	11,709	88.0	65.1	18,000	29,709	−11,709	238.0	165.1
1,000,000	20,000	10,769	2,700	13,469	88.0	67.4	21,000	34,469	−14,469	238.0	172.3
1,500,000	30,000	19,006	4,200	23,207	98.0	77.4	36,000	59,207	−29,207	248.0	197.4
2,000,000	40,000	27,306	5,700	33,006	98.0	82.5	51,000	84,006	−44,006	298.0	210.0
5,000,000	100,000	77,106	14,700	91,806	98.0	91.8	171,000	262,806	−162,806	348.0	262.8
Assuming Return of 5% to Wealth.											
50,000	2,500	619	75	694	48.0	27.8	0	694	1,806	48.0	27.6
100,000	5,000	1,444	450	1,894	48.0	37.9	0	1,894	3,106	68.0	37.9
200,000	10,000	3,913	1,200	5,113	73.0	51.1	1,000	6,113	3,887	93.0	61.1
300,000	15,000	7,150	1,950	9,100	73.0	60.7	2,000	11,100	3,900	113.0	74.0
400,000	20,000	10,769	2,700	13,469	88.0	67.4	4,000	17,469	2,605	128.0	87.3
500,000	25,000	14,856	3,450	18,307	88.0	73.2	6,000	24,307	693	148.0	97.2
600,000	30,000	19,006	4,200	23,207	98.0	77.4	9,000	32,207	−2,207	158.0	107.4
700,000	35,000	23,156	4,950	28,107	98.0	80.3	12,000	40,107	−5,107	158.0	114.6
800,000	40,000	27,306	5,700	33,007	98.0	82.5	15,000	48,007	−8,007	158.0	120.0
900,000	45,000	31,456	6,450	37,907	98.0	84.2	18,000	55,907	−10,907	158.0	124.2
1,000,000	50,000	35,606	7,200	42,807	98.0	85.6	21,000	63,807	−13,807	158.0	127.6
1,500,000	75,000	56,356	10,950	67,307	98.0	89.7	36,000	103,307	−28,307	158.0	137.7
2,000,000	100,000	77,106	14,700	91,807	98.0	91.8	51,000	142,807	−42,807	178.0	142.8
5,000,000	250,000	201,606	37,200	238,807	98.0	95.5	171,000	409,807	−159,807	198.0	163.9
Assuming Return of 10% to Wealth.											
50,000	5,000	1,444	450	1,894	48.0	37.9	0	1,894	3,106	68.0	37.9
100,000	10,000	3,913	1,200	5,113	73.0	51.1	0	5,113	4,887	83.0	51.1
200,000	20,000	10,769	2,700	13,469	88.0	67.4	1,000	14,469	5,531	98.0	72.3
300,000	30,000	19,006	4,200	23,207	98.0	77.4	2,000	25,207	4,793	118.0	84.0
400,000	40,000	27,306	5,700	33,007	98.0	82.5	4,000	37,007	2,993	118.0	92.5
500,000	50,000	35,606	7,200	42,807	98.0	85.6	6,000	48,807	1,193	128.0	97.6
600,000	60,000	43,906	8,700	52,607	98.0	87.7	9,000	61,607	−1,607	128.0	102.7
700,000	70,000	52,206	10,200	62,407	98.0	89.2	12,000	74,407	−4,407	128.0	106.3
800,000	80,000	60,506	11,700	72,207	98.0	90.3	15,000	87,207	−7,207	128.0	109.0
900,000	90,000	68,806	13,200	82,007	98.0	91.1	18,000	100,007	−10,007	128.0	111.1
1,000,000	100,000	77,106	14,700	91,807	98.0	91.8	21,000	112,807	−12,807	128.0	112.8
1,500,000	150,000	118,606	22,200	140,007	98.0	93.3	36,000	176,007	−26,007	128.0	117.3
2,000,000	200,000	160,106	29,700	189,807	98.0	94.9	51,000	240,807	−40,807	138.0	120.4
5,000,000	500,000	409,106	74,700	483,807	98.0	96.8	171,000	654,807	−154,807	148.0	131.0

The last three columns (Income after IT+WT, and IT+WT as per cent of Total – Marginal income and Total income) fall under the heading **Single person with minimum allowances**.

NOTE: Investment Income Surcharge is taken as 15 per cent. on investment incomes over £2,000. (The reduced rate on investment incomes between £1,000 and £2,000, introduced in the November 1974 Budget, has not been included.)

TABLE D11 UNITED KINGDOM: Income Tax at 1974–75 rates and Wealth Tax (at illustrative Scale B) for different levels of net wealth at different rates of return. The figures of combined Income Tax and Wealth Tax exclude Investment Income Surcharge (IIS).

Single person with minimum allowances

Net Wealth £	Income from Wealth £	(a) Basic + Higher rate IT £	(b) IIS £	(a)+(b) Total IT £	Rate of Income Tax (Total) Marginal %	Rate of Income Tax (Total) Average %	Wealth Tax WT £	Combined IT+WT £	Income after IT+WT £	IT+WT as per cent of Marginal Income %	IT+WT as per cent of Total Income %
Assuming Return of 2% to Wealth.											
50,000	1,000	124	0	124	33.0	12.4	0	124	876	33.0	12.4
100,000	2,000	454	0	454	48.0	22.7	0	454	1,546	83.0	22.7
200,000	4,000	1,114	300	1,414	48.0	35.4	1,000	2,114	1,886	83.0	52.9
300,000	6,000	1,836	600	2,436	58.0	40.6	2,000	3,836	2,164	143.0	63.9
400,000	8,000	2,784	900	3,684	68.0	46.1	4,000	6,784	1,216	153.0	84.8
500,000	10,000	3,913	1,200	5,113	73.0	51.1	6,000	9,913	87	208.0	99.1
600,000	12,000	5,141	1,500	6,641	73.0	55.3	9,000	14,141	—2,141	213.0	117.8
700,000	14,000	6,470	1,800	8,270	83.0	59.1	12,000	18,470	—4,470	218.0	131.9
800,000	16,000	7,830	2,100	9,930	88.0	62.1	15,000	22,830	—6,830	223.0	142.7
900,000	18,000	9,309	2,400	11,709	88.0	65.1	18,000	27,309	—9,309	223.0	151.7
1,000,000	20,000	10,769	2,700	13,469	88.0	67.4	21,000	31,769	—11,769	223.0	158.8
1,500,000	30,000	19,006	4,200	23,206	98.0	77.4	36,000	55,006	—25,006	233.0	183.3
2,000,000	40,000	27,306	5,700	33,006	98.0	82.5	51,000	78,306	—38,306	283.0	195.8
5,000,000	100,000	77,106	14,700	91,806	98.0	91.8	171,000	248,106	—148,106	333.0	248.1
Assuming Return of 5% to Wealth.											
50,000	2,500	619	75	694	48.0	27.8	0	619	1,881	33.0	24.8
100,000	5,000	1,444	450	1,894	48.0	37.9	0	1,444	3,556	53.0	28.9
200,000	10,000	3,913	1,200	5,113	73.0	51.1	1,000	4,913	5,087	78.0	49.1
300,000	15,000	7,150	1,950	9,100	73.0	60.7	2,000	9,150	5,850	98.0	61.0
400,000	20,000	10,769	2,700	13,469	88.0	67.4	4,000	14,769	5,231	113.0	73.8
500,000	25,000	14,856	3,450	18,307	88.0	73.2	6,000	20,856	4,144	133.0	83.4
600,000	30,000	19,006	4,200	23,207	98.0	77.4	9,000	28,006	1,994	143.0	93.4
700,000	35,000	23,156	4,950	28,107	98.0	80.3	12,000	35,156	156	143.0	100.4
800,000	40,000	27,306	5,700	33,007	98.0	82.5	15,000	42,306	—2,306	143.0	105.8
900,000	45,000	31,456	6,450	37,907	98.0	84.2	18,000	49,456	—4,456	143.0	109.9
1,000,000	50,000	35,606	7,200	42,807	98.0	85.6	21,000	56,606	—6,606	143.0	113.2
1,500,000	75,000	56,356	10,950	67,307	98.0	89.7	36,000	92,356	—17,356	143.0	123.1
2,000,000	100,000	77,106	14,700	91,807	98.0	91.8	51,000	128,106	—28,106	163.0	128.1
5,000,000	250,000	201,606	37,200	238,807	98.0	95.5	171,000	372,606	—122,606	183.0	149.0
Assuming Return of 10% to Wealth.											
50,000	5,000	1,444	450	1,894	48.0	27.9	0	1,444	3,556	33.0	28.9
100,000	10,000	3,913	1,200	5,113	73.0	51.1	0	3,913	6,087	68.0	39.1
200,000	20,000	10,769	2,700	13,469	88.0	67.4	1,000	11,769	8,231	83.0	58.8
300,000	30,000	19,006	4,200	23,207	98.0	77.4	2,000	21,006	8,994	103.0	70.0
400,000	40,000	27,306	5,700	33,007	98.0	82.5	4,000	31,306	8,694	103.0	78.3
500,000	50,000	35,606	7,200	42,807	98.0	85.6	6,000	41,606	8,394	113.0	86.0
600,000	60,000	43,906	8,700	52,607	98.0	87.7	9,000	52,906	7,094	113.0	88.2
700,000	70,000	52,206	10,200	62,407	98.0	89.2	12,000	64,206	5,794	113.0	91.7
800,000	80,000	60,506	11,700	72,207	98.0	90.3	15,000	75,506	4,494	113.0	94.4
900,000	90,000	68,806	13,200	82,007	98.0	91.1	18,000	86,806	3,194	113.0	96.5
1,000,000	100,000	77,106	14,700	91,807	98.0	91.8	21,000	98,106	1,894	113.0	98.1
1,500,000	150,000	118,606	22,200	140,007	98.0	93.3	36,000	154,606	—4,606	113.0	103.1
2,000,000	200,000	160,106	29,700	189,807	98.0	94.9	51,000	211,106	—11,106	123.0	105.6
5,000,000	500,000	409,106	74,700	483,807	98.0	96.8	171,000	580,106	—80,106	133.0	116.0

NOTE: Investment Income Surcharge is taken as 15 per cent on investment incomes over £2,000. (The reduced rate on investment incomes between £1,000 and £2,000, introduced in the November 1974 Budget, has not been included.)

TABLE D12 UNITED KINGDOM: Income Tax at 1974–75 rates and Wealth Tax (at illustrative Scale B) for different levels of net wealth at different rates of return. The figures of combined Income Tax and Wealth Tax take the larger of Wealth Tax OR Investment Income Surcharge (IIS).

Net Wealth £	Income from Wealth £	(a) Basic + Higher rate IT £	(b) IIS £	(a) + (b) Total IT £	Rate of Income Tax (Total) Marginal %	Rate of Income Tax (Total) Average %	Wealth Tax (WT) £	Combined IT+WT or IIS £	Income after IT+WT or IIS £	Single person with minimum allowances IT+WT or IIS as per cent. of Marginal income %	IT+WT or IIS as per cent. of Total income %
Assuming Return of 2% to Wealth.											
50,000	1,000	124	0	124	33.0	12.4	0	124	876	33.0	12.4
100,000	2,000	454	0	454	48.0	22.7	0	454	1,546	83.0	22.7
200,000	4,000	1,114	300	1,414	48.0	35.4	1,000	2,114(WT)	1,886	83.0	52.9
300,000	6,000	1,836	600	2,436	58.0	40.6	2,000	3,436(WT)	2,164	143.0	63.9
400,000	8,000	2,784	900	3,684	68.0	46.1	4,000	6,784(WT)	1,216	153.0	84.8
500,000	10,000	3,913	1,200	5,113	73.0	51.1	6,000	9,913(WT)	87	208.0	99.1
600,000	12,000	5,141	1,500	6,641	78.0	55.3	9,000	14,141(WT)	—2,141	213.0	117.8
700,000	14,000	6,470	1,800	8,270	83.0	59.1	12,000	18,470(WT)	—4,470	218.0	131.9
800,000	16,000	7,830	2,100	9,930	88.0	62.1	15,000	22,830(WT)	—6,830	223.0	142.7
900,000	18,000	9,309	2,400	11,709	88.0	65.1	18,000	27,309(WT)	—9,309	223.0	151.7
1,000,000	20,000	10,769	2,700	13,469	88.0	67.4	21,000	31,769(WT)	—11,769	233.0	158.8
1,500,000	30,000	19,006	4,200	23,207	98.0	77.4	36,000	55,006(WT)	—25,006	233.0	183.3
2,000,000	40,000	27,306	5,700	33,006	98.0	82.5	51,000	78,306(WT)	—38,306	283.0	195.8
5,000,000	100,000	77,106	14,700	91,806	98.0	91.8	171,000	248,106(WT)	—148,106	333.0	248.1
Assuming Return of 5% to Wealth.											
50,000	2,500	619	75	694	48.0	27.8	0	694(IIS)	1,806	48.0	27.6
100,000	5,000	1,444	450	1,894	48.0	37.9	0	1,894(IIS)	3,106	48.0	37.9
200,000	10,000	3,913	1,200	5,113	73.0	51.1	1,000	5,113(IIS)	4,887	73.0	51.1
300,000	15,000	7,150	1,950	9,100	73.0	60.7	2,000	9,150(WT)	5,830	98.0	61.0
400,000	20,000	10,769	2,700	13,469	88.0	67.4	4,000	14,769(WT)	5,231	113.0	73.8
500,000	25,000	14,856	3,450	18,307	88.0	73.2	6,000	20,856(WT)	4,144	133.0	83.4
600,000	30,000	19,006	4,200	23,207	98.0	77.4	9,000	28,006(WT)	1,944	143.0	93.4
700,000	35,000	23,156	4,950	28,107	98.0	80.3	12,000	35,156(WT)	156	143.0	100.4
800,000	40,000	27,306	5,700	33,007	98.0	82.5	15,000	42,306(WT)	—2,306	143.0	105.8
900,000	45,000	31,456	6,450	37,907	98.0	84.2	18,000	49,456(WT)	—4,456	143.0	109.9
1,000,000	50,000	35,606	7,200	42,807	98.0	85.6	21,000	56,606(WT)	—6,606	143.0	113.2
1,500,000	75,000	56,356	10,950	67,307	98.0	89.7	36,000	92,356(WT)	—17,356	143.0	123.1
2,000,000	100,000	77,106	14,700	91,807	98.0	91.8	51,000	128,106(WT)	—28,106	163.0	128.1
5,000,000	250,000	201,606	37,200	238,807	98.0	95.5	171,000	372,606(WT)	—122,606	183.0	149.0
Assuming Return of 10% to Wealth.											
50,000	5,000	1,444	450	1,894	48.0	37.9	0	1,894(IIS)	3,106	68.0	37.9
100,000	10,000	3,913	1,200	5,113	73.0	51.1	0	5,113(IIS)	4,887	73.0	51.1
200,000	20,000	10,769	2,700	13,469	88.0	67.4	1,000	13,469(IIS)	6,531	88.0	67.3
300,000	30,000	19,006	4,200	23,207	88.0	77.4	2,000	23,207(IIS)	6,793	98.0	77.4
400,000	40,000	27,306	5,700	33,007	98.0	82.5	4,000	33,007(IIS)	6,993	98.0	82.5
500,000	50,000	35,606	7,200	42,807	98.0	85.6	6,000	42,807(IIS)	7,193	98.0	85.6
600,000	60,000	43,906	8,700	52,607	98.0	87.7	9,000	52,906(WT)	7,094	113.0	88.2
700,000	70,000	52,206	10,200	62,407	98.0	89.2	12,000	64,206(WT)	5,794	113.0	91.7
800,000	80,000	60,506	11,700	72,207	98.0	90.3	15,000	75,506(WT)	4,494	113.0	94.4
900,000	90,000	68,806	13,200	82,007	98.0	91.1	18,000	86,806(WT)	3,194	113.0	96.5
1,000,000	100,000	77,106	14,700	91,807	98.0	91.8	21,000	98,106(WT)	1,894	113.0	98.1
1,500,000	150,000	118,606	22,200	140,007	98.0	93.3	36,000	154,606(WT)	—4,606	113.0	103.1
2,000,000	200,000	160,106	29,700	189,807	98.0	94.9	51,000	211,106(WT)	—11,106	123.0	105.6
5,000,000	500,000	409,106	74,700	483,807	98.0	96.8	171,000	580,106(WT)	—80,106	133.0	116.0

NOTE: Investment Income Surcharge is taken as 15 per cent. on investment incomes over £2,000. (The reduced rate on investment incomes between £1,000 and £2,000, introduced in the November 1974 Budget, has not been included.)

Selected Bibliography

BOOKS AND ARTICLES

ATKINSON, A. B., *Unequal Shares: Wealth in Britain,* Allen Lane, The Penguin Press, 1972.
'The Distribution of Wealth in Britain in the 1960s—the Estate Duty Method Re-examined' in *The Distribution of Personal Income and Wealth,* Ed. J. Smith, National Bureau of Economic Research, 1974.
'The Distribution of Wealth and the Individual Life Cycle', *Oxford Economic Papers,* July 1971.
BOSWELL, Jonathan, *The Rise and Decline of Small Firms,* Allen & Unwin, 1972.
BRACEWELL-MILNES, B., *Is Capital Taxation Fair?,* Institute of Directors, 1974.
BREAK, G. F., 'Effects of Taxation on Incentives', *British Tax Review,* June 1957.
CUTT, James, 'A Net Wealth Tax for Canada', *Canadian Tax Journal,* July/August 1969.
DALTON, H., *The Capital Levy Explained,* Labour Publishing Company, 1923.
DUE, John F., 'Net Wealth Taxation, *Public Finance,* XV, 1960.
FIELDS, D. B. & STANBURY, W. T., 'Incentives, Disincentives and the Income Tax', *Public Finance,* No. 3, 1970.
FLEMMING, J. S. & LITTLE, I. M. D., *Why We Need a Wealth Tax,* Methuen & Co. Ltd., 1974.
FORSYTH, M., *Property and Property Distribution Policy,* PEP, 1971.
GULATI, I. S., *Capital Taxation in a Developing Country,* Orient Longmans, 1957.
GOPAL, M. H., *Wealth Tax in India,* Economic and Scientific Research Foundation, New Delhi, 1970.
GUMPEL, H. J., *Taxation in the Federal Republic of Germany,* World Tax Series, Commerce Clearing House, 2nd Ed., 1969.
ILERSIC, A. R., 'Wealth Tax: Fiscal or Social Justice', *Canadian Tax Journal,* November/December 1968.
KALDOR, N., *Indian Tax Reform,* Ministry of Finance, Government of India, New Delhi, 1956.
'The Income Burden of Capital Taxes', *Review of Economic Studies,* 1942.
LYNCH, Thos. D., 'Capital Taxation in Eire', *The Accountants' Magazine,* May 1974.
MEADE, J. E., *Efficiency, Equality and the Ownership of Property,* George Allen & Unwin, 1964.
The Intelligent Radical's Guide to Economic Policy, George Allen & Unwin, 1975.
MERRETT, A. J., 'The Capital Gains Tax', *Lloyds Bank Review,* October 1965.
NORR, M., DUFFY F. J. & STERNER, H., *Taxation in Sweden,* World Tax Series, Commerce Clearing House, 1959.

PEACOCK, Alan, 'Economics of a Net Wealth Tax for Britain', *British Tax Review,* November/December 1963.
PEPPER, H. W. T., 'The Taxation of Wealth', *Bulletin of the International Bureau of Fiscal Documentation,* July 1967.
POLANYI, George & WOOD, John B., *How Much Inequality?,* IEA, 1974.
SANDFORD, C. T., *Taxing Personal Wealth,* George Allen and Unwin, 1971, *Hidden Costs of Taxation,* IFS, 1973.
SANDFORD, C. T., WILLIS, J. R. M. & IRONSIDE, D. J., *An Accessions Tax,* IFS 1973.
STERN, M., *The Needle's Eye of a Socialist Heaven,* Bow Group Memorandum, 1974.
STIGLITZ, J. E., 'The Effects of Income, Wealth and Capital Gains Taxation on Risk-Taking', *Quarterly Journal of Economics,* 1969.
STUTCHBURY, Oliver, *The Case for Capital Taxes,* Fabian Tract 388, December 1968.
TAIT, A. A., *The Taxation of Personal Wealth,* University of Illinois Press, 1967.
TANABE, Noboru, *The Taxation of Net Wealth,* International Monetary Fund Staff Papers, Vol. XIV, No. 1, March 1967.
THUROW, Lester C., 'Net Worth Taxes', *National Tax Journal,* September 1972.
TRESS, R. C., 'A Wealth Tax is a Wealth Tax', *British Tax Review,* November/December 1963.
TURVEY, Ralph & BREAK, Geo. F., 'The Taxation of Net Worth', *Studies in Greek Taxation,* International Publication Services, 1964.
WALLACE, Theo. & WAKEHAM, John, *The Case Against the Wealth Tax,* Bow Group, 1968.
WHEATCROFT, G. S. A., 'The Administrative Problems of a Wealth Tax', *British Tax Review,* November/December 1963.

REPORTS BY PRIVATE ORGANISATIONS

Confederation of British Industry, *Wealth Tax: A Report by the Wealth Tax Working Party,* 1974.
Country Landowners Association, *Constraints on Business Organisation in Agriculture,* Report of a Working Party, June 1974.
The Labour Party, *Labour's Economic Strategy,* 1969.
Skandinaviska Enskilda Banken, *The Tax System in Sweden,* Stockholm, 1972.

OFFICIAL PUBLICATIONS—UNITED KINGDOM

Capital Transfer Tax, Cmnd. 5705, 1974.
House of Lords, *Hansard,* 26 June 1974, HMSO (Debate on Wealth Tax Proposal and Historic Houses).
Inland Revenue Statistics, HMSO 1973.
Conditions Favourable to Faster Growth, NEDC, HMSO 1963.
Report of the Committee of Inquiry on Small Firms, Cmnd. 4811, HMSO, 1971.
Wealth Tax, Cmnd. 5704, 1974.

OFFICIAL PUBLICATIONS—OTHER COUNTRIES

Capital Taxation, White Paper issued by the Government of the Republic of Ireland, 1974.
EEC Report on Tax Harmonisation, Report of the Fiscal and Financial Committee, translated by International Bureau of Fiscal Documentation, Amsterdam, 1963.
Direct Taxation in Denmark, Finansministeriat, Copenhagen, 1974.
The Swedish Budget, 1974-1975, Ministry of Finance, Stockholm, 1974.
Revenue Statistics of OECD Member Countries 1965-1971, OECD, Paris, 1973.
Taxes in Norway, Royal Ministry of Finance & Customs, Tax Law Department, Oslo, 1970.
Three Taxes with Rules, (Indian Wealth Tax, Gift Tax, Estate Duty), Central Law Agency, Allahabad, 1974.
Draft Double Taxation Convention on Income and Capital, OECD, 1963.

Index

See Boats, Cars, Furniture, Jewellery, Work of Art, Collection